Do sentence strategies that
")

1) Compare
Petrarch + Bachman

Do sentence strategies that

- agency +
  self-actualization
  resourcefulness

"just the facts",
- Making the present
  critical to the
  past
- Focusing on how
  historical narratives
  work

- student government
- student newspaper

1.

2.

Learning Democracy

Monographs in German History

Volume 1
Osthandel and Ostpolitik: German Foreign Trade
Policies in Eastern Europe from Bismarck to Adenauer
Mark Spaulding

Volume 2
A Question of Priorities: Democratic Reform and
Economic Recovery in Postwar Germany
Rebecca Boehling

Volume 3
From Recovery to Catastrophe: Municipal Stabilization
and Political Crisis in Weimar Germany
Ben Lieberman

Volume 4
Nazism in Central Germany: The Brownshirts in
'Red' Saxony
Christian W. Szejnmann

Volume 5
Citizens and Aliens: Foreigners and the Law in
Britain and the German States, 1789–1870
Andreas Fahrmeir

Volume 6
Poems in Steel: National Socialism and the Politics of
Inventing from Weimar to Bonn
Kees Gispen

Volume 7
"Aryanisation" in Hamburg
Frank Bajohr

Volume 8
The Politics of Education: Teachers and School Reform
in Weimar Germany
Marjorie Lamberti

Volume 9
The Ambivalent Alliance: Konrad Adenauer, the
CDU/CSU, and the West, 1949–1966
Ronald J. Granieri

Volume 10
The Price of Exclusion: Ethnicity, National Identity,
and the Decline of German Liberalism, 1898–1933
E. Kurlander

Volume 11
Recasting West German Elites: Higher Civil Servants,
Business Leaders, and Physicians in Hesse between
Nazism and Democracy, 1945–1955
Michael R. Hayse

Volume 12
The Creation of the Modern German Army: General
Walther Reinhardt and the Weimar Republic,
1914–1930
William Mulligan

Volume 13
The Crisis of the German Left: The PDS, Stalinism
and the Global Economy
Peter Thompson

Volume 14
"Conservative Revolutionaries": Protestant and
Catholic Churches in Germany After Radical Political
Change in the 1990s
Barbara Thériault

Volume 15
Modernizing Bavaria: The Politics of Franz Josef
Strauss and the CSU, 1949–1969
Mark Milosch

Volume 16
Sex, Thugs and Rock 'N' Roll. Teenage Rebels in
Cold-War East Germany
Mark Fenemore

Volume 17
Cultures of Abortion in Weimar Germany
Cornelie Usborne

Volume 18
Selling the Economic Miracle: Economic Reconstruction
and Politics In West Germany, 1949–1957
Mark E. Spicka

Volume 19
Between Tradition and Modernity: Aby Warburg and
Art in Hamburg's Public Realm 1896-1918
Mark A. Russell

Volume 20
A Single Communal Faith? The German Right from
Conservatism to National Socialism
Thomas Rohkrämer

Volume 21
Environmental Organizations in Modern Germany:
Hardy Survivors in the Twentieth Century and Beyond
William T. Markham

Volume 22
Crime Stories: Criminalistic Fantasy and the Culture of
Crisis in Weimar Germany
Todd Herzog

Volume 23
Liberal Imperialism in Germany: Expansionism and
Nationalism, 1848–1884
Matthew P. Fitzpatrick

Volume 24
Bringing Culture to the Masses: Control, Compromise
and Participation in the GDR
Esther von Richthofen

Volume 25
Banned in Berlin: Literary Censorship in Imperial
Germany, 1871–1918
Gary D. Stark

Volume 26
After the 'Socialist Spring': Collectivisation and
Economic Transformation in the GDR
George Last

Volume 27
Learning Democracy: Education Reform in West
Germany, 1945–1965
Brian M. Puaca

Volume 28
Weimar Radicals: Nazis and Communists between
Authenticity and Performance
Timothy S. Brown

Volume 29
The Political Economy of Germany under Chancellors
Kohl and Schröder: Decline of the German Model?
Jeremy Leaman

LEARNING DEMOCRACY

Education Reform in West Germany, 1945–1965

Brian M. Puaca

Berghahn Books
New York • Oxford

Published in 2009 by
Berghahn Books
www.berghahnbooks.com

©2009 Brian M. Puaca

Library of Congress Cataloging-in-Publication Data

Puaca, Brian M.
   Learning democracy : education reform in West Germany, 1945–1965 / Brian M. Puaca.
   p. cm. — (Monographs in german history ; v. 27)
   Includes bibliographical references and index.
   ISBN 978-1-84545-568-2 (alk. paper)
   1. Education—Germany (West)—History. 2. Educational change—Germany (West)—
History. 3. Education—Political aspects—Germany (West)—History. 4. Education and
state—Germany (West)—History. I. Title.

LA721.82.P83 2009
370.943'09045—dc22

2009012812

British Library Cataloguing in Publication Data

A catalogue record for this book is available from the British Library

Printed in the United States on acid-free paper

ISBN: 978-1-84545-568-2 hardback

For my parents, Michael and Sally Puaca

CONTENTS

List of Figures   viii

Acknowledgements   ix

Abbreviations   xii

Introduction   1

Chapter 1   Rebuilding Education in a "New Spirit"
             The Challenges of the Immediate Postwar Period,
             1945–1947   13

Chapter 2   "We Learned What Democracy Really Meant"
             New Experiences Inside and Outside the Classroom,
             1948–1954   56

Chapter 3   Political Education
             Reforms Continue Beneath the Surface, 1955–1959   108

Chapter 4   Reform Reignited
             Ambitious Efforts in the New Decade, 1960–1965   153

Conclusion   193

Bibliography   203

Index   216

FIGURES

1 Berlin School, 1947   28

2 E&RA Officials, 1947   41

3 Chart of basic educational tracks in postwar Federal Republic   42

4 RIAS-Schulfunk-Parlament fifth anniversary announcement and
   admission ticket, 1953   57

5 Agenda for 46th meeting of RIAS-Schulfunk-Parlament, 1953   58

6 Newsletter of the RIAS-Schulfunk-Parlament, 1952   68

7 Newspaper article covering visiting German exchange teacher,
   Wilson High School Paper, Wilson City, NC, 1953   74

8 Front cover of Christmas Contest brochure for political
   education, 1953   109

9 Group work in a Hessian *Volksschule*, 1958   113

10 Front page of the *Schüler-Echo,* the student newspaper of
    West Berlin's Schadowschule, 1957   128

ACKNOWLEDGEMENTS

One of the greatest joys of finishing a book is the opportunity to thank all of the people who made the project possible. I would first like to extend my appreciation to the institutions and foundations that generously supported my work. My research in Germany was made possible by a grant from the Berlin Program for Advanced German and European Studies jointly administered by the Freie Universität Berlin and the Social Science Research Council with funds provided by the Freie Universität Berlin. A grant from the Georg-Eckert-Institut für internationale Schulbuchforschung facilitated an extended visit to its library in Braunschweig. The German Historical Institute in Washington, DC supported my work with American military government documents housed at the National Archives in College Park, Maryland. The Doris G. Quinn Fellowship awarded to me by the Department of History at the University of North Carolina–Chapel Hill provided the opportunity to write and revise the manuscript. Finally, a Dean's grant from the College of Liberal Arts and Sciences at Christopher Newport University provided additional support for revision and editing prior to publication. Naturally, the conclusions, opinions, and other statements herein belong to me, and I alone am responsible for any errors or omissions.

My project benefited from the expertise and assistance of archivists and librarians on both sides of the Atlantic. In Germany, I am deeply grateful to the staff of the George-Eckert-Institut für internationale Schulbuchforschung, the Landesarchiv Berlin, the Bundesarchiv Koblenz, the Hessisches Hauptstaatsarchiv, the Bibliothek für Bildungsgeschichtliche Forschung in Berlin, the Heimatmuseum Zehlendorf, the Archiv zur Geschichte von Tempelhof und Schöneberg, and the Heimatmuseum Neukölln. In particular, I would like to thank archivist Johann Zilien, who shared his knowledge of Hessian education with me during my time in Wiesbaden (and even found me an empty office to use there). Rudolf Roegler helped me set up interviews with former teachers in Berlin, while Gert Geissler, Hanna Schissler, and Heinz-Elmar Tenorth provided assistance navigating the academic landscape in the capital. In the United States, my work centered on the National Archives in College Park, Maryland, where I received guidance and advice from, among others, John Taylor.

In addition to those who helped with the research, I would also like to express my appreciation to those who were a part of it. The men and women who sat down with me and told me their stories made this book possible. Interviewing these remarkable individuals was one of the great pleasures of my work in Germany. In particular, I would like to thank Wilhelm-Dietrich von Thadden, who shared with me a wealth of personal files on the Berlin Student Parliament, several of which are included in this volume.

I am extremely grateful to those who assisted in the transformation of my original manuscript into this book. Blackwell Publishing allowed me to republish portions of two articles that originally appeared in the *History of Education Quarterly*. The Still Picture Reference Team at the National Archives helped me track down several photos and check on permissions. Marion Berghahn and her team at Berghahn Books have been wonderful. I would especially like to thank Kristine Hunt, Ann Przyzycki, and Melissa Spinelli for their assistance during the production process. Finally, I would like to thank the anonymous reviewers who devoted such careful attention to my work.

It is a great pleasure to finally have the opportunity to thank friends and colleagues who have contributed to this project over the past several years. Konrad Jarausch has supported my work from the very beginning. His guidance and wisdom has improved this study immensely. Christopher Browning, Don Reid, Jay Smith, Jim Leloudis, and Michaela Hoenicke-Moore have all provided valuable feedback on my work and challenged me to think in new directions. Kimberly Redding offered insightful comments on my work during my time in Berlin. Adam Seipp, Elana Passman, Michael Meng, Philipp Stelzel, Clara Oberle, Marti Lybeck, and Erik Huneke have served as sounding boards, sometimes saving me from my own ideas. Jim Albisetti, Arnd Bauerkämper, Benita Blessing, Bill Cutler, Dirk Schumann, Karl-Heinz Füssl, Charles Lansing, and Catherine Plum have all read portions of the manuscript and offered invaluable assistance and advice. Furthermore, I would like to express my gratitude to Eric Duskin, Andrew Falk, and Kurt Piehler for providing assistance at critical moments. I owe a final note of thanks to my research assistant, Alexandria Ruble, for her assistance in preparing the final version of the book.

Less visible in the finished product, but no less important to the creative process, was the hospitality and friendship I enjoyed while conducting my research. For their encouragement during my work in Germany, I would like to thank the Krügers, Markus Müller and family, Edith Raim, and the Wenzels. In particular, I would like to thank Martin Dienemann, his wife, Katrin, and his family, who have welcomed me with open arms every time I have visited Germany. Their warmth and kindness have reinvigorated me more times than I can count.

My greatest debt of gratitude goes to my family. My parents, Michael and Sally Puaca, provided much love and guidance. Their support made this project possible. I would also like to thank my sister, Deborah Puaca, and my in-laws, Rich and Ann Micheletti, for their love and encouragement every step of the way.

Finally, my wife, Laura, has been the greatest inspiration of all. She has read and reread draft after draft, attended countless talks and presentations, traveled halfway around the world, and even learned some German—all while conducting research of her own. And every day, she had a smile on her face.

ABBREVIATIONS

BSP	Berliner Schülerparlament (Berlin Student Parliament)
BVL	Berliner Verband der Lehrer und Erzieher (Berlin Association of Teachers and Educators)
CDU	Christlich Demokratische Union (Christian Democratic Union)
ECR	Education and Cultural Relations Division
EEC	European Economic Community
E&RA	Education and Religious Affairs Branch
EURATOM	European Atomic Energy Community
FRG	Federal Republic of Germany
GDR	German Democratic Republic
GEW	Gewerkschaft Erziehung und Wissenschaft (Trade Union for Education and Science)
GYA	German Youth Activities
HICOG	High Commission (US) for Germany
IfZ	Institut für Zeitgeschichte (Institute for Contemporary History)
KMK	Kultusministerkonferenz (Standing Conference of Culture Ministers)
LBA	Lehrerbildungsanstalt (normal school)
NATO	North Atlantic Treaty Organization
NSDAP	Nationalsozialistische Deutsche Arbeiterpartei (National Socialist German Workers' Party)
NSLB	Nationalsozialistischer Lehrerbund (National Socialist Teachers League)

OMGUS	Office of Military Government (US) for Germany
OPZ	Oberschule Praktischer Zweig (*Volksschule* in West Berlin)
OTZ	Oberschule Technischer Zweig (*Mittelschule* in West Berlin)
OWZ	Oberschule Wissenschaftlicher Zweig (*Gymnasium* in West Berlin)
PH	Pädagogische Hochschule (teacher's college)
PTA	Parent-Teacher Association
RIAS	Rundfunk im amerikanischen Sektor (Radio in the American Sector)
SED	Sozialistische Einheitspartei Deutschlands (Socialist Unity Party of Germany)
SFB	Sender Freies Berlin (Radio Free Berlin)
SMV	Schülermitverwaltung (student government)
SPD	Sozialdemokratische Partei Deutschlands (Social Democratic Party of Germany)
UN	United Nations
UNICEF	United Nations Children's Fund
WHO	World Health Organization
YMCA	Young Men's Christian Association
YWCA	Young Women's Christian Association

INTRODUCTION

As the Second World War drew to a close in Europe, many observers looked to the future of Germany with a mixture of anger and despair. Now that Germany had been defeated, the question on the minds of Allied leaders, as well as many Germans, was what should happen next. While various plans emphasized the breakup of large industrial concerns, the dissolution of banking giants, or the restructuring of the civil service, they all underscored the problems (and potential future dangers) of the German educational system. In perhaps the most infamous proposal for the postwar treatment of Germany, United States secretary of the treasury Henry Morgenthau spoke critically about the future of the German schools. In his 1945 treatise, *Germany Is Our Problem*, Morgenthau painted a bleak picture, asserting that

> for many years to come, [Germany's] schools and colleges will be nothing but a disappointment to believers in freedom. Such believers will be strongly tempted to attempt a revolution in German education. They can try, but they should not be too upset if they achieve little progress. They will cry out against the iniquity of allowing such and such heresies to be taught in German schools. They will perform a valuable service, too, in keeping our attention on the German problem. But they will not solve that problem. So far as education is concerned, the Germans will have to do most of that themselves.[1]

If Germany were to be transformed into a peaceful, democratic state, Morgenthau believed the schools would not be able to contribute to that process for many years. Furthermore, it would have to be the Germans, and not the Allies, who would bring about lasting change.

Notes for this section begin on page 10.

Twenty years later, the Federal Republic of Germany had become a stable democracy and close ally of the West. The schools of West Germany had helped create a new generation of Germans who cherished democracy and venerated peace. Through both modern textbooks and increased contact with other nations, West German pupils gained a knowledge of and appreciation for other cultures and peoples. A new cohort of young Germans entered the teaching profession, and they brought with them very different ideas about how a classroom should operate. Student government organizations emerged in almost every West German school, with pupil involvement in the administration of the classroom having become commonplace. Looking at German education twenty years after the end of the war, one could argue that a silent revolution had occurred in the schools of West Germany. Almost prophetically, Morgenthau's predictions had come true by the mid-1960s—at least in part. Reforms initiated after the war by Americans had resulted in only minor successes by the end of the occupation in 1949; it was the commitment of Germans and their hard work throughout the 1950s and early 1960s that was responsible for the postwar democratization of education in the Federal Republic.

Education serves as an excellent venue in which to examine how democracy took root in postwar Germany for several reasons. First, Americans and Germans both recognized the vital role of young people in the creation of a new, democratic state. Should the schools fail to instill the values of liberty, peace, and freedom in the youth of Germany, there was little hope for the stability of German democracy. Second, the schools are a key site for political socialization, where boys and girls learn how to interact with one another and the larger community. Yet many postwar studies have overlooked the schools of West Germany or depicted them as incapable of contributing to democratization in the postwar period.[2] Whether due to the organization of the school system, the age of the teaching profession, or the conservative politicians crafting policy, education has been marginalized by most scholars interested in the process of postwar German democratization. Finally, focusing on education allows one to examine how the process of democratization transpired at the most basic levels of society. This book does not investigate the effects of pedagogical reforms on some elite minority; it evaluates the influence of postwar pedagogical changes on an entire generation of Germans—those who would become lawyers and doctors, bankers and civil servants, and carpenters and mechanics.

It is no easy task to define what democratization, specifically "democratic education," meant in the postwar German schools. The American plan to democratize Germany had two major components. The first—and most obvious—aspect of this effort was the democratization of Germany's political institutions. A democratically elected parliament, a constitution, and separation of powers in government can be seen as products of this more overt process of political democratization. Reforming education, however, fell under the more complicated rubric of cultural democratization. As General Lucius Clay, American military governor for Germany during the last two years of the occupation, noted in his memoirs, the goal of cultural democratization was to instill in the Germans the idea of democracy as a way of life.[3] The schools, as envisioned by progressive American educators such as John Dewey and William H. Kilpatrick, could function as little democratic communities, instructing pupils in the benefits, perils, and responsibilities of citizenship in a democratic state.[4] It was this conception of democratic education that American education officials brought with them to Germany and that German educators latched onto after the war.[5] Postwar pupils were to gain knowledge and experience through their active participation in school activities and events. This conception of democratic education was not limited to any particular subject area; it became a principle of instruction (*Unterrichtsprinzip*) that extended to all subjects and activities. Democratic education thus influenced both the content and pedagogy of postwar classrooms. The schools were charged with providing a new generation of Germans with an understanding of democracy as a way of organizing society, a relationship between people, and an attitude regarding the way one leads life on an everyday basis.

This book intends to answer the riddle of how German educators were able to achieve democratic reforms in the schools, despite the fact that the organization of the educational system changed very little after the war. In order to do this, it concentrates on several related curricular and pedagogical innovations. First, new textbooks published after the war attempted to deconstruct the traditional authoritarian relationship between teachers and pupils. History texts, as well as a new breed of civics books, utilized new methods that emphasized the critical engagement of pupils in instruction and their responsibilities as citizens. Second, the advent of political education and social studies constituted a major change in the pedagogical landscape of the Federal Republic. The postwar commitment to creating active, democratic citizens contrasted with the passive civics instruction of the Weimar Republic that focused solely on the institutions of a democratic political state. Third, student government organizations that emphasized the everyday responsibilities of citizenship became commonplace in the West German schools during the 1950s. These organizations encouraged students to take part in the administration of their schools and afforded them the chance to experience democracy on a day-to-day basis. Fourth, exchange programs widened the horizons of West Germany's teachers and pupils, exposing them to the cultures of stable democracies throughout Western Europe, as well as in the United States. Fifth, teacher training programs began to prepare a new generation of educators committed to democracy that rejected the more authoritarian pedagogical approaches of the past. Although gradual, these reforms played a significant role in promoting democracy in the postwar Federal Republic.

Rethinking the "Restoration"

Not surprisingly, the subtle transformations in West German education have gone largely unnoticed, even by those who were most intimately involved in the process. Consequently, the impression that little, if anything, changed in the schools of the Federal Republic after the war is reflected in much of the scholarship on postwar education reform through the mid-1960s. Many of these works have portrayed the first two postwar decades as a time of "stagnation" and obscured the origins of the reforms that began to emerge in this period. Such an interpretation makes it seem as if the changes that occurred at the end of the 1960s appeared inexplicably and without warning. Only through examining the German schools of the first two postwar decades can one understand the pedagogical reforms that emerged in the late 1960s and beyond.

Both the Americans and the Germans have been indicted by scholars for an apparent lack of interest in reforming the schools following the Second World War. Traditionally, the years of the American occupation (1945–1949) have been viewed as a time of failed democratization.[6] Some have emphasized the chaos and destruction that came from the war itself, while others have stressed the intensification of the Cold War two years later.[7] In such an environment, these critics assert, the schools could not possibly have contributed to the process of building democracy. Following the end of the occupation, authority for education returned to the individual German federal states. Culture ministers and leading educators, much of the current scholarship suggests, seized this opportunity to push aside many of the reforms encouraged by American military officials. Scholars have thus labeled the 1950s as a time of "restoration." While political elites were working to rebuild Germany's economy, industry, and political institutions, education supposedly returned to the pre-Nazi traditions of the Weimar Republic.[8] Despite two major reform proposals in the 1950s, both of which sought to alter the basic organization of the educational system, the multitiered structure after 1945 looked very similar to the one that existed before 1933. Thus, the preoccupation with the organization of the school system and the political elites behind it has blinded many observers to the curricular and pedagogical changes that took place within the walls of postwar classrooms.

A handful of studies have appeared more recently suggesting that subtle changes indeed transpired in the postwar period. Hermann-Josef Rupieper has noted the apparent paradox of change occurring within a traditional structure.[9] Anselm Doering-Manteuffel, concurring with Rupieper, has cited the advent of group-oriented classroom discussions and student self-government in fomenting larger educational and cultural changes.[10] Comparing education reform in postwar Germany and Japan, Beate Rosenzweig has argued that implementing structural reform was by no means a guarantee for democratization. Although Japanese schools accepted organizational changes as demanded by American officials, it was the German schools—despite rejecting or evading similar proposals—that experienced more significant internal reform.[11] Interested in a variety of different issues, scholars such as these have offered provocative claims but little hard evidence to support their contentions regarding the ground-level transformation of postwar education.[12]

On a broader level, there is a large body of scholarship that asserts that postwar Germany experienced dramatic social and cultural changes after the war that can best be described as the result of Americanization. These studies underscore the influence of the United States on German attitudes toward politics, race, business, fashion, music, and popular culture.[13] Germans, however, were selective and did not adopt everything that America had to offer. A process of negotiation took place between Germans and Americans, as Volker Berghahn has explained, which resulted in a blending of new American ideas and German traditions.[14] Opponents of the Americanization argument emphasize the larger propagation of Western political, cultural, and social structures throughout the postwar world without placing special emphasis on the role of the United States.[15] It was this more general process of Westernization, they propose, that was critical in refashioning Germany's political and social institutions. The innovations that accompanied the Allied occupation, such as liberal democracy, the free market economy, and the social welfare state, should not be viewed as solely American influences. Proponents of this view contend that postwar reforms arose out of a larger Western tradition and not solely from America's postwar influence. This interpretation stresses the contributions of British and French military officials to the Allied occupation of Germany following 1945.

In the realm of education, it is only fair to acknowledge the impact of both American and other general Western influences in the postwar era. American military officials, education experts, and teachers left an indelible impression on German schooling that stretched far beyond the years of occupation. Student and teacher exchanges provided Germans the opportunity to visit America and study its political system, society, and popular culture throughout the 1950s. American philosophers, such as John Dewey, and American-modeled organizations such as student government, gained great influence among German teachers in the postwar decades. Yet the end of the war also marked the opening up of Germany to the rest of the outside world after more than a decade of isolation. German schools founded exchange programs and partnerships with their neighbors to the west—particularly France and Great Britain. Additionally, German educators gained access to the pedagogical publications and textbooks of other European countries. This development was particularly important, as German educators worked in conjunction with their colleagues in other European states on a number of collaborative projects. Thus, while the influence of the United States was strong in the educational sphere after 1945, it was not the only force contributing to the reform of the German schools.

Selecting Schools

Because of my interest in exploring the interactions between Germans and Americans in regard to education reform, I have chosen to concentrate on regions of

West Germany directly influenced by the United States after 1945. The first of these case studies—and the more significant of the two—is West Berlin. Admittedly, West Berlin is not emblematic of the other western federal states. Nevertheless, I would argue that it is a "hot spot" in the pedagogical debates of the postwar period, where debates on education and school reform were more intense than perhaps anywhere else in Germany. With an unfriendly, undemocratic regime staring at them from the other side of the city, educational questions took on enormous significance.[16] Additionally, many of the reforms that were initially introduced in West Berlin slowly began to be introduced in schools throughout the Federal Republic by the 1960s. Thus West Berlin serves as a pioneer or leader in educational reform in this investigation and not as an anomaly distinct from the rest of the Federal Republic. The second case study is Hesse, a less urban, more politically diverse venue.[17] Hesse offers a more balanced example, as school authorities and educators did not openly resist American proposals (as was the case in Bavaria). Yet, they did not meekly accept US suggestions either. Beginning with the policies of Culture Minister Erwin Stein in 1947 and continuing through the 1960s, Hesse followed a "middle road" in the realm of school reform, cautious on some issues and more reform minded on others. The Hessian example allows one to trace the continuing influence of American ideas first introduced during the occupation without the extreme magnification of the Cold War standoff. The examples drawn from Hesse serve to moderate the image provided by the trailblazing Berliners, while highlighting the widespread sentiment among educators that reform was necessary for the postwar reconstruction of West German education.

Within Hesse and West Berlin, I have concentrated on public schools, since they were without question the most widely attended educational institutions in the Federal Republic.[18] Although many American officials believed confessional schools to be inconsistent with the democratic values they hoped to instill in the educational system, they did not engage in a direct conflict with German authorities on this score during the occupation. Confessional schools thus maintained a notable—although weakened—presence in the Federal Republic after 1945, especially in Bavaria, southwestern Germany, and the Rhineland. While this book does not focus on areas with strong traditions of confessional schooling, it does include confessional schools in a limited fashion, most significantly through the participation of their teachers and students in exchanges and teacher training programs. Yet the larger conclusions drawn regarding changes in West German education are most applicable to the considerably more numerous public schools of the Federal Republic.

Narrowing my focus even further, I have decided to center my research on the emergence of reforms in late-primary and secondary education. The varying pace of reforms in the different types of schools is indeed part of the story, and it is particularly noticeable in certain areas, such as student government and student newspapers. The most dramatic changes in these fields are found in the *Gymnasien* of the Federal Republic. These most academically oriented secondary schools were home to the most active student government and student publications during the postwar period. Yet the other secondary schools also incorporated pedagogical innovations into the classroom. In this book, I explain how (and why) the nature of reforms and the timing of such changes varied among the different secondary schools. Finally, the emergence of reforms in elementary education highlights the postwar effort to encourage even the youngest pupils to accept new responsibilities and engage critically with Germany's troubled recent history.[19] New textbooks, better prepared teachers, and rudimentary student government groups all contributed to this process. Although the postwar reform process underway in the Federal Republic evolved differently within the various schools, they shared the ultimate goal of preparing pupils for their future responsibilities as citizens in a democratic society.

Looking at the Local Level

Due in part to a renewed interest in social history, there has been increasing attention to "teacher's-eye perspectives" in evaluating education reform.[20] Many American scholars of education have argued for a bottom-up approach in examining educational change, as it affords a more complete understanding of local variation and adaptation to central policies.[21] Such an approach also allows one to incorporate innovation and experimentation, which is often obscured by educational histories that revolve solely around policymakers and theorists. Measuring educational change from the bottom up also allows one to move past the policy planning stage and to focus on reforms as they are implemented in the schools. The relationship between state authorities and local schools is often a contentious one, and it can never be assumed that policy is instituted at the microlevel as it was formulated at the macrolevel. This suggests that interested parties at the local level have much greater control over school reforms than federal or even state bureaucrats. Additionally, complicated power relationships within the schools often hinder reforms mandated "from above," that is, legal and administrative change. Admittedly, there are differences in the organization of the American and German educational systems—local school districts exert great influence on schools in the US, while state education boards are responsible for regulating schools in Germany. The uniformity of state education policies, however, only makes the reforms introduced in the postwar German context all the more remarkable.

My focus on educational changes at the local and regional levels has required that I integrate a variety of sources into the project. Culture Ministry documents, coupled with American military government records, constitute one set of important sources for the project. These archival documents provide the broader framework for the subtle reforms transpiring at the local level. The greatest challenge of this project, however, has been to unearth how educational reforms played out on the small stages of individual West German schools. In order to measure the ideas and experiences of those most directly involved in the educational process, I first turned to the many pedagogical journals published in the postwar decades.[22] These publications give voice to the anxieties of postwar educators throughout the Federal Republic and recount their experiences with new curricula and pedagogical methods. Even more valuable to my analysis have been the records of individual schools. In these files, I have located pupils' essays and reports, teachers' lesson plans, and other instructional materials. Classroom assignments authored by pupils are particularly valuable, as they offer access into the thoughts and attitudes of those most affected by postwar innovations. Local archives, especially in Berlin, provided access to school documents from the locality that were unavailable elsewhere.[23] Here I discovered student newspapers, student government records, and yearbooks, all of which enhanced my understanding of how reforms evolved in the postwar schools. Likewise, private individuals allowed me to view and copy their relevant personal materials. This was especially useful in understanding such innovations as the Berlin Student Parliament (Berliner Schülerparlament), a remarkable organization that has received little attention from scholars of the postwar schools.[24]

Perhaps the most valuable sources relating to education at the local and regional level have been interviews with former teachers and pupils from this period. Oral history has been a critical tool for gaining insight into the ways in which Germans experienced the tumultuous years following the war.[25] Interviews with these teachers and pupils provide new insights into the history of education in the postwar period and call into question dominant narratives that focus primarily on social and political elites.[26] Speaking to individuals who taught in primary schools, as well as all three branches of the secondary schools, helped me differentiate the experiences of educators in the various levels of the West German educational system. While these oral histories are important to the project, they are used to complement and enrich the textual record. These interviews underscore the shared beliefs in democratization and curricular reform held by most postwar educators. At the same time, these discussions illustrate the varying levels of change experienced in the three forms of schools and the unique problems each possessed. Often glossed over in other studies of postwar education, these critical differences come to the fore as teachers and pupils recount their experiences in postwar classrooms.

Imperceptible Reform

A close reading of the rich sources available at the local and regional levels reveals the subtle reform underway in the two decades after 1945. Moving beyond the structure of the educational system, which largely retained its prewar appearance, this examination concentrates on the democratization of classroom practices, instructional materials, student organizations, and teacher training. It also evaluates schools at the local and regional level in order to move beyond the rhetoric of politicians and the bureaucratic proposals of Culture Ministry officials. Although the culture ministries of the federal states are an important part of the story, teachers and pupils are central to understanding change at the local level. Furthermore, this book underscores the process of negotiation that occurred as postwar German educators adopted and adapted some American educational ideas and methods while rejecting others. In emphasizing the role of Germans at the local level, I seek to underscore the process of "inner democratization" that took place in postwar society. Finally, this investigation pays special attention to the relationship between Americans and Germans in the postwar period and the trans-Atlantic exchange of ideas that occurred through the 1960s.

Although the two decades after 1945 have typically been labeled a monolithic period of nonreform, this book traces the evolution of West German education through four distinct phases. Chapter 1 focuses on the immediate aftermath of the Second World War (1945–1947). This period was a time in which material and professional concerns dominated the attention of American officials and German educators alike. Despite the significant problems locating useable classrooms, textbooks, and teachers, the foundation for future educational reform was laid during this chaotic time. Chapter 2 examines the years 1948–1954 and discusses the wealth of reforms initiated after physical and staffing issues subsided. This period witnessed the implementation of a variety of critical curricular and pedagogical reforms, such as the publication of the first new postwar textbooks. Exchange programs, for educators and pupils alike, expanded rapidly in these years as well. Chapter 3 turns a critical eye toward the apparent "stagnation" of the 1950s (specifically the years 1955–1959). It was during the late 1950s that reforms in the sphere of political education, such as student government and civics instruction, expanded and intensified in postwar classrooms. Postwar pupils increasingly gained personal experience with democracy through classroom instruction and extracurricular activities. Chapter 4 investigates the frenzy of initiatives introduced in the new decade (1960–1965), including *Zeitgeschichte* (the study of contemporary history) and the expansion and reform of teacher training programs. Student newspapers, too, had become established by this point, giving postwar pupils additional opportunities to prepare for their future responsibilities as citizens in a democratic state.

The temporal boundaries of this text—specifically the decision to conclude in the mid-1960s—arose from a combination of factors. First, by 1965 education had become a highly charged political issue as German academics, public intellectuals, and even some political elites began to criticize the educational system and linked it to the country's emerging economic difficulties.[27] This debate, however, focused largely on university and professional education and only obscures many of the issues emphasized here. Second, the mid-1960s witnessed a series of administrative reforms that prompted at least one scholar of German education to label these years "the end of the postwar period."[28] Many of the reforms emphasized in this book expanded and intensified further in the 1970s, but their formative years were undoubtedly those chronicled here. Third, I have intentionally avoided the use of more traditional temporal boundaries suggested by larger social and political developments: the founding of the Federal Republic in 1949; the building of the Berlin Wall in 1961; the student protests of 1968. Such dates would only shift the focus from the subtle reforms in primary and secondary schools to the larger political and social developments of the era. Nonetheless, I draw connections between the democratization of the postwar years and the student unrest of the late 1960s in the conclusion. The bold demands for change voiced by students in 1968, which were partly influenced by the curricular and pedagogical reforms encountered by these young Germans in the primary and secondary schools, further highlight the significant contribution of the schools to the postwar democratization of the Federal Republic.

Notes

1. Henry Morgenthau, Jr., *Germany Is Our Problem* (New York, 1945), 154. For additional proposals for the postwar treatment of Germany, see Walter Layton, *How To Deal With Germany* (London, 1945); Louis Nizer, *What To Do With Germany* (New York, 1944).

2. Anglo-American scholars have disagreed on the role of the schools in the political socialization of postwar German youth. American Sydney Verba has questioned the contributions of the educational system, while his British colleague, A. N. Oppenheim, praised the work of the West German schools a decade later. See Sydney Verba, "Germany: The Remaking of Political Culture," in *Political Culture and Political Development*, ed. Lucian W. Pye and Sydney Verba (Princeton, NJ, 1965), 130–70; A. N. Oppenheim, *Civic Education and Participation in Democracy: The German Case*, Contemporary Political Sociology Series, ed. Richard Rose, vol. 2 (London, 1977).

3. Clay emphasizes the contributions of education to the creation of a democratic consciousness among Germans and the value of American cultural examples to this process. See Lucius D. Clay, *Decision in Germany* (Garden City, NY, 1950), 303.

4. John Dewey, *Schools of Tomorrow* (New York, 1915); Dewey, *Democracy and Education* (New York, 1916); William H. Kilpatrick, *Group Education for a Democracy* (New York, 1940).

5. James Tent notes that most American officials responsible for education in Germany were proponents of Dewey's ideals. Stefan Bittner explains how Dewey was appropriated by German educators (despite a murky legacy in Germany due to his close identification with German nationalism before 1933) after the war. See Tent, *Mission on the Rhine* (Chicago, 1982), 5–6; Bittner, "German Readers of Dewey—Before 1933 and After 1945" *Studies in Philosophy and Education* 19 (2000): 83–108.

6. For general histories of the American military occupation in Germany, see Harold Zink, *American Military Government in Germany* (New York, 1947); Oliver J. Fredericksen, *The American Military Occupation of Germany* (Darmstadt, 1953). A more recent account that focuses on the first year of occupation is Klaus-Dietmar Henke, *Die amerikanische Besatzung Deutschlands* (Munich, 1995).

7. Jutta B. Lange-Quassowski argues that German education had not in fact begun before 1947, because denazification had prevented its implementation. Karl-Heinz Bungenstab offers a different interpretation, claiming that 1947 marked the end of positive reforms because the US shifted its priorities to containing communism. Henry Kellermann argues that reform, however limited through 1949, was not implemented based on Cold War ideological motives. See Jutta-B. Lange-Quassowski, "Amerikanische Westintegrationspolitik, Re-education

and deutsche Schulpolitik," in *Umerziehung und Wiederaufbau: Die Bildungspolitik der Besatzungsmächte in Deutschland und Österreich,* ed. Manfred Heinemann (Stuttgart, 1981), 53–67; Karl-Ernst Bungenstab, *Umerziehung zur Demokratie? Reeducation-Politik im Bildungswesen der US-Zone 1945–1949,* (Gütersloh, 1970); Henry Kellermann, "Von Re-education zu Reorientation: Das amerikanische Re-orientierungsprogramm im Nachkriegsdeutschland," in Heinemann, 86–102.

8. There is great consensus as to the "restoration" of pre-Nazi education after 1945. See Saul Robinsohn and J. Caspar Kuhlmann, "Two Decades of Non-reform in West German Education," *Comparative Education Review* 11, no. 3 (October 1967): 311–30; Hans-Georg Herrlitz, Wulf Hopf, and Hartmut Titze, *Deutsche Schulgeschichte von 1800 bis zur Gegenwart* (Regensburg, 1981); Arthur Hearnden, *Education in the Two Germanies* (Boulder, CO, 1974); Jutta-B. Lange-Quassowski, *Neuordnung oder Restauration? Das Demokratiekonzept der amerikanischen Besatzungsmacht und die politische Sozialisation der Westdeutschen* (Opladen, 1979).

9. Hermann-Josef Rupieper, *Die Wurzeln der westdeutschen Nachkriegsdemokratie. Der amerikanische Beitrag 1945–1952* (Opladen, 1993), 172.

10. Anselm Doering-Manteuffel, *Wie westlich sind die Deutschen? Amerikanisierung und Westernisierung im 20.Jahrhundert* (Göttingen, 1999), 64.

11. Beate Rosenzweig, *Erziehung zur Demokratie? Amerikanische Besatzungs- und Schulreformpolitik in Deutschland und Japan* (Stuttgart, 1998).

12. On the long-term effects of the occupation, see Tent, *Mission on the Rhine,* 312–18; H. J. Hahn, *Education and Society in Germany* (New York, 1998), 91; Karl-Heinz Füssl, *Die Umerziehung der Deutschen. Jugend und Schule unter den Siegermächten des Zweiten Weltkriegs 1945–1955* (Paderborn, 1995), 166–67, 183–84.

13. Kaspar Maase, *Bravo Amerika. Erkundigungen zur Jugendkultur der Bundesrepublik in den fünfziger Jahren* (Hamburg, 1992); Uta Poiger, *Jazz, Rock, and Rebels: Cold War Politics and American Culture in a Divided Germany* (Berkeley, CA, 2000); Volker Berghahn, *Americanization of West German Industry* (New York, 1986); Maria Höhn, *GIs and Fräuleins: The German-American Encounter in 1950s West Germany* (Chapel Hill, NC, 2002); Rupieper, *Die Wurzeln der westdeutschen Nachkriegsdemokratie.*

14. Volker Berghahn, "Conceptualizing the American Impact on Germany: West German Society and the Problem of Americanization," The American Impact on Western Europe, Conference, German Historical Institute, Washington, DC: 25–27 March 1999.

15. See Doering-Manteuffel, *Wie westlich sind die Deutschen?.*

16. Scholarship on postwar education in Berlin, specifically West Berlin, is voluminous. See Marion Klewitz, *Berliner Einheitsschule, 1945–1951,* Historische und Pädagogische Studien, ed. Otto Büsch und Gerd Heinrich, vol. 1 (Berlin, 1971); Karl-Heinz Füssl and Christian Kubina, *Mitbestimmung und Demokratisierung im Schulwesen. Eine Fallstudie zur Praxis von Beratungsgremien am Beispiel Berlins* (Berlin, 1984); Füssl and Kubina, *Zeugen zur Berliner Schulgeschichte (1951–1968)* (Berlin, 1981). The minutes of the meetings held by the Berlin school authorities until the division of the city in 1948 have recently been compiled and published in Gert Geissler, ed., *Schulreform und Schulverwaltung in Berlin. Die Protokolle der Gesamtkonferenzen der Schulräte von Gross-Berlin, Juni 1945 bis November 1948* (Frankfurt, 2002).

17. A brief account of the immediate postwar educational efforts in Hesse can be found in Birgitta M. Schulte, ed., *Die Schule ist wieder offen. Hessische Schulpolitik in der Nachkriegszeit* (Frankfurt, 1997). For two recent contributions to the history of postwar educational reform in Hesse, see Johann Zilien, *Politische Bildung in Hessen von 1945 bis 1965. Gestaltung und Entwicklung der politischen Bildung als schulpolitisches Instrument der sozialen Demokratisierung* (Frankfurt, 1997); Patricia Fedler, *Anfänge der staatlichen Kulturpolitik in Hessen nach dem Zweiten Weltkrieg, 1945–1955* (Wiesbaden, 1993). For a more general examination of postwar reform in all of the western states, with detailed coverage of the Hessian case, see Ludwig von Friedeburg, *Bildungsreform in Deutschland. Geschichte und gesellschaftlicher Widerspruch* (Frankfurt, 1989).

18. According to HICOG statistics, 98 percent of schools in the American zone were "public schools" in May 1949. This does not mean, however, that "public schools" refrained from religious instruction. See Office of Military Government for Germany, US—Education and Cultural Relations Division, *Second Handbook of Basic Education Statistics, U.S. Occupied Area of Germany* (Germany, 1950), 30; Christoph Führ, *Schulen und Hochschulen in der Bundesrepublik Deutschland* (Bonn, 1988), 212–13, 224–25.

19. For the purpose of classification, *Grundschulen*—that is, grades one through four of the *Volksschulen* (whether or not they are so termed)—are considered "primary schools" or "elementary education" in this book. In West Berlin, the *Grundschulen* include grades five and six. The upper grades of the *Volksschulen* (grades five through eight or nine in most of the FRG, or grades seven through nine in West Berlin), the *Mittelschulen,* and the *Gymnasium* constitute "secondary schools," despite their curricular differences.

20. See J. Little and Margaret J. McLaughlin, eds., *Teachers' Work: Individuals, Colleagues, and Contexts* (New York, 1993).

21. Milbrey W. McLaughlin, "The Rand Change Agent Study Revisited: Macro Perspectives and Micro Realities," *Educational Researcher* 19, no. 9 (December 1990): 11–16.

22. Interested in national publications with large circulations, I determined the following five to be the most representative: *Pädagogische Rundschau, Bildung und Erziehung, Westermanns Pädagogische Beiträge, Die deutsche Schule,* and *Die pädagogische Provinz.* These publications addressed pedagogical and professional concerns, represented the opinions of varying levels of educators, and offered discussion on all classroom subjects. In addition to these nationwide publications, I also examined the *Berliner Lehrerzeitung* and the *Hessische Lehrerzeitung* in order to examine specific debates in each of my two case study areas.

23. Archival sources at the district level *(Bezirk)* range from a handful of uncataloged boxes to the efficiently organized and vast holdings of the Heimatmuseum Neukölln. Besides the Neukölln holdings, I also consulted the collections of the privately administered Heimatmuseum Zehlendorf and the recently consolidated Archiv zur Geschichte von Tempelhof und Schöneberg.

24. Former West Berlin *Gymnasium* pupil Wilhelm-Dietrich von Thadden graciously allowed me to copy his personal files of the city's student parliament. He had participated in the organization from 1950–1955, and he still held all the meeting minutes, agendas, and related materials for his years of involvement.

25. For a general discussion of the field of oral history, see Paul Thompson, *The Voice of the Past: Oral History,* 3rd ed. (Oxford, 2000); Donald A. Richie, *Doing Oral History,* 2nd ed. (Oxford, 2003); David Henige, *Oral Historiography* (New York, 1982); Ken Howarth, *Oral History* (Stroud, UK, 1998).

26. Historians of modern Germany have increasingly embraced the use of oral history over the past three decades. Oral history played a vital role in *Alltagsgeschichte,* which underscored the subjectivity of all experience. See Alf Lüdtke, *The History of Everyday Life: Reconstructing Historical Experiences and Ways of Life* (Princeton, NJ, 1995). This trend has intensified since 1989, particularly in studies of life in East Germany. See Lutz Niethammer, *Die volkseigene Erfahrung: eine Archäologie des Lebens in der Industrieprovinz der DDR: 30 biographische Eröffungen* (Berlin, 1991); Dorothee Wierling, "Three Generations of East German Women: Four Decades of the GDR and After," *Oral History Review* 21/2 (Winter 1993): 19–30. For an excellent discussion of the debates regarding oral history in German historiography, see Kimberly Redding, "'We Wanted To Be Young': Hitler's Youth in Postwar Berlin" (PhD diss.: University of North Carolina at Chapel Hill, 2000), 17–25.

27. Georg Picht's series of articles in *Christ und Welt* initiated this wave of criticism in 1964.

28. Zilien, *Politische Bildung in Hessen,* 409.

Chapter 1

REBUILDING EDUCATION IN A "NEW SPIRIT"
The Challenges of the Immediate Postwar Period, 1945–1947

*I*n a 1946 article on the state of German education, an official in the Hessian Culture Ministry, Otto Appel, asserted that postwar educators must go about their task with a "new spirit." Embracing democracy, he argued, would bring about a "spiritual and political rebirth" for Germany's schools and its people.[1] A follow-up article written by Appel a few months later reiterated his point that nothing less than the "renewal of youth in a new spirit" would suffice for Germany's future.[2] Hessian culture minister Erwin Stein echoed this sentiment in a September 1947 speech, stating that "the rescue and the future of the *Volk*" hinged on ushering in a "new spirit" in the schools.[3] Culture Ministry officials, administrators, and teachers voiced similar claims throughout Germany in the immediate postwar period. They asserted that little, if anything, could be salvaged from the ruins of National Socialism and war. Declarations of a "new spirit" and of "looking to the future" were typical refrains in the postwar writings of German educators, administrators, and Culture Ministry officials. Most concluded, as Stein boldly asserted in his 1947 speech, that there could be "no going back."

This was no simple task, however, since most postwar educators were inclined to look to the past for guidance in mapping out the future of the German schools. The *Reformpädagogik* of the first third of the twentieth century was the educational tradition most often cited by German educators in the immediate postwar period.[4] Many postwar reformers envisioned the experimental schools of the empire and Weimar Republic as models for the postwar rebuilding of education. For these educators, a "new spirit" in education represented a rejection

---

of nationalism and militarism in the school, a less authoritarian relationship between teacher and pupil, and greater responsibility for young people within the classroom. Some colleagues who advocated more radical reforms recognized the possibilities suggested by their predecessors but deemed even the pedagogy of some interwar reformers as suspect and insufficiently democratic.

Reform-minded teachers, however, were not the only ones looking to the German past for assistance with the postwar educational crisis. Another group of postwar educators—often the eldest and most conservative—also looked to the empire and Weimar Republic, but they sought a return to the more traditional elements of German education, such as the teacher-centered classroom. They had few qualms about returning the schools to their pre-Nazi state. For these more conservative educators, a "new spirit" meant removing National Socialist ideology from the classroom, restoring the authority of the teacher, and avoiding politics within the school. Thus, the legacies of education during the empire and Weimar Republic were by no means clearly defined entities, as different segments of the teaching profession appropriated the past in accordance with their own convictions. Largely a generational conflict, these tensions were a hallmark of the immediate postwar years.[5] Although postwar educators quarreled about where to begin in 1945, there was one thing upon which they could all agree: after the ideological manipulation and instrumentalization of education under Hitler, fundamental change was absolutely necessary.

Discussions regarding the composition and content of a new postwar school system began among German educators as soon as the war ended. Their debates underscore the multiple legacies of education existent in Germany after the war. Could education begin anew after 1945 and turn its back on its history before 1933? If educators did look to Germany's pre-Nazi schools for guidance and inspiration, what aspects were appropriate for use in the postwar era? What changes were necessary to prevent the mistakes of Weimar from being repeated? Most postwar educators conceded that the schools of the empire and Weimar Republic had been imperfect, yet there was no consensus on how to draw on Germany's pedagogical traditions in order to build for the future. Thus German classrooms became contested terrain after 1945, as various approaches to rebuilding the schools circulated among postwar educators.[6]

Had Germany been spared from the destruction of war as has happened in World War I, these pedagogical discussions would have been much more meaningful when they began in May 1945. This was not the case, however, as massive material problems overshadowed the pedagogical and historical debates initiated after the war. These material concerns were largely responsible for the provisional nature of education in the immediate postwar years. Perhaps the most obvious challenge was locating adequate facilities for instruction. The combination of wartime bombings and postwar occupations of usable buildings for medical, municipal, or military government purposes put a strain on available classroom space. Another problem plaguing schools after the war was the shortage of necessary supplies. There was never enough coal to heat drafty classrooms, nor enough glass to replace broken windowpanes. Paper was hard to acquire for years after the war, even for local and regional government officials. Textbooks, too, posed a challenge to postwar educators, due to the fact that Nazi ideology had infiltrated virtually every subject by the end of the war. Further complicating the textbook problem was the hesitancy of OMGUS officials to reemploy books used during the Weimar Republic. This prompted the creation of temporary texts that could be used until German authors penned new volumes.

Another complication that had to be overcome in the immediate postwar period involved the composition of the German teaching profession. American officials initiated an ambitious denazification program in 1945 in order to remove former Nazis from positions of power. These denazification efforts struck the schools particularly hard; OMGUS officials removed an average of 50 percent of German teachers from their classrooms in the US zone by 1946. In some Nazi strongholds, this number reached as high as 90 percent.[7] The dismissal of experienced educators caused a series of problems for the German schools. First, it sparked a severe personnel shortage that forced remaining teachers to accept responsibility for unprecedented numbers of pupils. Second, reform efforts slowed because of the older, retired educators that returned to the schools in order to ease staff shortages. Third, in order to prepare new teachers, American officials established emergency teacher training programs that produced certified temporary teachers after only a few months, and in some cases, several weeks. All of these developments contributed to the instability of the schools, and in particular, the unsettled nature of the postwar classroom.

A final contribution to the tumultuous postwar environment was the presence of American occupation officials. The goals and beliefs of these OMGUS officials complicated the debates currently underway among German educators and administrators. US occupation officials had very strong opinions about the history of German education when they arrived in 1945, and unlike the Germans, they did not identify any indigenous traditions worth reviving in the postwar schools.[8] To the contrary, OMGUS officials believed that German education possessed a long history of antidemocratic instruction. The schools, they argued, had not suddenly been corrupted under Hitler; education under the Kaiser had facilitated the nationalism that sparked World War I, while the schools of the Weimar Republic had paved the way for the Nazi seizure of power. The goal of these young, idealistic American education officials was to reshape the very basis of the German schools. Only through meaningful, fundamental reform could the postwar schools overcome the nationalist, militaristic traditions that OMGUS education officials traced back to the nineteenth century.

It was in this chaotic environment that schools began to reopen in late 1945. It would certainly be inaccurate to characterize these first years of the postwar period as a time of successful reform. *Destruction, uncertainty,* and *shortage* are the words used most often by teachers and pupils describing their experiences in the first few postwar years.[9] In this environment, meaningful reform was virtually impossible. Nevertheless, this period serves as a critical time of recovery and stabilization for the German schools. The foundation was laid for changes that would begin to emerge before the end of the decade. Renovated buildings, adequate supplies, and in many cases, new teachers were a precondition for this process. So, too, was the dialogue initiated among German educators regarding the nature of postwar reform. Likewise, the denazification and professional training efforts undertaken by American officials were critical to the creation of a "new spirit" in the schools of Germany. Thus the first postwar years, despite their many hardships, should be viewed as a time of gradual rebuilding in German education—physically, pedagogically, and professionally. Despite the fact that rebuilding efforts began as soon as the war ended, the years 1945–1947 might be best described as a prologue in the history of German education reform after World War II.

The Multiple Legacies of German Education after 1945

Unable or unwilling to reject the traditions that they had experienced and to which they had contributed before the war, many postwar teachers looked into their past for guidance in rebuilding Germany's educational system. The oldest educators cast their gaze to the schools of the empire in search of inspiration for the postwar schools. These typically more conservative educators looked back upon the schools of the empire as a time of stability; they remembered the teacher as a figure of respect and the pupil as obedient and well disciplined. Struggling with the uncertainty and challenges of the postwar period, these teachers highlighted aspects of education in the empire that they believed would be useful in the postwar period. First, there was a great fear after 1945 of the upheaval and lack of control over youth in the chaos of the surrender period. While their younger colleagues rejected the authoritarian nature of teacher-pupil relationships before 1918, older educators suggested that these traditions might help postwar teachers maintain control in the classroom. These experienced educators favored stability and control over innovation or experimentation.[10] Second, *Frontalunterricht* appealed to these educators, as they once again called for order and control in the classroom. This style of teaching placed the teacher at the center of the classroom while pupils listened passively to the lecture. The rigid ordering of the classroom into banks of attentive pupils held greater attraction for some postwar educators than the group work and child-centered instruction advocated by reformers.

Many of the most experienced educators looking to the schools of the empire also sought guidance for teaching various subjects in the chaos of the immediate postwar period. The two subjects that held the most appeal were history and civics instruction (*Staatsbürgerkunde*). The main reason for this was a desire among many to avoid dealing with the complicated and divisive events of the Weimar Republic and the authoritarianism of the Third Reich. They based their argument in part on the misuse of education, especially political instruction, in the schools of the Third Reich. For those educators nearing the end of their careers,

"forgetting" the last thirty years seemed to be the easiest solution. Naturally, this translated into incomplete instruction in history and political education after 1945. Some teachers simply refused to incorporate recent history into their lessons, disdainfully remarking that "contemporary events" had no place in their courses. Others who were more clever scheduled their calendars in such a manner that no time would remain for the study of post-World War I events.[11]

Another factor in the reluctance of some teachers to address Germany's development in the twentieth century was the belief that instruction in several subjects had become overly politicized after 1945. Although both history and civics instruction had become increasingly politicized by the turn of the century, many of these older educators remembered the empire as a time devoid of the political and ideological debates of the post-World War II world.[12] Instead of emphasizing the need for critical analysis of politics and the importance of the individual, *Kaiserreich* educators had focused on loyalty to the monarch and his regime. An infamous example occurred in a Bavarian classroom in 1946. Brought back as a temporary instructor after the war, an elderly, retired teacher in the small village of Tegern Lake lectured to seventy-five eight-year-old boys about Bismarck. "Boys," he began his lecture, "I have told you that the dreams of the so-called imperialists as personified by Bismarck are evil. Very evil. The Americans have told us to say that and we are saying it—as long as the American flag is here."[13] The white-haired teacher grinned at the American in the room who recorded his comment. This brazen episode illustrates the influence that the training and experience of teaching before 1918 continued to have on the oldest postwar educators. Many older educators also argued that since they had their own political views, they could not possibly be expected to teach political education.[14] Finally, after the Nazi experience, many Germans, not just teachers, wanted to withdraw from the world of politics and retreat into the safety of their families and private lives.[15] Some hoped to avoid the simmering political tensions of the postwar era, while others felt a sense of complicity for their actions during the Third Reich. For these reasons, many older teachers refused to teach history in the postwar schools, even after it was once again allowed to be taught, and avoided political education entirely.[16]

These eldest and most conservative educators were also more likely to cling to the nationalist and militaristic lessons of the empire. Despite the ravages of war that Germany had experienced, many older teachers refused to alter their lessons after 1945, or they made only superficial changes in order to satisfy occupation officials. Teachers age fifty-five and older at the outset of the occupation had attended school, received their professional training, and spent their formative years teaching in the classrooms of the German Empire. They were accustomed to a certain style of instruction that placed Germany's interests above those of other European nations and often in direct conflict with its neighbors' aspirations. The legacy of conservative nationalist education under the Kaiser stretched beyond the ruptures of two military defeats by virtue of the continued presence (or recent arrival) of these most senior teachers in the postwar classroom.

In contrast to the yearning for tradition and stability exhibited by many looking to the schools of the empire, postwar reformers highlighted a more innovative pedagogical tradition beneath this apparently conservative exterior. Even this
period of authoritarian instruction, nationalism, and empire did not possess a
monolithic legacy, since those postwar reformers could look to the *Reformpädagogik* movement that began in the early twentieth century for inspiration. Specifically, educators recalled the reform efforts of Gustav Wyneken and Paul Geheeb,
who established experimental private schools around the turn of the century.[17]
German pedagogues had also formulated a new pedagogical approach in the first
decade of the new century, "pedagogy from the perspective of the child," emphasizing a pupil-centered style of instruction. This method of teaching contrasted
sharply with *Frontalunterricht,* which confined pupils to a passive role in the classroom. In the first issue of the post–World War II pedagogical journal *Bildung und
Erziehung,* the editors referred to this legacy in their introduction. They reminded
their readers that it had been German pedagogues who promoted child-centered
education in an age when the state and society had become overpowering in areas
of pedagogy.[18] Yet as attractive as it was for postwar German educators to point
to such precedents in the history of German education before World War I, even
they were forced to admit that the impact of these reformers had been limited
and that their ideas had exerted little influence on most schools.

Reform was indeed rare in the schools before World War I. Many older educators, administrators, and Culture Ministry officials had resisted the introduction
of new ideas in the prewar schools. Pedagogical innovation before 1918 had been
further hampered by the conditions in many German classrooms. Facilities were
poor and overcrowded, and teachers often had to work around shortages of basic
classroom materials. This was particularly true in the most crowded schools of
the empire, the *Volksschulen.* Recognizing how such shortages hampered classroom instruction, Johannes Tewes, perhaps more than any other *Kaiserreich*-era
reformer, brought the problems of education to the attention of the public. In
addition to his pedagogical reform proposals, Tewes advocated the repair of rural
schoolhouses, a reduction of class sizes, and a greater investment in public education.[19] Only through these basic changes could his larger goals of providing all
of Prussia's pupils an equal education in a unitary school system be achieved.
Tewes's most basic desire was to move beyond the class system that dominated
German society and create a classroom where educational goals and levels—not
social rank or class—dictated classroom organization. Bold aspirations shared
with many reform-minded contemporaries, these proposals remained largely unrealized before 1918. Nevertheless, the ideas of Tewes and his criticisms regarding the inequalities of compulsory education resonated with many teachers who
pursued similar goals two world wars and four decades later.

The ideas of Geheeb, Wyneken, and Tewes provide evidence that German
education was not without its pre–World War I innovators. They proposed both
pedagogical and material reforms for the improvement of Germany's schools.
Looking back on the schools of the empire after 1945, however, most educa-

tors saw a legacy that might best be described as one of pedagogical frustration. Politicians, members of the clergy, and conservative educators either prevented the introduction of reforms altogether or forced progressive educators to create experimental schools of their own, as was the case with Wyneken, Geheeb, and another noted reformer during the empire, Hermann Lietz. Forced to open their own private boarding schools, these innovators had only a limited impact on public education.[20] Even the moderate changes promoted by Wyneken or the basic improvement of German schools proposed by Tewes had been too radical for the majority of educators and administrators. Public schools during the empire were more concerned with combating Social Democracy, molding loyal subjects of the Kaiser, and preserving the educational traditions of the nineteenth century than they were with introducing new ideas or offering pupils a more active role in their education.[21] The legacy of education in the empire thus represented exclusion and rejection for many teachers after 1945.

It was the schools of the Weimar Republic that held perhaps the broadest appeal for many educators after 1945. Undoubtedly, the Weimar years represented a contentious period in which conservative educators thwarted the reform efforts of their more liberal colleagues.[22] Yet there were a number of small and incomplete changes that occurred after World War I that many German educators cited in 1945 as a foundation for postwar reform. Perhaps the most significant of these post–World War I experiments was a fundamental restructuring of the school system's structure. In an attempt to erode the elitism they identified in Germany's schools, liberal educators advocated an obligatory four-year primary school that all pupils must attend. No longer could the children of the wealthy enroll in private preparatory schools, apart from the large majority of the nation's pupils. Additionally, a new type of secondary schools (*Aufbauschulen*) was established that linked primary education directly to secondary schooling. As Marjorie Lamberti has argued, Prussian officials, who instituted these new schools in 1922, hoped they would "bridge over the chasm that had separated working-class people and the educated class in Germany for centuries."[23] This effort could be perceived as a first step toward realizing the dreams of *Kaiserreich* reformers such as Tewes. It would be inaccurate, however, to argue that this reform made the school system considerably more egalitarian. Throughout the Weimar Republic, the *Gymnasium* remained an elite secondary school admitting approximately 5 percent of fifth-grade pupils, while the *Volksschule* remained the only institution of education for over 80 percent of the population. Thus this structural reform was an important, though limited, advance.

As significant as such structural changes were, the Weimar legacy was more attractive to post-World War II educators because of curricular reforms first instituted after 1918. Progressive Weimar educators came to believe that education should focus on individual development, social interaction, and educating students for practical reality.[24] This belief, held by a small number of reformers, led them to place greater emphasis on preparing pupils for their future roles as citizens in the young republic. Encouraged by official decrees from various culture ministries, among them Prussia and Bavaria, progressive teachers charged their students with a host of newfound responsibilities after 1918.[25] Pupils undertook a variety of new tasks, including the organization of school festivals and the composition of itineraries for field trips. In some schools, progressive teachers established student associations in order for pupils to participate in the administration of the classroom and school. Limited to mundane tasks and rarely involving important decisions, these early attempts at student governance nonetheless offered pupils new opportunities to participate in the organization of school life. These activities represented a belief in an "educational spirit" founded on a closer relationship between teachers and pupils.[26] Because these new organizations seemed to diminish the authority of the teacher, they raised the ire of some Weimar educators. This opposition prevented such organizations from gaining a foothold in most areas, and as late as 1933, they remained confined largely to more academically focused secondary schools.[27] Nevertheless, these student organizations represented a small success to teachers wanting to give their students more responsibilities in the classroom and school.

In addition to the involvement of pupils in the administration of the classroom, progressive teachers in the Weimar era looked for other ways to bring education more in tune with the new republic created after 1918. Realizing that the authoritarian teacher-pupil relationship had facilitated the seamless movement of Germany's youth from school to military service, many reformers cultivated a new image in the classroom. These teachers rejected the use of severe punishments to maintain order.[28] They also realized that portrayals of Germany's military, and warfare more generally, as glorious and courageous had encouraged many of their pupils to embrace the outbreak of war in 1914. The gallantry of war espoused in history texts coupled with a blind faith in the Kaiser had proved a seductive combination for many pupils. Thus, progressive educators hoped to highlight the mistakes and weaknesses of the military and the monarchy. War could no longer be idealized; Weimar pupils had to learn from the lessons of their parents. This resonated particularly strongly with educators after 1945, many of whom saw a long tradition of militarism in the schools that predated the Third Reich.

A more widespread curricular reform of the Weimar era was the advent of civic education. Carrying the same name as it had before the war, *Staatsbürgerkunde* had its roots in the geography (*Erdkunde*) and local history (*Heimatkunde*) lessons of the empire. Yet the *Staatsbürgerkunde* instruction of the interwar period focused on the composition and function of the new democratic governmental system, as called for by Article 148 of the Weimar constitution.[29] New textbooks devoted to the subject typically outlined Germany's political history, recapitulated Germany's struggle for freedom, and concluded with a full version of the Weimar constitution. Progressive proponents of a new *Staatsbürgerkunde*, however, were left disappointed. They had advocated a departure from the traditional narrative focused on elites, military officials, and politicians. Additionally, these educators hoped that the subject would prepare Germany's youth for their future duties as citizens in a democracy. Instead of emphasizing the responsibilities and duties of citizenship in the postwar era, the overwhelming majority of texts merely stressed the institutions and leaders of the new state. The subject stressed the "apolitical alignment" of the citizen and, as the 1920s advanced, it betrayed an increasingly nationalistic reverence for the state.[30] Some post-World War I history texts even claimed that the monarchy was gone "for the time being," while a popular *Staatsbürgerkunde* text published in 1923 still included a foreword proclaiming "love for the royal houses."[31] Support for the new republic was lukewarm at best. Thus interwar *Staatsbürgerkunde* lessons, although officially supporting the new republic, maintained their prewar emphasis on compliance with authority and the rigid structure of German society.[32] The legacy of *Staatsbürgerkunde* after 1945 was thus a checkered one, offering perhaps more insight into what the subject might avoid in the new democracy than what it should actually encompass.

Despite the ambivalent legacy of education in the interwar period, it is hardly surprising that many German educators recalled the pedagogical innovations of Weimar in the years after 1945. Coerced by American military officials to adopt democratic reforms in their postwar classrooms, teachers hoping to salvage some aspects of Germany's pedagogical traditions looked back to indigenous reforms initiated during the country's first republic. Realistically, there were few other places to look.[33] These educators returned to the pedagogical reformers of the Weimar era as a guide for the postwar reconstruction of education. One of the most cited German pedagogues after the war was Georg Kerschensteiner, who was heralded for his work in the field of *Staatsbürgerkunde* both before and after 1918. Influenced by John Dewey's writings as well as the theories of nineteenth-century German pedagogues such as Johann Herbart and Friedrich Fröbel, he was also remembered for promoting the involvement of pupils in the administration of the classroom.[34]

Another much-heralded Weimar reformer in the postwar period was Peter Petersen. Petersen's "Jena Plan" of 1927 broke many of the orthodoxies of German school structures. Hoping to help pupils gain greater experience working with their peers, Petersen's revolutionary plan rejected the rigid organization of German education by entry year. He proposed that pupils be instructed in age groupings; there would be four cohorts: an *Untergruppe* (classes 1–3), a *Mittelgruppe* (classes 4–6), an *Obergruppe* (classes 7–8); and a *Jugendgruppe* (grades 9–10).[35] Additionally, Petersen deemphasized the role of the teacher in the classroom. He believed that the teacher should function as a discussion leader, or facilitator. Petersen, like Kerschensteiner, was also heavily influenced by the writings of John Dewey, particularly his *Schools of Tomorrow* (1915) and *Democracy and Education* (1916).[36] Concurring with his American colleague, Petersen envisioned the schools primarily as centers of community life—places of socialization. Revisiting these ideas after World War II, many German educators saw in Petersen's ideas, as well as those of Kerschensteiner and others, the seeds of an indigenous reform movement that could serve as a guide in the chaotic postwar period.

Whereas the reform efforts of Weimar pedagogues provoked real discussion after 1945, the legacy of education during the Third Reich was much less debated.

Virtually all educators agreed that the schools under Hitler had become a propaganda tool for the Nazi regime. The curriculum showcased the *völkisch* ideology of National Socialism, glorifying rural life, idealizing manhood, and elevating the military above all other spheres of society. The extreme nationalism, xenophobia, expansionism, and militarism of the National Socialists found their way into the textbooks and curricula of schools throughout Germany. As Gilmer Blackburn has argued, "the very core of the movement's educational program was the preparation for war."[37] Because of the emphasis on athleticism and the body, schools in the Third Reich were required to extend the amount of class time dedicated to physical fitness courses. Hitler also politicized the schools in order to indoctrinate young people with the party's ideology. Yet the Nazi refashioning of education was by no means a complete success. Few teachers openly defied National Socialist educational policies, but many avoided them or did not implement them as intended.[38] Thus, while Hitler enjoyed notable achievements in transforming the curriculum, his control over the classroom was never complete.

Hitler also introduced a number of other initiatives designed to undermine the integrity of the educational system. The most notable of these was the Hitler Youth, which eroded the authority of the teacher in the classroom.[39] Homework often went undone because the local Hitler Youth leader had organized mandatory evening or weekend activities. The authority of the Hitler Youth leader came at the expense of educators and parents, both of whom increasingly had to work around the organization's activities. Further eroding the importance of education was Hitler's 1938 decision to abbreviate secondary education.[40] In need of young men to fill the ranks of the army, Hitler shortened secondary education by one year. Finishing their education a year sooner would mean that Germany's young men could enter military service more quickly. Although not implemented, the National Socialists drafted additional provisions for reducing secondary education to be introduced at a later date.[41]

It is hardly surprising that education reforms initiated during the Third Reich were almost universally repudiated after 1945. Not only had Hitler's educational reforms been implemented in order to promote political and military goals, but educators after the war claimed that they were also pedagogically unsound. The reduction in the number of years of compulsory instruction had set Germany behind other Western nations. The continued emphasis on the teacher's authority within the classroom (even though it had diminished due to the regime's youth organization) prevented open discussions and the sincere exchange of opinions among pupils.[42] In terms of political education, those who had been educated during the Third Reich had received a perverse understanding of the nation, citizenship, and government. A particular shortcoming often cited by German educators after 1945 was that Nazi instruction provided no conception of the relationship between the state and its citizens. Arguably a continuation of Weimar civics instruction, political education under the Nazis had placed citizens beneath the state. In light of the experiences of the past twelve years, German educators quickly realized the imperative for a new political education curriculum after

1945. Thus in citizenship instruction, as in other areas, the educational policies of the Third Reich served as a foil against which postwar teachers and administrators forged a new curriculum.

Looking back on this ambiguous mixture of educational legacies, many postwar educators were uncertain about the actual value of Germany's pedagogical traditions after 1945. Young, idealistic educators who entered the profession after World War II refused to take their cue from the schools that—in the most biting indictments—had abetted Hitler's rise to power. Added to these were more experienced educators who saw the legacy of Weimar not so much in specific reforms but as a more general lesson about how to avoid future failure. Reforms in the Weimar schools had been incomplete, half-hearted, and extremely limited, they realized. Making changes at the margins would be inadequate for meeting the challenges of the postwar era. Merely resurrecting the ideas, however innovative, of turn-of-the-century pedagogues would likewise be insufficient. Putting "new wine in old containers," as Hessian culture minister Stein phrased it near the end of the occupation, would not meet the challenges of the postwar era.[43] Serious, ground-level reform would be required in order to educate students in a way that prepared them for their duties and responsibilities in a new democratic state.

This belief in fundamental change expounded by Stein was shared by many educators hoping to right the failures of the past. These teachers recognized that the approaches and innovations of the *Reformpädagogik*—while a useful starting point—needed to be expanded and strengthened in the postwar situation. Thus while the ideas and methods of pre-Nazi reformers could provide guidance, merely adopting them could not guarantee meaningful change. A 1947 address given by Hessian Culture Ministry official Theo Fruhmann illustrates precisely this concern. Fruhmann asserted that previous German educators were well versed in the ideas of such pedagogues as Dewey, Kerschensteiner, Hugo Gaudig, and Maria Montessori, but that they "had made no *practical* use of this theoretical knowledge."[44] Fruhmann thus looked to the progressive ideas of the Weimar reformers, but he insisted that their ideas must be put into practice within the schools:

> What Germany has created with the help of the occupation powers are democratic structures. It will be our job to fill these structures with spirit and life, so that model and life gradually grow into a way of life (*Lebensform*). In the family, on the sports field, in the overflowing streetcars, in offices, and last but not least, in the schools, it must be shown whether we Germans can realize what the Americans call (in an untranslatable fashion): "Democracy in action." Give an example! A single example of democratic conduct works better than a thick book about democracy.[45]

Even at the beginning of the occupation, some German educators realized that the ideas of German reformist pedagogues could only be used as a starting point. At the same time, however, they did not want to accept American methods and ideas unquestioningly. This sentiment is expressed most clearly near the end of his speech, as Fruhmann concluded that German educators should not merely copy American practices. Discussing student government as one example, he suggested German educators should "adopt its spirit and find out for themselves" what works in their circumstances.[46] Initiating democratic reforms in the schools did not mean that German educators would simply adopt American practices. This process of negotiation, as Fruhmann so succinctly described it here, is central to understanding the reforms of the postwar schools.

Calls for fundamental reform and specific proposals for achieving it were not limited solely to the speeches and writings of Culture Ministry officials. In a 1948 article, educator Kurt Debus addressed his colleagues in the pages of *Die pädagogische Provinz*. He wrote, "If we want to win the future, we must mold the young. The old educational principles have failed—to a large degree they have actually been harmful—and a reform must be thorough and drastic if it really wants to shape things anew."[47] Even in the first years of the occupation, many teachers recognized that time was of the essence, especially considering the pedagogical setbacks experienced under Hitler. Debus suggested that the old approach of imparting increasing amounts of information in docile pupils was not the true pedagogical goal of the postwar educator. Like Fruhmann, Debus intimated that postwar teachers needed to devote themselves to initiating new approaches and techniques in the classroom. If "thorough and drastic" change were to occur in the schools, postwar educators would need to formulate new ideals and innovative methods to which they would dedicate themselves.

Virtually all postwar educators agreed that reforms of some kind were necessary. The major question remaining in the immediate postwar period was where German educators could look for guidance in implementing reforms. As Fruhmann's article explained, there was some hope in the ideas of Weimar-era reformers. Yet as the Germans themselves indicated, these reforms had been limited and incomplete. Debus's article went further than Fruhmann's text, echoing the bold statement of Culture Minister Stein in its call for "thorough and drastic reform." Unfortunately, German educators did not have the luxury of holding long pedagogical discussions in the first years after 1945. In the aftermath of twelve years of authoritarian rule and six years of war, there were a number of more fundamental concerns with which educators had to grapple. And with the conclusion of the war in 1945, German educators had to face the occupation of their country by the victorious Allies. These occupation forces, particularly the United States, arrived in Germany with strong beliefs regarding the troubled history of German education and bold ideas for its reconstruction. Yet before any pedagogical discussions could take place, a number of basic material issues needed to be resolved so that education could resume.

Problems at the Outset of the Occupation

Before German educators could worry about broader curricular matters, they had to address more immediate concerns. Similarly, once the occupation actually began, American officials did not have the luxury of engaging in discussions of pedagogical theory with German educators. Material problems dominated the attention of American officials in the immediate aftermath of the war and over-shadowed most other issues, since they had to be addressed before the schools could resume their tasks. Not even the experience many of the OMGUS educa-tion officials had working in large American cities could have prepared them for the challenges of rebuilding education in the ruins of Germany. Locating adequate facilities for classroom instruction was the first assignment many edu-cation officers encountered. There was also a severe shortage of supplies—paper, chalk, heating materials, and food. American officials faced a slightly more peda-gogical problem as they dealt with German textbooks after 1945. Between the wholly unacceptable Nazi texts and the problematic books of the Weimar Re-public, OMGUS officials had to decide how German educators should instruct pupils with imperfect materials. This host of material problems plagued German schools throughout the first two years of the occupation.

Reaching agreement at the February 1945 conference at Yalta, the victorious powers divided Germany into four zones for postwar occupation.[48] The US zone of occupation was territorially the largest of the three western occupation zones, stretching from the Bavarian Alps westward and northward past Kassel toward the industrialized areas near the Ruhr. The American zone also included the city of Bremen and the southwest quarter of Berlin, which was placed under quad-ripartite administration. Including both urban centers (such as Frankfurt and Munich) and large rural areas, the US zone contained just over 17 million people placing it third behind the British zone (22.3 million) and the Soviet zone (17.3 million).[49] Although it was home to the largest Catholic population in Germany, the US zone also included many regions that were a mixture of confessions as well as Protestant areas in the north. Additionally, the American zone contained states with distinct educational traditions of their own, most notably, Bavaria.[50] The diversity of the American zone of occupation, coupled with its sheer size and the magnitude of the destruction, posed a colossal challenge to the young education officials whose assignment it was to rebuild the schools.

Because of an effective Allied bombing campaign initiated in the last years of the war, many German cities in the American zone were virtually destroyed. Thus the first problem faced by American education officials was shared by their colleagues in the other occupation zones: locating adequate facilities for class-room instruction.[51] Conditions were particularly bleak in urban areas, where the bombing had been most severe. The situation was dire in Berlin, which had bore the brunt of countless Allied bombing raids.[52] Of the 608 schools existent in Berlin before the war, 124 were totally destroyed and another 111 were in need of serious repair before they could be reopened.[53] In the American sector of the city, the schools in Steglitz, Kreuzberg, Schöneberg, and Neukölln were hardest hit, although the situation in other districts was not much better.[54] Classroom shortages were particularly hard to deal with in Berlin because by 1947, there were almost 10 percent more pupils in need of instruction than there had been before the war. Even in more rural Hesse, over five thousand damaged classrooms were unavailable for use.[55]

Adding to the crippling effects of wartime bombings were the requisitions of useable schools for noneducational purposes. Both American military officials and German authorities occupied school buildings that were still standing after May 1945. Although utilized for a variety of purposes, the most common uses for these buildings were medical facilities, office space for occupation officials and German governmental agencies, and housing for displaced persons.[56] This further complicated the postwar situation, since the schools that were ordinarily housed in these facilities had to seek out other classroom space. In Berlin, the occupation of eighty-one schools for noneducational purposes further restricted the available classroom space in the city. These confiscations, in addition to the schools that were unusable due to bombing, meant that only 3,044 classrooms—approximately 23 percent of the prewar number—were available for instruction in the fall of 1945.[57] Similar requisitions occurred throughout the American zone in the immediate postwar period, as German authorities and American military officials tried to balance their medical and staffing requirements with educational needs. The situation was somewhat better in rural areas. Not including Berlin, only 380 schools in the American sector were used for purposes other than instruction as of 1 October 1945—approximately 6 percent.[58] The use of classrooms for noneducational purposes, however, continued, and actually intensified in many areas throughout the occupation. As late as January 1949, 1,024 classrooms in Wiesbaden were still being used for office, medical, and living space, continuing to put a strain on the other schools in the city.[59]

The shortage of classrooms in Germany after 1945 forced German educators to seek instructional space in other facilities. These educators, in conjunction with administrators and Culture Ministry officials, formulated several possible responses. One option was to shift instruction into buildings that were not designated for classroom use. In the immediate postwar period, teachers held classes in "emergency schoolhouses," which included theaters, restaurants, and even private domiciles.[60] This, however, was not ideal, and classes were sometimes disrupted by the surroundings in which they were conducted. A temporary classroom in the Bavarian city of Regensburg serves as a revealing example. According to OM-GUS reports, 460 pupils from a local *Volksschule* received instruction inside the Karthaus Pruel Insane Asylum during the first years of the occupation. The borrowed classroom space had no electric lights, in some rooms pews had to be used as desks for the pupils, and bathroom facilities were shared with inmates of the asylum.[61] While the Regensburg case is an extreme example, as OMGUS records note, it highlights the potential problems that "emergency schoolhouses" posed. As with the requisition of schools for noneducational purposes, these emergency facilities were most common in urban areas. American officials asserted in October 1945 that only 265 schools in their zone were operating in temporary quarters, yet 69 of these were in the US sector of Berlin.[62] This means that more than one-third of schools in the American sector in Berlin reopened in temporary facilities.

The more common—and much longer-lasting—solution to the classroom shortage after 1945 was the creation of *Schichtunterricht*, or teaching in shifts. This development was actually less a new solution as it was a return to the situation during the war, when governmental organizations and hospitals had commandeered classrooms for other uses. After the war, schools that had operational facilities would share their classrooms with neighboring schools that had no instructional space available to them. Typically, *Schichtunterricht* meant that one school would hold classes in the morning and the other would have the classrooms for the afternoon or evening. In the immediate postwar years, some schools were shared by three institutions, so that the school day had to be divided up into thirds in order for all pupils to receive instruction. While it did allow larger number of pupils to receive instruction in an educational setting, *Schichtunterricht* also limited the amount of class time postwar pupils received. In addition to a lack of facilities, schools also scheduled classes in shifts due to material shortages. One such example is the Dreilindenschule in Berlin-Zehlendorf, which had to shorten classes, and in some cases cancel instruction, because of power shortages throughout the late 1940s.[63] The complications involved in *Schichtunterricht* outlived the American military occupation, as the practice continued in West Berlin into the 1950s and only ended in Hesse in 1956.[64]

Even if schools were still standing and classroom space was available, German educators faced the prospect of having few if any supplies with which to teach. Many schools did not have adequate heating materials, which prompted their closure (or an "extended recess" as it was phrased by many administrators) in the harsh winter of 1946–47. Teachers also complained of shortages of other basic materials: desks, pencils, and slates. Particularly problematic was the lack of paper, which restricted instruction in the classroom, as well as the homework that could be assigned. The severe shortage of paper throughout the first few occupation years also hindered the extracurricular activities of pupils. One postwar educator remembered "begging for paper at the Amerikahaus" in order to help his pupils begin a school newspaper.[65] This is not to mention shortages of other basic necessities—shoes, clothes, and coats—that prevented many pupils from traveling to school at all in inclement weather. Additionally, disease and malnourishment forced thousands of pupils to miss school. In the Berlin district of Neukölln alone, 770 pupils were suffering from tuberculosis in June 1946.[66] Thus shortages of classroom supplies and appropriate clothing, as well as poor health, all contributed to the educational uncertainty of the first years of peace after 1945.

Hardships caused by supply shortages marred the experiences of both teachers and their pupils. Reflecting on his experiences in a recent Abitur-Zeitung commemorating the fiftieth anniversary of his graduation, Wiesbaden pupil Gerd Moos remembered the challenges of attending school in the initial postwar period. He recalled that

Figure 1. School in the American sector of Berlin, 1947. Overcrowding, damaged facilities, and shortages of food and supplies (note starving child at far left) all plagued the schools in the immediate postwar period. Courtesy National Archives, photo no. RG260-MGG-Box 10–312.

when instruction resumed in the Gutenbergschule in February 1946, it was restricted to fewer subjects and less hours of coursework. There was little, if any, heat; the windows were temporarily patched up with wired glass. The wind howled through the halls and the rain dripped through the roof. There were no books. … There was no chalk; no paper. We stole pencils from the "Amis" [Americans] at the GYA on Friedrichsstrasse. There were only a few teachers, since most had been dismissed.[67]

Moos's recollection indicates that even if classrooms were useable after the war, they were by no means an environment conducive to learning. In addition to his later reflections, Moos also included passages from his postwar journal. In an excerpt dated 23 August 1946, the fourteen-year-old noted that he "with seven other strong guys had to shovel coal at school. Six tons in four hours." Moos and his classmates had used three wheelbarrows and a few shovels, and, he added, that "it [had] worked perfectly."[68] As Moos's journal illustrates, sheer survival took priority over instruction.

The problems caused by a lack of everyday items took a severe toll on the postwar schools. American officials were shocked to see that malnutrition continued to affect children in the zone throughout the first few years of the occupation, in many cases preventing them from attending school. Poor nutrition continued to plague the schoolchildren of Germany despite the efforts of American and other Allied officials, such as the provision of a hot meal to all children in the Berlin schools beginning in September 1945. American officials also learned that the children's teachers were by no means immune to the ravages of disease either. Reports from school authorities throughout the American zone explain the lengthy absences of teachers and administrators from their workplaces on account of illness. For example, in his May 1948 report, the school superintendent of the Kreuzberg schools in the American sector of Berlin informed Main School Office administrators (and OMGUS officials) that the health of the district's teachers had improved only because of the warmer weather. Despite this temporary improvement, the report added that "the number of sicknesses, especially those of a longer nature, is still high." It also noted that many teachers required new shoes. "If, at the very least, the neediest teachers cannot be supplied with shoes, some teachers, because of a lack of shoes, will no longer be able to report for service when bad weather arrives."[69] Basic health and supply needs continued to be a significant concern for both Germans and Americans well into the occupation.

As if the lack of facilities and supply shortages were not enough, the German schools faced a third—and longer-lasting—problem in the immediate aftermath of the war. American officials knew even before they arrived that the schools could not merely revert to the textbooks of the Weimar Republic. Planning for the textbook needs of German schools thus began in the middle of the war. As early as 1944, American officials in Aachen had prepared temporary "new" texts for use in the schools under American control.[70] With an initial printing of a paltry forty thousand copies, these books, which were reproductions of editions in the collections of Columbia University Teachers College, were designed to serve as useable texts until new ones could be printed on a large-scale basis. Refusing to allow German émigrés to the United States to author new textbooks, OMGUS officials bolstered their case that they were not trying to "Americanize" the German schools. This decision, however, delayed the introduction of new, useable textbooks until at least the end of the 1940s.

Explaining the necessity of a new generation of texts in the postwar schools, OMGUS Education and Cultural Relations chief Alonzo Grace quipped in 1948, "unbridled nationalism usually buries its roots in the dishonest school textbook."[71] Fearing the continuation of nationalistic instruction, American officials could take little solace in the fact that most Nazi texts were removed from classroom use in 1945.[72] OMGUS officials identified a nationalistic, militaristic tradition in the German schools that extended back to the nineteenth century. This made the reversion to Weimar-era texts after 1945 particularly problematic, since many of the shortcomings of Nazi textbooks built on those found in their pre-1933 predecessors. Thus once the occupation began, American officials began a monumental operation to review and vet Weimar-era texts in order to produce an adequate supply of books for the first phase of the occupation. Removing passages that were nationalistic, militaristic, expansionist, racist, or questionable on social, political, or religious grounds, OMGUS officials worked tirelessly to create a supply of useable texts large enough to meet the needs of the pupils in the zone. Paying no attention whatsoever to pedagogical merits, American officials vetted Weimar texts solely on the basis of content.[73] By the end of 1945, American education officials had vetted over 5 million texts and approved them for use in the schools of the zone. There were twenty volumes in total: eight readers, five arithmetic books, three history texts, and four editions in the sciences. These "emergency textbooks" did not meet the needs of all pupils, and they were by no means a permanent solution. Nevertheless, as problematic as they were, these books would serve as the basis of instruction through 1948.[74]

American officials and German educators alike recognized that virtually all subjects would require new, revised texts. Certainly mathematics, foreign languages, and the sciences posed problems, but OMGUS officials were most concerned about reemploying Weimar history textbooks.[75] American officials believed that since most Weimar history texts were in need of such serious revision, it would be best to delay the reintroduction of history instruction in the schools.[76] Further complicating the use of Weimar history texts was the fact that they were often targeted at a regional audience. Combining local events and traditions with the larger history of Germany, these texts sometimes emphasized regional identities. Naturally, this led to questionable interpretations of historical events. One such example can be found in a Bavarian text, which criticized the Frankfurt Parliament of 1848 for asking a Prussian to serve as Kaiser.[77] Even in the immediate postwar period, American officials likely wanted to avoid an emphasis on regional identity, which might come at the expense of allegiance to a future West German state.

Although American officials arrived with an awareness of the content of German texts, they must have been startled to learn how pervasive such problems actually were. History, German language, and geography books—even those authored before 1933—contained nationalistic, militaristic, and xenophobic content that American officials could not allow to reenter German classrooms. For example, a 1927 geography text embodies the lingering tensions regarding territories lost after World War I. Regarding "the old German border state" Alsace-Lorraine, pupils learned that "in Alsace in 1910 perhaps 95% of the population was German; in Lorraine 73.5%. German culture has put its stamp on this land. At present a stubborn defensive against Frenchifying is taking place there."[78] The First World War was indeed a troubling issue for German textbook authors in the years after the war. In many cases, German texts in the Weimar era vilified the French for the outbreak of hostilities. G. Bader's 1932 history textbook for the *Volksschulen* of Württemberg serves as one example. Bader stressed France's excitement at the outbreak of the Great War, since it would allow her to humiliate her despised neighbor.[79] The text asserted that French leaders such as Poincaré and Clemenceau had "pressed for war." Such depictions of the outbreak of World War I reflected a belief in Germany's encirclement by hostile neighbors seeking to instigate war for selfish aims.

The ubiquity of militaristic and nationalistic passages extended to less overtly political or historical subjects as well. American officials vetted troubling passages from Latin, foreign language, and arithmetic texts in the first years of the occupation.[80] Latin readers were particularly problematic, as they were indicted for glorifying strong leaders, emphasizing individual sacrifice for the state, and exalting the fighting spirit of the Romans and ancient Germanic peoples. Among passages to be translated by pupils in a 1929 Latin reader were the following: "Many names of brave leaders are immortal. Brave men love an honorable death, not a dishonorable life;" "Germany above all. German valor is the highest;" "It is cowardly and disloyal not to obey the leader."[81] Additional translations included in Latin texts after 1933 only intensified these sentiments. Assignments that included declarations such as "our life belongs to our country" and "surrender of the Fatherland brings eternal disgrace" could not be allowed to appear after 1945.[82] Arithmetic textbooks also received the ire of American officials because of their emphasis on the military and the political doctrine of the National Socialists. Calculating the speed of a bullet, the distance a military unit could cover in a day, or the decline in unemployment since Hitler's appointment as chancellor were all standard fare.

Aware that vetting German texts and publishing "emergency" books could only serve as a stopgap solution, American officials implemented plans that would facilitate the creation of a new generation of textbooks. Designed to offer adequate writing facilities to postwar educators, Curriculum and Textbook Centers first opened their doors in 1946.[83] These centers offered German authors all that they would need to produce new texts: a library, basic supplies, contact with colleagues working on similar projects, and a warm office in which to write. OMGUS officials hoped that these new facilities would bolster the dismal number of approved texts in the American zone. As of August 1946, only two new history textbook manuscripts had been submitted to OMGUS officials.[84] Of old textbooks that were submitted after (one assumes) revision, 17 of 27 were approved in 1945, while only 22 of 66 were approved in 1946.[85] Thus the textbook situation remained dire throughout the first two years of the postwar period.

This chaotic textbook situation hampered instruction in the schools throughout the first part of the postwar period. American-authorized texts, even in 1947, were in short supply. Further complicating the situation was the fact that many German educators deemed these temporary replacements as inadequate for use in their classrooms. This left German educators with three alternatives: illicitly using an older publication, teaching without a text, or writing a book of their own. Even in the immediate aftermath of the war, most educators felt that some kind of text was necessary for instruction. These teachers would sometimes edit older texts themselves and then redistribute them to their pupils for classroom use. This, however, did not last long, as both American officials and German administrators endeavored to centralize the vetting of books under OMGUS authority. Other educators did choose to instruct some subjects without a classroom text. A third group, certainly the most resourceful teachers, decided to create "texts" of their own and issue them to their pupils. For example, Berlin educator Gerd Poeschke authored his own mathematic books for his classes in the immediate postwar period. Although he initially reused mathematics books published after 1933 in his postwar classroom, he soon authored his own "textbook" and made copies for his pupils.[86] Many postwar educators did the same thing, writing pamphlet-style "textbooks" for a variety of subjects. In the case of Poeschke, his textbook-writing experiences during the occupation led him to author a mathematics textbook with Diesterweg in the 1950s.

The picture of the educational environment in postwar Germany painted here is admittedly a rather dreary one. The lack of basic instructional supplies, classroom space, and texts unarguably hampered education in the first years of the occupation. The situation was not static, however, as things began to improve by 1947. While education clearly suffered from the effects of the war after 1945, these first postwar years served as a time of gradual recovery and stabilization. Germans and Americans worked together to repair classrooms and rebuild schools. As we have seen, Americans endeavored to help German educators write new texts. Necessity being the mother of invention, ingenious German teachers cobbled together "textbooks" of their own in the interim. It is true that the physical carnage of the immediate postwar period is an important part of the postwar experience, yet it is not the whole story. These shortages and complications did not prevent the introduction of curricular and pedagogical reforms, they merely delayed them. This period was a necessary rebuilding phase, which helped lay a stable foundation for more meaningful reforms initiated in the years ahead.

Denazification and the Teaching Profession

In addition to material shortages, the German schools faced at least one more crisis in the immediate postwar period: denazification. American officials, similar to the other occupying powers, believed that the teaching profession required serious investigation. Those educators deemed by American officials to have been Nazis would be removed from the classroom in order to prevent their continued influence in the postwar era. Despite the fact that this process of denazification was intended to assist in the rebuilding of German education, its short-term effect was the further paralysis of the schools. Denazification prompted several important educational developments immediately after the war, many expected and a few unanticipated. While most Germans conceded that some sort of denazification was necessary after the war, they were unprepared for the encumbrances it would place on the already-overburdened educational system.

German historian Georg Franz-Willing has asserted that the first act of "reeducation" after the war was denazification.[87] Franz-Willing is correct, insofar as American officials believed the removal of Nazis from the schools to be a precondition for meaningful education reform. As it was envisioned by American officials in 1945, denazification was designed to remove all National Socialists from positions of influence and restore the pre-1933 social order.[88] Although this did not ensure the success of reform in the German schools, OMGUS officials asserted that any subsequent change was dependent upon thorough denazification. Much of the work of education officers in the immediate postwar period, therefore, consisted of removing "politically unreliable teachers" and replacing them with those more amenable to American aims. Despite their mission of removing Nazis from all aspects of public life, OMGUS did not implement a uniform, coherent denazification program. Denazification efforts depended largely on the priorities and needs of local and regional military government officials, as well as their capabilities.[89] Further highlighting the problems of the denazification process is the fact that the definition of "Nazi" according to American policy changed at least three times in 1945 alone.[90] This unmethodical—sometimes almost random—system of removing individuals from their jobs made the German public increasingly skeptical about the fairness and effectiveness of denazification. Adding to the distrust of some Germans was the fact that denazification policy differed among the Western Allies.

In few other fields was the problem of denazification more complicated than in education. Perhaps the greatest challenge that authorities examining the questionnaires (*Fragebogen*) of German educators faced in 1945 was how to evaluate the level of their participation in the Nazi teachers association.[91] This was no small problem. The National Socialist Teachers League (NSLB) was a compulsory Nazi professional organization for teachers, which absorbed democratic, women's, and other teacher associations after 1933. Virtually all educators were compelled to join the NSLB, and few resisted for fear of losing their positions. Charged with infusing the teaching profession with Nazi ideology, the NSLB claimed 97 percent of German teachers as members in 1936. Of these NSLB members, 32 percent also belonged to the Nazi Party (which was more than three times higher than the average population).[92] It would have been virtually impossible for American authorities to dismiss the entire teaching profession in 1945. At the same time, OMGUS officials were convinced that some sort of purge was necessary. American officials thus attempted to remove teachers based on whether their participation in the NSLB had been "active" or "passive," the degree of their involvement in other Nazi organizations, and whether they had publicly spoken out or acted in favor of National Socialism.

The fact that the cases of many educators, as with other professionals, were "gray" meant that it was hard for American officials to adhere to uniform standards. The almost universal membership of educators in the NSLB and the rather arbitrary means for the evaluation of their cases after the war highlight the problems of denazification. How does one define a Nazi teacher? What distinguishes an "active" Nazi from a "passive" one? These were the very questions that the German public asked of the Americans after the war. As German political-scientist Jutta-B. Lange-Quassowski rightly argues, the inconsistencies of denazification efforts underscore the fact that American officials had no clear answer. More importantly, Lange-Quassowski asserts, US officials had difficulty winning the full support of the population because individuals who had only been minimally involved with the Nazi regime were often removed while others, often higher-ranking party members, went unpunished.[93] It was this inconsistency and the apparent concentration on average people that caused denazification to become increasingly unpopular with the German population throughout the occupation.[94]

Further contributing to its unpopularity was the fact that the intensity and thoroughness of American denazification efforts wavered during the first postwar years. After an initial flood of dismissals, American officials relaxed denazification efforts and focused their attention on other matters. With the appearance in mid-1946 of articles in American publications such as the *New York Times* and the *New Republic* that proclaimed the continued existence of a Nazi threat in the US zone, American officials reintensified their denazification efforts.[95] This rededication to the elimination of Nazi educators prompted the reexamination of questionnaires already approved earlier in the occupation. In a 1946 report, Education and Religious Affairs (E&RA) officials in Bavaria reported that a spot-check in several counties (*Kreise*) revealed that almost one-fifth of educators in those areas would have to have their questionnaires reevaluated because of questionable actions that passed through while the denazification process had been more relaxed. The report concluded that "a considerable number of these will probably be dismissed as a result."[96] This came at a time when the pupil-to-teacher ratio stood at the stratospheric level of 79:1.

American denazification efforts were further susceptible to criticism because of the fact that decisions were rarely final. Hesse serves as a perfect example of this process of incremental amnesty, which gradually allowed previously dismissed teachers to return to their classrooms.[97] Initial denazification efforts in Hesse resulted in the dismissal of almost 66 percent of the teaching profession by early 1946. By July 1946, 26 percent of those who had been dismissed were once again teaching in Hessian schools. As the occupation came to a close in 1949, approximately 21 percent of Hessian teachers had ultimately lost their jobs due to denazification proceedings.[98] Thus, two-thirds of those teachers initially judged by OMGUS officials to be Nazis were once again teaching in Hessian schools. Perhaps the most likely explanation for this development is the expansion of amnesty to an increasing number of Germans during the first years of the occupation. This fact, coupled with the American decision to relax and eventually halt denazification proceedings in some cases as early as 1947, illuminates the somewhat haphazard nature of the process.

Denazification was part of a long-term strategy to improve the schools, but its immediate impact proved highly detrimental to the effectiveness of the educational system. The first of these consequences appeared as soon as the schools reopened. Already suffering from shortages dating from as early as 1939, the teaching profession was further decimated by the denazification process.[99] By June 1946, 52 percent of all Hessian *Volksschullehrer* had been dismissed due to denazification policies.[100] Not surprisingly, class sizes began to balloon. The ratio of pupils to teacher in the *Volksschulen* of many *Kreise* in Hesse was over 60:1 in

November 1946. *Kreis* Ziegenhain, for example, had 8,497 registered pupils and only 98 teachers, resulting in a pupil-to-teacher ratio of 86:1. In all but one *Kreis* in the Kassel region, the *Volksschulen* requested additional teachers, with one, Kassel-Stadt, demanding 100 more.[101] In total, this region was in need of 754 teachers at the end of 1946. The other two Hessian administrative regions turned in similar requests, asking for 722 and 789 respectively.[102] Thus, the Hessian *Volksschulen* alone required an additional 2,200 teachers over a year and a half after the end of the war.

The Hessian *Gymnasien* did not fare much better, as most schools dismissed a third or more of their teachers before reopening in early 1946. The Staatliche Oberschule für Jüngen in Weilburg illustrates the difficulties the war and denazification caused secondary schools in the American zone. In the required petition to reopen the school, principal J. W. Ferdinand Bergmann informed OMGUS officials that of the school's four buildings, one had been destroyed and another was only partly useable.[103] Only four of the school's full-time teachers who had taught in the 1944–45 school year were still available to teach. The other seven had been dismissed in accordance with military government denazification policy. All seven of these dismissed educators—and they were all men—had been Nazi Party members, including three who joined as early as 1933. In their place, Bergmann informed OMGUS officials, seven temporary instructors (*Hilfslehrer*) had been hired to teach courses upon the school's reopening. Of these seven new teachers, six were women. And with but one exception, all of these new recruits had been born in the nineteenth century; the average age of these replacements was 54.[104]

The situation was much the same in Berlin, where schools suffered similar staffing shortages. In the immediate aftermath of the war, Berlin authorities reported that only 2,663 teachers were available to teach in Berlin's schools, whereas the number of teachers before the war had been over 13,000. Approximately 2,500 of those missing teachers had been removed due to the denazification efforts of all four occupying powers. Several thousand more were undoubtedly lost to the war. Over a year later, in October 1946, the *Volksschulen* of Berlin were still missing over 350 teachers in comparison to 1938. When the *Mittel-* and *Oberschulen* of the city were considered, the city was still lacking almost 3,000 educators at the end of 1946—roughly 22 percent of its prewar total.[105] This statistic, however, obscures the level of training that those in the classroom possessed. In the American sector of Berlin, only 42 percent of those in classrooms were fully trained teachers, while the remaining 58 percent consisted of temporary or partially trained assistants.[106] These figures indicate the provisional nature of the teaching profession in the immediate postwar years. Overcrowded and often staffed by instructors possessing limited experience, the classrooms of postwar Germany could hardly be considered fertile ground for reform in the immediate aftermath of the war.

A second consequence of the denazification activities undertaken by American military officials was the return of older, typically more conservative educators to postwar classrooms. The gradual aging of the teaching profession, however, began years before the occupation. After the outbreak of World War II in 1939, increasing numbers of men of military age were drafted and sent to the front. A twelve-year-old pupil in Berlin at the time, Joachim Matysiak recalled that "the teachers that we really liked, the ones who were young, the ones that were dynamic and that we respected, were all sent off to the front by 1940."[107] The removal of young and middle-aged teachers from the classrooms had two major effects on the teaching profession. First, older educators returned to the classrooms in droves, many coming out of retirement. Second, women entered the schools in ever-greater numbers. The gradual transformation of the teaching profession in Berlin highlights this trend. Before the war, men dominated the ranks of educators in the *Oberschulen,* and they had a significant majority in the classrooms of the *Volksschulen.*[108] After the war, men held onto a smaller—but still considerable—advantage in the *Oberschulen,* yet women now comprised over 58 percent of the teachers in the *Volksschulen* of West Berlin.[109] While American denazification efforts contributed to a change in the composition of the teaching profession in Germany's schools, they built upon a legacy begun before the war ended in 1945.

American denazification policies intensified the transformation of the teaching profession that had begun during the war. The dismissal of thousands of younger and middle-aged teaching professionals forced American officials and German administrators to call on the services of older, often retired educators. Many of these educators had attended teacher training schools during the empire. Their background and age made many of them particularly unlikely to support any of the reform initiatives then being discussed by both Americans and Germans. As we have already seen, many of these older educators clung to the more rigid, authoritarian pedagogical ideas and methods of the empire. As a whole, these educators were unreceptive to new pedagogical methods or curricular reforms. The need for these teachers slowly declined after 1945, yet two years after the war had ended, almost 50 percent of teachers in the American zone were over sixty years of age.[110]

Significantly, the problems posed by the return of older educators to the classroom (or the continued employment of the longest-serving teachers) did not go unnoticed by postwar pupils. Germany's youth recognized a paradox of their own in examinations of their classrooms after the war. How could the educators who had only a few years earlier indoctrinated pupils in National Socialism so quickly remove Nazi ideology from their heads? How could those that had so fiercely clung to traditional ideas and methods now suddenly claim to embrace new ones? *Abitur* essays from the class of Karl Basler in the American sector of Berlin (Neukölln) underscore these concerns. One pupil argued in his 1948 examination essay that

> it is mostly old men, who have already taught for forty years or more—something one cannot blame them for—that continue to hold their old views and unfortunately teach according to the old methods. The youth of today, however, cannot share these old views for perfectly understandable reasons. Thus, especially in the most advanced classes, there is

often a considerable difference of opinions between the old teacher and the pupils, since no one wants to give up his views.[111]

Criticisms such as these highlight the fact that teachers were not the only parties discussing their role and methods in the postwar classroom. Pupils, too, expressed an interest in reform and voiced reservations about the ideals of their instructors. Additionally, comments such as these indicate the critical engagement of some pupils with the educational questions under discussion at this time.

Those pupils who did not indict older educators for their past sometimes questioned their commitment to the future of democracy in Germany. A female pupil in Basler's class boldly discussed the lack of confidence pupils had in their teachers in her *Abitur* examination. Perhaps even more important was her recognition that the newfound commitment to democracy on the side of many remaining in postwar classrooms might be superficial or opportunistic:

> The trust of youth in those who now want to lead is not great. This lack of trust is not surprising. In most cases, this concerns people who two years ago still taught young people to hate the enemy, to regard him as an inferior being, and to despise everything having to do with democracy. Suddenly these people have become the best democrats and want to prove to the youth that they have done wrong and now "finally" must turn around. It is thus understandable that the young want to construct their own future.[112]

This pupil's biting critique could have just as easily been voiced by American officials skeptical about an older educator's commitment to reform. Her 1948 essay emphasizes at least two important aspects of postwar reform efforts. First, she highlights the continuing (or increased) presence of older, compromised educators in the classroom. Second, this pupil raises the much more fundamental question of authority and sincere belief in reform. While younger educators would increasingly return to the schools by the late 1940s—or early 1950s in the case of West Berlin—this question of commitment to democratic reform and the legitimacy of older teachers calling for such change would linger throughout the postwar decades.

A third consequence of American denazification efforts was the unavoidable influx of underprepared temporary instructors into the postwar classroom. The *Schulhelfer* program was the American short-term solution for the German teaching crisis and played a vital role in the reopening of elementary schools in October 1945. With initial denazification removal rates for teachers reaching as high as 90 percent in some *Kreise*, almost anyone who had passed through the denazification process could enroll and become a teacher in many areas. Exposed to lessons in theory, *Schulhelfer* were also given hands-on experience in the classrooms of the US zone. Training in this program lasted from two weeks to three months depending on the area and the need for teachers, but it most often provided approximately six weeks of intense instruction. The *Schulhelfer* program was dominated by women, who made up over 80 percent of its participants. Although American officials deemed the program insufficient for the successful achievement of long-term goals and terminated it in 1947, its influence continued to be felt for several more years. Three years after the war, over 6 percent of Hessian *Volksschullehrer* had only completed the six-week *Schulhelfer* course, and an additional 6.5 percent had received virtually no training at all. The most startling figures come from Berlin, as over 30 percent of teachers were *Schulhelfer* and an additional 7.8 percent had received no training as of 1948.[113] These statistics, combined with the fact that many more teachers who were recalled from retirement and who had been educated during the *Kaiserreich* were still teaching in 1948, only further underscores the provisional nature of education in the first years after 1945.

While staffing concerns plagued the schools through the first postwar years, the situation did improve as the decade neared an end. Hesse gained almost two thousand *Volksschullehrer* between 1947 and 1948, an impressive increase of 20 percent. Similar increases occurred in the teaching staffs of *Volksschulen* throughout the US zone, with the largest, a 33 percent increase occurring in Bavaria. In fact, in all of the areas of the US zone (except for Bremen), the number of *Volksschullehrer* in 1948 met or exceeded the number who were teaching at the outbreak of the war. Subsequently, pupil-to-teacher ratios declined significantly by 1948. Between 1947 and 1948, the pupil-to-teacher ratio declined from more than 76:1 to 53:1. In Hesse, the ratio dropped from 64:1 to less than 50:1.[114] The number of teachers in the more advanced secondary schools also increased significantly in 1947 and 1948. During this period, the number of secondary school teachers in Bavaria, Württemberg-Baden, and Hesse increased 23 percent, 24 percent, and 28 percent, respectively. Although not quite yet at its prewar level, the number of educators in the secondary schools of the American zone recovered before the end of the occupation in 1949.[115] Following on the heels of the significant rise in the number of teachers was a significant increase in their pedagogical training. By 1948, the number of teachers with substandard or no teacher training had shrunk to less than 13 percent in Hesse and under 5 percent in Bavaria.[116] West Berlin, however, continued to be an enclave of underprepared teachers into the 1950s.[117]

The teaching profession that was rebuilt during the occupation was not only younger than it had been before the war, it was also less dominated by men. The war had taken its toll on the profession, as had denazification, with both disproportionately removing men from the classrooms.[118] It is true that men still accounted for a statistical majority of all teachers in Germany, yet they had become minorities in some schools and areas. Whereas in 1939 men constituted almost 70 percent of the *Volksschullehrer* in what would become the American zone of occupation, by 1947 they held only 45 percent of teaching positions in these schools. In Bavaria and Berlin, women constituted over 60 percent of *Volksschullehrer*, with Bremen following closely with 58 percent. The women teaching in *Volksschulen* were also, on average, younger than their male counterparts. For the American zone as a whole, it was almost twice as likely that a teacher under twenty-five years of age was female.[119] In the secondary schools of the US zone, the transformation was less dramatic, yet it was still noticeable. In 1942, women had held less than 10 percent of teaching positions in the secondary schools of Hesse, Bavaria, and Württemberg-Baden. By 1947, that figure had risen to 20 percent.[120]

The influx of women into the profession, coupled with the flood of young blood after 1945, provides evidence for two distinct postwar trends. First, as the 1940s came to a close, the teaching profession had virtually returned to prewar levels, in terms of the number of teachers and level of training they possessed. This was due in no small part to the increased employment of women in the classrooms. Thus it is misleading to overemphasize continued shortages, staffing crises, and lack of training in discussions of German education in the 1950s. Admittedly, problems still existed, yet the staffing crises of 1945 and 1946 had largely been solved as the decade came to a close. Second, many of the educators who entered the schools after 1945—male or female—had little professional experience from before upon which they could rely. Likewise, these young teachers had no personal stake in the traditions of the past. If anything, young teachers were the most vocal in indicting the old system for the political and pedagogical mistakes of past. While resistance to change continued through subsequent decades, most notably in the more elite secondary schools, younger educators often navigated their own course and simply worked around their colleagues. It was these young teachers, both American officials and German educators agreed, that would be most likely to fulfill the promise of a "new teacher" in the postwar era.

American Perceptions of German Education and Their Plans for the Future

The beliefs that American officials held regarding German education and their bold plans for reform constituted a final complication for the schools in the immediate postwar period. These officials, few of whom had much experience with German education, nevertheless held a very poor image of the schools with which they would be working. Alonzo Grace, who became chief of the Education and Cultural Relations Division responsible for German schools in 1948, asserted that German education "had never been democratic." He cited an authoritarian heritage that long predated the advent of the Third Reich.[121] The American military officers who worked with Germany's schools after the war largely shared his opinion. These military officials were faced with a number of dilemmas in the first years of the occupation. The most obvious one, yet the one they only gradually realized, was the paradox of forcing German teachers to initiate democratic reforms in the schools. Democracy, they slowly recognized, could not be imposed on others. A second dilemma had to do with the nature of the reforms proposed. While many German educators looked to the reforms of the interwar era for guidance, American officials did not see educational traditions that would be useful in the postwar period.[122] Yet OMGUS officials hoped to avoid the impression that the changes they advocated were American in origin. Therefore, they connected the democratization of German schools with broader European pedagogical trends. This, it was hoped, would avoid making OMGUS suggestions appear as an effort at "Americanizing" the German schools. A final dilemma was the more general question of "reeducation," as the Americans termed their mission. What did it mean to "reeducate" the German people? Was there a "German mind-set" that could be altered? American military officials grappled with these questions throughout the first years of the occupation.

Given responsibility for these enormous questions of education and cultural politics in 1945 were twenty-eight young military officers in the OMGUS branch of E&RA. With a small, inexperienced staff at the outset of the occupation, the responsibilities of E&RA seemingly did not command great importance; it was initially organized as a subdivision under Public Health and Welfare.[123] Education officials came from a wide variety of organizations during the first years of the occupation, with few of them having had previous experience in the European theater of war or with Germany.[124] A small number were recruited from civilian agencies in the US, with the remainder coming from organizations such as the Strategic Bombing Survey, Field Information Agency, Technical (FIAT), and the United Nations Relief and Rehabilitation Agency (UNRRA).[125] As James Tent notes in his seminal study of education during the American occupation, *Mission on the Rhine*, most education officers in the military government were educational administrators, "the majority of whom tended to be suspicious of educational practices that varied from their own."[126] These men were mostly New Deal liberals whose only experience was in an urban setting. Their ideas of "democratic education" were largely formed by the pedagogical writings of John Dewey, William Kilpatrick, and other Progressives.[127] They were largely unprepared for the types of problems they would face in the schools of the defeated former enemy. The composition and background of OMGUS education officials in the immediate postwar period does not indicate any great significance given to education on the part of the American government. Yet this small branch of OMGUS was charged with the monumental task of rebuilding the German educational system, democratizing the schools, and "reeducating" the German people. Secondary status in the hierarchy of the military government and a lack of manpower would complicate the tasks of these education officials throughout the first years of the occupation.

The American education officers who arrived in 1945 came to their new positions with a long list of specific complaints regarding the nature of German schooling. Perhaps their most fervent belief was that the organizational structure of the German educational system upheld the divisions of German society. The elitist character of the educational system reinforced social distinctions and was, they argued, inherently undemocratic. Although undergoing moderate reform during the Weimar Republic and minor changes under Nazi rule, the organization of the German school system in 1945 remained virtually unchanged from the time of the empire.[128] After four years of common elementary schooling, termed the *Grundschule,* pupils were separated into one of three separate schools

Figure 2. OMGUS education officials discussing policy, 1947. From left: Alonzo Grace; John P. Steiner (E&RA chief, Württemberg-Baden); Vaughn R. DeLong (E&RA chief, Hesse); Walter Bergman (E&RA chief, Bavaria); Harold H. Crabgill (E&RA chief, Bremen); R. T. Alexander (deputy director, E&RA); John W. Taylor (director, E&RA); Fritz Karsen (E&RA higher education specialist). Courtesy National Archives, photo no. RG 260-MGG-Box 16–568.

at age ten: the *Gymnasium,* the *Mittelschule* (later *Realschule*), or they continued their stay in the *Volksschule* (later *Hauptschule*).[129] The *Gymnasium* prepared its pupils for study at the university and future careers as doctors, lawyers, scientists, and professors. Retaining its emphasis on classical languages—specifically Latin and Greek—after the war, the *Gymnasium* was most selective in which pupils would be admitted. Although by the mid-1960s, roughly 25 percent of West Germany's pupils attended the *Gymnasium,* the number of pupils moving from the *Grundschule* to the *Gymnasium* in the immediate postwar period ranged from 5 to 10 percent.[130] Slightly less selective was the *Mittelschule,* which admitted approximately 15 to 20 percent of Germany's fifth-grade pupils and prepared them for careers in business and industry. The remaining pupils would complete their compulsory education after the eighth grade in the *Volksschule* and then move on to vocational training. Both American officials and many German educators feared that this would become a "school of leftovers" (*Restschule*) where the vast majority received a second-rate education. Thus reforming the structure of Germany's educational system would be the highest priority of American officials throughout the first years of the occupation.[131]

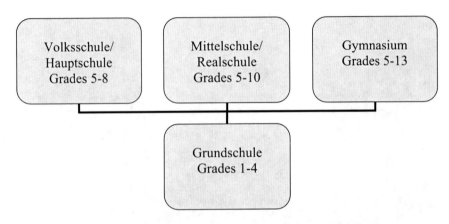

Organizational Structure of the Hessian Schools, early 1950s

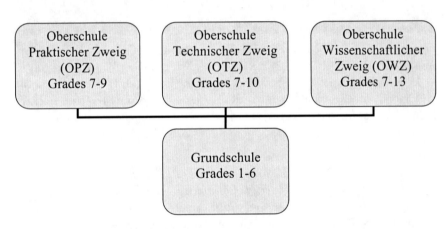

Organizational Structure of the West Berlin Schools, 1951

Figure 3. The organization of the postwar schools in West Berlin and Hesse.

The OMGUS critique of Germany's educational structure would capture many headlines throughout the years of occupation, but it was only one of the Americans' concerns. US officials arrived after the war with a list of specific pedagogical and curricular issues that they felt German educators needed to change. The idea of the schools reverting to the pre-Nazi status quo alarmed American officials, particularly because the faults they identified in the German schools were not linked solely to Nazi pedagogy. Naturally, National Socialist ideology would have to be removed from textbooks and the obvious glorifications of Hitler, Göring, Goebbels, and other Nazi minions would have to be deleted. American officials, however, identified a number of problematic trends in German education that predated the rise of Hitler. In order for the schools to educate a new generation in the spirit of democracy, peace, and international cooperation, German schools would have to undergo several significant changes.

One of the strongest preconceptions Americans had regarding German schools in 1945 was that they were authoritarian in design. Believing that Germans tended to subordinate themselves to a strong leader, American officials indicted German schools for instilling this unquestioning deference to authority from an early age. A postwar handbook for those involved with the German Youth Activities (GYA) organization informed American military men that many Germans "follow a leader and respect only the leader, who demands obedience."[132] Specifically in relation to the schools, OMGUS officials questioned the rigid relationship between pupil and teacher. No longer should a teacher be seen as an authoritarian figure that lorded over the class. Many American officials believed that this only reinforced the tendency of Germans to respect strong leadership and to obey unquestioningly the person in charge. The personification of the teacher with the state raised additional concerns. Both American officials and many German teachers agreed that there was a history of education placing the priorities of the state before the welfare of the individual. The pupils' perception of the teacher as a representative of the state also made him less approachable. American officials thus wanted to deconstruct the rigid relationship between pupils and teachers and facilitate a more relaxed classroom environment.

German educators, too, recognized the need for a new pupil-teacher relationship and voiced their concerns in the pages of postwar pedagogical publications. Emil Fuchs, calling for a "new teacher" in 1947, demanded an end to the strict authoritarianism that ruled German classrooms before and during the Third Reich. He saw the greatest opportunity for change in the building of strong relationships with pupils. He argued that "the great task of the teacher currently lies particularly in that he recognizes that he is the first figure in which the child, the growing citizen, meets the state … and it is crucial that the child meets the state in a form in which he can respect and love it."[133] Fuchs's concern sounds quite similar to that of US military officials. His proposal was likely welcomed by American officials as a sign of German willingness to move beyond the traditions of prewar pedagogy.

Another complaint voiced by American officials in the immediate postwar period was the tendency of the schools to emphasize the community at the expense of the individual. This sentiment can be seen in the "Report of the U.S. Education Mission to Germany," authored by ten American educators who spent almost four weeks evaluating Germany's schools in the autumn of 1946. The report served as both a diagnosis of and treatment plan for the German schools. It asserted that before the war, teachers displayed "a complete disregard of the ideals of equal opportunity, respect for the individual, [and] the sharing of ideas through discussion."[134] The report argued that tolerance for a variety of opinions and awareness of individual needs would facilitate the creation of a more democratic environment for pupils. OMGUS officials agreed, and they encouraged postwar educators to develop the intellect, curiosity, and distinct personality of each and every pupil. Many German educators shared the concerns of American officials regarding the depersonalization and loss of individuality (*Vermassung*) in the schools. After the experience of the Third Reich, many Germans recognized the dangers in blindly adhering to the will of the group. In a 1951 article published in one of West Germany's leading pedagogical journals, educator Paul Lotz claimed "the dangers of depersonalization threaten every one of us hourly." If German educators allowed such practices to endure in the postwar period, he concluded, they would lead only to ruin.[135]

As the occupation began, American officials also expressed concern that German educators were wholly unprepared for teaching political education and the responsibilities of citizenship. Although civics instruction had officially entered the curriculum after the First World War, occupation officials concluded that German teachers did not understand the requirements of teaching the subject, especially in a newly democratic state. These concerns were openly expressed in a January 1947 publication provided to German teachers, entitled "Twenty Proposals for Social Studies." OMGUS officials used this pamphlet to encourage educators to move beyond the pedagogical approaches of old and employ new strategies for teaching citizenship:

> The theoretical knowledge of all processes in a democratic state is not enough, even if it is indispensable; it must be brought to completion through deeply-rooted habits as well as through corresponding outlook. These habits and this outlook can only be achieved through many years of experience and participation in group work of a democratic character and through the development of individuality, self-reliance, and initiative in every individual. It is the responsibility of the schools to offer as many opportunities as possible that lead to this goal.[136]

This quote clearly distinguishes between knowledge of democratic processes and practical experience. Whereas learning about the constitution and president of the Weimar Republic may have been central to the *Staatsbürgerkunde* courses of the interwar period, American officials hoped that postwar pupils would acquire personal experience with democracy in the classroom.

A related concern American officials possessed regarding the instruction of political education after the war was the unwillingness of many German educators to engage in any discussion of politics or contemporary issues. Many educators felt a sense of complicity for the crimes of the Third Reich; others simply wanted to avoid sensitive discussions regarding Germany's recent history. Still others saw the tensions of the Cold War as a reason to remain silent on political questions in the classroom. American awareness of this tendency and their frustration with it is clear in the speech of American educator (and OMGUS "visiting expert" from the University of Wisconsin) Burr Phillips at a 1948 social studies conference in Hesse. He issued a word of caution to those educators in the room who were fearful that providing social studies instruction would be tantamount to "throwing the youth into the chaos of the present." Phillips countered that pupils already faced this chaos on a daily basis. He concluded that it was the responsibility of "teachers to give them the leadership which they need so sorely and to help them in the formation of a philosophy of life and action which will save their generation … and the world for future generations."[137] Contrary to the views of some German teachers, Phillips suggested that in the emerging Cold War world, political education was an indispensable instrument in the construction and protection of democracy.

In order to give German pupils experience with "everyday democracy" in postwar classrooms, American education officials came armed with a number of suggestions taken from the schools they knew back home. Among the many proposals were a few that illustrate American ideas about the shortcomings of German education after the war. First, student government received high praise from American officials in the hopes that it would actively involve pupils in the administration of their classroom. The aforementioned 1947 social studies pamphlet targeted at teachers encouraged them to have their classes elect officers that would represent the interests of the pupils and operate according to parliamentary procedure. American officials asserted that "[e]very boy and girl should be so familiar with parliamentary procedure through repeated experience that he will feel perfectly at home in any public assembly and will know how to make motions and take the floor to express his views."[138] A second, and related, suggestion was that teachers should encourage pupils to hold debates in the classroom. This, OMGUS officials were convinced, would help pupils sharpen their critical thinking skills and gain experience in evaluating both sides of an argument. These debates served a double purpose for the American officials who proposed them, since they envisioned these events as an opportunity to convey both relevant classroom material and practical experience with democratic methods and concepts.[139]

Moving beyond classroom instruction, OMGUS officials also suggested a number of extracurricular activities that would prepare young Germans for their future responsibilities as citizens. Again drawing on American traditions, OMGUS officials advocated the creation of clubs organized around specific interests. In order to motivate pupils to take part in the life of their school and to give them experience working in groups with peers, American officials suggested the formation of theater, chess, and sports clubs. These clubs were intended to "promote a spirit of enterprise and voluntary cooperation" among German pupils.[140] Another proposed reform centered on pupils familiarizing themselves with the functioning of democracy in their locality. Teachers were encouraged to organize field trips to various governmental offices and civic organizations and have pupils conduct interviews with those people they encountered. This was supposed to help pupils understand the responsibilities and daily functions of government in a democratic state. Such activities sought to demystify the workings of democracy, making them immediate and comprehensible to postwar pupils. These proposals underscore the emphasis on presenting democracy as a process that affected all citizens instead of an abstract theory or distant institutions far removed from everyday life.

Despite their protests to the contrary, OMGUS officials clung to a rather narrow conception of democratic education throughout the occupation. Not surprisingly, they viewed American schools as a guide for Germany. OMGUS officials, however, could not tell German educators that American schools were the benchmark for democratic schools. This tricky situation is where American officials encountered an operational dilemma. How could they convince German educators that their ideas were not foreign? The most typical refrain employed by US officials was that the democratic reforms they advocated were those same pedagogical methods common to democracies in Europe as well as America. Therefore, returning Germany to the larger European and global community was a common theme among American officials. Sometimes OMGUS officials went even further in their appeals, allowing their suggestions to be interpreted as a reawakening of Weimar-era reforms. In retrospect, this may have made more sense than American officials realized, since the reformers they highlighted or to whom they indirectly referred—Kerschensteiner, Petersen, and Fritz Karsen, to name a few—were themselves influenced by the pedagogical writings of American educators, particularly John Dewey. Although only occasionally mentioning pedagogues by name, American officials made proposals that German teachers often associated with specific domestic reformers.[141] For example, an American professor addressed an assembly of Berlin-Neukölln educators in 1947 and outlined numerous reform proposals. The teachers listening to the speech believed that they were being asked to introduce some of the very same pedagogical approaches begun in the Neukölln schools of the 1920s and 1930s. With this connotation in mind, it is little surprise that the 1947 report written by the German educators after the assembly explained that the approaches advocated by the American professor received "much encouragement."[142]

The most common pedagogical concern expressed by American officials during the occupation was that the German schools failed to make democracy a real, palpable process to their pupils. Even if pupils had received instruction in political education before the war, US officials asserted, it had been only theoretical and unrelated to the day-to-day responsibilities of citizenship in a democracy. Abstract, theoretical instruction in the institutions of democracy, Americans asserted, would be insufficient for the democratization of German education. Largely unrealized—or only modestly established—by the end of 1947, many of the proposals cited here would become commonplace in the schools of the Federal Republic in the 1950s. In some ways, the proposals American education officials outlined during the first years of the occupation served as a partial blueprint for the future reform of education in West Germany.

* * * * * *

The period from May 1945 to December 1947 might best be characterized as a time of recovery and rebuilding in the German schools. Rudimentary concerns such as repairing facilities dominated the agenda. Textbooks were in short supply. Denazification sparked a shortage of professional teachers, thus further paralyzing the schools. Yet addressing these issues was a necessary precondition for the longer-term reforms that began to appear at the end of the 1940s. By early 1948, the situation had stabilized, as pedagogical concerns began to eclipse material and staffing shortages. First, teacher-pupil ratios began to decline as a new generation of fully trained teachers entered the classrooms. Second, the militaristic, nationalistic textbooks of the Nazi era and before disappeared from German classrooms. Finally, many pupils began to engage in the practical experiences of democracy that their reform-minded teachers had suggested. Taken together, developments such as these signal the inauguration of significant, if subtle, pedagogical reforms.

The presence of American occupation forces in Germany after the war added yet another variable to the postwar equation. OMGUS proposals for education reform would play an important role in postwar schools, even if their suggestions could not be implemented immediately due to more pressing concerns. Admittedly, American proposals for the alteration of the three track school system did not receive much support among German educators. While there was tension in some instances between American officials and German educators and administrators, there was also much consensus. As we will soon see, American interests in education reform did not disappear in the face of an intensifying Cold War in 1947. Instead, US officials shifted their attention to less tangible issues, such as personal exchanges and student organizations. The heating up of the Cold War underscored how important educational change would be in a newly divided world. It was only through the material and professional restructuring of the early occupation period that made possible the longer-term curricular and pedagogical reforms that extended into the next two decades and beyond.

Notes

1. Otto Appel, "Vom Neuen Geist des Erziehers," *Der deutsche Lehrer* 2 (1946): 4.
2. Otto Appel, "Die deutsche Schule. Ihr Neubau nach den Plänen des Hessischen Kultusministeriums," 7 February 1947, 1, Abteilung 1178, No. 75b, Hessisches Hauptstaatsarchiv (HHstA).
3. Erwin Stein, "Pläne zur Schulreform und Lehrerbildung in Hessen," speech given in Bad Herzfeld, 13 September 1947, 2, Abteilung 1178, No. 72, HHstA.
4. Debates on what precisely constitutes *Reformpädagogik* and, perhaps more significantly in this context, what influence it had on post–World War II education continue unabated. Wolfgang Keim maintains that *Reformpädagogik* exerted a largely restorative influence on the schools of West Germany after 1945. See Wolfgang Keim, "Reformpädagogik als restaurative Kraft," in *Erziehung und Erziehungswissenschaft in der BDR und der DDR,* vol. 1, ed. Dietrich Hoffmann and Karl Neumann (Weinheim, 1994), 221–48.
5. Horst Kollat, interview by author, tape recording, Berlin-Reinickendorf, 23 April 2003.

6. Many recent studies question the traditional American-focused examinations of postwar education reforms in Germany. These authors emphasize the active role of German educators in the postwar debates. See Wolf-Arno Kropat, "Amerikanische oder deutsche Schulreform?" *Nassauische Annalen* 112 (2001): 541–68.

7. See James Tent, *Mission on the Rhine* (Chicago, 1982), 50–57.

8. See Harold Zink, *American Military Government in Germany* (New York, 1947) and *The United States in Germany, 1944–1955* (New York, 1957).

9. Entering the schools as a teacher in 1945, Horst Kollat remembered the immediate postwar years as a "hard but wonderful time." As with others of his generation, his decision to become a teacher was influenced by financial concerns. Horst Kollat, interview, 23 April 2003.

10. See Gottfried Stein, *Die pädagogische Provinz* 5, no. 1 (1951): 8–11.

11. This problem was most common in the early 1950s. Yet it took more than a decade for this reluctance in addressing the Weimar Republic and Third Reich in history and political education classes to disappear. Berndt Roland, interview by author, tape recording, Berlin-Mitte, 29 May 2003.

12. See James Albisetti, *Secondary School Reform in Imperial Germany* (Princeton, NJ, 1978), 171–291.

13. Gregor Ziemer, "Our Educational Failure in Germany," *American Mercury* 62, no. 270 (June 1946): 726–33.

14. Herbert Broermann, "Gemeinschaftskunde in geschichtlicher Sicht," *Pädagogische Rundschau* 9, no. 11 (1954–55): 500.

15. Johann Zilien, *Politische Bildung in Hessen von 1945 bis 1965. Gestaltung und Entwicklung der politischen Bildung als schulpolitisches Instrument der sozialen Demokratisierung* (Frankfurt, 1997), 33–34.

16. Horst Kollat, interview, Berlin-Reinickendorf, 23 April 2003.

17. A brief examination of Geheeb's pedagogical ideas can be found in Dennis Shirley, *The Politics of Progressive Education: The Odenwaldschule in Nazi Germany* (Cambridge, MA, 1992).

18. Franz Hilker and Erich Hylla, "Zur Einführung," *Bildung und Erziehung* 1, no. 1 (1948): 3.

19. Marjorie Lamberti, *The Politics of Education: Teachers and School Reform in Weimar Germany* (New York, 2002), 16–17.

20. See Marjorie Lamberti, *State, Society, and the Elementary School in Imperial Germany* (New York, 1989).

21. For more on the role of the schools in fighting the influence of the SPD, see Marjorie Lamberti, "Elementary School Teachers and the Struggle against Social Democracy in Wilhelmine Germany," *History of Education Quarterly* 32, no. 1 (Spring 1992): 72–97.

22. For an excellent discussion of the debates between liberal and conservative educators during the Weimar Republic, see Lamberti, *The Politics of Education*. Lamberti emphasizes the role of *Volksschullehrer* in these discussions and the modest but important successes they achieved.

23. Lamberti, *The Politics of Education*, 119.

24. John Edward Harrington, III, "Weimar Educators' Views of American Educational Practices" (PhD diss., University of North Carolina, 1979), i. See also Val Rust, "The Image of American Education through the Weimar Period," *Paedagogica Historica* 33, no. 1 (1997): 25–44.

25. Friedrich Bran, "Schülermitverantwortung," *Bildung und Erziehung* 15, no. 2 (1962): 95.

26. Jobst Werner, *Schülermitwirkung in den öffentlichen Schulen Deutschlands nach 1945 unter besonderer Berücksichtigung der Entwicklung in Berlin. Eine Darstellung der Entwicklung in der Zeit von 1945 bis 1994* (Berlin, 1995), 26.

27. See Wolfgang Scheibe, *Schülermitverantwortung* (Berlin, 1962). For further examples of postwar educators reflecting on the trials of *Schülermitverwaltung* in the interwar period, see Marie Quade, "Schülermitverwaltung? Ja.—Aber richtig." *Die pädagogische Provinz* 7, no. 5 (1953): 255–60; Bran, "Schülermitverantwortung," 94–105.

28. Lamberti, *The Politics of Education*, 120.

29. Karin Kitowski, "Ein warmer Hauch der Liebe zu Volk und Staat … Anspruch und Wirklich-

keit der Staatsbürgerkunde in der Weimarer Republik," in *Die Liebe zu Volk und Vaterland. Erziehung zum Staatsbürger in der Weimarer Republik,* ed. Karin Kitowski and Rüdiger Wolf (Dortmund, 2000), 9–29. See also Paul Roehrig, *Politische Bildung. Herkunft und Aufgabe* (Stuttgart, 1964).

30. Zilien, *Politische Bildung in Hessen,* 27.

31. Gerald L. Buckhout, "The Concept of the State in Modern Germany: History Textbooks, 1918–1933," *Internationales Jahrbuch für Geschichtsunterricht* 9 (1963/1964): 15–30; A. Bodesohn, *Handbuch der Staats- und Bürgerkunde,* 3rd ed. (Wittenberg, 1923).

32. Wolfgang Geiger, "Geschichte und Staatsbürgerkunde vor und in der Weimarer Zeit," in *Geschichte und Geschichtsdidaktik vom Kaiserreich bis zur Gegenwart,* ed. Paul Leidinger (Stuttgart, 1988), 99–109.

33. See Thomas Ellwein, "Die deutsche Gesellschaft und ihr Bildungswesen. Interessenartikulation und Bildungsdiskussion," in *Handbuch der deutschen Bildungsgeschichte,* vol. 4/1, ed. Christoph Führ and Carl-Ludwig Furck (Munich, 1998), 90.

34. Hermann Röhrs, "Progressive Education in the United States and its Influence on Related Educational Developments in Germany," *Paedagogica Historica* 33, no. 1 (1997): 45–68.

35. Theo Dietrich, *Die Pädagogik Peter Petersens. Der Jenaplan: Beispiel einer humanen Schule,* 4th ed. (Bad Heilbrunn, 1986), 65.

36. Röhrs, "Progressive Education in the United States," 57. See also Jürgen Heideking, "Mutual Influences on Education: Germany and the United States from World War I to the Cold War," *Paedagogica Historica* 33, no. 1 (1997): 9–23.

37. Gilmer Blackburn, *Education in the Third Reich* (Albany, NY, 1985), 102.

38. See Marion Klewitz, *Lehrersein im Dritten Reich* (Weinheim, 1987), 219; Harald Scholtz, *Erziehung und Unterricht unterem Hakenkreuz* (Göttingen, 1985); Hermann Schnorbach, ed., *Lehrer und Schule unterem Hakenkreuz. Dokumente des Widerstands von 1930 bis 1945* (Königstein, 1983).

39. Peter Stachura, "Das dritte Reich und Jugenderziehung: Die Rolle der Hitlerjugend 1933–1939" in *Erziehung und Schulung im Dritten Reich,* ed. Manfred Heinemann (Stuttgart, 1980), 90–112. See also H. W. Koch, *The Hitler Youth: Origins and Development 1922–1945* (New York, 1975); Peter Stachura, *The German Youth Movement 1900–1945* (New York, 1981).

40. Mathias Homann, "Schulalltag im Dritten Reich—Erfahrungen am Kaiser Wilhelms-Realgymnasium," in *Schulreform—Kontinuitäten und Brücke. Das Versuchungsfeld Berlin-Neukölln,* vol. 1, ed. Gerd Radde and Werner Korthaase, et al. (Opladen, 1993), 366–86. See also James Tent, "Mission on the Rhine: American Educational Policy in Postwar Germany: 1945-1949, *History of Education Quarterly* 22, no. 3 (1982): 255-276.

41. Arthur Hearnden, *Education in the Two Germanies* (Boulder, CO, 1976), 28.

42. See Heinz Meissner, "Diskussion über das Diskutieren! Bericht über die Durchführung einer Unterrichtsstunde im Fach 'Bürgerkunde' der Berufsschule," *Pädagogische Rundschau* 2, no. 8 (1948): 362–64; Gottfried Bussard, "Das Unterrichtsgespräch," *Pädagogische Rundschau* 3, no. 1 (1949): 19–24.

43. "Richtlinien für den politischen Unterricht," 30 June 1949, *Amtsblatt des Hessischen Ministeriums für Kultus und Unterricht* 2, no. 7 (July 1949): 229.

44. Theo Fruhmann, "Demokratisches Leben und Schülerselbstverwaltung," undated (likely 1947), 1, Abteilung 1178, No. 122, HHstA, my emphasis. See also Zilien, *Politische Bildung in Hessen,* 170–72. Fruhmann was a member of "Die Neue Schule," a committee in the Hessian Culture Ministry dedicated to formulating a new social studies curriculum.

45. Fruhmann, "Demokratisches Leben," 2.

46. Ibid., 17.

47. Kurt Debus, "Ein kleiner Beitrag zur grossen Schulreform," *Die pädagogische Provinz* 1, no. 2 (1948): 96–100.

48. Christoph Klessmann, *Die doppelte Staatsgründung* (Bonn, 1991), 30.

49. Ibid., 67.

50. For an examination of the tense relationship between the American occupation authorities and the Bavarian Culture Ministry after the war, see Winfried Müller, *Schulpolitik in Bayern im Spannungsfeld von Kultusbürokratie und Besatzungsmacht 1945–1949* (Munich, 1995), 111-272. See also Hubert Buchinger, *Volksschule und Lehrerbildung im Spannungsfeld politischer Entscheidung 1945–1970* (Munich, 1975), 17–79.

51. Education in the other Western occupation sectors has received less attention than reforms in the American zone. For the British zone, see Arthur Hearnden, *The British in Germany: Educational Reconstruction after 1945* (London, 1978); Günther Pakschies, *Umerziehung in der Britischen Zone, 1945–1949* (Weinheim, 1979). For the French zone, see Angela Ruge-Schatz, *Umerziehung und Schulpolitik in der französischen Besatzungszone, 1945–1949* (Frankfurt, 1977). An excellent recent investigation of Soviet education efforts in their zone of occupation can be found in Benita Blessing, *The Antifascist Classroom: Denazification in Soviet-occupied Germany, 1945–1949* (New York, 2006).

52. *Zahlen aus dem Berliner Schulwesen,* 22 January 1948, C. Rep. 120, No. 3304, Landesarchiv Berlin, (LAB).

53. "Die Berliner Schulen vor und nach dem Kriege," Letter from Magistrat von Gross-Berlin (Hauptschulamt), 13 February 1948, C. Rep. 120, No. 3304, LAB.

54. "School Survey—U.S. Sector, Berlin," Box 75; Records Relating to Cultural Exchange and School Reopenings; Records of the Education Branch; Records of the Education and Cultural Relations Division; Records of the US Occupation Headquarters, WWII, Record Group 260, National Archives, College Park (NACP).

55. Birgitta M. Schulte, ed., *Die Schule ist wieder offen: Hessische Schulpolitik in der Nachkriegszeit* (Frankfurt, 1997), 7.

56. OMGUS, *Education and Religion—Monthly Report of Military Governor,* No. 2, September 1945, 2.

57. "Die Berliner Schulen vor und nach dem Kriege," C. Rep. 120, No. 3304, LAB.

58. OMGUS, *Education and Religion—Monthly Report of Military Governor,* No. 2, September 1945, 2.

59. Patricia Fedler, *Anfänge der staatlichen Kulturpolitik in Hessen nach dem Zweiten Weltkrieg, 1945–1955* (Wiesbaden, 1993), 76. She emphasizes here that both American and German authorities were responsible for this problem.

60. Protokollbuch der 32.Volksschule, Protokoll vom 12 October 1945, Heimatmuseum Neukölln, quoted in Dietmar Schiller, "Schulalltag in der Nachkriegszeit," in *Schulreform—Kontinuitäten und Brücke. Das Versuchsfeld Berlin-Neukölln,* vol. 2, ed. Gerd Radde and Werner Korthaase, et al. (Opladen, 1993), 33.

61. "Investigation made 5 January 1949 of the Deplorable Conditions in a Bavarian School at Regensburg," 6 January 1949; Box 74; Records Relating to Cultural Exchange and School Reopenings; Records of the Education Branch; Records of the Education and Cultural Relations Division; Records of the US Occupation Headquarters, WWII, Record Group 260, NACP.

62. OMGUS, *Education and Religion—Monthly Report of Military Governor,* No. 2, September 1945, 2.

63. Vereinigung der Freunde der Dreilinden-Oberschule, *Schulzeit 1939 bis 1999. Festschrift anlässlich des 60-jährigen Bestehens der Dreilinden-Oberschule Berlin-Zehlendorf* (Berlin, 1999), 50–51.

64. Reinhold Skoecz, who taught in the 12.Volksschule in Neukölln, remembers teaching in shifts until 1951. One week, he would have the morning shift and the next week he would teach after lunch. Reinhold Skoecz, interview by author, tape recording, Berlin-Lankwitz, 28 May 2003. For more on the Hessian context, see Fedler, *Anfänge der staatlichen Kulturpolitik in Hessen,* 73.

65. Otto Hundsdorfer, "Demokratie lernen. Erfahrungen eines Junglehrers nach dem Krieg," in *Münchner Nachkriegsjahre. Lesebuch zur Geschichte des Münchner Alltags,* ed. Angelika Baumann (Munich, 1997), 123–133.

66. Schiller, "Schulalltag in der Nachkriegszeit," 35.
67. Gerd Moos, "Aus der Mittelstufe unserer Klasse," *O' KPATHP, Der Mischkrug, Abitur-Zeitung Dilthey-Schule 1953,* ed. Hans-Rudolf Horn et al. (Wiesbaden, 2003), 73. The GYA was an American organization that offered young Germans the opportunity to participate in organized extracurricular activities. For more on the GYA, see Karl-Heinz Füssl, *Die Umerziehung der Deutschen. Jugend und Schule unter den Siegermächten des Zweiten Weltkriegs 1945–1955* (Paderborn, 1995), 148–67.
68. Moos, "Aus der Mittelstufe unserer Klasse," 74.
69. Hanke, Zehlendorf Schulamt, to Magistrat von Gross-Berlin, Volksbildung, "Monatsbericht für Mai 1948," 8 June 1948, 2; Box 127; General Records, 1945–1950; Records of Education and Cultural Relations Division; Records of the Berlin Sector; Records of the US Occupation Headquarters, WWII, RG 260, NACP.
70. Education and Religious Affairs Branch, *Textbooks in Germany-American Zone,* August 1946, 2; Box 702; Education Reports of the Education Branch, 1947–1948; Education and Cultural Relations Division; Records of Office of Military Government, Hesse; Records of the US Occupation Headquarters, WWII, RG 260, NACP.
71. Alonzo Grace, "Democratizing Textbooks," undated (likely 1948), 1; Box 38; Records Related to Policy and Planning; Records of the Education Branch; Records of the Education and Cultural Relations Division; Records of the Office of Military Government, US Zone; Records of the US Occupation Headquarters, WWII, RG 260, NACP.
72. Even the removal of Nazi texts was incomplete in 1945, as some schools continued to use Nazi-era books with pages torn out or with blacked-out sections. One Berlin teacher remembered that in his *Gymnasium* in Berlin-Lichterade, the Ulrich-von-Hütten-Schule, some colleagues simply reused old Nazi texts with problematic passages crossed out. Gerd Poeschke, interview by author, tape recording, Berlin-Marienfelde, 12 May 2003.
73. Education and Religious Affairs Branch, *Textbooks in Germany-American Zone,* 2–3.
74. See Jürgen Bennack, "Volksschulbücher der Nachkriegszeit zwischen Erneuerung und Restauration," in *Zwischen Restauration and Innovation. Bildungsreform in Ost und West nach 1945,* ed. Manfred Heinemann, in *Bildung und Erziehung,* Beiheft 9 (1999): 1–15.
75. Through August 1946, OMGUS officials disapproved 49 history texts (67 percent of those submitted). At the same time, 50 Latin books (58 percent), 51 geography books (58 percent), 59 arithmetic books (39 percent), and 124 German books (21 percent) were disapproved. Education and Religious Affairs Branch, *Textbooks in Germany-American Zone,* 8.
76. Officially, history instruction was forbidden in the American zone until 1948. Even then, many postwar educators were hesitant to teach history well into the 1950s because they believed the subject to be overly politicized. Horst Kollat, interview, 23 April 2003. See also Gregory Wegner, "The Power of Tradition in Education: The Formation of the History Curriculum in the Gymnasium of the American Sector in Berlin, 1945–1955," (PhD diss., University of Wisconsin, Madison, 1988), 207.
77. August Eichelsbacher, ed., *Geschichte des deutschen Volkes—Aufgabe für Nordbayern* (Munich, 1927), 97. Regionally focused texts were quite common in schools before 1933. See also G. Bader, *Geschichte für württembergische Volks- und Mittelschulen,* vol. 2 (Stuttgart, 1932).
78. Seydlitz, *Geographie,* vol. 8, quoted in *Textbooks in Germany-American Zone,* 6.
79. Bader, *Geschichte für württembergische Volks- und Mittelschulen,* 159.
80. Arithmetic and Latin books received some of the highest disapproval ratings from Americans through the summer of 1946. Fifty-eight percent of Latin books were disapproved, while 39 percent of arithmetic texts were not allowed in the classrooms. See *Textbooks in Germany-American Zone,* 5.
81. Herzog-Planck, *Lateinisches Übungsbuch für die erste Lateinklasse,* 10th ed. (1929), quoted in *Textbooks in Germany-American Zone,* 13.
82. Heiter, *Elementa Latina,* Part I, 5th ed. (1942) quoted in *Textbooks in Germany-American Zone,* 14.

83. "Manual for Curriculum-Textbook Centers," 1948, 2; Box 32; Records Related to Policy and Planning; Records of the Education Branch; Records of the Education and Cultural Relations Division; Records of the US Occupation Headquarters, WWII, RG 260, NACP.

84. Education and Religious Affairs Branch, *Textbooks in Germany-American Zone*, 30.

85. Education and Cultural Relations Division, *Report on Textbook Evaluation, 1945–1949* (Germany, 1950).

86. Gerd Poeschke, interview, 12 May 2003.

87. Georg Franz-Willing, *Umerziehung: Die de-Nationalisierung besiegter Völker im 20. Jahrhundert* (Coberg, 1991), 131.

88. Jeffrey S. Gaab, *Justice Delayed: The Restoration of Justice in Bavaria under American Occupation, 1945–1949* (New York, 1999), 62.

89. Tent cites Hesse as an excellent example of the limitations on denazification due to OMGUS staffing shortages. At the outset of the occupation, three American officials were responsible for the entire process. See Tent, *Mission on the Rhine*, 168–69.

90. Ibid., 50.

91. *Fragebogen* were questionnaires used by OMGUS officials to gauge political reliability and to determine whether or not Germans would be allowed to reenter their professions. These questionnaires requested a full account of one's activities during the Third Reich, as well as those of family members. On the basis of these *Fragebogen*, American military officials removed teachers from the schools of the US zone.

92. See Ottwilm Ottweiler, *Die Volksschule in Nationalsozialismus* (Weinheim, 1979), 24–32. According to American statistics, 98 percent of teachers—totaling 360,000 individuals—belonged to the NSLB by 1942. See "Supreme Headquarters Allied Expeditionary Force G-5 Division Education and Religious Affairs Handbook," February 1945, 17, Entry 16, File 129966; Box 1497; Intelligence Reports (XL Series), 1941–1946; Research and Analysis Branch Divisions; Records of Office of Strategic Services, RG 226, NACP. See also Konrad H. Jarausch, *The Unfree Professions: German Lawyers, Teachers, and Engineers, 1900–1950* (New York, 1990), 164–65.

93. Jutta-B. Lange-Quassowski, *Neuordnung oder Restauration? Das Demokratiekonzept der amerikanischen Besatzungsmacht und die politische Sozialisation der Westdeutschen: Wirtschaftsordnung—Schulstruktur—Politische Bildung* (Opladen, 1979), 159–70.

94. Support for denazification activities in the US Zone decreased from 57 percent in March 1946 to 34 percent by December 1946. See Richard and Anna Merritt, *Public Opinion in Occupied Germany* (Chicago, 1970), 304.

95. See Raymond Daniell, "Nazi Virus Thrives in U.S. Zone," *New York Times*, 22 April 1946, 1–2; Irving Wolfson, "The AMG Mess in Germany," *New Republic* 114 (6 March 1946): 312.

96. "Quarterly Report of Education and Religious Affairs Branch," December 1946, 121; Box 4; Education Mission Thru Re-education; Administrative Records of the Director's Office, 1945–1949; Records of the Education and Religious Affairs Division; Records of OMGUS—Bavaria; Records of the Office of Military Government, US Zone; Records of the US Occupation Headquarters, WWII, RG 260, NACP.

97. For a detailed discussion of the denazification process in Hesse, see Armin Schuster, *Die Entnazifizierung in Hessen 1945–1954*, Veröffentlichungen der Historische Kommission für Nassau, vol. 66, Vorgeschichte und Geschichte des Parlamentarismus in Hessen, vol. 29 (Wiesbaden, 1999).

98. Fedler, *Anfänge der staatlichen Kulturpolitik in Hessen*, 144.

99. There were two reasons for shortages during the Third Reich. The first, and most obvious, is the drafting of men to fight in the *Wehrmacht*. Second, Hitler Youth propaganda that mocked and belittled "old-fashioned teachers" played a role in the reduction in the number of youths entering the profession. The number of teachers in all of the areas under American occupation had begun to decline by 1939. See Susanne Charlotte Engelmann, *German Education and Re-education* (New York, 1945), 113.

100. Wernfried Schreiber, "Auf den Wege zur universitären Lehrerbildung in Hessen von 1945–1950," (PhD diss., Goethe Universität Frankfurt, 1978), 21.

101. "Bericht über den Stand der Volksschulen vom 1.November 1946, Regierungsbezirk Kassel," Abteilung 504, No. 553b, Fiche 3207, HHstA.

102. After a second reorganization under American occupation in September 1945, Hesse came to consist of three *Regierungsbezirke:* Kassel, Wiesbaden, and Darmstadt. For further explanation, see Fedler, *Anfänge der staatlichen Kulturpolitik in Hessen,* 20–23.

103. "Formular für Berichtserstattung und Unterlage für das Gesuch zur Wiedereröffnung der Mittel und höheren Schulen," Der Staatlichen Oberschule für Jungen, Weilburg, 15 October 1945; Box 62; Records Relating to Cultural Exchange and School Reopenings; Records of the Education Branch; Records of the Education and Cultural Relations Division; Records of the US Occupation Headquarters, WWII, Record Group 260, NACP.

104. Ibid.

105. "Zahlen aus dem Berliner Schulwesen, 22.1.1948," C. Rep. 120, No. 3304, LAB.

106. *Volksschulen* were much more likely to rely on temporary assistance. Of the 1,292 *Hilfslehrer* and *Schulhelfer* in the American sector of Berlin in November 1946, only 77 taught in *Oberschulen.* See "Zahlen aus dem Berliner Schulwesen, 22.1.1948," C. Rep. 120, No. 3304, LAB.

107. Joachim Matysiak, interview by author, tape recording, Berlin-Dahlem, 27 June 2003.

108. In 1931, the *Oberschulen* of Berlin were not yet coeducational. In male *Oberschulen,* men held 99 percent of the teaching positions. In female *Oberschulen,* of which there were only two-thirds as many, men still held almost 38 percent of the positions. See Statistisches Amt der Stadt Berlin, *Statistisches Jahrbuch für der Stadt Berlin,* 9th edition (Berlin, 1933).

109. "Volksschulen, Statistisches Übersicht—Stand 1.10.1949," B. Rep. 015, No. 18/2, LAB.

110. Karl-Ernst Bungenstab, *Umerziehung zur Demokratie? Reeducation-Politik im Bildungswesen der US-Zone 1945–1949* (Gütersloh, 1970), 75.

111. Quoted in Ekkehard Meier, "In einer neuen Zeit—Abiturarbeiten 1946 bis 1948," in *Schulreform—Kontinuitäten und Brücke. Das Versuchungsfeld Berlin-Neukölln,* vol. 2, ed. Gerd Radde and Werner Korthaase, et al. (Opladen, 1993), 26.

112. Ibid.

113. Office of Military Government for Germany, US—Education and Cultural Relations Division, *Handbook of Education Statistics : (U.S. occupied area of Germany)* (Germany, 1949), 30.

114. Ibid., 40. It should be noted that this report does not distinguish between the elementary and secondary grades of the *Volksschule* in its statistical analysis.

115. Ibid., 20.

116. Ibid., 29.

117. For a brief examination of the teacher shortage and temporary training new teachers received in one district of American-occupied Berlin, see Angelika Schmidt, "Lehrer gesucht—Zur Ausbildung der Schulhelfer und Hilfslehrer," in *Schulreform—Kontinuitäten und Brücke. Das Versuchungsfeld Berlin-Neukölln,* vol. 2, ed. Gerd Radde and Werner Korthaase, et al. (Opladen, 1993), 48–53.

118. See Müller, *Schulpolitik in Bayern,* 73.

119. Office of Military Government for Germany, US—Education and Cultural Relations Division, *Handbook of Education Statistics: (U.S. occupied area of Germany),* 33.

120. Ibid., 21.

121. This is true of almost all education officials, including military government leadership. See Alonzo G. Grace, "Education," in *Governing Postwar Germany,* ed. Edward H. Litchfield (Ithaca, NY, 1953).

122. Heinz-Elmar Tenorth, *Zur deutschen Bildungsgeschichte 1918–1945,* Studien und Dokumentationen zur deutschen Bildungsgeschichte, ed. Christoph Führ and Wolfgang Mitter, vol. 28 (Cologne, 1985), 2.

123. Christoph Weisz, ed., *OMGUS-Handbuch: Die amerikanische Militärregierung in Deutschland*

1945–1949 (Munich, 1994), 16–17. The Education & Religious Affairs Branch received division status and became the Education and Cultural Relations Division in 1948.

124. Significant exceptions were the first two leaders of E&RA, John W. Taylor and R. T. Alexander. Taylor obtained his PhD from Columbia University's Teachers College after completing a dissertation on the Weimar youth organizations. His successor as E&RA chief was Alexander, who had been his doctoral advisor as well as dean of Teachers College at Columbia. See Tent, *Mission on the Rhine*, 48.

125. Ibid., 49.

126. Ibid., 8.

127. See Otto Schlander, "Der Einfluß von John Dewey und Hans Morgenthau auf die Formulierung der Re-educationspolitik," in *Umerziehung und Wiederaufbau. Die Bildungspolitik der Besatzungsmächte in Deutschland und Österreich,* ed. Manfred Heinemann (Stuttgart, 1981), 40–52.

128. See Bernd Zymek, "Schulen, Hochschulen, Lehrer," in *Handbuch der deutschen Bildungsgeschichte,* vol. 5, ed. Dieter Langewische and Heinz-Elmar Tenorth (Munich, 1989), 155–208; Margret Kraul, *Das deutsche Gymnasium 1780–1980* (Frankfurt, 1984), 140–44.

129. It is important to note that West Berlin used different labels for its schools beginning in 1951. The *Oberschule Praktischer Zweig* (OPZ) corresponded to the *Volksschule,* the *Oberschule Technischer Zweig* (OTZ) to the *Mittelschule,* and the *Oberschule Wissenschaftlicher Zweig* (OWZ) to the *Gymnasium.* Additionally, common schooling extended through the sixth grade in West Berlin, with pupils entering separate tracks two years later than most of the Federal Republic. For a detailed examination of the Berlin School Law of 1948 and its revision in 1951, see Marion Klewitz, *Berliner Einheitsschule 1945–1951,* Historische und Pädagogische Studien, ed. Otto Büsch and Gerd Heinrich, vol. 1 (Berlin, 1971); Karl-Heinz Füssl and Christian Kubina, *Berliner Schule zwischen Restauration und Innovation* (Frankfurt, 1983). This study will refer to the upper grades of the *Volksschule,* as well as the *Mittelschule,* and the *Gymnasium* as "secondary education."

130. See Christoph Führ, *Schulen und Hochschulen in der Bundesrepublik Deutschland* (Bonn, 1988), 100, 212–13.

131. The restructuring of the school system indeed dominated the attention of American education officials until the end of 1947. It was also perhaps the least successful aspect of the many American-proposed reforms, as Culture Ministry officials throughout the US zone delayed or refused American proposals. On Bavaria, see Tent, *Mission on the Rhine*, 110–63; Buchinger, *Volksschule und Lehrerbildung,* 49–68. For Hesse, see Fedler, *Anfänge der staatlichen Kulturpolitik in Hessen,* 87–99. The situation was more complicated in Berlin due to the quadripartite occupation of the city.

132. EUCOM, OPOT Division, Training and Education Branch, *German Youth Activities Guide* (Germany, 1947), 33. This handbook for officers involved with the GYA lists an assortment of German "character traits."

133. Emil Fuchs, "Der Lehrer im Neuen Staat," *Der Deutsche Lehrer* 3 (1947): 49–54.

134. "Report of the United States Education Mission to Germany," 1946, 21; Box 4; Education Mission Thru Re-education; Administrative Records of the Director's Office, 1945–1949; Records of the Education and Religious Affairs Division; Records of OMGUS—Bavaria; Records of the Office of Military Government, US Zone; Records of the US Occupation Headquarters, WWII, RG 260, NACP.

135. Paul Lotz, "Reform oder Restauration?" *Die Pädagogische Provinz* 5, no. 3 (1951): 115–18. See also J. J. Welsch, "Zum Problem der Vermassung," *Westermanns pädagogische Beiträge* 3, no. 5 (1951): 193–97.

136. Education and Religious Affairs, Office of Military Government (US) for Germany—Hesse, 14 January 1947, 1, Abteilung 1178, No. 81b, HHstA. This document was first issued in 1946 and expanded for recirculation in 1947.

137. Burr W. Phillips, "Address at Social Studies Conference," 24 May 1948; Box 700; Education Reports of the Education Branch, 1947–1948; Education and Cultural Relations Division; Records of Office of Military Government, Hesse; Records of the US Occupation Headquarters, WWII, RG 260, NACP. Emphasis in original.

138. "Nineteen Suggestions for Citizenship Education," undated (likely December 1946), 2; Box 702; Education Reports of the Education Branch, 1947–1948; Education and Cultural Relations Division; Records of Office of Military Government, Hesse; Records of the US Occupation Headquarters, WWII, RG 260, NACP.

139. Ibid., 3.

140. Ibid., 2.

141. See "Secondary Schools in Germany—American Zone," Box 702; Education Reports of the Education Branch, 1947–1948; Education and Cultural Relations Division; Records of Office of Military Government, Hesse; Records of the US Occupation Headquarters, WWII, RG 260, NACP.

142. Protokollbuch der 32. Volksschule, Protokoll vom 20 February 1947, Heimatmuseum Neukölln, quoted in Dietmar Schiller, "Schulalltag in der Nachkriegszeit," 36.

Chapter 2

"WE LEARNED WHAT DEMOCRACY REALLY MEANT"
New Experiences Inside and Outside the Classroom, 1948–1954

On 28 January 1953, the RIAS-Schulfunk-Parlament (Berlin Student Parliament) celebrated its fifth anniversary. Despite the distractions of having important West Berlin and West German politicians in their midst as a sign of support, the young parliamentarians handled that day's business with their usual mix of enthusiasm and determination. These elected secondary school pupils debated five bills that afternoon, passing four of them. Among those that passed was a commitment to assist in the construction of a new library for pupils living in East Berlin. Wilhelm-Dietrich von Thadden, a member of the cabinet, reported on his successful work with school authorities to institute the parliament's proposal for changes in school menu offerings. Another representative, Hanna Gätke, informed her colleagues about the Christmas activities of the parliament, which had raised DM 450 for charity and provided over nine hundred gifts to elderly Berliners. The young Berliners also had a "lively discussion" about the conduct of parliamentary debate. Before adjourning the meeting, the pupils reported on the activities of student government in each section of the city and continued their debate about the parliament's larger goals.[1]

The Berlin Student Parliament is but one example of the ways in which West German pupils gained practical experience with democracy in the postwar era. While German educators deemed the production of new textbooks and the expansion of teacher training programs as critical, many believed that new activities

RIAS-SCHULFUNK-PARLAMENT

Berlin-Schöneberg · Kufsteiner Straße 69 ·· Telefon 71 02 71 / 469

Berlin, den 16. Januar 1953

Liebes PM!

Ver-fünf Jahren — am 25. Januar 1948 — trat das RIAS-Schulfunk-Parlament zum ersten Male zusammen. Eine "Festsitzung"
wollen wir aus diesem Anlass nicht abhalten. Vielmehr wollen
wir uns bemühen, auf unserer <u>46. Sitzung am Mittwoch, dem
28. Januar 53, um 15,00 Uhr im Titania-Palast</u> durch unsere
Haltung und durch den Ernst unserer Beratungen einen besonders
wertvollen Beitrag zur Förderung der Schülermitverwaltung
zu leisten.

Wir erwarten auf dieser Sitzung eine Anzahl prominenter Gäste,
darunter unseren Regierenden Bürgermeister.

Eine Tagesordnung fügen wir bei. Gastkarten können ab sofort
täglich zwischen 10,00 und 17,00 Uhr in unserem Sekretariat
abgeholt werden (ausser sonnabends).

In Erwartung eines anregenden und würdigen Verlaufes dieser
Sitzung sind wir mit den besten Grüssen

R I A S
SCHULFUNK
PARLAMENT

Das Präsidium

gez. Harry Schulz, Hanna Gätke, Harry Baum.

- -

<u>A u s w e i s</u>

Dieser Ausweis gilt für den Besuch der 46. Sitzung des RSP
am 28.1.53 und ist am Saaleingang abzugeben, bei Verhinderung
bitte einschicken!

Name: _____

Privatanschrift: _____

Abgeordneter der Schule _____ im Bezirk _____

PM sitzen im I.Parkett ab Reihe 4.

RIAS - 186 - P

Figure 4. Announcement of fifth anniversary of Berlin Student Parliament and
admission ticket for pupils, 1953. The letter notes that a number of prominent
guests are expected at the meeting, including the city's mayor, Ernst Reuter.
Courtesy Wilhelm-Dietrich von Thadden.

T a g e s o r d n u n g
-.-.-.-.-.-.-.-.-.-.-.-.-.-.-

der 46. Sitzung des

R I A S

SCHULFUNK-PARLAMENTES

Mittwoch, den 28. Januar 1953, 15,00 Uhr im

Titania-Palast

1.) 4 Minuten für den Schulfunkvater

2.) 5 Jahre RIAS-Schulfunk-Parlament

3.) Bericht des BSA und des Präsidiums

4.) Berichte der Bezirks-Arbeitskreise

5.) Aus der Schülermitverwaltung

    a) Klassenpatenschaften
                (Hanna Gätke, Oberschule f. Mädchen,Kreuzberg)

    b) Muss es erst ein Höflichkeits-Wettbewerb sein?
                (Herbert Ludz, Schadow-Schule)

6.) "10 Minuten" Selbstkritik

7.) Wahl eines neuen Schiedsausschusses

8.) Anträge:

    296) Der BSA möge sich dafür einsetzen, dass alle Klassen der Schulen
    die ihnen entsprechenden Hausaufgaben bekommen, so dass die
    9. Klasse nicht die Arbeiten der 5. bis 7. Klassen aufbekommen.
                (Hans-Jürgen Mantey, 2. OPZ, Charlottenburg)

    297) Der BSA möge sich an das Hauptschulamt oder die sonst zuständigen
    Stellen mit der Bitte wenden, dass im kommenden Schuljahr neben
    der Schulspeisung der Verkauf von Milch und Kakao durchgeführt
    wird.
                (Ernst-Georg Metz, Schiller-Schule, Charl.)

    298) Das RSP möge den Schulen empfehlen, zur Unterstützung der vom
    RIAS geplanten "Bibliothek für Ostschüler" eine Sammlung alter
    Schulbücher durchzuführen.
                (Olaf Paeschke, Rheingau-Schule, Friedenau)

    299) Der BSA möge sich beim HSA dafür einsetzen, dass auch den Ober-
    schulen des Technischen Zweiges ein zweiter aufgabenfreier Nach-
    mittag eingeführt wird.
                (2. OTZ, Kreuzberg)

    300) Der BSA möge das Theater der Schulen bitten, jedem Schüler vor
    dem Besuch eines Konzertes eine schriftliche Einführung in das
    jeweilige Programm zusammen mit der Eintrittskarte zu übergeben.
    Dafür könnten dann die mündlichen Einführungen direkt vor dem
    Konzert fortfallen.
                (Georg Karsunke, Rheingauschule Friedenau)

9.) V e r s c h i e d e n e s .

- - - - -

Figure 5. Agenda for 46th meeting of BSP, 1953. The agenda highlights the various tasks in which the young parliamentarians engaged, including the discussion and debate of five new bills. Courtesy Wilhelm-Dietrich von Thadden.

offering pupils hands-on experience in democracy were even more important. In the vein of expanded political education, student government (*Schülermitverwaltung*, or SMV) became increasingly commonplace in the schools of West Germany in the early 1950s. Exchange programs, too, offered West German educators and their pupils the chance to observe and participate in democratic societies throughout Europe and in the United States. Initiated in the closing years of the occupation, these programs reached their zenith in the early 1950s. Developments such as these underscore the new emphasis on experiencing democracy first-hand. Likewise, they highlight the growing awareness that such lessons could be learned outside the walls of the traditional classroom and in environments not dominated by the teacher. These sorts of activities offered participants the chance to learn from peers, as well as to gain experience in a variety of new settings.

Innovation, however, was not limited solely to extracurricular activities after 1945. Important educational reforms also took place within West German classrooms throughout the last years of the occupation and the first years of the new decade. A new postwar generation of textbooks began to appear as the occupation came to a close, which departed from traditional texts both in terms of content and pedagogy by virtue of their design. Admittedly, troublesome features remained in some of these new books, and there were undoubtedly continuities between postwar publications and their interwar predecessors. Nevertheless, the postwar generation of schoolbooks utilized new pedagogical methods and incorporated different perspectives than those used in previous decades. This period also witnessed the widespread adoption of new pedagogical practices, including the principle of pupils working in independent groups of their own. Another method gaining greater influence at this time was classroom debate, which removed the teacher from the center of activity and required pupils to express their opinions and respect the ideas of their classmates. Finally, teacher training programs began to offer increased training to future educators. Newly trained educators received expanded training in social studies and political education, and in most cases, they were required to attend continuing education seminars throughout their careers.

Focusing on the years 1948 to 1954 as a cohesive period in its own right, this chapter crosses over one of the most fundamental divisions in postwar German history. The foundation of the Federal Republic in May 1949 has distracted many scholars from the educational developments that bridge this gap. Drawing a line in 1949 makes it easy to characterize the occupation as a self-contained period, as well as to describe it as a time of "failure." As we have seen, education reform in the first postwar years was hampered by material and staffing problems. Many of the reforms discussed here germinated before the occupation ended but only began to flourish in the early 1950s. At the same time, beginning a study of postwar education only in 1949 reinforces a view of the 1950s and early 1960s as a time of conservative domination. Looking only at the organization of the West German school system in the first postwar decade, one could conclude that this period was a time of restoration. Yet the focus here will be on curricular and extracurricular reforms that transpired within—and often in spite of—this rigid structure. Examining such postwar developments as student government, exchange programs, new textbooks, and enhanced teacher training activities highlights the subtle yet meaningful changes that have been ignored in so many other studies of West German education.

Admittedly, the reforms discussed here did not affect all the schools of West Germany evenly. There were at least two important variables in the educational equation: location and school type. Education was the responsibility of the individual states in West Germany, with the federal government playing only a minimal role. This was to guard against any interference in cultural affairs from a strong national government, as had been the case under Hitler. The sovereignty of the states in the sphere of education naturally meant that reforms entered the schools at different times and with varying levels of intensity across the country. Some areas were more willing to introduce changes in postwar classrooms than others. Although there was a concerted effort among the culture ministers to coordinate the curricula of the different states more closely in the 1950s, notable differences still existed among the West German schools. Nevertheless, the broader pedagogical and curricular trends discussed here hold true for much of the Federal Republic.

The second variable affecting the spread of reforms in the postwar schools was school type. Student government organizations were most common in secondary schools in this period, specifically the *Gymnasien*. Yet this should not obscure the fact that such organizations evolved in schools of other levels as well. Exchanges targeted university students and the oldest pupils in secondary schools, since most funding agencies (including the US government) did not believe that youths under age sixteen could truly appreciate the opportunities of the programs. This does not mean, though, that the *Volksschulen* (in particular the *Grundschulen*) were left out of this process. Teachers in *Volksschulen,* particularly young ones, were actively recruited to participate in exchange programs beginning in 1950. Textbook reforms ushered in various changes in both primary and secondary schools. The most widely circulated new history books of this period targeted not the upper echelons of the *Gymnasien* but the seventh and eighth grades of the *Volksschule.* Finally, postwar teacher training courses introduced a new generation of educators to social studies and political education, while experienced teachers, particularly *Volksschullehrer,* benefited from enhanced continuing education programs. Thus it is inaccurate to describe educational reform in the postwar Federal Republic as a "trickle-down process." While many changes did indeed begin in the most academically focused secondary schools and then later gained acceptance elsewhere, others began in the classes of the *Volksschulen* among more liberal and reform-minded educators. Through examining both classroom and extracurricular reforms, this chapter investigates the ways by which West German pupils and educators—at all levels—gradually began to learn first-hand what democracy actually meant.

"Live Properly!"[2]: The Rise of Student Government

In the years after the war, many German educators recognized the importance of political education in the postwar schools. It was within the context of political education that most debates about the potential of student government organizations took place. Many educators saw SMV as a critical tool in cementing the ideals of the new democracy among the young. Educators throughout West Germany openly discussed the merits of involving pupils in the administration of the classroom and school in the pages of pedagogical journals.[3] In contrast to much of the civics and political education instruction before 1933, student government offered pupils the opportunity to gain first-hand experience with the processes of democracy at the everyday level. The growing interest in student government in this period prompted the organization of conferences dedicated to examining its pedagogical value, as well as the creation of new associations committed to the growth of SMV.[4] Culture Ministry officials throughout West Germany also latched onto these pedagogical innovations before the end of the occupation. Hesse, for instance, actually called for the introduction of student government in secondary schools "as soon as possible" in May 1946.[5] Supported by American military officials who promoted the values of student government, culture ministries throughout western Germany outlined new curricula in which the self-governance of pupils played a significant role. Hesse and West Berlin were by no means exceptions to this trend.

Hessian culture minister Erwin Stein published his pioneering *Lehrpläne für den politischen Unterricht in den Schulen des Landes Hessen* (Curriculum for Political Education in the Schools of the State of Hesse) in August 1948. Although the Hessian Culture Ministry officially required the introduction of political education beginning in the seventh grade in some schools as early as 1946, these 1948 guidelines proposed that pupils in all schools would have instruction in the new subject.[6] In this document, Stein called for a mixture of "experience, instruction, and practical application." At the same time, he encouraged open classroom debates, and demanded a spirit of tolerance within the school.[7] This curriculum offered Hessian educators detailed instructions for political instruction beginning in the seventh grade for all schools. In 1949, Stein expanded political education in Hesse through his *Richtlinien für den politischen Unterricht* (Guidelines for Political Education). Political education would now be a required course of instruction beginning in the fifth grade. Significantly, this document also reemphasized Stein's commitment to SMV, which he had first delineated in a brief decree the year before.[8] Stein recognized that student government offered pupils precisely that "practical application" of democratic values for which he had called in the past. "Political education," Stein asserted, would "promote student government and fill it with life from within, so that it does not remain an empty model; rather it will become a practically experienced and exercised democracy in the life of the pupil."[9] Stein envisioned student government activities as aiding in the creation of a new generation of citizens who had personal experience with the mechanisms and techniques of democracy.

While Stein praised the value of student government, he was nevertheless concerned about how Hessian pupils might express their newfound freedoms. His fears appeared to be confirmed when, in August 1948, the pupils of Wiesbaden's *Gymnasien* crowded onto the streets in front of the Culture Ministry with signs and handbills. The thousand or so protesters, who had organized into student councils (*Schülerräte*) in their respective schools and then formed an overarching organization for all of the city's *Gymnasien*, gathered to voice their opposition to the recent lengthening of the school year. Angered by the "tone" of the demonstration, Stein made clear his beliefs that pupils should not organize into associations beyond the school level and that they did not have the right to strike.[10] This rather hostile response to the activism displayed by the pupils of Wiesbaden's *Gymnasien* was incorporated into Stein's decree on SMV issued in September 1948.[11] Although Stein wanted to promote SMV within the schools, he endeavored to limit its power and ensure that it did not challenge established authorities. Thus while officially supporting the creation and growth of student government in Hesse, Stein's policies prevented the establishment of stronger organizations, such as regional or even statewide parliaments. While Stein welcomed democratic reforms, he was also careful to make sure that the powers of the Culture Ministry and other educational authorities were not openly challenged by Hessian pupils.[12]

This is not to say that student government failed to take root in Hesse after the war. Its growth was more limited than in other areas, since the organization of larger student government groups beyond the individual school was forbidden by Stein's decree.[13] Yet within the schools, pupils and educators alike soon recognized the potential offered by SMV. This realization sparked a dramatic growth spurt for student government in postwar Hesse. By the middle of 1949, 52 percent of *Volksschulen* had some sort of elected student organization.[14] Student government grew at an even higher rate in the upper-level schools through the early 1950s, due at least in part to the 1946 decree requiring secondary schools to introduce SMV. Student government organizations in these schools played a more active role in the administration of the school than their colleagues in the *Volksschulen*. Whereas pupils in the *Volksschulen* held elections, voted for classroom representatives, and took responsibility for a variety of classroom and schoolwide tasks, pupils in the *Gymnasien* accepted additional duties and privileges, such as drafting a formal constitution, organizing their own extracurricular clubs, and publishing a school paper. Thus while student government grew in all of the Hessian schools, there was a qualitative difference between *Volksschulen* and more academically focused secondary schools in the functioning of SMV.

Wiesbaden's Dilthey-Schule, a *Gymnasium*, provides an excellent example of how pupils envisioned the responsibilities and organization of student government during this period. In a written statement, the pupils outlined the four key goals they had for their new organization: to improve life in the school and make it more harmonious; to create a more personal and trusting relationship between pupils and teachers; to ensure that all members of the school community act in a friendly manner and respect one another; and finally, to contribute to the education of pupils for their duties as "responsible and conscientious citizens."[15] According to the guidelines the pupils drafted, student government in the school consisted of the student council, the student court, the editors of the school newspaper, and the school community. The student council of the Dilthey-Schule consisted of two bodies—an organization for the lower grades and another for the upper classes. The guidelines provided great detail for the election of representatives, the passing of legislation, and even for a possible vote of no confidence for the leadership of the parliament. The pupils also created a pupil-operated judicial board under the auspices of SMV. This court consisted of three judges, a prosecutor, a defense attorney, and other necessary representatives and operated on the basis of its own charter. Additionally, the chairmanship of the student government approved the editorial staff of the school's newspaper, which was also an organ of SMV.[16] The fact that an organization as complicated as the SMV of the Dilthey-Schule could be founded so shortly after 1945 highlights the undercurrent of change promoted by both educators and pupils in the aftermath of the war.

While the documents of the Dilthey-Schule provide evidence for the existence of efficient and well-intentioned student government organizations in postwar Hesse, they are less helpful in determining how pupils measured the importance of this process. Fortunately, *Abitur* essays authored in this period provide some insight on this question. The Gymnasium Philippinum in Weilburg had founded its own SMV in the late 1940s, and it had quickly gained the respect of both pupils and teachers in the school. Citing the growth of SMV in the school, the spring 1952 *Abitur* examination in German offered pupils the opportunity to respond to a question on how student government served as a training ground for democratic order.[17] Either out of a sense of duty to address this contemporary pedagogical issue or a sense of relief that they did not have to expound on the writings of Detlev von Liliencron, several pupils responded to this question. Almost taking a page out of John Dewey's *Democracy and Education,* Ruth Kunz remarked in her response that "what the state is in large, that is what the school is in small; namely an order." She continued in that same paragraph, "The democratic order gives rights, but it requires things as well; it places claims on every individual person, which everyone must carry out himself." In her conclusion, Kunz reminded the reader that the characteristics required to make a democratic order a reality are "no longer or not yet present" in Germany. This, she argued, justified the need for student government in the schools, since it could serve as a model for the future.[18] Kunz's essay indicates that at least the most advanced pupils recognized the historical shortcomings of German education in preparing the young for democracy and the possibilities that SMV offered to the new generation.

The essays of other pupils reinforced and expanded upon the ideas expressed in Kunz's essay. At the same time, these essays also voiced criticism of some aspects of SMV. Irmgard Hofmann briefly recounted the plight of young people socialized under the Third Reich and voiced the fear that West Germany's only democrats will be the gray old men of the Weimar era. Her essay supported the cause of SMV as a means to provide the youngest Germans first-hand experience with the workings of democracy, yet she criticized the institution as it operated in her school. She objected to the participation of a faculty advisor in the meetings, since she feared that the presence of a teacher might prevent pupils from expressing their true opinions. She also asserted that SMV needed to expand its influence and address larger issues that affected the school.[19] Another pupil, Eberhard Weber, relied on his extended experience as a member of student government in writing his response. Weber criticized several aspects of SMV, specifically the exclusion of the younger classes in the school from voting, which he deemed "a break with democratic principles."[20] These essays suggest that while pupils recognized the value of SMV, they also realized that they had the right to criticize the institution and suggest ways to improve its effectiveness. This constructive criticism of student government shows that many pupils—specifically those in the upper echelons of the *Gymnasien*—had begun to internalize the ideas expressed in political education lessons and the democratic principles of SMV.

The situation in Berlin was much more complicated than Hesse due to the quadripartite administration of the city. Yet the year 1948 marked an important turning point for the growth of student government in the former capital as well. One of the last agreements finalized before the blockade that summer was a new School Law that called for fundamental reform in the Berlin schools.[21] The importance of political education did not go unnoticed by school officials, as they cautiously endorsed the principles of political education and student government. Article 17 of the School Law stated, "The pupils' self-administration to be established in all schools shall consciously cultivate their communal life and their self-responsibility."[22] There was no other mention of SMV or political education anywhere else in the document. Thus Berlin school authorities had produced a new School Law that embraced the fundamental ideas of the new political education, yet they appeared hesitant about legislating for specific practices or proposing a concrete schedule for its introduction. This is undoubtedly due in part to political differences between the occupation powers and differing conceptions of what education reforms should be pursued.

Despite the rather vague stipulations of the Berlin School Law, student government nonetheless experienced remarkable growth in the schools of West Berlin. As was the case in Hesse, school officials believed student government offered pupils the chance to gain practical experience with the workings of democracy. In order to gauge whether SMV was living up to these expectations, city school officials conducted a detailed survey in the schools at the beginning of 1954. This survey offers valuable insight into the growth of student government throughout this period. Of the 212 primary schools (*Grundschulen,* incorporating grades one through six in Berlin) that responded to the survey, 150 confirmed that their classes elected a class representative. City officials deemed the election of a class representative as the most embryonic form of student government. The number of schools in which classes elected representatives was significantly higher at the secondary level. In the upper levels of the *Volksschulen,* the OPZs, 64 of 65 schools responded that elections were held for class representatives.[23] In the OTZs (*Mittelschulen*) and the OWZs (*Gymnasien*), all the schools that responded asserted that they had introduced some form of student government.[24] This survey also confirmed that pupils had at least some knowledge of the actions of their student governments, since more than two-thirds of all SMVs reported on their activities during the school day. Quantitatively, at least, SMV had cemented a place in the schools of West Berlin.

Fortunately, these reports also highlight the quality of pupils' participation in the schools through involvement of SMV. According to survey responses, the most common responsibilities of student government in the OPZs were: planning and hosting school celebrations; social service inside and outside the school; coadministration of the school library; assisting in the determination of school discipline; arranging class trips; and coordinating theatrical productions.[25] For pupils in the schools of the OTZ, their key responsibilities included many of those of their counterparts in the OPZ, as well as the creation of sports clubs and voluntary academic groups.[26] The duties of SMV in the OWZ were the most advanced of all the schools. In addition to most of the tasks already mentioned, these pupils also formed theater clubs and were the most likely to have founded a school newspaper (nineteen of sixty-three had already done so by this relatively early date).[27] In addition to these most popular duties, the student government organizations of the city's schools also formed youth Red Cross societies, decorated classrooms and school grounds, assisted in the organization of the school schedule and teaching plans, and served as sponsors to pupils in lower classes. The results of this survey indicate that not only had SMV become an established presence in the early 1950s, but that these organizations offered pupils the chance to become involved with a wide variety of activities and responsibilities in the life of the school.

Despite the expansion of student government in the schools of the city, there was also widespread awareness that SMV continued to face a number of challenges. Like the authors of the *Abitur* essays in Hesse, pupils—and teachers—in West Berlin criticized SMV and highlighted many of its shortcomings. A 1953 report to the senator for education (West Berlin's title for the culture minister) from the principal of the Schadowschule alluded to the fact that SMV did not experience the level of success many teachers had hoped for because pupils were more interested in getting through school and finding a job as soon as possible.[28] This was a particularly challenging problem in the earliest years of the postwar period, and judging from the reports received by city school authorities, it lingered well into the 1950s. Another challenge faced by SMV was apathetic pupils. Taking it upon themselves to respond to the 1954 inquiry from city education officials, the elected leaders of the Getraudenschule's student government expressed frustration with their classmates. "Only those pupils who had already felt responsible for the school and had accepted related duties took part; the others remained passive or came along only after complaining," they noted in their report to city school authorities.[29] This passivity on the part of many pupils was also noted by educators. A teacher in the Droste-Hülshoff-Schule in Zehlendorf cited progress in the growth of SMV in his school, but he lamented the fact that "the involvement of the pupils to the degree desired has not yet been achieved."[30] Student government had become commonplace in the West Berlin schools by the mid-1950s, but it was by no means without its flaws.

In its final summation of the state of student government in West Berlin, city school authorities expressed mixed feelings. Like most of the teachers who had commented on their experiences with SMV, they were optimistic for the future, yet they realized there were immediate problems that needed to be addressed. The largest problems loomed in the schools of the OPZs. School officials explained that the pupils in these schools were only together for three years, which in many cases was insufficient for building a strong foundation for SMV. Additionally, pupils in these schools were often cited as lacking the initiative and perseverance necessary for a stable student government organization.[31] City school officials also detected a lack of initiative in the OTZs, and noted that in some instances, student government groups could not acquire the necessary classroom space for their activities. Yet the report concluded "that in many cases, good experiences have been had with SMV, so that a slow but steady positive development of SMV is to be seen."[32] The report on the OWZs was the most positive, as it highlighted the many strong student government organizations created in these schools. City school officials were undoubtedly surprised to find that many student government groups from these schools included appendices with their questionnaires. The fact that thirty-three of the sixty-three respondents enclosed detailed reports on their activities—in addition to the survey forms—speaks volumes about the growth of student government in the most academic secondary schools. That nineteen organizations also included their constitutions with their questionnaires further underscores this point.[33]

Unlike in Hesse, student government organizations were not limited to the individual school in West Berlin. This more flexible policy on student government permitted the creation of the RIAS-Schulfunk-Parlament, the most advanced student government organization of its time in the Federal Republic. Founded by the American-sponsored radio station in West Berlin, RIAS, the city's school authorities, and interested secondary school pupils in January 1948, this body stood atop the city's student government pyramid.[34] The organization was sponsored and coordinated by Hermann Schneider, who was in charge of educational programming at RIAS. The initial goal of the organization was actually quite limited: it was designed to provide criticism and suggestions to RIAS for future educational programming. Its attention and goals expanded rapidly and by the end of its first year of existence, it took on the mantle of student parliament for the city's secondary school pupils. Although initially limited to a handful of *Gymnasien,* it expanded to include elected members from all three types of West Berlin's secondary schools by the mid-1950s. This organization fostered relationships with other student government associations throughout West Germany, passed bills regarding educational and political topics, and raised money for charities and aid organizations. These young parliamentarians corresponded with leading West German politicians, often inviting them to observe and address their meetings.[35] The parliament debated developments within the schools and even made recommendations to city school officials regarding issues it had discussed. Additionally, the BSP formed a variety of committees to deal with important topics. One such committee promoted the discussion of contemporary political issues in the classrooms of the city, while another spearheaded charity efforts sponsored by the organization.[36]

The activities of one BSP meeting offer insight into the sorts of experiences pupils received through their participation in the organization. The agenda for the thirty-third meeting of the parliament on 28 October 1951 was quite full, as were the thousand or so seats of the auditorium.[37] Meeting in the mid-afternoon at the Titania-Palast, a large city theater, the parliament opened its meeting as it always did—with a four-minute address from the "founding father" of the organization, Hermann Schneider. Following this, the parliament engaged in ten minutes of reflection, discussing long-term issues with which it had grappled. The leaders of the parliament—Wolfgang Bernhardt, Doris Schultz, and Harry Schulz—then gave their report, which was followed by the reports of preexisting committees. The fifth item on the agenda was the announcement of a new exchange program with England for the pupils involved in the RIAS-sponsored orchestra. The representatives were requested to take news of this new program back to their schools and identify possible candidates for this four-week trip.[38]

At this point, the parliament finally addressed the legislative business on its agenda. First, it agreed to submit a letter of protest to the East German minister of education in response to the punishment of fifteen secondary school pupils in Werdau for having publicly expressed their displeasure with the government. Turning their attention to more practical matters, the parliament passed a bill requesting that a low score (a "5") in one subject on the *Abitur* would not prevent a pupil from achieving a better final grade than "passing." Another bill passed asking that city school authorities devote more days in the 1952–53 school year to field trips. Bill number 198 passed after "lively discussion." It requested that school authorities no longer require a grade for handwriting in the secondary schools. Another bill, one proposing the rescheduling of parliamentary meetings to Saturdays, was rejected. In total, the parliament passed seven bills, rejected two, and tabled a further three for discussion at the next meeting. The meeting concluded with reports on the activities of school-level student government organizations within the city's various districts.[39]

Much of the legislation passed by the BSP was conditional, in the sense that it requested changes from others that it could not enact on its own. Naturally, this makes it easy to dismiss its activities and to label the parliament ineffective or perhaps overly idealistic. Skeptics might even argue that the BSP wielded little if any power of its own, and that the teenage parliamentarians were simply "going through the motions." Yet this is precisely what made the BSP such a meaningful organization. For the first time in the lives of most of these pupils, they gained experience with the techniques and mechanisms of democracy. These pupils were

M I T T E I L U N G E N
D E S
S C H U L F U N K - P A R L A M E N T S

XV   MÄRZ 1952

Vier Jahre RIAS-Schulfunk-Parlament

Der Bundesbevollmächtigte für Berlin, Herr Dr. Vockel, spricht auf der 32. Sitzung
vom 22. 9. 51 im Berliner Abgeordnetenhaus

Figure 6. Newsletter of the Berlin Student Parliament, 1952. Heinrich Vockel, West Berlin's special representative to the federal government, addresses the young parliamentarians. Courtesy Wilhelm-Dietrich von Thadden.

elected by their peers, and they in turn elected parliamentary leaders who were responsible for directing the organization. The first generation of BSP members authored a constitution, which was a detailed document outlining the rules, goals, and responsibilities of the body. Those who came after them supplemented the constitution, abided by it, and enacted new rules for the conduct of business in the monthly meetings.[40] Members of the parliament gained experience in debating issues, expressing and defending their own ideas, and accepting the ideas of others. These were all critical skills that made the value of the student parliament much more than merely the sum total of the legislation it passed.

It is challenging to measure the effect that participation in the BSP had on its members, but this organization clearly served as a formative experience for many who were involved. As one former participant remembered years later, the BSP "decisively formed" his life. "We who had been in the *Jungvolk* or Hitler Youth learned here what democracy and democratic relations with one another meant."[41] Another stated that "for the exercise not merely of democratic methods but of democratic values, the Berlin Student Parliament was invaluable."[42] Berlin's citywide student parliament, one of a handful of such postwar creations in the FRG, made democracy a real, palpable process to the pupils who participated. This organization was an extension of the instruction offered in the classroom and indeed, as a former teacher advisor noted years later, "practical political education."[43] The BSP underscored the growth of student government and an accompanying interest in the functioning of democracy among secondary school pupils after the war. It also highlights the fact that these reforms originated at the local level among teachers, pupils, and other members of the community.

Although it is relatively easy to dismiss the influence of the BSP as meaningful only to the most academically oriented secondary school pupils, this is an oversimplification. First, pupils from a variety of schools participated in the organization in increasing numbers throughout the 1950s. Attendance figures for the BSP as the 1950s came to a close indicate the growing participation of all secondary schools in the organization. Of the 79 OPZs in West Berlin, 46 had representatives in attendance—almost 60 percent. The statistics for the OTZs were still better, as 39 of 48 were represented. The participation of OTZs— roughly 80 percent—actually matched that of the OWZs, of which there were 55 represented in the parliament.[44] Second, sensitive to concerns that the parliament catered to the concerns of only the eldest pupils (and typically those in the OWZs), the BSP worked for the creation of a separate organization that would represent vocational schools. Founded as a chamber of the BSP, the Berufsschul-Parlament met for the first time in April 1950 at the Amerikahaus located at Nollendorfplatz.[45] It too consisted of pupils elected by their schools to serve in the citywide organization. The Berufsschul-Parlament also passed a constitution of its own, although it remained in close contact with the BSP throughout its existence.[46] Thus the new opportunities generated by the BSP enabled a growing number of the city's pupils to gain practical experience with the methods—and responsibilities—of democracy.

The last years of the occupation and first years of the new decade witnessed remarkable changes in the participation of pupils in the life of their schools. In Hesse, the Culture Ministry promoted the active involvement of pupils in the administration of their classrooms through student government. In West Berlin, the participation of pupils in student government organizations was even stronger, as the activities of the Berlin Student Parliament reveal. This is not to suggest that pupils became the ultimate arbiters of educational policy in the postwar schools. Nevertheless, their involvement in school affairs, even in regard to minor decisions regarding class trips, school menu offerings, and fundraising efforts, gave these young Germans personal experience with the mechanisms of democracy. Through their involvement in student government, pupils throughout the Federal Republic acquired an intimate understanding of the rights and responsibilities of citizens in a democratic state. It was not what pupils accomplished that was significant; rather the value of their labors came out of the process in which they participated. For the first time in their lives, young Germans became actively engaged in the workings of a democratic society.

Exchange Programs Reunite Germany with the World

Designed to expose Germans personally to American democracy, the US government inaugurated a slate of new exchange programs for them in the last years of the occupation. These "exchange of persons" programs, as they were officially titled by the State Department, began in the last years of the occupation and reached their peak in the first half of the 1950s. Government-sponsored exchange programs were responsible for the visits of thousands of Germans to the United States in the postwar period. American officials hoped to use these exchange programs to influence the thinking of leading Germans about democracy and American society. Business leaders, politicians, journalists, professors, attorneys, and other prominent Germans were the first to take part in these exchanges. By 1950, however, the number of educational exchanges expanded tremendously, as American officials recognized these programs as yet another means to instill an appreciation for democracy (as well as for America) in the postwar schools. Budget figures for "leader" programs show that education surpassed politics and government to become the leading group for federally funded exchanges to the United States by the early 1950s. When one considers the additional specialized programs that targeted educators directly, it becomes clear that American officials envisioned exchanges as a key tool for the promotion of continued reform in the German schools.[47]

Almost without exception, participants in educational exchanges with America viewed their visits to the US as a critical learning experience in their lives. Participants often noted that their visit to the US allowed them to glimpse life in a democracy for the first time. It is indeed challenging to quantify the influence that exchange programs had on a new postwar generation of teachers and pupils; even former participants often admit to having difficulty in explaining how their visits to the United States changed them. While some specific reforms in German education can be cited as direct results of these trips, the much more important effects are the changes in thinking and openness to new ideas that developed in participants after their return home. West Berlin secondary school educator and teacher education exchange program participant Ulrich Kledzik serves as a telling example. Recalling his experiences in the US fifty years after his first visit, Kledzik remarked that his trip allowed him "to see the world anew."[48] A twenty-six-year-old teacher at the time, Kledzik remembered being astonished by the endless optimism of his American colleagues. In a report written at the end of his stay in the US in 1953, Kledzik asserted that after the isolation of the Nazi era, the most pressing task of the German educator was to reconnect "to international pedagogical development as quickly as possible."[49] Significantly, Kledzik returned from his trip and continued his career, first as a teacher and then as a principal, specifically working on introducing student government in his schools.[50] Statements such as these can only begin to illustrate the impact that exchange programs had on a new generation of German educators and their pupils as the first postwar decade began.

With the passing of the Smith-Mundt Act in 1948, a large sum of US tax dollars became available to fund a variety of exchange opportunities throughout the world. It was the exchanges with West Germany, however, that propelled the program to unprecedented levels.[51] By the end of 1949, less than 1,200 Germans had visited the United States as a part of official US government programs. This number grew dramatically beginning in the new decade, with the number of visiting Germans rising above 2,000 per year from 1950–1952. Making the growth of the early 1950s even more impressive is the fact that Fulbright grants were not made available for US-German exchanges until 1953. Particularly striking about the expansion of these programs in the new decade was the increased emphasis on education. American officials consciously targeted teachers, administrators, and secondary school pupils in these programs, sometimes even creating specialized exchanges for educational purposes. University students also participated in postwar exchanges, and they actually accounted for more visitors to the US through 1948 than the "leaders" program. Yet as the 1950s began, university students were consistently outnumbered by visiting teenagers, denoting a change in emphasis on the part of American officials. The explosion of teenage participants indicated a desire for "winning the hearts and minds" of the youngest Germans, those in the secondary schools who had been born and socialized under the Third Reich.[52]

Initiated under OMGUS and expanded under the High Commission (HICOG), a variety of State Department exchange programs brought Germans to the US in this period. These exchanges were divided into four main branches, under which there were often numerous subprograms targeting specific professional groups. The first—and largest—of these four was the aforementioned "German Leaders" program. This broadly defined exchange provided a variety of German leaders—in business, law, medicine, science, journalism, politics, and education—the opportunity to cross the Atlantic as early as 1947. Education did not assume major significance in this program until later, and the initial educators who visited the United States as part of this program were overwhelmingly university faculty. A second exchange program targeting university students also began at this early date, bringing 219 visitors to the US by 1948.[53] A third program, dedicated to "German Trainees," began in 1949. It facilitated the visits of young professionals (such as attorneys, social workers, and trade union leaders) who were either at the end of their period of training or who had only just recently begun their careers. American officials especially targeted groups whose work would involve broad social and civic responsibilities. Primary and secondary school educators would become a critical part of this program by 1950. A fourth exchange opportunity, also added in 1949, was for German teenagers. Focused on sixteen- to eighteen-year-olds, this exchange had a more general goal of promoting cultural understanding and instilling "a knowledge of and respect for the democratic way of life" in the youth of Germany.[54] Although initiated later than other programs, it quickly became one of the most popular exchanges, both in terms of the number of Germans who participated and in its reception by American politicians, educators, and citizens.

An excellent example of the type of professional programs initiated during this period is one of the largest: the "German Teacher Trainee Program." Founded in 1950 under the rubric of the "trainee programs," this exchange brought young West German teachers to the United States to study American education.[55] Annually, this program brought an average of 140 young West German educators to the US for approximately seven months.[56] American officials specifically targeted young educators for this program—those between the ages of twenty and twenty-nine—believing that they would be the most valuable in influencing West Germany's schools over the coming decades. As stipulated in an early policy report, the goals of the German Teacher Trainee Program were "to bring German teachers into close contact with educational and community life in the United States [and] to help them observe the administration, curriculum, and educational practices of our schools in action."[57] American officials added that they hoped the young teachers would be in the position to "make a real contribution to the college, the cooperating schools, and to the community" they were visiting.[58] In effect, these young educators were supposed to become typical college students and active community members, as well as involved educators during their visits to the US.

The German Teacher Trainee Program was divided into two main parts. The first four to five months of their visits were spent in small groups of ten to fifteen Germans at a variety of American universities offering excellent programs in education. On campus, the visiting Germans enrolled in education courses, where they studied pedagogical theory and methods. The Germans also had the opportunity to observe schools in the area, and in some cases, laboratory schools affiliated with the university. In addition to coursework, they were encouraged to become active members of the university and local communities. The young educators took part in intramural sports, various campus clubs, and student government while at their respective institutions. The final two months of their programs allowed the Germans to experience American schools in an individual setting. Each guest had the opportunity to visit two different American schools for a one-month period. These visits allowed the Germans to witness American classroom and intraschool relationships, the role of the community in education, the content of textbooks, equipment and facilities, and extracurricular activities such as student government and club sports. American teachers sometimes offered their German colleagues the chance to teach, although this was not required by program authorities. Superintendents, principals, teachers, and parents all worked to make their German guests feel as comfortable as possible during this final part of their visits.

Although the classroom aspect of the exchange played an important role in the experiences these Germans had in the United States, the extracurricular activities in which they engaged impressed them as the most significant aspect of their exchange. The institutions and organizations that opened their doors to the Germans allowed them the unique opportunity to participate personally in American civic life. Cultural institutions such as symphonies, museums, preservation societies, conservatories, and art museums invited the German educators to their meetings. Social agencies such as the YMCA and the YWCA did likewise, as did local government and business associations. Perhaps of more direct relevance to their careers, local Parent-Teacher Associations entertained the German educators and invited them to their meetings. While many of these events cannot be strictly construed as "educational" in a pedagogical sense, the visiting Germans deemed these experiences as a valuable opportunity to see first-hand how democratic community organizations operated.

American officials also believed that these trips offered German educators the opportunity to experience participatory democracy in action. Campus officials in particular believed that the program was much more than a preordained, imposed schedule of activities; the exchange should serve as an opportunity for German educators to contribute to the decision-making process. Within their own ranks, each group of exchange teachers operated their own mechanisms of self-governance. Groups typically elected a chairman for a period of one month. The Germans usually met among themselves and discussed their needs, desires, and problems, and then the elected representative met with university officials on a weekly basis to share the group's concerns. In his end-of-program report in 1953, University of Cincinnati coordinator Gordon Hendrickson noted that the German groups "allowed freedom of discussion and encouraged participation by the whole group. The democratic process operated effectively within the group itself."[59] In this example, the American ideal of self-government as it applies to the schools is evident. It is hard to doubt that American officials, hoping that this experience would leave a deep impression on the participants, wanted German educators to introduce similar approaches to their pupils upon returning to Germany.

German Teacher Leaves For Washington

Pictured above, just before he boarded the train to Washington, is Mr. Gerhart Voelker, the German exchange teacher, with a group of students. Pictured left to right: Joe Rand, Barbara Jean Deans, Mr. Voelker and Margaret Tyson. Second row: Joe Williams, Royce Matthews, Richard Ward, and the Rev. Robert W. Bradshaw.

Figure 7. Wilson High School Newspaper, Wilson City, North Carolina, 1953. The newspaper covers the visit of Gerhart Völker, a *Gymnasium* teacher from Osnabrück, to the school as part of the German Teacher Trainee Program. Courtesy National Archives, RG 59, Bureau of Public Affairs, International Educational Exchange Service, Reports on German Teacher Program 1951–1953, Box 1.

GERMAN SCHOOL TEACHER LEAVES AFTER MONTH'S STAY IN SCHOOLS

Mr. Gerhart Voelker, German exchange teacher f r o m Osnabrueck, spent four weeks in the Wilson City schools completing a project of visitation and observation which he and 110 other German exchange teachers began in September.

The purpose of Mr. Voelker's visit was to see at first hand the American schools and institutions, to learn how students live in and out of school, and to know and understand the American way of life.

Orientation Followed Arrival

Following his arrival in New York city September 10, Mr. Voelker spent two weeks of orientation in Washington before going to the University of Illinois for a general background seminar. From the university, he spent a month studying the schools of Arizona before coming to North Carolina for further study.

The State Department of Public Instruction chose Wilson for Mr. Voelker's study of North Carolina schools. Mr. Voelker teaches Latin, Greek, and geography in a high school in Osnabrueck. He mentioned that although their classes are not as informal as those of the American

schools, they are not as strict and dull as one might imagine. The girls attend a separate high school from the boys.

Mr. Voelker's impression of America prior to his visit was somewhat false. From books, movies and advertising he had received, as many Europeans have, a wrong impression of America and its way of life. Now that he has visited in homes, seen various schools, and the community life of an American small town he related that he was much impressed by the hospitality and naturalness of the American people.

Leaves March 24

Mr. Voelker left March 24, f o r Washington, D. C. where he will meet the other exchange teachers. There they will conclude their study in the office of Education by evaluating what they have learned. In April the group will sail for Germany by way of Genoa, Italy.

While in Wilson, Mr Voelker stayed in the homes of Rev. and Mrs. Robert Bradshaw and Mr. and Mrs. Oliver G. Rand.

The essays that the visiting Germans authored before their return to West Germany illuminate how the program influenced them as educators. Although one must be cautious when evaluating these writings since they were written before their authors returned to Germany, they nevertheless provide valuable insight into the young Germans' impressions of American education and society. These young teachers identified a number of practices that they believed could be useful in their own classrooms. One of the features that particularly impressed German educators was the close cooperation of parents and teachers. The reports of the young educators indicate a sincere respect for the work of the Parent-Teacher Associations (PTAs), which they had so often visited during their stays. Many Germans asserted that the close relationships forged by American PTAs could ameliorate communication problems at home. Gertrud Schweier, a Bavarian *Volksschullehrer,* noted in her report that, as her highest priority upon her return, she would work to facilitate *"closer cooperation* between parents and teachers [emphasis added]" in the school.[60] Another strength that the young educators identified in American schools was the early preparation of pupils for their responsibilities as citizens in a democracy. Heinrich Beck noted this in his 1952 report, asserting that he would return home "with the belief that education for good citizenship starts right in the school." In order to realize this goal, Beck explained that he could use a variety of approaches he observed on his visit, including "group working, participation of students in planning of work, more student responsibilities, student government, [and] informal relations between students and teacher."[61]

While the Germans were highly receptive to many American pedagogical practices, they did not adopt everything they encountered in a wholesale fashion. The negative comments of the visiting educators illustrate that American education could not simply be copied and transferred to German schools. One of the strongest criticisms of the US system was that it did not devote enough emphasis to the mastery of skills and information. Some German teachers believed that American educators devoted too much time to group work, "fun" activities, and extracurricular events than to the basic understanding of important facts and skills. Related to this was the suggestion that American schools simply offered too many extracurricular activities. Roland Wallisch, a participant in the Kentucky program, claimed in his report that many of these activities were "unprofitable" and "take the time of the students, which they could use either for serious studies if necessary, or to enjoy themselves in a good recreation program."[62] Another criticism common among visiting German educators was that the American educational system did not offer adequate accommodations for gifted pupils.[63] Unable to realize their full potential, these advanced pupils simply stagnated in their local schools. Thus the reports authored by the young German educators indicate a critical engagement with the educational surroundings they encountered in America.

More valuable than these essays written at the end of the program were unsolicited letters from young German educators explaining how their American experiences had translated into changes in their classrooms after returning home. For example, in a July 1952 letter, Adelheid Sailer informed the State Department that she had instituted some of her American experiences in her school in Ludwigsburg. US officials were undoubtedly pleased to learn that the school's new PTA was very active. It was working to improve classroom equipment and had begun to plan a new exchange program.[64] Another educator, Margaret Wissmann, contacted State Department officials and informed them that she was attempting to introduce voluntary subjects in the schools of her town. Examples as specific as these, however, are exceptional. Much more common are those letters that underscore a psychological change. Impressed by the responsibility of pupils in American schools, Brigitte Scholz, a teacher in West Berlin, informed American authorities that she was trying to change the "whole atmosphere" of her classroom. "Children have to be taught to be more self-reliable, to find out from their own opinions," she asserted.[65] Another teacher, Johann Strobl, informed American officials that former participants met regularly after their return. He stated that he and his colleagues were no longer content with the educational conditions in their local schools and that small progress was being made from year to year. These responses from the teacher trainee program suggest that, in some cases at least, exchanges to the US sparked modest change in the 1950s. Albeit fragmentary, evidence such as this underscores the psychological—and to a lesser extent, curricular—impact that exchange programs began to have on the schools in the early 1950s.

In terms of sheer numbers, one of the largest educational exchange programs of the postwar period was devoted to teenagers. Begun in 1949, these exchanges brought almost 1,900 secondary school pupils to America through 1953.[66] The teenager programs matched participants with a host family and required that they attend high school in their temporary American hometowns. These young Germans typically stayed in the US for a year and, separated from other German participants, quickly forged friendships with their host families and classmates. Unlike other major programs, teenage exchanges were operated in conjunction with private organizations. The American Field Service, the Brethren Service Committee, the National Grange, the National 4-H Club Foundation, the National Catholic Welfare Conference, Rotary International, and the Ann Arbor Council of Churches—to name only the most active sponsors—increasingly organized these youth exchanges with their own staff and funds as the 1950s progressed.[67] The involvement of these private organizations undoubtedly strengthened and enlarged the program, but perhaps more importantly, it ensured the continued existence of teenager exchanges after federal interest in the project had waned.

Arguably one of the largest and most successful "teenager" programs was the "German Teenagers in Michigan Program." A variety of local civic organizations in Michigan organized and operated these exchanges and offered supplementary funding, with the State Department covering most of the costs during the program's early years. For example, two Michigan Rotary International clubs sponsored seventy-five German teenagers in the 1951–52 program, while the

Michigan Council of Churches and Ann Arbor Council of Churches coordinated the visits of twenty youths the following year. The purpose of the program, as outlined in a 1952 report, was twofold. First, the program hoped to foster international cooperation and understanding by having teenagers live as a member of a family in a Michigan community. Second, the program aspired to provide the visiting Germans with a demonstration of democracy as a "living process" in the community. Justifying the creation of the program, the report's author asserted that "[d]emocracy is a living thing. It lives in the hearts of people. It is only in a living experience that it can be truly appreciated. Once experienced, it is never forgotten."[68] Civic leaders in Michigan believed, much as did State Department officials, that visits to the US could serve as a "proving ground for democracy."[69]

Although there was no formalized program for the visit of German teenagers to the US, the 1951–52 Michigan program provides a revealing glimpse into the sorts of activities these exchanges offered. Arriving in July 1951, the young Germans spent four days sightseeing in New York before traveling to the Midwest. Once in Michigan, they took part in a three-day orientation in Dearborn as guests of the local Rotary Club and the Ford Motor Company. The young visitors then spent two weeks at an orientation camp where they held discussions about American family life, dating, high school, politics, money, and clothes. After the Labor Day holiday, they began classes in their respective high schools. The visiting teenagers took part in athletic teams, speech and debate clubs, and choral and drama groups. Many received special positions on student councils, in order to gain a better understanding of student government in the American schools. All of the young Germans enrolled in government, American history, and social studies courses during their stay. Many also took part in local church groups, worked part-time jobs to earn money, and even spoke to civic organizations about their experiences. Finally, they graduated in the spring of 1952, many of them having attained high grades and scholastic honors in their respective schools.[70] In short, these teenagers lived the lives of American high school seniors, insofar as that was possible.

Virtually all of the Americans involved in the program saw the exchange as beneficial. Specific evidence of how the exchange affected the visiting German youths, however, was hard for State Department officials to assemble. The annual report of the Michigan program proved helpful, since it did offer evidence of changes in the thinking of its participants. According to its findings, the high level of responsibility accorded to pupils in American schools was one of the most striking aspects of the exchange for many Germans. One visiting German pupil noted that if

American youngsters want to found a new club in school, "all right," says the principle [*sic*], "go ahead and do it." So they set up a committee, so the [*sic*] work together, bear the responsibility together and enjoy the result of their common effort together. In a German school everything is out-lawed what [*sic*] is not inspired and led by a teacher, an attitude, which is a very great mistake, according to my personal experience.[71]

The eagerness of American high school students to undertake work on their own initiative and, perhaps more importantly, the willingness of teachers to cooperate in these endeavors left a deep impression on the German teenagers.

State Department officials appreciated this evidence of a change in thinking among German teenage exchangees, but they were more interested in connecting the exchange of young Germans to America with specific social developments in the Federal Republic. Linking government-sponsored teenager exchange programs with social changes in Germany, however, was even harder to do than in the case of teacher exchanges. One of the rare examples of these teenagers initiating tangible changes in his homeland is Ludwig Jagla, a teenager from northwestern Germany. Jagla had spent the 1951–52 academic year in Michigan as a participant in the Teenager Exchange Program. In an unsolicited letter to US officials, he wrote that a program targeting teenagers was precisely what West Germany needed. He asserted that "one thing [was] certain" about German teens once they returned home: "the memory of America is permanent in their heads. Along with this memory goes a strong belief in democracy. This feeling is penetrating families and friends as well, and since most returnees go back to school they will spread the knowledge gained also there."[72] Better than merely asserting such positive changes, Jagla offered a number of concrete ways in which he had put his American experiences to use in his homeland. After returning to Germany, he organized a workshop to promote "German-American friendship." This course soon led to the introduction of two specific programs in the commercial and vocational schools of Gladbeck (Ruhr): "Democracy in Action" and "Information on America." In addition to this, Jagla had formed a similarly themed workshop for the youth group of the local trade union, as well as the city's YMCA. He also organized these workshops in three neighboring towns, and had begun to work for their introduction in the city of Essen. Plus, his relations with local youth officials had led to at least two new opportunities for exchanges with the United States.[73]

American officials only gradually came to terms with the fact that the greatest results of exchange programs were virtually impossible to calculate. A 1952 report of the US Information Administration Educational Service Exchange notes that the comments of returning teenagers to Germany represent "intangibles. They don't really prove anything but they indicate an attitude; an attitude which is based on strong personal ties. The attitude is there. It can grow and develop."[74] This attitude, American officials believed, could also be passed on from program participants to friends, family, colleagues, and even the community at large. Although applicable to virtually all Germans who visited the US under the auspices of formal exchange programs, the term *multiplier* became most intimately linked to teenagers and educators in the 1950s. These two groups, perhaps more than any others, were expected to return to their communities and share their experiences, thoughts, feelings, and ideas with others.

Even though the greatest impact of the exchange programs was invisible, American officials endeavored to measure the "intangibles," insofar as that was possible. The State Department and HICOG thus conducted numerous surveys in the early 1950s in an attempt to gauge the multiplier phenomenon. Phrased rather crudely, officials at the State Department wanted to determine the "value" that the United States gained from exchangees once they returned home. According to a 1952 HICOG report, American officials estimated that each exchange program returnee had spoken with an average of 150 Germans after returning from the US. Of those Germans who had had contact with a returnee from America, 93 percent believed that a visit abroad allowed an individual to contribute more to his country's future, as opposed to the support of only 63 percent of those who were not familiar with the exchange program. Similarly, 83 percent of those familiar with the exchange program were convinced that Germany could learn from other nations, while only 35 percent of those who were unfamiliar with the exchange programs held such beliefs.[75]

As HICOG came to a close three years later, new surveys highlighted the expanding influence of the exchange programs with Germany. By 1955, American officials calculated that the average returnee had contact with 210 Germans, with face-to-face relations being more frequent than other forms of contact. Only 8 percent of those who had met with returnees from America held the opinion that their experiences abroad would be of no use in Germany. Of even greater interest for American officials was the revelation that 51 percent of exchangee contacts reported that they had been "favorably influenced" through contact with a returnee.[76] Specifically, those who had met exchangees had gained the most favorable "new ideas" in relation to education (22 percent), technology, economy, and agriculture. As the report summarized in its conclusion, there was "substantial evidence that the Exchange of Persons Program is a successful one in terms of creating pro-American orientation among those exposed to returnees' dissemination and that this dissemination is an ever-widening circle among the public."[77] Positive impressions circulated by former program participants, American officials argued, made many Germans more receptive to change.

A decade after the Second World War ended, few could dispute that German education had been the greatest beneficiary of US government-sponsored exchange programs. Of those participants in the leaders and trainee programs, 1,345 came from the field of education. Only exchange participants categorized as "political and governmental leadership" came close—claiming just over 1,000 exchanges. The statistics for leaders and trainees in education, however, pale in comparison to the number of university students and teenagers who visited the US through 1955. Over 3,600 of these young Germans had traveled to America—for a year-long visit, in most cases—and they hailed from all areas of West Germany, not just those that had been in the American zone of occupation.[78] And these HICOG statistics do not include exchangees who visited the United States as part of the Fulbright Program. If one groups those labeled as "educators" together with students and teenagers who came to the US under American auspices, then the broadly conceived field of education accounted for just under 50 percent of all federally funded exchanges. And 46 percent of program participants were under thirty years of age.[79] Undoubtedly, American officials believed that exchange programs could play a significant role in the reform of German education. Beyond these specific goals, exchange programs helped reconnect Germany to the outside world after twelve years of isolation, provided young Germans with first-hand experience in the everyday workings of a democratic society, and as many participants noted in postprogram essays and letters, offered them ideas for initiating change in their own society upon their return.

A New Generation of Textbooks

In addition to the extracurricular reforms initiated during this period, the West German schools also experienced several significant changes within the classrooms. One of the most visible of these intraschool reforms was the introduction of new textbooks. As we learned in chapter 1, American occupation officials experienced limited success in their cultivation of new texts in the first years of the occupation. Yet as the postwar situation stabilized and German educators had more supplies and time to work, new textbooks gradually began to appear in the schools. These texts represented a departure from the militarism and xenophobia of the Third Reich, as well as a moderation of the fervent nationalism of the Weimar Republic. Many of these books employed new pedagogical methods—such as posing assignments for in-class group work or offering questions for debate—and encouraged pupils to take a more active role in their education. Even the design of postwar textbooks, with many more photos, maps, charts, and review sections, catered to the interests of pupils more than those of the interwar era. This new generation of texts, however, was not entirely without its faults. At least through the mid-1950s, most books overlooked the enormous crimes of the Third Reich. In many narratives, Hitler was a lone figure who, assisted by only a handful of accomplices, led Germany to destruction. A number of texts overemphasized German resistance to the Third Reich and devoted as much attention to it as they did to the injustices of the regime. Even the most innovative texts contained questionable passages or omitted troubling material from their pages.

History was undoubtedly the most challenging discipline for postwar Germans to address in the classroom. The authors of new textbooks faced the challenge of explaining Germany's tumultuous twentieth century, including the outbreak of World War I, the short-lived experience with democracy after the war, the Third Reich, and the crimes of the Nazi regime, especially the Holocaust. Unwilling to return to the nationalist and militarist traditions of the past, many history textbook authors offered a new narrative to postwar pupils. These texts presented a vibrant, if not always successful, tradition of democracy in German history that legitimated the Federal Republic. This new narrative presented the struggle for freedom and democracy as the key theme in German history; these texts indicated that the authoritarianism of the Third Reich marked a departure from (and not a culmination of) Germany's modern development. Just as important as this democratic narrative was the fact that many of these postwar texts incorporated new pedagogical approaches designed to involve the pupil more actively in the educational process. As we will see, innovations such as debating classmates, working together in groups, and critically analyzing important historical events provided another means for pupils to obtain experience with democratic practices within the classroom. These new textbooks employed democratic procedures and techniques in an effort to teach pupils about German democracy.

As was the case in postwar exchange programs, American officials also played an active role in the creation of new postwar texts. These officials deemed textbook reform to be critical to the larger mission of democratizing Germany's schools. In order to facilitate the publication of new German textbooks, American officials adopted a number of policies to assist in the process. First, throughout the last years of the occupation, they continued to review and approve only texts authored by Germans living in Germany. While émigrés living throughout the world—especially in the United States—submitted manuscripts, these were not introduced into the schools. US officials believed that books written by those outside Germany would undermine the legitimacy of reform efforts already underway.[80] Second, American officials drafted a host of general policies targeting the major problems they identified in German texts of the Third Reich and Weimar Republic. Those of the most problematic subject—history—nicely encapsulate the broader goals of US officials. Postwar texts were to deemphasize war, and when the subject was broached, authors were encouraged to stress the costs in lives and resources. American officials realized that nationalism could not be removed entirely from texts (nor did they aspire to do so). Yet they asked German authors to illuminate Germany's relationship with other countries, as well as to underscore the "mixture of races" that inhabited Germany. Shifting the focus from Germany and devoting attention to achievements and developments in other countries struck American officials as another way to challenge traditional German-centric narratives. An American postwar report on history textbook guidelines concluded that "the final goal of history teaching should be to build responsible citizens, not only Germans but also Europeans and human beings."[81]

OMGUS officials exercised direct control over textbooks through the occupation period by virtue of their position as "gatekeepers" in regard to the German schools. American officials held a tight grip on the review and vetting of textbooks during the initial years of the occupation, only allowing German authorities to participate in this process as the occupation neared its conclusion. The careful evaluation of all textbooks conducted by OMGUS officials through 1949 meant that militarism, extreme nationalism, and racism disappeared from old editions still in use in the German schools. By 1947, newly printed—and carefully edited—editions of older texts began to replace the crudely blackened-out passages of books used in the immediate postwar period. Additionally, American oversight of the process prevented repackaged books from the Weimar Republic from reentering the classrooms under the guise of a new edition. While this sweeping power helped US officials control the content of history lessons, it did not assist in the production of new postwar textbooks.

American officials exerted a more subtle influence on the writing of postwar textbooks through the creation of Curriculum and Textbooks Centers. These centers offered German educators a warm, comfortable facility in which they could work on their projects. OMGUS officials opened nine centers throughout the American zone in 1946 to assist German educators in the writing of "new democratically oriented textbooks and to plan curricula reforms."[82] With the shifting of emphasis away from structural reform toward curricular changes around 1947, these centers drastically expanded their services. Renamed Education Service Centers in 1948, these facilities greatly increased their services for educators and also offered their resources to the community. In a 1948 manual, eight major activities were highlighted as "main functions" for these institutions: curriculum making, teacher education, research, textbook revision and development, library services, audio-visual materials, publications, and public relations.[83] With the expansion of its services and opening of its doors to the German population at large, the Education Service Center became a "main point of contact with the German people."[84] By the time the occupation came to a close in 1949, these centers had become the public face of the American educational mission to Germany.

Education Service Centers had an immediate impact on the production of new, "democratically oriented" textbooks in the American zone. First, these centers provided German educators with guidance in the preparation of manuscripts. Offering textbook authors reference materials, workspace, and a forum in which they could interact with colleagues, American officials hoped, would lead to a decrease in the number of rejected proposals. Statistics for the year after these facilities opened indicate an impressive level of success. The number of disapproved history texts for 1947 declined from 50 percent to 17 percent.[85] Not surprisingly, these numbers continued to decline through 1950. While not the only explanation for this trend, the Education Service Centers undoubtedly contributed to the higher number of accepted textbook manuscripts. Second, and perhaps more importantly, these centers could cite specific successes in the publication of new textbook titles (and series) that embodied the sorts of reforms Americans had advocated. US officials could claim that two series had been drafted almost solely at the centers: an eight-title history series called *Wege der Völker* (*Paths of the Peoples*), and a fourteen-volume social studies series named *Unsere Schule* (*Our School*). Although the Educational Service Centers supplied critical materials and American officials worked closely with German authors in the composition of these series, they ultimately represent the coordinated efforts of German educators. These books, particularly the *Wege der Völker* volumes, underscore the sincere efforts of German authors to break with pedagogical traditions deemed problematic by American officials and many German teachers.

The *Wege der Völker* series signaled a milestone in the production of postwar textbooks. These books were written by German educators who, after being selected by American officials, labored in the Education Service Center in Berlin.

The series consisted of volumes for use in grades five through twelve and entered production in late 1947. The first volumes began appearing in West German classrooms in the last months of 1948. The most contentious volumes were those that focused on Germany's most recent development. Volume 3 (for the seventh grade) and volume 4 (for the eighth grade) addressed German history from the end of the Middle Ages to 1848 and from 1849 to the post–World War II period, respectively. Their strategic placement in the curriculum meant that even pupils who left school after the eighth class—the minimum requirements of the educational system—would nonetheless have studied Germany's recent history. The penultimate volume of the series reexamined many of these issues in greater depth for those pupils in the eleventh class who were returning to Germany's nineteenth- and twentieth-century history in the more advanced classes of the secondary schools.

The *Wege der Völker* series marked the creation of a new narrative that centered on Germany's struggle for democracy. Rejecting the nationalist, militaristic narratives of the past, the authors of this series legitimized the West German state through their focus on the historic struggle for democracy and rule by the people.[86] Pupils reading the *Wege der Völker* books would encounter the most vivid expression of Germany's desire for democracy in discussions of the revolution of 1848. In this event, pupils were exposed to one of the earliest and most valiant attempts of the Germans to throw off the oppression of monarchy and authoritarian rule. Yet as volume 3 of the series explained, this was the not first time that Germans had voiced such sentiments. It noted that the fight for "German freedom, similar to the Peasants' War, was a revolution from below."[87] The yearnings of Germans for freedom and unity reappeared during the Napoleonic Wars in the hearts of Germany's youth. It was for these beliefs, the authors argued, that young Germans had enlisted in the effort against the French emperor.[88] The Germans could thus claim a legacy of struggle for democracy and freedom that long predated even the American Revolution.

The revolution of 1848 was the key component to postwar narratives focused on Germany's democratic lineage. The constitution of 1849 served as the cornerstone of German democracy—even into the post–World War II period. In the final pages of volume 3, the authors asserted that the constitution of 1919 "breathed the same liberal and democratic spirit as the work of the years 1848–49." The German *Volk*, however, had not succeeded in "filling the constitution with life and protecting it." In the aftermath of the Third Reich, the authors argued, the German people once more "confronted the task of 1848: the creation of a free German state with internal freedom and external unity."[89] Despite the fact that the revolution had not brought democracy in 1848, the authors did not want pupils to believe that the revolution had been wholly unsuccessful. "Even if the German peoples' revolution remained uncompleted, it nevertheless played an important role in Europe's wider fight for freedom. ... The centuries-long struggle of people for spiritual and political freedom was not without success even in Germany."[90]

In tracing Germany's history after 1871, the authors of the *Wege der Völker* series continued to emphasize the struggle for democracy. Anticipating possible questions from pupils regarding the unification of Germany, the authors differentiated Bismarck's constitution from that of 1848. The German Empire founded by Bismarck constituted "unification 'from above,' a royal state, but not a people's state, as the revolution of 1848 had set out as its goal."[91] Certainly Bismarck's ideals differed from those of the men of 1848, but, in this new postwar narrative, the Iron Chancellor's new empire served as a stepping stone towards a future democratic state. The book informed pupils that "the constitution of 1871 was perhaps the best that could be achieved in the circumstances of that time." Perhaps most notably, the textbook explained that Bismarck's efforts indicated "progress was being made on the road to democracy."[92] While the work of Bismarck no longer served as the glorious realization of unity that it had been in the past, neither was it rejected as the antithesis of freedom and democracy. The authors of the *Wege der Völker* series conceived of the constitution and the construction of a new German state as a bridge between the events of 1848 and 1919.

The Weimar Republic was an even a greater challenge for the young historians who authored this series. It represented a realization of democracy but also its subsequent failure. The authors praised the Weimar Republic for incorporating women into government, as well as for encouraging cooperation in the forging of ruling coalitions. Both of these advances are presented as highly democratic developments. The republic could not, however, withstand the constant attacks from conservative and nationalist groups. In a striking passage that recounted Hitler's rise to power, the German people are described as unable to maintain their patience for the successful recovery of the young republic. Hitler and the Nazi movement are represented as a departure from the democratic ideals of German history, specifically the constitution of the Weimar Republic. Thus, the Third Reich does not represent the culmination of German history in the authoritarian tradition of Luther and Bismarck, as many Americans envisioned it in the postwar period. For the authors of the *Wege der Völker* series, Hitler's Third Reich stood as a disruption—not a continuation—of Germany's historical development.

In addition to a new narrative, the authors of the *Wege der Völker* series also incorporated a variety of new pedagogical methods in their texts. The most important of these pedagogical innovations was the inclusion of assignments for group work and topics for classroom debate. Utilizing these new methods afforded pupils the opportunity to engage in democratic practices within the classroom through the use of the text. A section entitled "Questions and Suggestions" located at the end of each section provided material for discussion. These questions moved beyond simple factual queries and encouraged pupils to take a position on a potentially divisive issue. A question addressing the political chaos of the Weimar Republic asked pupils to "give examples for nonviolent resistance in modern history. What do you think is the value of this manner of struggle in comparison to more violent resistance (war)?"[93] A later question on the post–World War II period required pupils to consider the validity of the Soviet claim that the Marshall

Plan contributed to the division of Europe.[94] Questions such as these encouraged pupils to discuss their opinions, as well as to listen to the ideas of their classmates. Other questions pushed the idea of group work even further—prompting pupils to seek assistance from family members, teachers, and people in the community. One such example relating to the Weimar Republic asked pupils to interview grandparents or other older people about their time in school. The question continued: "How is the school of today different from before and what is the purpose of changes in the contemporary school? What changes would you propose?"[95] These examples might seem trivial, but the creation of closer student-teacher and student-parent relationships was another goal of postwar reformers.

Just as important as the group work sparked by the design of the *Wege der Völker* books was the critical analysis it prompted on the part of pupils. Unlike previous German textbooks, this series did not stress the mastery of information above all else. The *Wege der Völker* books emphasized critical analysis and active evaluation of complex issues by pupils. One such example is an assignment prompting pupils to evaluate Hitler's actions during the war. Indicating a continuing sense of victimization on the part of Germans, a question near the end of volume 4 read: "In what ways was the Second World War a crime against humanity and at the same time a crime against the German people?"[96] Another example can be found in the closing analysis of the Third Reich. The book encouraged pupils to ponder the nature of war, asking them to think about the passages they had read about World War II and to answer a complicated question: "Is the verdict 'War is a crime' valid for all conflicts? Give reasons for your answer."[97] Whether it was defending one's position on a controversial question such as this, respecting the opinions of others, or collaborating on a group assignment, postwar textbooks offered the opportunity to learn democratic conduct while engaged in classroom instruction. The *Wege der Völker* series was a pioneer in this regard, as textbook authors from the Weimar period made no effort to include these sorts of practices in their publications.

The significance of this new narrative—and the *Wege der Völker* series more broadly—extends beyond the mere number of volumes the authors produced. First, with an initial printing before the end of the occupation, these texts were among the first entirely new history books of the postwar period. The broad swath of time covered by the series and the praise it received from American officials and German educators alike meant that these texts soon became staples of postwar history instruction. Unlike many textbooks of the postwar period, the *Wege der Völker* series was adopted by culture ministries throughout the Federal Republic. Although published by the Berthold Schulz publishing house, a small press in West Berlin, the series targeted a broad audience and received approval for classroom use in several states by 1953, including Lower Saxony, North Rhine-Westphalia, Rhineland-Palatinate, Schleswig-Holstein, and Hamburg. The series dominated history instruction in classrooms throughout West Berlin and the Federal Republic until the mid-1950s, when other history textbook series published by the Klett and Diesterweg publishing houses gained a greater share of the market. Nevertheless, the *Wege der Völker* books remained in German classrooms throughout the first two postwar decades. The second, and perhaps even more important, impact of the series was its role as a model for subsequent history texts. Many textbook authors drafted their own volumes that incorporated a narrative and features similar to that of the *Wege der Völker* books.

A number of new history texts containing the ideals represented in the *Wege der Völker* series began to appear in this period. One such text was Otto Müller's *Deutsche Geschichte in Kurzfassung* (*German History in Abridged Form*), approved by OMGUS in December 1948 and first published in 1949, which targeted secondary school pupils.[98] Müller worked in the Hessian Culture Ministry and, like many of his colleagues working for Erwin Stein, was receptive to calls for reform in the schools. His textbook project is best characterized as a collaborative effort of the history committee of the Hessian School Advisory Council and American officials.[99] The text is a remarkably concise one-volume synthesis of German history from the Pax Romana to 1945. Similar to the *Wege der Völker* series, Müller emphasized the democratic traditions of German history and the struggle for freedom. For example, Müller's text devoted six pages to the events of 1848, emphasizing the actions of the political leaders as well as their ideas. His text explained that the parliament desired by the democrats was not to be a "parliament of professors" that was ignorant of the wishes of the people. Instead, it was to be a selection of educated individuals (but not solely academics), who sought "unity, justice, and freedom" for all.[100] Müller offered the example of Dresden, where professor Theodor Mommsen, composer Richard Wagner, and architect Gottfried Semper fought side-by-side on the barricades. Müller made clear to the pupil that the actors of 1848 were not confined to any one social group or profession. The yearning for freedom indeed extended to men of all classes.

In a manner similar to his colleagues in Berlin, Müller connected the legacy of 1848 to the Weimar Constitution and the challenges of the post–World War II period. For Müller, the constitution of 1849 served as evidence for Germany's democratic legacy. More importantly, he saw the document as the foundation of Germany's two republics, representing the "great ideas" of rule by the people and national self-determination. "Even Bismarck," Müller concluded, "could not marginalize the work of the *Paulskirche*, which the Weimar Constitution took as its guideline; the present is now given the task of granting continuance to its basic thoughts."[101] While earlier events in German history, such as the Peasants' War or the fight against Napoleon, could be cited as preparation for liberty and democracy, it was 1848 that most clearly indicated the Germans' own democratic heritage. Müller's narrative also emphasized that democracy was an indigenous development and not merely imported into Germany after World War I and once again after World War II.

As in the *Wege der Völker* series, the Weimar Republic, despite its many flaws, represented the long-desired achievement of democracy in Müller's narrative. "The November Revolution," he explained, "reached the goal that had been laid out four hundred years earlier by some of the leaders of the Peasants' War, who were far beyond their time: the princes lost their power and Germany became a republic."[102] More direct connections, however, were drawn to 1848. Müller's presentation of the Weimar Constitution in the text closely paralleled that of his discussion of the 1849 constitution. Direct passages from the Weimar Constitution revolving around democracy and citizenship were incorporated into the textbook. Thus the language and the explicit references to earlier events made it clear to the pupil that Germany's newfound democracy was actually the realization of hundreds of years of struggle between German democrats and those who wanted to silence the voices of the people. Yet Müller concisely explained to pupils why the new republic did not succeed. Despite the economic recovery of the mid-1920s and the social advances made by the Weimar government, "inner development" did not proceed at the same pace. Romanticized memories of life under Wilhelm I, the continued influence of elites hostile to democracy, and the frustrations prompted by military defeat translated into a "democracy without democrats."[103] Müller added that the stability and support required for the young republic to succeed were absent. Ending his narrative with the defeat of 1945, Müller concluded the volume with the words of Franklin Roosevelt and his own hopes for the future.

In a manner similar to the *Wege der Völker* books, Müller's text encouraged pupils to work together and debate a variety of issues in German history. At the end of each chapter, Müller prompted pupils to expand and deepen their knowledge of issues addressed in the book through reading literature, writing reports, producing charts, and analyzing "myths." Perhaps more importantly, each chapter included "Themes for Discussion," which, in a fashion similar to the *Wege der Völker* texts, proposed topics for classroom debate. For instance, a discussion question at the end of the chapter on 1848 required pupils to discuss what significance the work of the Paulskirche had for contemporary Germany.[104] Perhaps a more controversial subject is broached in the section covering World War I, where Müller asserts: "It has been said that modern German history has been a chain of 'missed opportunities.' Name facts from the period 1890–1914 that speak for this interpretation."[105] A final example of Müller's desire to prompt debate can be found after his analysis of the Weimar Republic. In this section, pupils are queried as to whether they believe Hitler's seizure of power to have been avoidable. If it could have been prevented, the prompt continued, what forces would have had to act?[106] Examples such as these underscored Müller's hope that pupils could interact not only with the text but with their classmates as well.

A final example of these textbook reforms can be found in Hans Ebeling's postwar series entitled *Deutsche Geschichte* (*German History*). A Braunschweig secondary school teacher troubled by the textbooks of the past, Ebeling drafted a sweeping new set of texts that presented a new narrative of German history.[107] His ambitious 1950 series, which consisted of a three-volume edition produced in association with the Geschichtspädagogischer Forschungskreis Braunschweig (a group of educators dedicated to history textbook research), a five-volume edition for older pupils, and a ten-volume thematic edition for younger readers, covered more than two millennia of German history. As was the case with the *Wege der Völker* series and Müller's text, Ebeling's work rejected the nationalist and militaristic traditions of older textbooks, preferring instead to focus on Germany's struggle for a stable democracy. The events of nineteenth- and twentieth-century German history in the *Deutsche Geschichte* series fall into a narrative structure similar to Ebeling's postwar colleagues. The revolution of 1848 and the subsequent constitution serve as key moments in Germany's progress toward democracy. Only after 1918 was democracy actually realized in Germany, Ebeling explained, yet—in an explanation more forthright than those found in other postwar books—he described the lack of support among many Germans that led to its failure. Ebeling nonetheless devoted a five-page section to the economic, social, and cultural contributions of the first German republic. The last two chapters of volume 5 chronicled the Third Reich, its crimes, and the destruction of World War II. The book concluded with a reserved juxtaposition of East Germany and West Germany and an impassioned call for peace and global cooperation.

Although Ebeling's series does not incorporate discussion questions, it nevertheless marks a departure from the history books of the past. In addition to the new perspective on Germany's development offered by Ebeling, his text also incorporated a multitude of primary sources for pupils to examine. In his treatment of the Third Reich, Ebeling included a variety of primary documents illustrating the nature of the regime. Among the documents incorporated in his volume are: a 1937 speech of Hitler to his confidants addressing his territorial ambitions; a 1938 Göring speech on industrial planning; passages from Hitler's wartime correspondence on military issues, the uses of propaganda, and his leadership; and finally a few lines from his infamous final political testament on the failures of the German people.[108] The inclusion of these documents in Ebeling's volume encouraged pupils to evaluate Hitler's regime based on its own words. Such an approach not only encouraged critical analysis, but it also lent itself to a reevaluation of the Third Reich among the young whose knowledge of Hitler's regime came mostly through parents and older siblings.

Admittedly, not every textbook produced in this period embraced the aforementioned curricular and pedagogical reforms. Likewise, many educators may have opted not to utilize the innovative methods contained in their pages. Nevertheless, a number of widely distributed books did alter the traditional narratives of Germany's development. Many of these major textbook series also introduced new techniques to encourage the active participation of pupils. Moving beyond mere memorization, these books encouraged pupils to think critically about complicated historical questions, to express their opinions and defend them before their classmates, and to collaborate with others on group assignments. Many younger educators also seized the opportunities presented by these texts and encouraged their pupils to debate complex historical issues in the classroom. The advent of new history textbooks in the early 1950s recentered the curriculum on the democratic continuities of German history, while at the same time offering a host of new approaches to the educator. These books rejected the problematic nationalist and militaristic content of the Weimar Republic and the Third Reich in favor of a more European and international scope. As a part of the larger reform process underway in the postwar era, a new generation of history textbooks played an important, if subtle, role in the reorganization of West German education after 1945.

Teacher Training, Pedagogical Innovation, and Continuing Education

Recognizing the enormous powers of the teacher in the classroom, Americans and Germans alike called for changes in the training of educators after the war. American officials deemed the construction of a new teacher training system as fundamental to the democratization of the German schools. If there was not a new generation of well-trained and committed teachers to instruct Germany's youth, other reforms such as new textbooks and student government would not have their desired effect. In essence, the newly trained teacher was the proverbial glue that held the entire educational reform program together. The period of stabilization after the immediate postwar years, however, proved rather disappointing to many who had hoped for fundamental change in the structure of the teacher education system. Although not a complete reversion to the teacher training programs of the past, the programs constructed in the states of West Germany in the late 1940s and early 1950s shared many similarities with their prewar predecessors. Yet there were important changes that took place beneath the surface of this restorative structure. Having first gained experience with new approaches during their professional training, teachers introduced a variety of new pedagogical methods in their postwar classrooms. At the same time, a new subject—social studies, or political education—slowly entered the curriculum and commanded more attention from young teachers. Finally, continuing education programs for West German teachers encouraged the sharpening of pedagogical skills while at the same time expanding the horizons of experienced educators. These significant reforms in the sphere of teacher training, although subtle, complemented other changes already underway in the schools of the Federal Republic.

In January 1947, OMGUS officials issued a concise directive to the various culture ministries in their zone: "All teacher education shall be on the university level." After almost two years of emergency training programs for teachers, American officials desired the construction of a new, permanent teacher training system, which they deemed critical to the democratization of the educational system.[109] There were many factors in their decision to work toward the unified teacher training system at the university level. First, American officials hoped to break down the "almost insurmountable caste system between elementary and secondary teachers" created by virtue of their distinct tracks of education.[110] American officials deemed this double standard in the realm of teacher training inherently undemocratic.[111] Second, OMGUS officials believed that elementary teachers were well-trained pedagogically but lacked adequate knowledge in many subject areas. The reverse was supposedly true of secondary school teachers, who mastered facts but did not acquire the same level of pedagogical preparation. American officials believed that a single training system at the university level would alleviate these discrepancies. A third reason was the American belief that shifting teacher training to the university level would loosen the control of the church over young educators in some areas. This was particularly true in Catholic areas such as Bavaria, where the clergy expressed worries that the university might divert some rural *Volksschullehrer* from their intended careers. American officials argued to Culture Ministry officials throughout their zone that a unified system of teacher training at the university level would erase the professional divide between elementary and secondary educators, provide a more balanced pedagogical program, and contribute to the broader goals of democratization.

American officials and German education reformers promoted a new program of teacher training as a solution to the complicated, multitracked system of the Weimar Republic and Third Reich. Although the Weimar Constitution had mandated the "higher education" of all teachers—even elementary educators—in 1919, the culture ministries of the various German states interpreted this in different ways. The result was a convoluted system in which there were roughly three sets of institutions offering training to aspiring German elementary educators. The first was the *Fachschule,* or technical school, which could be considered the lowest track. It was a lengthy program consisting of several years of study following the completion of the *Volksschule* after the eighth grade. This was a continuation of the denominational "normal schools" of the empire and existed only in Bavaria and Württemberg after 1918.[112] The most common form of teacher training in the Weimar Republic was the pedagogical academy, which differentiated itself from the technical school by requiring prospective teachers to have completed the *Abitur.*[113] Elementary and secondary teachers often studied jointly in these institutions, which typically required two years of study. The pedagogical academy, however, lacked direct connections to the universities. The third and final form of elementary teacher training was the two- and three-year university-level programs in select areas before 1933, such as Hamburg, Jena, Leipzig, Dresden, and Rostock.[114] The preparation of elementary teachers after 1933 took place largely in the pedagogical academies, renamed *Hochschulen für Lehrerbildung* by the National Socialists. These were dissolved by 1941 into the *Lehrerbildungsanstalten* (LBAs), or normal schools, which represented a further deterioration of the preparation and standards for elementary educators. While calls for the equal training of all educators at the university level had begun around 1800 and reached a crescendo in 1848 and again in 1919, they remained unrealized before 1945.

American military officials were not the sole proponents of a new system of teacher training at the university level. Many German educators advocated fundamental reform to their system of professional training. They believed that the inequalities of the training system discouraged interested young men and women from becoming teachers. This, they argued, contributed to the continued aging of the profession. A 1952 report from the Federal Office of Statistics (Statistisches Bundesamt) confirmed these fears. It indicated that over a quarter of the profession was over fifty-five years of age in 1950, whereas only an eighth had been so old before the war.[115] There was a call for new blood, yet many German educators realized that the teaching profession—particularly at the level of the *Volksschule*—was unattractive to many. These experienced *Volksschullehrer* asserted that improved training on an equal footing with that of advanced secondary school teachers would entice more young Germans to pursue careers in the school.[116] Perhaps the most vocal supporters of a new teacher training system at the university level for all prospective educators were the unions. The most prominent of these was the Gewerkschaft Erziehung und Wissenschaft (GEW), the largest teachers' union in West Germany and the standard bearer for educators in the country's *Volksschulen* and technical schools.[117] The Hessian branch of the GEW emphasized the need for teacher training reform in the pages of its weekly publication, the *Hessische Lehrerzeitung*. For example, in a 1950 article outlining the "pressing program of the GEW," the leaders of the Hessian organization listed "the integration of teacher training at the university and postsecondary level" as a key goal.[118] It reiterated these demands throughout the postwar period, as a 1954 interview with new Hessian culture minister Arno Hennig indicates. Hennig faced some critical questions regarding the failure of state authorities to provide university-level instruction for young teachers.[119] Thus as 1955 began, virtually ten years after the end of the war, the Hessian GEW maintained its demands for equal training for Hessian educators, placing a new law for teacher training at the top of its list of necessary legislation in its front page appeal to the Hessian state assembly.[120]

The political environment may have been different in the former capital, but the pedagogical situation was similar to that of Hesse. The Pädagogische Hochschule (PH), responsible for training the city's *Volksschul-* and *Mittelschullehrer*, was located inside the Soviet zone of occupation after 1945. Because of the increasing tensions in teacher training courses by the autumn of 1948, city school officials decided to separate the institution into two parts.[121] Despite the protests of educators in the Soviet sector, as well as many others in the city who still hoped for a compromise, a group of students and teachers transferred essential materials from the facility to a temporary location in West Berlin.[122] The PH remained in its temporary quarters in Berlin-Lankwitz until moving to a permanent facility in 1950. The other main institution for teacher training in the city—beginning in late 1948—was the Free University, which prepared the city's *Gymnasiallehrer*. While the PH and Free University both possessed strong facilities for the training of the city's teachers, their separation reflected the continued divide between the "two castes" of educators to which American officials referred in their 1947 directive. This distinction in the preparation of the city's teaching professionals continued throughout the 1950s.

As in Hesse, there was much discussion among educators and administrators in West Berlin regarding the fundamental reform of the city's teacher training program. Administrators, educators, and school authorities openly discussed whether (and how) to create a uniform, university-level system for all of the city's educators. Recognizing the need to eliminate differences in the training of the city's teachers, authorities in the Main School Office (Hauptschulamt) outlined a series of policies and goals for the Pädagogische Hochschule in West Berlin designed to erase the double standard. While this document was framed by the city's desire to institute an integrated, comprehensive school—the *Einheitsschule*—it nevertheless echoed debates taking place elsewhere in the Federal Republic. The authors noted that "the difference between the former teacher of the secondary school and the teachers of the elementary school … in fact still remains and is a substantial impediment on the path toward the preparation of a unified teaching profession."[123] A 1950 report from a commission organized by the Hauptschulamt reiterated this point and called for equal training for the city's teachers. The commission consisted of representatives from the city's Pädagogische Hochschule, the Free University, and a Berlin teachers' union (the Berliner Verband der Lehrer und Erzieher, or BVL). Their report called for equal training for all levels of teachers and proposed an eight-semester period of study, in which pedagogical theory was not to be sacrificed for content.[124] Yet resistance to these goals remained among some secondary school teachers, university professors, and conservative political leaders. The absence of the Free University's representatives from the final committee meeting that produced this report symbolizes the resistance of some university members to the reform of the teacher training system in the city.

Because of the disparities between the teacher training programs of the various federal states, it is difficult to make generalizations regarding the course of study for prospective teachers. Yet the Hessian model serves as a good example of the basic construction of this system. By 1950, aspiring *Volksschullehrer* enrolled in teacher training courses in Hesse completed a six-semester program after obtaining the *Abitur*.[125] They completed this course of study at one of the two pedagogical institutes located in Jugenheim and Weilburg. These institutions were dedicated to the instruction of educators of the *Volksschule, Mittelschule,* and the *Berufsschule,* and they were distinct from facilities preparing teachers for careers in the advanced secondary schools. Students in these institutions typically spent the first semester of their study in an internship at a local school, with the following five semesters consisting of instruction at the pedagogical institute. At this point, applicants would complete the first professional exam and enter the schools as *Lehramtsanwärter,* or teaching candidates. After three years of experience in the schools, these young teachers would complete their second exam and become full-fledged teachers, eligible for official recognition as civil servants.[126] Thus by age twenty-five, elementary educators could have completed their mandatory three years of teaching, passed their second professional exam, and become civil servants for life, all without ever having attending the university.

Teacher training in the former capital was unarguably more complicated due to the quadripartite occupation and pedagogical experimentation with the *Einheitsschule*. Fortunately for the city's educators, after the founding of the Free

University in November 1948 and the establishment of the PH in Lankwitz the following month, the situation stabilized. Training for *Volksschullehrer,* as well as for trade and technical school teachers, took place at the PH, which offered a six-semester program. Prospective educators were expected to excel in three main areas during their professional training: pedagogy, subject specialization, and practical experience. The PH stressed the value of classroom training from its inception, requiring students to teach in the city's classrooms for several weeks at a time every semester during their preparation. This emphasis on practical training became a defining difference between the PH and the Free University. It also ensured the continued separation of teacher training during this period, as preparation of advanced secondary teachers at the Free University concentrated on research and theory. The two competing teacher training institutions in West Berlin proved frustrating both to American officials who aspired to a unified system and German educators who believed all prospective educators would benefit from a more balanced program of instruction. These tensions continued into the late 1950s, with both sides unwilling to yield to demands for change. As the president of the Free University informed West Berlin senator for education Joachim Tiburtius in a 1953 letter, the Department of Philosophy (responsible for teacher training) "recognized no equal instruction for teachers of all school forms. It maintains the belief that … the training of elementary school teachers must remain separate from that of secondary school educators."[127]

The question of teacher training was a state-specific issue, meaning that the Hessian and West Berlin cases did not necessarily represent the state of the entire Federal Republic. Yet virtually all of the states of West Germany constructed a teacher training system similar to the antiquated programs of the Weimar Republic. By 1952, only Hamburg could claim a unitary system of training for all teachers with connections to the university.[128] Excluding Hamburg, there were seventy-five teacher training facilities in West Germany during the 1950–51 academic year, with the individual states operating all but twelve (the exceptions being in Bavaria) with every one being separate from the university.[129] Although there were a variety of differences in terms of qualifications, length of study, and course instruction, the structure of these teacher training programs closely resembled those of the Weimar era. Thus, although German educators and school officials called for changes to the teacher training system that paralleled those proposed by American officials, structural reforms were slow to materialize through the first half of the 1950s.

Despite the fact that the reform of the teacher training system fell short of the goals elucidated by American officials and many German educators, it was not a mere restoration of the pre-Nazi status quo. OMGUS officials sought ambitious changes to the content of the professional preparation of educators in three distinct areas. First, they sought to reduce the amount of time devoted to religious study and redirect these energies toward a better knowledge of pedagogy and child psychology.[130] This was of particular concern in southern Germany, although American officials believed that all young educators could benefit from a more concentrated study of educational theory. A second reform promoted by OMGUS officials was the adoption of new pedagogical methods in the classroom. As we have already seen, many believed that breaking down the traditional authoritarian relationship between teacher and pupil was critical to the success of other reforms. The third American reform objective was the introduction of social studies and political education into the teacher training curriculum. Whereas the teacher education curriculum had largely ignored political education before 1933 and had sought to indoctrinate new teachers during the Third Reich, postwar programs encouraged prospective teachers to introduce such issues in their classrooms. The combination of social studies with a variety of pedagogical innovations fostered a new idea of how citizenship should be taught in the postwar schools, both in terms of content and method. As city school officials in West Berlin phrased it in their 1950 report, "the highest principle is that they [the next generation of teachers] must be educators of youth (*Jugenderzieher*) above all else, and that they become … not only teachers but also citizens."[131]

Teachers who prepared for their teaching careers after the war also gained experience with the values of in-class debate and discussion. Horst Kollat, a West Berlin teacher who completed his training in 1950 and then enrolled in continuing education courses in the early 1950s, utilized these methods after being exposed to them during his studies. Interested in shifting the focus of the classroom from himself to his pupils, Kollat encouraged pupils to analyze their readings critically and discuss them openly in his classroom. Specifically, Kollat recalled the significant role that Friedrich Oetinger's 1951 book *Partnerschaft als pädagogische Aufgabe* (*Partnership as Pedagogical Principle*) had on his lessons.[132] While the new emphasis on political education impressed Kollat, he was fascinated by the conception of partnership and collaboration between pupil and teacher presented in Oetinger's work. Kollat was not alone. This evolving relationship between pupil and teacher facilitated the introduction of debate and discussion in classrooms throughout West Germany. Postwar pedagogical journals lauded the new methods and saw them as particularly valuable for use in regards to political questions. "Under no circumstances should a proposed topic be avoided because it is 'political' or too political," asserted H. H. Pauly in a 1950 article published in *Die pädagogische Provinz*.[133] Even more traditional questions regarding politics and citizenship could be converted into discussion topics. Pauly suggested "the right to vote," a fundamental component of political education that dated back to the empire, as one such example. Instead of traditional textbook recapitulations of the topic, however, Pauly suggested it be turned into a discussion on "why we vote" with the Third Reich serving as an obvious backdrop.

American officials, too, assisted in introducing classroom discussion and debate to West German teachers and pupils even after 1949. US educators and administrators participated in conferences of pupils and teachers organized by German culture ministries, such as one held in Ruit, near Stuttgart, in 1950. This event brought together thirty teachers and sixty pupils to examine the role of discussion in the postwar classroom. After a week of collaboration, the participants agreed on the pedagogical value of classroom discussions, that they should receive a certain amount of time in each school, and that family, community, and politics were the most suitable topics.[134] Similar conferences were held throughout West Germany in the late 1940s and early 1950s. In their reviews of these events, American officials cited mixed results in the receptiveness of teachers and pupils to the new ideas that ranged from open hostility to "active enthusiasm."[135] American officials could nevertheless cite specific successes. For example, a Ludwigsburg *Gymnasium* pupil informed HICOG officials that after taking part in these organized seminars, "our teachers show their reception of the new methods by allowing us to express our own opinions in class discussions and have also encouraged the formation of a student council group, so that we will also have an opportunity to express ourselves on school problems."[136] This example underscores the interconnectedness of postwar reforms: young teachers encouraging a closer pupil-teacher relationship were more likely to introduce new pedagogical approaches such as classroom discussions, as well as to promote the work of student government.

Whereas changes in pedagogical approach surfaced quickly among postwar educators, the emergence of social studies was less dynamic. OMGUS officials did not cite significant successes in introducing social studies to West German teachers as they looked back upon their work in the mid-1950s. In fact, Henry Pilgert, employed with the Historical Division of HICOG, asserted in 1953 that social studies was "virtually non-existent in the present German curriculum and [is] little understood by teachers and school officials."[137] This claim, however, is overly critical; American officials often expressed their frustration with the slow speed of change in the curriculum. Nevertheless, the subject gradually gained acceptance during this period as younger educators entered the profession and their colleagues recognized the need for preparing pupils for their future social and political responsibilities. As a consequence, it also slowly made its way into German teacher training facilities. The curriculum for emergency teachers indicates that the subject entered the teacher training program already in the late 1940s. One notable example was the Hessian curriculum, which provided instruction in both "Political Discussion" (*Politische Aussprache*) and "social studies" (*Gemeinschaftskunde*) as early as 1946.[138] At the time, these two subjects together received as much attention as the four key concentrations for emergency teachers: pedagogy, psychology, religion, and German. With the Hessian Culture Ministry requiring instruction in *Gemeinschaftskunde*—an entirely new postwar concentration—in all seventh-grade classes in January 1946, it was only logical that emergency teachers receive some instruction in the subject.

Social studies officially entered the curriculum of those who would pursue their careers as professional teachers soon after 1945. The subject became mandatory in the Hessian schools in 1946 and was integrated into history instruction in West Berlin by 1948. As a result, the subject became a part of the teacher training curriculum in both areas during the occupation. Despite the American emphasis on social studies as a new creation after 1945, much of the earliest instruction in the subject resembled the older civics lessons of the prewar era. Although subtle, there were nevertheless important innovations that accompanied social studies training for young teachers by the early 1950s. Classroom discussions, unusual in the preparation of prospective teachers in specific subject areas, began to appear in training seminars. Young educators also began to address contemporary social and political issues and acquire experience with the importance of student involvement in the school community through student government and extra-curricular activities.[139] Admittedly, preparation in the subject was uneven in both states; while many educators fondly recalled their training in social studies, others could not remember having taken any such courses. Yet on the whole, the new ideas and approaches introduced in these seminars would gradually translate into meaningful classroom changes by the end of the 1950s.

Social studies instruction for young educators in West Berlin evolved steadily in this period, as it moved away from the traditional imposition of knowledge toward an expanded curriculum that emphasized the active participation of pupils. A 1951 draft of the requirements for *Volksschullehrer* in the field of *Sozialkunde* underscores the continued influence of traditional ideas of the subject, listing "exceptional knowledge of the geographical, morphological, and biological composition of German areas, [and] knowledge of the economic, social, and cultural development of the city of Berlin."[140] Complementing these aspects of teacher training, however, were new lessons dedicated to student government and contemporary issues. The intensifying trend toward introducing contemporary topics into the classroom was particularly strong in the former capital due to its unique location behind the Iron Curtain. As a consequence, debates and discussions gained a greater role in the classroom. Educators increasingly organized politically themed activities for pupils, providing them practical experience with the concepts of collaboration and group work so often broached in teacher training courses. For example, pupils in the West Berlin schools examined the plight of Germans living in the lost territories of the East, discussed how these people could best be helped, and then collected and shipped food and supplies to them. With an expanded curriculum and a premium placed on the active involvement of pupils in the life of the school, young German teachers hoped to avoid the pitfalls of political education instruction as it was practiced during the Weimar Republic.

The development of social studies among teachers in Hesse closely mirrored that of West Berlin. A gradual broadening of the curriculum accompanied a heightened emphasis on the involvement of pupils in the life of the school. While the official integration of the subject into the curriculum of both teachers and pupils is well known, it is less clear what effects this change had on Hessian education. One of the most insightful accounts of this process comes from Burr W. Phillips, who examined progress in the teaching of social studies in the schools in a report for American authorities. Phillips, a professor of history and pedagogy at the University of Wisconsin, expressed satisfaction with the integration of the new subject into the Hessian curriculum. Advances in teacher training for teachers in the realm of social studies stood at the top of his list. For example, Phillips was "especially impressed" with a group of prospective secondary school teachers he met on his 1954 visit. After several semesters of study and a challenging examination in the subject, these teachers engaged in a discussion of "very high quality," Phillips noted in his report. He was particularly pleased to see a "highly praiseworthy amount of student participation" in Hessian classrooms and teacher training courses, which stood in marked contrast to what he had experienced during prior visits.[141] Mirroring American discussions on the subject of social studies in the 1950s, instruction in the subject in Hessian classrooms also considered contemporary social and political issues. In a telling summation, Phillips advised American officials that "one detects little external structural change, but the 'inner school reform' seems … to be making good progress."[142]

The other venue in which professional training experienced significant reform is continuing education programs for teachers. Postwar changes in continuing education signified departures from the past both in the target audience for such activities, as well as in their content and emphasis. First, education officials in the various states composed continuing education courses that appealed to both elementary and secondary school educators. While educators in the more academically focused secondary schools had garnered most of the attention of officials organizing continuing education courses in the past, *Volksschullehrer* participated in postwar programs in increasing numbers. Second, the curriculum of continuing education courses placed a newfound emphasis on political education and social studies. State-level education officials organized entire seminars and courses around questions of political education. These new courses meant that even older teachers whose careers bridged the divide of 1945 would have the opportunity to participate in seminars and short-term courses in the emerging discipline. Additionally, seminars and courses on pedagogical questions encouraged the adoption of new strategies in the classroom and provided greater psychological and professional training for postwar educators. Continuing education thus served as a means to expand the scope of reform to established educators, equalize the training provided to elementary and secondary school teachers, and introduce new themes and approaches to the profession.

Hesse's most important institution for continuing education, the Reinhardswaldschule, attracted educators from across the professional spectrum. In particular, officials of the Reinhardswaldschule were interested in bringing *Volksschullehrer* to the facility. Attendance figures from the first eight months the institution was open (from May 1951 to the end of the year) indicate that the Reinhardswaldschule experienced great success in this endeavor. Of the 1,449 educators who participated in the institution's course offerings for 1951, almost 60 percent were *Volksschullehrer* and *Mittelschullehrer*.[143] The three branch facilities claimed similar results in their efforts to bring educators from outside the *Gymnasium* to their programs. This pattern continued to hold throughout the first half of the decade, with 53 percent of participants during the first three-quarters of 1954 hailing from these schools.[144] From its opening to the end of September 1954, the Reinhardswaldschule could claim to have hosted over 7,600 participants in its 208 courses (*Lehrgänge*).[145] The three branch facilities accounted for an additional 5,700 participants in their 205 courses. These figures do not include educators who participated in shorter seminars or workshops in these facilities. Admittedly, the number of elementary educators in the Hessian schools was much greater than that of secondary school teachers. This increase is nevertheless remarkable because the participation of elementary educators showed signs of dramatic growth in comparison to their involvement in similar programs during the Weimar Republic, when a similar ratio of primary-to-secondary educators had existed. In less than four years, the Hessian institutions for continuing education had provided over 13,000 educators, administrators, and, in select cases, parents the opportunity to improve their knowledge in courses covering a variety of issues.

More than in perhaps other areas, education reform in the realm of teacher training was decidedly mixed through the mid-1950s. Structural reforms to the teacher training system did not materialize either under the American military occupation or during the High Commission. The organization of teacher training for West Germany's postwar teachers closely mirrored that of the Weimar Republic. Curricular and pedagogical changes, however, slowly entered the curriculum after 1945. Most striking was the introduction of new pedagogical methods of group work and classroom discussion and debate. These were introduced as new approaches in the pedagogy study of young teachers, and they subsequently began to appear in the postwar schools during this period. Social studies and political education, although garnering new attention, still contained many traditional ideas of the prewar era. Change was nevertheless afoot, as the Hessian emphasis on *Sozialkunde* as a new subject of study indicates. Notably, experienced teachers were not left out of these reforms, as continuing education programs grew impressively after 1950. Not only did these programs introduce older educators to a variety of new pedagogical methods and subject matter, they also concentrated on elementary school teachers, a group traditionally overlooked in professional training. As in other aspects of the educational system, changes did not occur precisely as American officials and German reformers hoped. Reforms in teacher training nevertheless facilitated the preparation of a new generation of educators, many of whom helped create a more relaxed classroom in which pupils actively engaged with a variety of contemporary issues.

* * * * * *

"It was not a revolution, rather an evolution," former West Berlin secondary school teacher and now university instructor Ulrich Kledzik maintained. Reflecting on his more than fifty years as an educator in the city, Kledzik described the first postwar decade as a time of "prereform," when new ideas and methods still competed for attention with more basic problems of supplies and facilities. Nevertheless, he added, there were still important changes that took place within the schools even at this early point.[146] As we have seen, a variety of significant yet subtle changes entered the West German schools from 1948 to 1954. Perhaps the most visible were extracurricular activities. New student government organizations allowed pupils to gain experience in the mechanisms of democracy—parliamentary procedure, debate, speaking one's opinion, and respecting the views of others. *How* pupils practiced student government is just as meaningful as *what* they actually achieved. Exchange programs, another extracurricular reform, allowed German pupils and teachers to study abroad—particularly in the United States—and to experience the workings of a democratic society for themselves.

Less visible, but no less important, were the curricular reforms that began during this period. The publication of a new generation of history textbooks around 1950 signaled important changes within the walls of the conventional classroom. These books deemphasized the nationalism and militarism of the Weimar Republic and Third Reich in favor of a new narrative that underscored the struggle for democracy. At the same time, many of the new postwar history texts embraced a variety of innovative methods designed to give the pupil a more active role in the classroom. These texts offered group work assignments and debate questions, both of which encouraged pupils to think critically about many problematic issues in German history. The expansion and intensification of teacher training constitutes another important curricular reform initiated in this period. Teachers embraced a host of new pedagogical methods during their professional training and acquired personal experience with political education and social studies. In these classes, seminars, and meetings, West German educators also gained a better knowledge of extracurricular reforms—such as student government, school newspapers, and exchange programs. These courses also exposed veteran teachers to the same sorts of new methods being advocated in teacher training courses and in the pages of professional education journals.

Viewing the years 1948 to the mid-1950s as a coherent, if brief, period, it becomes clear that meaningful reform did not end with the American military occupation. The founding of the Federal Republic in 1949 was a key moment in the postwar period, but it had little effect on educational reforms already underway. Changes ignited during the occupation actually intensified in the 1950s unaffected by the creation of a new state. Naturally, these reforms sparked some disagreement and debate among those involved. There was widespread agreement that the schools needed to change in the postwar period, but there was not always consensus on what needed to be done. Despite these tensions, subtle reform initiated during the occupation continued into the early 1950s and would intensify in the years that followed.

Notes

The title of this chapter comes from an interview with a former participant in the Berlin Student Parliament. See Wilhelm-Dietrich von Thadden, interview by author, tape recording, Berlin-Lichterade, 19 May 2003.

1. Minutes of the RIAS-Schulfunk-Parlament, 46.Sitzung on 25 January 1953, 9 February 1953.

Document from private collection of Wilhelm-Dietrich von Thadden. Also Wilhelm-Dietrich von Thadden, interview by author, tape recording, Berlin-Lichterade, 19 May 2003.

2. This was the motto of the Berlin Student Parliament from its foundation in 1948.

3. There were numerous articles published in this period regarding political education, many of which discussed the merits of student government. See Alfred Ehrentreich, "Wege zur inneren Schulreform," *Bildung und Erziehung* 2, no. 9 (1949): 665–71; "Geht es auch ohne? Zum Problem der Schülermitverwaltung," *Pädagogische Rundschau* 7, no. 6 (1952–53): 222–24; Marie Quade, "Schülermitverwaltung?" *Die pädagogische Provinz* 7, no. 5 (1953): 255–60.

4. West Berlin hosted one such conference in 1953. See "Freunde der Schüler-Mitverantwortung," *Berliner Lehrerzeitung* 7, no. 17 (1953): 372. In Hesse, educators and community members founded the Hessischer Arbeitskreis für Schülermitverantwortung in 1951. This organization hosted yearly conferences for teachers (and to a lesser extent, pupils) who were interested in the possibilities of student government in their schools.

5. See Abteilung 504, No. 644, Fiche 3807, Hessisches Hauptstaatsarchiv (HHstA).

6. Johann Zilien, *Politische Bildung in Hessen von 1945 bis 1965. Gestaltung und Entwicklung der politischen Bildung als schulpolitisches Instrument der sozialen Demokratisierung* (Frankfurt, 1997), 138.

7. "Lehrpläne für den politischen Unterricht in den Schulen des Landes Hessen," 21 August 1948, *Amtsblatt des Hessischen Ministeriums für Kultus und Unterricht* 1, no. 6 (October 1948): 149–70.

8. Student government was made mandatory in secondary schools in May 1946, while another decree issued in late May recommended its introduction in *Volksschulen* and vocational schools. See Zilien, *Politische Bildung in Hessen*, 162–63.

9. "Richtlinien für den politischen Unterricht," 30 June 1949, *Amtsblatt des Hessischen Ministeriums für Kultus und Unterricht* 2, no. 7 (July 1949): 252.

10. Zilien, *Politische Bildung in Hessen*, 187–89.

11. "Schülermitverwaltung in den Schulen," 14 September 1948, *Amtsblatt des Hessischen Ministeriums für Kultus und Unterricht* 1, no. 7 (November 1948): 184–87. See also "Schulzeitungen," 24 September 1948, *Amtsblatt des Hessischen Ministeriums für Kultus und Unterricht* 1, no. 7 (November 1948): 188–91.

12. The Hessian context provides further support for Dirk Schumann's recent claim that this period was one in which "conservatism prevailed, but this should not be mistaken for unquestioned acceptance of authority." See Schumann, "Authority in the 'Blackboard Jungle': Parents, Teachers, Experts and the State, and the Modernization of West Germany in the 1950s," *Bulletin of the German Historical Institute* 33 (Fall 2003): 65–78.

13. West Berlin was already home to a citywide student parliament by the time Stein issued his 1948 decree. Other cities home to citywide student government organizations by the early 1950s included Hamburg, Bremen, Stuttgart, and Munich.

14. Zilien, *Politische Bildung in Hessen*, 212.

15. "Schülermitverwaltung des staatliches Gymnasiums und Realgymnasiums Dilthey-Schule Wiesbaden," undated, Abteilung 429/5, No. 1248, HHstA. Although undated, this document was likely written in 1952 or 1953.

16. Ibid., "Geschäftsordnung," 2–4 (unnumbered). See also *O' KPATHP, Der Mischkrug, Abitur-Zeitung Dilthey-Schule 1953* (Wiesbaden, 2003).

17. "Vorschläge für die schriftlichen Aufgaben in Deutsch," Ostern 1952, Abteilung 429/7, No. 810, HHstA.

18. Ruth Kunz, "Die Schülermitverwaltung als Übungsfeld demokratischer Ordnung," 25 January 1952, Abteilung 429/7, No. 810, HHstA.

19. Irmgard Hofmann, "Die Schülermitverwaltung als Übungsfeld demokratischer Ordnung," 25 January 1952, Abteilung 429/7, No. 810, HHstA.

20. Eberhard Weber, "Die Schülermitverwaltung als Übungsfeld demokratischer Ordnung," 25 January 1952, Abteilung 429/7, No. 810, HHstA.

21. For a detailed discussion of this Berlin School Law of 1948, see Marion Klewitz, *Berliner Einheitsschule 1945–1951,* Historische und Pädagogische Studien, ed. Otto Büsch and Gerd Heinrich, vol. 1 (Berlin, 1971); Benno Schmoldt, ed., *Das Schulwesen in Berlin seit 1945* (Berlin, 1996).

22. Translation of "School Law for Greater Berlin," appendix 3, "Report on the Progress of the School Reform," 1 August 1948; Box 122; General Records, 1945–1950; Records of Education and Cultural Relations Branch; Records of the Berlin Sector; Records of the US Occupation Headquarters, WWII, RG 260, National Archives College Park (NACP).

23. In West Berlin, the *Oberschule Praktischer Zweig* (OPZ) corresponded to the *Volksschule,* the *Oberschule Technischer Zweig* (OTZ) to the *Mittelschule,* and the *Oberschule Wissenschaftlicher Zweig* (OWZ) to the *Gymnasium.*

24. "Gesamtergebnis der Rundfrage über den Stand der Schülermitverwaltung in den Berliner Schulen," 6 January 1954, B. Rep. 015, No. 427, LAB.

25. "Auswertung der Fragen III/1–27, OPZ; Rundfrage an aller Berliner Schulen," 1954, B. Rep. 015, No. 427, LAB.

26. Ibid.

27. Ibid.

28. Jauernig, Schadowschule, "Report an den Senator für Volksbildung," 23 February 1953, B. Rep. 015, No. 689, LAB.

29. Getraudenschule (4.OWZ Dahlem), "Auswertung der Erfahrungen in der SMV," 26 February 1954, B. Rep. 015, No. 689, LAB.

30. A. Jahr, Droste-Hülshoff-Schule, "Report an den Senator für Volksbildung," 1 March 1954, B. Rep. 015, No. 689, LAB.

31. "Zu den Erfahrungsberichten und Fragebogen der Oberschulen PZ," undated (likely April 1954), B. Rep. 015, No. 427, LAB.

32. "Zu den Erfahrungsberichten und Fragebogen der Oberschulen TZ," undated (likely April 1954), B. Rep. 015, No. 427, LAB.

33. "Zu den Erfahrungsberichten und Fragebogen der Oberschulen WZ," undated (likely April 1954), B. Rep. 015, No. 427, LAB.

34. The organization changed its name in 1954 to the Berlin Student Parliament in recognition of the fact that it had become the independent representative for the pupils of all of Berlin (not just the American sector). For the sake of consistency, this study will refer to it as the Berlin Student Parliament (or BSP) throughout. See "Arbeitsgemeinschaft Berliner Schülervertretungen, BSP Verfassung und Geschäftsordnung," undated, B. Rep. 015, No. 430, LAB. See also Hermann Schneider to J. C. Thompson, "The Development of RIAS-Schulfunk from September 7, 1947 to August 15, 1948," 10 September 1948, 5; Box 125; General Records, 1945–1950; Records of Education and Cultural Relations Branch; Records of the Berlin Sector; Records of the US Occupation Headquarters, WWII, RG 260, NACP.

35. A number of influential West German officials indeed visited the student parliament during its first years. Among the guests of the BSP were: Bundestag president Hermann Ehlers; Berlin mayor Ernst Reuter; president of the West Berlin Parliament Otto Suhr; and West Berlin senator for education Joachim Tiburtius. See "Prominente Gäste im RSP," *Mitteilungen des Schulfunk-Parlaments* 15 (March 1952): 4. Document from private collection of Wilhelm-Dietrich von Thadden.

36. "Berliner Schülerparlament. Mitteilungen der Arbeitsgemeinschaft Berliner Schülervertretungen," 15 June 1959, B. Rep. 015, No. 431, LAB.

37. Thadden explained that the meetings of the BSP were always packed with interested pupils from the city's schools. There was no charge for tickets, which were distributed in the schools by representatives. Wilhelm-Dietrich von Thadden, interview by author, tape recording, Berlin-Lichterade, 19 May 2003.

38. "Tagesordnung der 33.Sitzung des RIAS Schulfunk-Parlaments," 28 October 1951. Document from private collection of Wilhelm-Dietrich von Thadden.

39. Report of the RIAS Schulfunk-Parlament, 33.Sitzung, 31 October 1951. Document from private collection of Wilhelm-Dietrich von Thadden.

40. The parliament first promulgated a constitution in 1948 and agreed on a revised one at its thirty-first sitting in 1951. The BSP officially agreed on rules for the conduct of business at the thirty-ninth meeting in June 1952. See "Geschäftsordnung des RIAS-Schulfunk-Parlaments," 29 June 1952. Document from private collection of Wilhelm-Dietrich von Thadden.

41. Wilhelm-Dietrich von Thadden quoted in Jobst Werner, *Schülermitwirkung in den öffentlichen Schulen Deutschlands nach 1945 unter besonderer Berücksichtigung der Entwicklung in Berlin. Eine Darstellung der Entwicklung in der Zeit von 1945 bis 1994* (Berlin, 1995), 80.

42. Hans-Jörg von Jena quoted in Werner, *Schülermitwirkung in den öffentlichen Schulen Deutschlands,* 80.

43. Horst Kollat quoted in Werner, *Schülermitwirkung in den öffentlichen Schulen Deutschlands,* 80.

44. "Berliner Schülerparlament. Mitteilungen der Arbeitsgemeinschaft Berliner Schülervertretungen," 15 June 1959, B. Rep. 015, No. 431, LAB.

45. See "Entstehung und Aufgaben des RIAS-Berufsschul-Parlaments," *Mitteilungen des Schulfunk-Parlaments* 15 (March 1952): 7. Document from private collection of Wilhelm-Dietrich von Thadden.

46. The Berufsschul-Parlament did not formally separate itself from the BSP until the beginning of the 1967–1968 school year. See Werner, *Schülermitwirkung in den öffentlichen Schulen Deutschlands,* 78.

47. See Henry J. Kellermann, *Cultural Relations as an Instrument of U.S. Foreign Policy: The Educational Exchange Program Between the United States and Germany 1945–1954* (Washington, DC, 1978), 99, 118–23.

48. Ulrich Kledzik, interview by author, tape recording, Berlin-Charlottenburg, 8 May 2003.

49. Ulrich Kledzik, "Report for the Period from September 10, 1952 to January 31, 1953," 5; Box 3; Entry 3027; International Educational Exchange Service—Reports on the German Teacher Exchange Program, 1951-53; Bureau of Public Affairs; Records of the Department of State, RG 59, NACP.

50. Kledzik has published several articles and books on school reform, especially the *Gesamtschule.* For two early examples of his work related to student government in his West Berlin school, the Ernst-Reuter-Schule, see "Lebendige Schülermitverwaltung I: Ein englischer Schüler besucht Berlin," *Berliner Lehrerzeitung* 13 (28), no. 11 (15 June 1959): 244–45; "Lebendige Schülermitverwaltung II: Wir wählen unseren Schülerpräsidenten," *Berliner Lehrerzeitung* 13 (28), no. 23/24 (15 December 1959): 518–19.

51. Kellermann, *Cultural Relations as an Instrument of U.S. Foreign Policy,* 9–10.

52. Ibid., 264–65.

53. Ibid.

54. Fifteenth Semiannual Report to the Congress by the United States Advisory Commission on Educational Exchange, Department of State, for the Period 1 July to 31 December 1955, 84th Congress, 2nd session, H. Doc. 335, 8, quoted in Kellermann, *Cultural Relations as an Instrument of U.S. Foreign Policy,* 121.

55. Officially titled the "German Teacher Trainee Program" upon its founding, State Department officials changed the name of the program to the "German Teacher Education Program" in 1952. See Marvin Pittman, "The German Teacher-Trainee Program," February 1951; Box 3; Entry 230; Records of the German Teacher Education Program; Cultural Exchange Program, 1951-53; Cultural Exchange Programs; Records of Special Projects and Programs; Records of Office of Education, RG 12, NACP.

56. See "Semiannual Report on the Activities of the Professional Activities Division (1 July to 31 December 1953)," 1 February 1954, 21; Box 1; Entry 3024; International Educational Exchange Service—Misc. Staff and Fulbright Program Reports, 1947-1954; Bureau of Public Affairs; Records of the Department of State, RG 59, NACP. For a detailed discussion of the

"German Teacher Trainee Program," see Brian M. Puaca "'Missionaries of Goodwill.' Deutsche Austauschlehrer und –schüler und die Lehren der amerikanische Demokratie in den frühen 1950er Jahren," in *Demokratiewunder. Transatlantische Mittler und die kulturelle Öffnung Westdeutschlands 1945–1970*, ed. Arnd Bauerkämper, Konrad H. Jarausch, and Markus Payk (Berlin, 2005), 305–31. See also Karl-Heinz Füssl, *Deutsch-amerikanischer Kulturaustausch im 20.Jahrhundert* (Frankfurt: Campus, 2004), 219–24.

57. Report on Project in Foreign Teacher Education, German Teacher Education Program 1952–1953, 1–2; Box 2; Entry 3027; International Educational Exchange Service—Reports on the German Teacher Exchange Program, 1951-53; Bureau of Public Affairs; Records of the Department of State, RG 59, NACP.

58. Ibid., 12.

59. See "Toward Understanding and Goodwill," Report of the Coordinator of the German Teacher Education Program, 3; Box 1; Entry 11; Records Relating to International Teacher Development Programs, 1951-1976; Division of International Education and Exchange; Records of US Office of Education, RG 12, NACP.

60. "Report on German Teacher Education Program 1952–1953," Director of Program, Washington State College at Pullman; Box 2; Entry 3027; International Educational Exchange Service—Reports on the German Teacher Exchange Program, 1951-53; Bureau of Public Affairs; Records of the Department of State, RG 59, NACP. Emphasis in original.

61. "University of Kentucky Final Report, German Teacher Trainee Program, 1951–52," 24 May 1952, Report of Heinrich Beck; Box 2; Entry 3027; International Educational Exchange Service—Reports on the German Teacher Exchange Program, 1951-53; Bureau of Public Affairs; Records of the Department of State, RG 59, NACP.

62. "University of Kentucky Final Report, German Teacher Trainee Program, 1951–52," 24 May 1952, Report of Roland Wallisch, 10; Box 2; Entry 3027; International Educational Exchange Service—Reports on the German Teacher Exchange Program, 1951-53; Bureau of Public Affairs; Records of the Department of State, RG 59, NACP.

63. "University of North Carolina Report on German Teacher Trainee Program," Final Report, March 1952, 27 (unnumbered); Box 1; Entry 3027; International Educational Exchange Service—Reports on the German Teacher Exchange Program, 1951-53; Bureau of Public Affairs; Records of the Department of State, RG 59, NACP.

64. "German Teacher Program, 1951–1952," 2; Box 3; Entry 11; Records Relating to International Teacher Development Programs, 1951-1976; Division of International Education and Exchange; Records of the US Office of Education, RG 12, NACP.

65. "Evidence of Effectiveness," undated (likely 1953); Box 3; Entry 3024; International Educational Exchange Service—Misc. Staff and Fulbright Program Reports, 1947-1954; Bureau of Public Affairs; Records of the Department of State, RG 59, NACP.

66. See Henry P. Pilgert, *The Exchange of Persons Program in Western Germany* (Bonn, 1951).

67. Kellermann, *Cultural Relations as an Instrument of U.S. Foreign Policy*, 122.

68. "Annual Program Report, German Teenagers in Michigan," 23 July 1952, 1; Box 3; Entry 3024; International Educational Exchange Service—Misc. Staff and Fulbright Program Reports, 1947-1954; Bureau of Public Affairs; Records of the Department of State, RG 59, NACP.

69. "Program Report—German Teenagers in Michigan," 15 February 1953, 1; Box 3; Entry 3024; International Educational Exchange Service—Misc. Staff and Fulbright Program Reports, 1947-1954; Bureau of Public Affairs; Records of the Department of State, RG 59, NACP.

70. "Annual Program Report, German Teenagers in Michigan," 23 July 1952, 2–5; Box 3; Entry 3024; International Educational Exchange Service—Misc. Staff and Fulbright Program Reports, 1947-1954; Bureau of Public Affairs; Records of the Department of State, RG 59, NACP.

71. Ibid., 6.

72. Letter from Ludwig Jagla, Gladbeck, 2 August 1952; Box 3; Entry 3024; International Educational Exchange Service—Misc. Staff and Fulbright Program Reports, 1947-1954; Bureau of Public Affairs; Records of the Department of State, RG 59, NACP.

73. Ibid., 2.

74. "Program Report: German Teen-Agers in Michigan," United States International Informa-tion Administration Educational Exchange Service in cooperation with Michigan Council of Churches and Ann Arbor Council of Churches, 15 February 1953; Box 3; Entry 3024; Inter-national Educational Exchange Service—Misc. Staff and Fulbright Program Reports, 1947-1954; Bureau of Public Affairs; Records of the Department of State, RG 59, NACP.

75. "West German Receptivity and Reactions to the Exchange of Persons Program," Research Re-ports on German Opinion Series 2, 25 August 1952, Report No. 151; Box 4; Records of the United States Information Agency, RG 306, NACP.

76. "A Study of the Extent and Nature of Exchangee's Contact with the German Population," 22 November 1955, Report No. 221; Entry 3020; International Educational Exchange Ser-vice—European Country Files 1951-56; Bureau of Public Affairs; Records of the Department of State, RG 59, NACP.

77. Ibid., ii.

78. "Status Report on German Exchange Grantees," 1 July 1955, 1; Box 3; Entry 3020; Interna-tional Educational Exchange Service—European Country Files, 1951-56; Bureau of Public Affairs; Records of the Department of State, RG 59, NACP.

79. Ibid., 18.

80. It should be noted, however, that émigrés did publish new German history textbooks, but they were not introduced into the schools of the American zone of occupation. Perhaps the best known example is Fritz Karsen's *Geschichte Unserer Welt* project, on which six other expatriates collaborated. This series appeared in the schools of the British zone shortly before the end of the occupation. See Gregory Wegner, "The Power of Tradition in Education: The Formation of the History Curriculum in the Gymnasium of the American Sector in Berlin, 1945–1955," (PhD diss.: University of Wisconsin, 1988), 240–43.

81. "General Rules for the Preparation of New History Texts," undated, 2; Box 94; Records Re-lated to Education, 1945–1948; Records of the Education Branch; Records of the Education and Cultural Relations Division; Records of the US Occupation Headquarters, WWII, RG 260, NACP.

82. "Manual for Curriculum-Textbook Centers," 1948, 2; Box 32; Records Related to Policy and Planning; Records of the Education Branch; Records of the Education and Cultural Relations Division; Records of the US Occupation Headquarters, WWII, RG 260, NACP.

83. Ibid., 3.

84. "Minutes of Textbook Officers' Meeting," 18–19 November 1948, 1; Box 110; Records Re-lating to Textbooks and Other Publications, 1947-1951; Records of the Education Branch; Records of the Education and Cultural Affairs Division; Records of the Office of Military Gov-ernment, US Zone; Records of the US Occupation Headquarters, WWII, RG 260, NACP.

85. Office of Military Government for Germany, US—Education and Cultural Relations Divi-sion, *Report on Textbook Evaluation, 1945–1949* (1950).

86. This study will avoid debates about the validity of this new narrative. Undoubtedly this inter-pretation focusing on the traditions of German liberalism and the centuries-long struggle for democracy was problematic. For a detailed analysis of the problems with this interpretation, see Wegner, "The Power of Tradition in Education," 244–45.

87. Harald Scherrinsky, Elisabeth Berger, and Georg Müller, *Wege der Völker*, vol. 3, *Ringen um Freiheit* (Berlin, 1950), 263.

88. Ibid., 217.

89. Ibid., 258.

90. Ibid., 263.

91. Ibid., 258.

92. Gertrud Schulze et al., *Wege der Völker*, vol. 4, *Demokratie im Werden* (Berlin, 1950), 20.

93. Ibid., 252.

94. Ibid., 332.

95. Ibid., 265.
96. Ibid., 317.
97. Ibid., 298.
98. O. H. Müller, *Deutsche Geschichte in Kurzfassung* (Frankfurt, 1950).
99. Henry P. Pilgert, *The West German Educational System With Special Reference to the Policies and Programs of the Office of the U.S. High Commissioner for Germany* (Germany, 1953), 58. See also "The Work of the History Committee 1947/48 in its Suppositions and Results," undated; Box 698; Education Reports of the Education Branch, 1947–48; Education and Cultural Relations Division; Records of Office of Military Government, Hesse; Records of the US Occupation Headquarters, WWII, RG 260, NACP.
100. Müller, *Deutsche Geschichte in Kurzfassung*, 166.
101. Ibid., 170. The Paulskirche, in Frankfurt, is where the assembly met to draft the constitution.
102. Ibid., 233.
103. Ibid., 239.
104. Ibid., 171.
105. Ibid., 227.
106. Ibid., 243.
107. See Elizabeth Ebeling, *Erinnerungen an Hans Ebeling: 1906–1967* (Braunschweig, 1997).
108. Hans Ebeling, *Deutsche Geschichte,* Edition A, vol. 5 (Braunschweig, 1952), 124–28.
109. For a detailed examination of the *Schulhelfer* and *Hilfslehrer* programs constructed immediately after 1945 and designed to prepare an emergency cadre of teachers in the western occupation zones, see Wernfried Schreiber, "Auf den Wege zur universitären Lehrerbildung in Hessen von 1945–1950," (PhD diss., Goethe Universität Frankfurt, 1978), 42–87.
110. "Reorganization of Teacher Education in Hesse, Germany," undated, 4; Box 77; Records Related to Cultural Exchange and School Reopening; Records of the Education Branch; Records of the Education and Cultural Relations Division; Records of the US Occupation Headquarters, WWII, RG 260, NACP.
111. This reference to castes reflects the deep divisions that separated elementary and secondary educators. The differences were not just in training, but also corresponded to palpable social, ideological, and economic tensions. Secondary school teachers held an elevated status in German society; by midcentury, these educators had entered the lowest echelons of the upper class. Elementary educators had made gains in the twentieth century, yet they were still considered part of the lower-middle class. Differences in salary confirmed this divide. American officials had some recognition of this fact, yet they largely ignored social and professional traditions and believed that equalized training could be a panacea for tensions that dated back to the nineteenth century.
112. Pilgert, *The West German Educational System,* 67.
113. Albert Reble, *Lehrerbildung in Deutschland* (Henn, 1958), 16–17.
114. Elisabeth Lippert, "Zur Lehrerbildung," *Die pädagogische Provinz* 3, no. 3 (1949): 204–11.
115. "Die lehrerbildenden Anstalten und Einrichtungen den Bundesgebietes und West-Berlins im Winterhalbjahr 1950/51," 30 June 1952, 3, Abteilung 504, No. 553a, Fiche 3202, HHstA.
116. Another factor explaining the shortages of young educators that continued into the 1950s was the poor salary they received. See "Übersicht über die Besoldung der Lehrer an den allgemein-u. berufsbildendenden Schulen nach dem Siebenten Gesetz zur Änderung des Besoldungsrechtes in Hessen (Jahresbesoldung)," *Hessische Lehrerzeitung* 7, no. 10 (15 May 1954): 128–29.
117. See Wolfgang Kopitzsch, *Gewerkschaft Erziehung und Wissenschaft (GEW) 1947–1975. Grundzüge ihrer Geschichte* (Heidelberg, 1983)
118. "Dringendes Kurzprogramm der GEW," *Hessische Lehrerzeitung* 3, no. 10 (15 May 1950): 165.
119. "Minister Hennig über aktuelle kulturpolitische Fragen des Landes Hessen," *Hessische Lehrerzeitung* 7, no. 12/13 (15 June 1954): 167–68.
120. "Die dringlichsten Erfordernisse für das hessische Schulwesen," *Hessische Lehrerzeitung* 8, no. 1–2 (1 January 1955): 1.

121. Michael-Sören Schuppan, *Berliner Lehrerbildung nach dem Zweiten Weltkrieg. Die pädagogische Hochschule im bildungspolitischen Kräftspiel unter den Bedingungen der Vier-Mächte-Stadt (1945–1958)*, (Frankfurt, 1990), 240–43, 248.

122. Reinhardt Crüger, interview by author, tape recording, Berlin-Lankwitz, 10 June 2003.

123. "Vorschläge der Pädagogische Hochschule," undated (likely 1949), 4, B. Rep. 015, No. 148, LAB.

124. "Abschliessender Bericht über Vorarbeiten zum Lehrerausbildungsgesetz," 12 April 1950, 2, B. Rep. 015, No. 148, LAB.

125. Karl August Bettermann and Manfred Gössl, *Schulgliederung, Lehrerbildung, und Lehrerbesoldung und der bundesstaatlichen Ordnung* (Berlin, 1963), 57.

126. Schreiber, "Auf den Wege zur universitären Lehrerbildung," 186–187.

127. Letter from Rektor, Free University to Senator für Volksbildung, 10 July 1953, quoted in Schuppan, *Berliner Lehrerbildung nach dem Zweiten Weltkrieg*, 357.

128. "Die lehrerbildenden Anstalten und Einrichtungen den Bundesgebietes und West-Berlins im Winterhalbjahr 1950/51," 30 June 1952, 2, Abteilung 504, No. 553a, Fiche 3202, HHstA. See also Bettermann and Gössl, *Schulgliederung, Lehrerbildung, und Lehrerbesoldung*, 56–57.

129. Eleven of these were cloister schools for the instruction of female teachers, and the remaining facility prepared teachers of home economics. See Hubert Buchinger, *Volksschule und Lehrerbildung im Spannungsfeld politischer Entscheidung 1945–1970* (Munich, 1975), 495.

130. Marvin Pittman, "Teacher Education in Bavaria," 12–14; Box 73; Records Relating to Cultural Exchange and School Reopenings; Records of the Education Branch; Records of the Education and Cultural Relations Division; Records of the Office of Military Government, US Zone; Records of the US Occupation Headquarters, WWII, RG 260, NACP.

131. "Abschliessender Bericht über Vorarbeiten zum Lehrerausbildungsgesetz," 12 April 1950, 2, B. Rep. 015, No. 148, LAB.

132. Friedrich Oetinger was the pen name for Theodor Wilhelm, professor at the *Pädagogische Hochschule* in Flensburg and later faculty member of the University of Kiel. See Friedrich Oetinger, *Wendepunkt der politischen Erziehung. Partnerschaft als pädagogische Aufgabe* (Stuttgart, 1951). Subsequent editions of the book were published with the shortened title *Partnerschaft als pädagogische Prinzip*.

133. H. H. Pauly, "Der Lehrer und die Diskussion im Unterricht," *Die pädagogische Provinz* 4, no. 2 (1950): 65–74. See also Gottfried Bussard, "Das Unterrichtsgespräch," *Pädagogische Rundschau* 3, no. 1 (1949): 19–24; H. Hartwig Fiege, "Die Aufgabe des Lehrers im Unterrichtsgespräch," *Westermanns Pädagogische Beiträge* 5, no. 6 (1953): 291–96.

134. Noble Hiebert, "Classroom Discussions," in *Educational and Cultural Activities in Germany Today*, Reprints from *Information Bulletin*, ed. High Commission (US) for Germany (Office of), (Frankfurt, 1950), 41.

135. Ibid., 43.

136. Ibid.

137. Pilgert, *The West German Educational System*, 50.

138. These courses were targeted at emergency teachers who already had some university study. See Schedule for *Schulhelfer*, 7 August 1946, Abt. 504, No. 589, Fiche 3470, HHstA.

139. Burr W. Phillips, "Der Sozialkunde-Unterricht in den Schulen," 9 June to 8 September 1954, 2, Abt. 504, No. 10316, Fiche 6502, HHstA.

140. "Vorläufige Prüfungsordnung über die wissenschaftliche und pädagogische Prüfung für das Lehramt an der Grundstufe der Gemeinschaftsschule Gross-Berlins," undated (likely 1951), appendix 1, 4, B. Rep. 015, No. 153, LAB.

141. Burr W. Phillips, "Der Sozialkunde-Unterricht in den Schulen," 9 June to 8 September 1954, 2, Abt. 504, No. 10316, Fiche 6502, HHstA.

142. Ibid., 3.

143. Protokoll, "Arbeitsausschusses des Kuratorium für Lehrerbildungsheime," 17 January 1952, Abt. 504, No. 1505, Fiche 9308, HHstA.

144. "Hessisches Lehrerfortbildungswerkes—Bericht über die Tätigkeit im Jahre 1954," December 1954, 1, Abt. 504, No. 1505, Fiche 9308, HHstA.
145. This does not mean that 7,600 educators took part in the courses, since courses in all four institutions in Hesse typically included parents, university educators, local school administrators, and "guests," accounting for approximately 20 percent of the total enrollment.
146. Ulrich Kledzik, interview by author, tape recording, Berlin-Charlottenburg, 8 May 2003.

Chapter 3

POLITICAL EDUCATION
Reforms Continue Beneath the Surface, 1955–1959

*A*fter months of waiting, the pupils in the combined seventh and eighth grades of the Gossfelden *Volksschule* (near Marburg in Hesse) were overjoyed to hear that they had won. A letter from federal officials to the class president, Johanna Heine, informed them that their entry in the Fourth Great Christmas Prize Competition had been completed perfectly and was chosen as one of the grand prize winners.[1] The contest, an annual affair sponsored by the Bundeszentrale für Heimatdienst (later the Bundeszentrale für politische Bildung, or Federal Office for Political Education), required that pupils work as a class on a multitude of activities related to political education. The contest encouraged pupils to collaborate on assignments such as studying the constitution, learning significant political events in German history, completing a European map, and deciphering clues to answer economic questions. Winning the competition was no small feat by 1955, due to the tremendous increase in submissions. The Gossfelden pupils had triumphed over 25,000 other entries submitted by classes throughout the Federal Republic, which was an increase of more than 100 percent over the 1953 competition. In total, more than one million pupils had taken part.[2] The reward for this class of thirteen boys and seventeen girls was a trip to Bonn. During this visit to the capital, they would observe the Bundestag in session, visit the offices of several federal departments, and even have the opportunity to meet with the president, Theodor Heuss. This trip, federal officials hoped, would instill a deeper understanding of and greater appreciation for the West German democracy in its youngest citizens.

Notes for this section begin on page 148.

ZWEITES

großes
Weihnachts-

PREISAUSSCHREIBEN

Liebe Schüler und Schülerinnen!

Das große Interesse, das die Lehrer und Schüler im Bundesgebiet und in Westberlin unserem vorjährigen Weihnachtspreisausschreiben entgegengebracht haben, veranlaßt uns, auch in diesem Jahre wieder im Einvernehmen mit der Bundeszentrale für Heimatdienst einen ähnlichen Wettbewerb zu starten.

Wieder wird es für Euch wertvolle Preise zu gewinnen geben: Als Spitzenpreise für mindestens zwei Klassen eine mehrtägige gemeinschaftliche Reise nach Bonn und Umgebung. Für mindestens 50 Klassen je ein Rundfunkgerät. Im ganzen werden mindestens 150 wertvolle Preise und außerdem viele Trostpreise verteilt werden. Die Bundeszentrale für Heimatdienst setzt dafür

40 000.- DM

aus. Sie behält sich aber vor, die Anzahl der Preise wie im vorigen Jahre wesentlich zu erhöhen, wenn sich besonders viele Klassen beteiligen.

Teilnahmebedingungen:

1. Teilnahmeberechtigt sind alle Schulklassen im Gebiet der Bundesrepublik und Westberlins, in denen die Jahrgänge 1937, 1938 und 1939 vertreten sind. Teilnehmer sind die Klassen, nicht einzelne Schüler! Jede Klasse darf nur eine Lösung einsenden! Darum soll sich auch die ganze Klasse an der Bearbeitung der Rätselaufgaben beteiligen.

2. Die ausgefüllten Vordrucke sind im verschlossenen Briefumschlag bis spätestens 20. Dezember 1953 (Datum des Poststempels) an den Informationsdienst zur politischen Bildung, Universum-Verlagsanstalt, Wiesbaden, Roesslerstraße 7, einzusenden.

3. Bei Eingang mehrerer richtiger Lösungen entscheidet eine Verlosung unter Aufsicht des Direktors der Bundeszentrale für Heimatdienst. Der Rechtsweg ist ausgeschlossen.

Die Gewinner werden gleichzeitig mit der Lösung der Preisaufgabe in einem späteren Informationsdienst bekanntgegeben. Außerdem wird die Wochenzeitung „Das Parlament" über das Preisausschreiben berichten. Der Preis, den eine Klasse gewinnt, gehört der ganzen Klasse. Wird die Klasse durch Beendigung der Schulzeit oder aus anderen Gründen aufgelöst, so wird von den Gewinnern erwartet, daß sie den etwa gewonnenen Gegenstand ihrer Schule überlassen.

Versucht, den Vordruck so sauber wie möglich auszufüllen, sobald Ihr Euch über die Lösung völlig im klaren seid. Wir empfehlen, die Aufgaben und Rätsel zunächst abzuschreiben und erst am Schluß, wenn die ganze Preisaufgabe gelöst ist, den Vordruck durch einen von Euch gewählten Schüler ausfüllen zu lassen.

Und zuletzt noch eine wichtige Bitte: Vergeßt beim Eintragen Eurer Lösung nicht, auch die Rubrik am Kopf dieser Seite genau und deutlich lesbar in Blockschrift auszufüllen, sonst ist es uns nicht möglich, Eure Mühe mit einem vielleicht besonders wertvollen Preis zu belohnen. Und das wäre doch für beide Seiten ärgerlich.

Und nun frisch ans Werk!
Wir wünschen Euch viel Erfolg!

Informationsdienst zur politischen Bildung
Wiesbaden, Roesslerstraße 7

Figure 8. Cover of the Second Great Christmas Prize Competition, 1953. The contest application features a photo of last year's winners meeting Federal President Theodor Heuss. Courtesy Bundesarchiv, File B168, Nr. 275.

Teachers and federal officials alike regarded the contest as a successful endeavor. In a report after the second competition in 1953, a Bonn official praised the competition as a valuable means of political education, as well as a subtle tool for instructing pupils in practical democracy. He asserted that the contest promoted self-sufficiency and tolerance. The end result, this official concluded, was that "pupils report not just their knowledge about the problems of our democracy, but they are unknowingly placed in the position of experiencing and living practical democracy themselves."[3] Many postwar educators expressed similar sentiments. Willi Bratge, a *Volksschullehrer* in Udenhausen (near Kassel), praised the contest in an unsolicited letter to federal officials in 1955.[4] The young teacher concurred with federal officials that the contest contributed to the education of pupils toward "a democratic attitude" through the process of completing the required politically themed tasks.

The annual Christmas Competition nicely illustrates the growth of many of the educational reforms promoted since the end of the war. First and foremost, the contest emphasized an engagement with Germany's recent history. Admittedly, some sections of the contest were of more limited value, asking pupils to recapitulate dates or names. Yet other parts encouraged pupils to ponder their rights and responsibilities as citizens, drawing from their study of Germany's troubled past—including the Third Reich—and offering everyday situations as examples. Second, the contest prompted pupils to organize into groups and collaborate on their entry as a class project. Teachers were to play only a supervisory role in the completion of these entries. Third, as the report above notes, pupils engaged in discussions with classmates en route to completing their entry. In a manner similar to that of participating in student government, pupils learned to express their opinions and defend them, as well as to respect and evaluate the ideas of others. Fourth, the Christmas Competition addressed contemporary international issues—social, political, and economic—which was a new development in the postwar curriculum. Questions related to the European Coal and Steel Community (and later the European Economic Community), the division of Europe as part of the Cold War, and the peoples living in the former German lands of the East were just a few of the topics broached in the annual contest.

In addition to these pedagogical innovations, the Christmas Competition also underscores the newfound enthusiasm for political education by the late 1950s. As we saw in chapter 2, political education had begun to establish a place for itself in the schools in the early 1950s. At this early point, however, it still had not yet secured a stable place in the postwar curriculum. This was due in part to the ways the new subject contrasted with its prewar precursor. Unlike the civics lessons of the Weimar Republic, political education after 1945 stressed the active participation of the pupil in classroom instruction. Postwar classes underscored the everyday activities of the citizen in a democratic state—both rights and responsibilities. If democracy was to succeed in West Germany after World War II, German educators believed that pupils would have to have a personal connection to the young state. Political education further solidified its place in the postwar curriculum in this period, yet as we will soon see, educators continued to struggle with a variety of problems that had plagued the subject since the end of the war.

In order for this new curriculum in political education to gain hold, educators relied on a variety of reforms already existent in the postwar schools. The first of these was student government, which had already been established in many postwar schools by the mid-1950s. SMV (*Schülermitverwaltung*, or student government) and a growing number of student newspapers both played important roles in providing pupils hands-on experience with the rights and responsibilities of life in a democratic society during this period. Because they encouraged pupils to take an active role in the functioning of the school, German teachers increasingly linked these two innovations to political education. A second reform contributing to the preparation of postwar pupils for life in a democracy was the evolution of a new generation of textbooks for political education. These books, building on innovations in earlier postwar history texts, were critical for instruction in the new subject. Postwar texts sought to overcome the gap between the pupil and seemingly distant democratic institutions by emphasizing the various responsibilities of citizens and their applicability in daily life. A third postwar reform that facilitated the growth of political education in this period was the study of recent history and contemporary events, or *Zeitgeschichte.* The new subject had first appeared during the American occupation, but it took another decade before it had become an established part of the curriculum. Instruction in *Zeitgeschichte* encouraged pupils to examine recent German history, as well as contemporary domestic and international political topics. To realize these objectives, instructors utilized classroom debates and discussions, radio programs, and local and national newspapers as tools for instructing pupils. All of these approaches, teachers believed, made political education more accessible to young pupils.

The 1950s is traditionally considered a decade of conservative dominance in the Federal Republic, and such claims are not without basis. Consequently, this has prompted many observers to portray the late 1950s as a time of pedagogical stagnation, with reform stifled by politicians, administrators, and educational elites. As was the case in the first postwar decade, the West German schools did not experience meaningful organizational change in this period. The three-track system of schooling remained a defining characteristic of the German system. Yet this does not mean that the schools failed to change during the height of the Adenauer years; subtle curricular reforms continued to take place in the schools beneath the surface. Political education, a new subject spawned in the immediate postwar period, finally secured its place in the West German schools as the 1950s came to a close. Relying on reforms already underway in the postwar schools— student government, new civics textbooks, and the study of recent history and contemporary events—political education expanded and intensified during this period. Not surprisingly, the growth of political education prompted controversy and debate in the West German schools. Some educators resisted certain innovations or attempted to avoid controversial topics. Pupils, too, displayed differing feelings about political instruction. Some embraced the new subject while others remained apathetic. There can be little doubt that instruction in political education was uneven in the schools of the Federal Republic. Nevertheless, the late 1950s marked a significant period of development in the history of West German political education.

Political Education in the Postwar Classroom

In January 1955, the Deutscher Ausschuss für das Erziehungs- und Bildungswesen (German Committee for Education and Schooling) published its much-anticipated recommendations for political education in the Federal Republic. The committee, created to address national educational questions, was composed of a variety of leading West German citizens—mostly educators, but also lawyers, journalists, and business professionals. The central purpose of the committee's report was to reaffirm the importance of political education in the postwar curriculum. In a concise introduction that suggested a sense of urgency, the report reminded readers that the political responsibilities of people were greater than ever. The committee also recognized that political education was particularly troubling for many educators and parents, especially after their experiences in the Third Reich. These realizations, however, made political education all the more important in the postwar schools. In the pages that followed, the committee outlined several themes to be integrated into classroom instruction. Stressing the value of "cooperation, group education, and partnership," the report prompted teachers to promote activities that fostered attitudes that would be helpful to pupils in their future responsibilities as citizens.[5] Teaching methods that emphasized relations among pupils also received praise for contributing to political education. In this vein, the committee promoted group work in the classroom, the delegation of specialized assignments to pupils, and the creation of *Arbeitsgemeinschaften* (study groups). Student government, student judicial courts, and schoolwide forums also garnered accolades from the committee for reinforcing the values of political education. In a passage that clearly enticed many newspaper editors searching for a snappy headline, the report asserted that "political education has therefore never been as urgent as it is today."[6]

Virtually everyone agreed that some form of political education was critical for the future of the Federal Republic, but it was less clear what actually constituted this new discipline. The 1955 national report echoed the views of many postwar educators in eschewing the Weimar emphasis on a factual mastery of the organization of the state, or *Institutionskunde*. It seemed that determining what was undesirable for political education was often easier than deciding what features it should actually possess. Certainly knowledge of the state and its institutions was important. Yet the Deutscher Ausschuss emphasized the value of practical experience in teaching pupils the techniques of living in a democratic society. To the committee, behavior, experience, and attitude were as much a part of political education as knowledge. Activities that provided pupils with opportunities

Figure 9. Group work in a Hessian *Volksschule*, 1958. The pupil speaking in this photo is reporting the findings of her group to the entire class. Courtesy Bundesarchiv, Signatur B 145 Bild-F005512–0020.

to work independently and in groups facilitated the acquisition of attitudes and skills necessary for citizens in a young democracy. Integrating political education into the classroom and removing teachers from their traditional position at the center of instruction were two key themes in the report. It became the task of the individual state culture ministries, however, to translate the recommendations of the national committee into actual classroom practices.

It is difficult to make generalizations regarding the state of political education in the Federal Republic during the late 1950s. Each of the eleven western states (including West Berlin) had its own curriculum in the subject, which was known by at least half a dozen different names.[7] Hamburg and Saarland chose not to specify political education as an independent subject, instead labeling it as an educational principle and outlining themes to be addressed in each grade in a variety of disciplines. Much more common, however, was the creation of a distinct subject concentration for political education, even if it was merged into history instruction, as it was in many West German states. In most of the *Volksschulen* of the Federal Republic (and the OPZs of West Berlin), instruction in the subject started in the seventh grade. This format was by no means universal, however. By 1960, pupils in Lower Saxony, Hesse, and Baden-Württemberg began studying the subject in the fifth grade. Pupils received anywhere between one and six hours of instruction in the subject during their final year in school. The curriculum for political education in the *Mittelschulen* (or OTZs) mirrored that of the *Volksschulen* with instruction beginning in the seventh grade, except for Hesse and Baden-Württemberg, where study again started in the fifth grade. The amount of time devoted to political education was similar to that of the *Volksschulen*. There was less consensus on political education in the *Gymnasien* (or OWZs), with the subject taught at various times during the nine years of study. Most pupils received two hours per week of instruction in these schools, with additional hours dedicated to political education in the tenth and thirteenth classes.[8] Despite the glaring differences in the scheduling and integration of political education in the postwar schools, educators were largely of one mind regarding the underlying mission of the subject: making democracy tangible to their pupils.

Interested in obtaining a better picture of the state of political education in the schools of West Berlin, senator for education Joachim Tiburtius commissioned a citywide survey in 1958. Tiburtius undertook this survey in the face of a series of neo-Nazi episodes, in which buildings and graveyards in the Federal Republic were vandalized. Seeking a scapegoat for these embarrassing crimes, politicians cited the failure of the schools to create responsible and knowledgeable citizens. Public opinion became more critical of political education at this point, with the press scrutinizing the instruction that pupils received in their schools. With the lens focused so sharply on education, Tiburtius decided to evaluate not just the content of the political education curriculum in the schools of West Berlin but also the actual lessons provided in each school. As was the case in many states of the Federal Republic, the schools of West Berlin taught political education as a component of the history curriculum. Because of this, the two subjects were typically interwoven in school reports. Virtually all of the respondents recognized the value of political education in the school curriculum, yet they recounted vastly different experiences with the subject. The 1958 surveys present a mixed picture of political education in the city.

Many of the reports cited shortcomings in the instruction pupils received in the classroom. Not surprisingly, most of these problems appeared in the classes of the city's OPZs. The reports indicate that one of the greatest challenges to political education in these schools was a lack of interest and engagement on the part of pupils. In his report on political education in the Westpreussenschule in the district of Charlottenburg, the school's director, Herr Trojahn, explained that the pupils in the ninth grade "have little interest in the political events of the time." Pupils in the eighth grade "are even less interested," while the interest of those in the class behind them is "hardly detectable."[9] Due in large part to an apparent disinterest in the subject, as well as the belief of educators that pupils could not grasp many of the pivotal concepts, political education in many of the West Berlin OPZs fell short of expectations.

The paternalism of school officials and the apparent lack of interest on the part of pupils did not sabotage political education in all of the city's OPZs. While political education by no means thrived in these schools, there were OPZs in the city in which educators reported great success. The two teachers of political education in the 10.OPZ in Reinickendorf, Herr Voigt and Herr Kusch, presented a different picture to Senator Tiburtius in their report. Their pupils, they reported, had the "opportunity to gain practical experience in the cultivation of a community, to learn to respect the opinions of other pupils, and to subordinate oneself to the common task [of the group]." They did this through a variety of activities, such as accepting supervisory duties during the school day, organizing art exhibitions in the school, participating in theater and youth conferences, and working with student government. The "crowning achievement" of the ninth-grade classes of this school was a fourteen-day trip through West Germany. "Success is possible," even in the lower classes, these two educators asserted. One could transform the chaos of school breaks into sensible, shared lessons in political education. Group work, too, assisted in introducing pupils to a "democratic 'community lifestyle' of classroom life."[10] As the report of the Deutscher Ausschuss had suggested three years before, activities such as these contributed to the development of democratic attitudes and values that provided a solid basis for their future responsibilities as citizens of the West German state.

The experiences of teachers in the OTZs inspired greater confidence in political education than did those of their colleagues in the OPZs. In a particularly thorough report, four teachers at the Gustav-Stresemann-Schule (OTZ) in the district of Kreuzberg illustrated how they sought to make political education more immediate and practical for pupils. Among the activities they listed were: student involvement in the administration of the class, school, and grounds; special projects including the annual Christmas Contest sponsored by the Bundeszentrale für Heimatdienst; listening to radio programs devoted to political education; regular assemblies of all pupils for the discussion of such topics as new rules and school donations to charities; the organization of "Europe Evenings" for parents; the planning for memorial events in the school (such as 17 June, the date upon which East German workers rose against the SED in 1953); visits to the Berlin House of Representatives; and a partnership with a school in one of the western states, which included a yearly visit to the Bundestag.[11] This OTZ in Kreuzberg was not unusual, as most other schools offered some combination of similar activities. Some noted that they had started new *Arbeitsgemeinschaften* dedicated to political topics, or that they had initiated partnerships with schools in other countries that furthered the possibilities of political education, while at the same time increasing pupils' interest.

As the survey commissioned by Tiburtius indicated, political education could often be even stronger in the OWZs. In the report of the Schadowschule in Zehlendorf, Dr. Galmof, the teacher responsible for political education in the school, focused on how he had connected the subject to the everyday life of his pupils.[12] More strongly than most, his report highlights several of the reforms introduced to the political education curriculum since 1945. First, Galmof explained the several exchange partnerships that existed between the Schadowschule and schools in Great Britain and the United States. These partnerships increased "friendship and human understanding between both peoples." The school had also founded a "Political Room," in which pupils could peruse publications dedicated to contemporary historical and political issues. Notably, the Landeszentrale für politische Bildungsarbeit, the state-level office dedicated to political education in West Berlin, assisted the school in securing publications for this special room. Third, pupils visited many of the city's political institutions, such as the mayoral and governmental offices of their local district. Several pupils, Galmof added, had the opportunity to participate in different courts in the city as part of their political education. Finally, he also encouraged pupils to contribute to the school's newspaper, "Das Schüler-Echo," as another aspect of their instruction in political education.

Instruction in political education in the OTZs and OWZs of West Berlin, however, cannot be considered an unqualified success. Many senior educators still clinging to their jobs in these schools viewed political education as a distraction from true history instruction. Whether an excuse or a sincere criticism, these sentiments appeared frequently in reports filed in response to Tiburtius's query. Since these feelings could not be expressed in official correspondence with Tiburtius and the city's education officials, teachers veiled their resistance in other ways. Some explained that the amount of information they were required to cover prevented as full a discussion of political themes as they had planned. Others complained that city officials had simply devoted too few hours to the newly enlarged subject of "History and Political Education." Another commonly expressed excuse was that teachers did not find the courage to leave enough out of their lesson plans ("der Mut zur Lücke"). Extended absences from school because of sickness also surfaced in many reports as explanation for inadequate attention to political topics. While some of these reports are likely true, there is little doubt that a significant number of these educators hoped to avoid the problems of Germany's recent history and a discussion of the new political scene of the Federal Republic. Political education had secured a place in the curriculum of the postwar schools, but instruction in the young subject was irregular, even in the most academically focused institutions.

While these reports recount experiences in political education that run the gamut from thinly veiled resistance to remarkable success, many of them do share a common underlying theme. Almost four years after the publication of the 1955 Deutscher Ausschuss report, a significant number of the educators who detailed their experiences in the classroom still remained uncertain about what precisely constituted political education. Nowhere is this more apparent than in the report of Carl-Heinz Evers, school superintendent for Tempelhof, whose report summarized the 193 pages of text submitted to him by the teachers of his West Berlin district. In a report to Senator Tiburtius, Evers explained that measuring success or failure hinged on how one defined political education:

> If one conceives of the term broadly and understands education toward human behavioral patterns as well as knowledge of institutions and contemporary events as part of it, then there is no doubt that much has been achieved in the scope of history instruction and political education in the final classes. If one conceives of the term in a more narrow sense,

however, as the acquisition of facts, forms, and connections of personal, social, state, and supranational relations, then instruction appears to be somewhat superficial.[13]

As was the case in other districts in the city, Evers's report revealed a variety of experiences with political education in the classrooms of Tempelhof. Considered as a whole, these reports indicate that although some teachers possessed a narrow conception of political education, others envisioned the subject much more broadly. A basic knowledge of facts was necessary, but many reports suggest that classroom experiences and community activities assumed considerable importance in the city's schools. This realization further reinforces claims that postwar teachers understood political education as a new subject, not confined by the same boundaries as civics instruction had been in the interwar period.

Like West Berlin, Hesse also faced a host of challenges in strengthening the curriculum in political education during this period. Perhaps the most important move was the 1956 decision to introduce a new curriculum in the subject. Responding to debates among teachers and pedagogues since the end of the war, the Hessian Culture Ministry announced new requirements that made political education an *Unterrichtsprinzip*, or teaching principle, applicable in all subject areas. The 1956 guidelines also established *Weltkunde* as a new subject in the Hessian schools, officially combining social studies, history, and geography into one academic unit. While this seemed like a solution to the problem of how to unite these subjects, debates continued among Hessian teachers about the soundness of the pedagogy behind this decision. Some educators viewed this as a successful combination of three related subjects, while others resisted it as an unworkable compromise and retained former distinctions in their lessons.[14] In another important decision, the Culture Ministry called for the expansion of political education to the fifth and sixth grades of the *Volksschule*. Whereas the 1949 guidelines authored by Stein had proposed that pupils receive four hours of weekly instruction in civics-related topics in grades five and six, the new guidelines formalized this requirement and made it part of the new subject concentration. These pupils addressed topics relating to family, work, school, and the community in their first encounters with the postwar discipline.

More important than the changes to the title and scheduling of political education was the fact that Hessian officials endorsed a more balanced approach to the subject in the 1956 directive. Increased attention to the practical application of lessons in the subject offset the traditional emphasis on knowledge and factual information. A revealing analysis of the reforms can be found in a 1958 thesis written by Renate Glufke, a young Hessian *Volksschullehrer*. Her examination criticized the political education guidelines drafted in the late 1940s under Stein for devoting too much attention to the transfer of factual knowledge. She asserted in her thesis that "a realistic worldview must be conveyed to young people, and theoretical knowledge must be combined with practical activity."[15] While Glufke praised the recent emphasis on practical activities, as well as the attempt to craft a comprehensive new subject concentration, she recognized the difficulties that political education continued to face. Nevertheless, the infusion of new teachers into the profession, such as Glufke, coupled with improvements in teacher training solidified the place of political education in the Hessian schools and contributed to its growth throughout this period.[16]

Another important factor in the growth of political education in Hesse was the state's Landeszentrale für Heimatdienst. The Hessian Landeszentrale für Heimatdienst, which promoted political education at the state level, sponsored a variety of educational activities throughout this period. Perhaps its most significant work was the organization of politically themed seminars for teachers at Hessian universities. Notably, a significant number of *Volksschullehrer* took part in these courses; these educators typically accounted for more than a third of seminar participants. The lectures they attended dealt with themes such as problems in the West German economy, the legacies of National Socialism, and epochs of political education in Germany.[17] These lectures attracted not only interested elementary and secondary school teachers but serious scholars as well. For instance, at the 1954 session in Frankfurt, Max Horkheimer and Theodor Adorno both offered lectures on political topics to interested primary and secondary school educators.[18] The Landeszentrale also organized a similar seminar at the university in Marburg, offering lectures and discussions on such topics as "Germany in Contemporary Europe," "The Current Status of Political Education in Germany," and "The Special Nature of Social Studies Instruction."[19] Finally, the Hessian continuing-education facility in Kassel, working in conjunction with the Landeszentrale, offered educators instruction on such themes as "Social Studies and Modern History in the Final Year of the *Volksschule*."[20] Attendance at these seminars was usually modest, typically ranging from twenty to one hundred participants. Nevertheless, developments such as these further underscore the continuing commitment to political education in Hesse and its gradual growth through the first full postwar decade.

Despite the highly touted successes of Hessian political education in this period, lingering problems continued to affect instruction in the subject. The three major challenges to political education that Johann Zilien cites in his examination of the subject in Hesse can be applied to the entire Federal Republic. First, teachers of political education could use their classroom as a forum to express dissatisfaction with the curriculum. The most common instance of this was an emphasis on predemocratic notions of community, which reflected Nazi ideas of the individual subsumed by the whole. This is something that Culture Ministry officials continued to see in the reports of history and social studies teachers throughout this period. Second, instruction in the subject could turn a blind eye toward the active participation of pupils and return instead to the teacher-centered style of the past. Third, teachers uninterested in group work, discussion, and debate could transform the class into a fact-based course, which relied on the memorization of names, dates, and laws in a fashion similar to the Weimar Republic.[21] This final problem was perhaps the greatest challenge of all. Some educators spoke openly about their fears of a return to the civics instruction of the Weimar Republic, with political education becoming merely a study of institutions.[22]

Teachers did receive much of the blame for the problems of political education in the schools, but they were not the only variable in the equation. In the pages of the *Berliner Lehrerzeitung,* Erich Frister admitted that some teachers in the city continued to dodge instruction in political education. There were other reasons, however, that Frister found just as important to the perceived failings of the subject in West Berlin. First, he held pupils accountable for their own education. Many pupils, he claimed, did not learn or quickly forgot material addressed in class. Politicians, too, raised the ire of Frister. He encouraged them to become more active in the education of pupils, since as supposedly neutral figures, teachers could not possibly answer all of their pupils' questions. Third, Frister criticized the interference of city school administrators and the public. Constant media attention and hurried policy responses only further hindered effective political education.[23] Finally, Frister (albeit briefly) indicted parents for their failure to incorporate political themes in their discussions at home. This criticism reiterated a concern voiced in the city's surveys of the year before: in most cases, parents were either a nonfactor or negative influence in the political education of their children. This article was undoubtedly motivated by the increasing criticism of schools and teachers by the public as the 1950s came to a close. Frister's terse response turned the spotlight on other groups whose contributions to political education he deemed less than admirable.

Thus our understanding of political education as the 1950s came to a close should not be overly romanticized. The subject did solidify its place in the postwar curriculum during this period, and it did offer many pupils a new means by which to prepare for their future responsibilities as citizens in a democracy. Innovative pedagogical techniques, school trips, and extracurricular activities all contributed to the instruction provided in the classroom. Political education became an important part of the curriculum and assisted in teaching postwar pupils about life in a democratic state. Nevertheless, the subject continued to face challenges. As we have seen, confusion regarding the definition and requirements of political education lingered. Divisions among some of these teachers limited the effectiveness of instruction in the subject. Finally, politicians, parents, and the media, anxious to find a scapegoat for embarrassing outbreaks of anti-Semitic vandalism or neo-Nazi activity, accused teachers of failing their charges. In reality, all of these groups contributed to the difficulties in the field of political education, with superfluous and overly theoretical legislation, lack of reinforcement at home, and biting critiques in the mainstream press all complicating the work of postwar teachers.

Headline: Student Government Flourishes; Student Press Arises

In his 1955 *Abitur* essay, Kurt Sauerborn, a pupil finishing his secondary education in Wiesbaden's Dilthey-Schule, examined the role of student government in the school. He recapitulated the usual statements about the efforts to strengthen the teacher-pupil relationship and the duties of organizing activities and organizations in the school. At the same time, Sauerborn also saw the broader picture and connected the experiences he had had in student government to his responsibilities as a citizen of the young West German democracy. "The higher mission and the main goal [of SMV], however, is to familiarize pupils during their time in school with the 'ways of life' [*Lebensformen*] that will be of help to them in the future."[24] Of the utmost importance, he asserted, was the fact that student government provided each pupil with responsibilities that he or she must accept in order for the work of the school to be completed successfully. The words "responsibility" and "cooperation" appear several times in Sauerborn's essay, as he described the activities of the school's student government and the lessons he drew for the future from his participation in the organization. Four years later, another pupil from the Dilthey-Schule, Eckhard Pilz, completed his *Abitur* essay on the advantages and disadvantages of democracy. He underscored a fundamental truth about democracy that American occupation forces required years to comprehend fully: "One cannot impose democracy; this contradicts its character."[25] Like Sauerborn, Pilz drew on his experiences in student government to discuss the everyday responsibilities of citizenship and one's duties in a democratic society. The responses of these two pupils illuminate the practical lessons drawn from their experiences in SMV and how they conceived of the contributions of these activities for the future.

The essays of these Hessian pupils and their classmates highlight the vital relationship that existed among political education, student government, and the burgeoning student press in the postwar era. Both student government and the student press continued to grow in the late 1950s, and as they did, their contributions to the practical preparation of pupils in political education also increased. While SMV had already taken root by mid-decade, it expanded to an even greater number of schools in the years that followed. The years before 1960 also witnessed a remarkable expansion in the number of student newspapers. In this period, one can identify the creation of a genuine student press in the Federal Republic, with the establishment of publications in *Gymnasien, Mittelschulen,* and even some *Volksschulen.* These papers provided a voice to pupils wishing to express their ideas on a variety of school issues. Not surprisingly, they did not limit the scope of their interests to the events taking place in their respective schools. Despite restrictions imposed by the culture ministries of the Federal Republic, pupils continued to address social, political, and cultural issues, in addition to topics related to the life of the school. These papers, like SMV, became another means for providing pupils practical experience in the field of political education.

As the first full postwar decade came to a close, student government continued its expansion throughout the Federal Republic. Nowhere was this more visible than in the former capital, where the membership of the Berlin Student Parliament expanded to over 75 percent of the city's secondary schools by the end of the decade. On the occasion of its tenth anniversary in January 1958, the parliament welcomed a collection of local and national officials, whose praise for the organization was effusive. The city's mayor, Willy Brandt; senator for education, Joachim Tiburtius; and the federal minister responsible for West German-East German relations, Ernst Lemmer, were all in attendance and lauded the BSP for its commitment to democracy and its work on behalf of the people of Berlin. The first president of the BSP, Heribert Schätze, returned to the assembly in order to speak about the legacy of the organization. The Berlin Student Parliament, he asserted, had become a place for the free exchange of ideas for all pupils. Just as important, Schätze claimed, was the fact that the parliament also served as an educational site for the exercise of practical democracy.[26] The organization also endeavored to improve communication between pupils on both sides of the city. The BSP not only established formal contact with East Berlin schools via official correspondence but also assisted in fostering relationships between members of the parliament (and other West Berlin pupils) and counterparts on the other side of the city.

As the BSP evolved throughout the 1950s, it increasingly engaged broader social and political issues. The bills debated at the hundredth meeting of the BSP in December 1958 underscore this development, as the parliament explicitly addressed several issues of contemporary political relevance. The first of these was Bill 399, which requested that Senator Tiburtius use his influence to discourage theaters on the border with East Berlin from showing "so many Wild West films."[27] The pupils likely raised this issue for several reasons. First, they might have hoped to ease tensions between the East German government and the Federal Republic and its Western allies regarding border crossings sparked by showing these films. Second, many pupils might have desired that youths in East Berlin gain a different impression of life in the West. A third possibility is that the parliament was influenced by the CDU's campaign against "smut," which was well underway by the late 1950s. Regardless of their motivations, the mere fact that the BSP addressed this issue indicates a willingness to engage with contemporary political and social concerns. The very next proposal under discussion that day further underscored the value of the parliament as a tool for political education, as well as its potential to affect the instruction of its constituents. Bill 400 requested that city school authorities investigate the possibility of showing a recently released documentary on the Nuremberg war crimes trials to all older pupils throughout the city.[28] The young parliamentarians believed that these sorts of film showings would be a valuable addition to the political education instruction of all West Berlin pupils over the age of ten. Although the parliamentarians debated many sweeping topics such as these, they did not neglect their traditional agenda. At this same meeting, the BSP also discussed bills related to the selection of reviewers for *Abitur* exams and financial assistance for needy pupils preparing for these tests.

The BSP did not limit its political education activities to its regular meetings. In 1957, the parliament founded a "Political Committee" that further encouraged political education in the classrooms of West Berlin.[29] In particular, this committee advocated the analysis and debate of contemporary political issues. To realize this objective, the pupils who were members of this committee sent information to the city's teachers on such topics as "The Existence of the United Nations," "Night of the Broken Glass," and "East Germany." These topical reports encouraged teachers to devote greater attention to such issues in their lessons. In its 1959 report, the BSP claimed that the efforts of the "Political Committee" had led to the founding of several extracurricular organizations in the city's schools devoted to the study of contemporary political questions.[30] The committee also inaugurated a new series of meetings dedicated to the discussion of political themes. Devised as a means to improve the knowledge of young West Berliners on a host of political subjects, these meetings brought leaders in the fields of government, education, and economics into the schools and made them accessible to postwar pupils.

This attention to broad political issues might lead one to dismiss the BSP as a body of overzealous pupils from the most academically focused West Berlin secondary schools. Yet as we saw in chapter 2, the parliament undertook efforts to integrate pupils from all secondary schools from an early date. Perhaps the most visible sign of the BSP's continuing desire to represent all of the city's schools in its meetings was the so-called gavel wielder. The position of gavel wielder typically belonged to one of the youngest representatives in the BSP, whose job it was to pound his hammer when a foreign phrase, unclear metaphor, or stilted manner of argument required clarification. As the parliament's founding father, Hermann Schneider, explained it, this position was designed so that "no pupil of the *Volksschule* or OPZ would need to feel himself to be a 'second-class parliamentarian.'"[31] This position had existed from the parliament's earliest days but had disappeared by the mid-1950s. Because pupils from the city's OPZs and OTZs expressed their dismay with the rhetorical techniques and language of their colleagues from the OWZs, the position was reestablished in 1957.[32] After the gavel wielder once again became a fixture in the monthly meetings of the BSP, the speeches of all those who spoke before the BSP were liable to be challenged—from Norbert Götz, the representative of the Tannenburg-Schule, to the city's highest official, Willy Brandt, whose speech as a distinguished visitor was once interrupted by the gavel. This rather simple parliamentary procedure reinforced the BSP's commitment to representing pupils from all schools, working together on an equal footing, and aiding those in need of assistance.

Further illustrating the growth student government in the *Volksschulen* (and OPZs of West Berlin) during this period are the expanded activities in which these organizations engaged. Admittedly, student government activities were less diverse in these schools than in *Mittelschulen* or *Gymnasien,* but the burgeoning endeavors of SMV in West German *Volksschulen* became increasingly visible as the 1950s came to a close. The Westendschule in Frankfurt serves as a telling example. The pupils in this school claimed a student government organization founded in 1954. The school had a student president, a council, class representatives from grades four through eight, and several committees. Among the activities in which the school's student government were involved: a quarterly student newspaper; aid packages to East Germany; exchanges with American military schools in Frankfurt; toy donations for children of refugees from the East; and collection drives for UNICEF.[33] While this would have constituted a remarkable accomplishment for virtually any school, it was particularly impressive for a *Volksschule*. Yet by the end of the 1950s, many *Volksschulen* could claim achievements in the realm of student government that had once limited to the most academically oriented schools. In West Berlin, all of the OPZs responding to the 1959 query of the BSP had an elected student government.[34] Sixty percent of the city's OPZs were represented in the BSP, and almost all of these schools allowed their representatives to give reports on the organization's activities during class time. These examples underscore the growing involvement of pupils in the life of the school. Pupils from *Volksschulen* benefited from the practical political education provided by student government in increasing numbers as the decade came to a close.

Although statistics like those in West Berlin are unavailable for the Hessian schools, the written work of pupils during this period indicates increasing connections between political education and student government. Questions appearing on Hessian *Abitur* exams reveal that student government and political education became increasingly popular themes in the late 1950s. Hessian pupils prepared for *Abitur* exams in German that by the mid-1950s consisted of multiple subsections; concentrations in "Literature," "Social Studies," "Cultural History," and "General Themes" were most common. Almost without fail, there would be a question from each subject area, with the social studies question frequently asking pupils to expound on the values, responsibilities, and contributions of student government in their response. Questions related to social studies or SMV, however, were by no means an easy way to circumvent tougher questions on literature or history. Scores on responses to such questions were similar to those given to pupils who wrote on more traditional themes.

The replies of young West Germans to these queries illustrate how pupils viewed the role of SMV, as well as their responsibilities in the school and in society as a whole. For example, in his 1955 *Abitur* essay, Dilthey-Schule pupil Heinrich Moos recounted the numerous tasks of SMV. Among the duties of student government, he cited cooperation between teacher and pupil, support for the school's administration, extracurricular groups, and assisting sports clubs. These were all important, Moos asserted, but there was one task that student government provided that eclipsed the others. "The decisive thing is that the young person learns to take responsibility and to act independently through his work and the fulfillment of his tasks in student government."[35] He later noted that such lessons were more important for young Germans than ever before. In the opinion of Moos, student government provided preparation for active citizenship in West Germany's young democracy through teaching pupils about responsibility and encouraging them to become more involved in their school and community. Addressing the issue of how to educate young citizens four years later, Michael

Thomas examined the role of the school and SMV in the preparation of German pupils for their future societal responsibilities. He asserted that the school was charged with the mission of awakening an interest in politics in the postwar pupil. He continued, the school "familiarizes him with state events. In the student council, responsibility is placed in his hands. Even if it is modest, it should nonetheless serve as a model for his future activities."[36] Once again we see the convergence of student government activities and political education. This was not lost on pupils, as they conceived of SMV as practical political education both in the issues they addressed, as well as the methods they employed. Likewise, they were under no delusions about their authority in student government. As was the case in the BSP in West Berlin, it was not what these pupils achieved in the way of policies or tangible reforms that mattered most. The processes and activities in which they engaged constituted the most pedagogically valuable aspect of SMV.

In addition to the everyday activities of student government, a blossoming student press contributed to the continuation of political education outside the classroom. The increasing number of student publications as the 1950s came to a close signifies a growth in the participation of postwar pupils in the life of their schools. Just as important is the variety of issues addressed by student newspapers. These publications devoted attention to important political questions in the life of the school, including the activities of student government, election campaigns, and pupil-teacher relationships. At the same time, they committed themselves to enhancing the knowledge of pupils on a variety of larger political issues. In some papers, pupils analyzed Germany's troubled relationship with Jews and how these tensions reappeared in the late 1950s. In others, they criticized the policies of local, regional, and national political leaders. Particularly in West Berlin, pupils challenged the authority of school officials and raised troubling questions about the Cold War status quo in the divided city. Engaging this spectrum of political topics sparked discussions, ignited debate, and encouraged pupils to investigate many controversial questions in greater detail. These school publications extended political education in the schools and provide evidence for the interest of postwar pupils in local, national, and international political issues.

The student press required more than a decade before it cemented a secure place in the life of the West German schools. Whereas there had been a handful of newspapers founded as early as 1946, few came into existence before the end of the occupation in 1949. Yet as the involvement of pupils in the life of the school expanded, as well as their desire to express their views on political and social issues, student newspapers began to sprout up in schools across the country. Nevertheless, these publications were most common in the *Gymnasien* and experienced more gradual growth in other schools during the 1950s. West Berlin provides an excellent example of both of these trends. A June 1959 survey of the city's secondary schools conducted by the BSP shows that while the number of student publications had increased significantly, they were still largely limited to the most academically focused institutions. Of the 38 OWZs that responded to the survey, 28 could claim a student newspaper. The situation was less impressive in the OTZs, where roughly a third of the 28 schools that responded had a paper. Unsurprisingly, only one of the 28 responding OPZs had a newspaper.[37] Based on the files of the Culture Ministry and individual schools in Hesse, it is reasonable to believe that the growth of its student press followed a similar pattern throughout West Germany. It would not be until after 1960 that student newspapers cemented their place in the OPZs and *Volksschulen* of the Federal Republic.

Naturally, intraschool issues continued to hold a prominent place in the pages of postwar school newspapers. This, however, did not preclude a discussion of questions of political education in their pages. Many articles addressing the everyday activities of pupils in the school contributed to their preparation for democratic citizenship at the same time. One such example comes from the Dilthey-Schule in Wiesbaden. On the front page of the school's newspaper, *Der Funk,* the editors posed an interesting question: "Whose trust?" This November 1955 article was a response to the complaints of pupils that a teacher had interfered in the election of a class president. The editor rhetorically asked if the elected pupil was in fact first and foremost a trusted representative of the teacher. If so, then pupils did not need to vote. The editor continued:

> We, as pupils, have a different interpretation of this office. Thus we speak of a class president. That actually says it all: we determine the comrade of our trust, the one who should speak on our behalf. And this is where *democracy* begins for us, which everyone should know. … We can, I think, expect understanding, [when we ask] that our vote be respected.[38]

This article demonstrates that pupils utilized the student press to address problems that existed within the schools, as well as to seek resolutions to these tensions. The editor stated at the beginning of the piece that his criticisms would not likely be well received by many of the school's teachers, yet he believed it to be his duty to inform pupils of the problem and encourage discussion and action.

Perhaps the best indication that student newspapers had secured a place in the life of the postwar schools in Hesse was the announcement of a statewide contest for such publications in 1957. The newspapers evaluated for this contest provide insight into the state of the Hessian student press as the 1950s came to a close. Culture Ministry officials received entries from all across Hesse, running the gamut from a four-page *Volksschule* paper to a sophisticated twenty-page *Gymnasium* biweekly. As in West Berlin, the most advanced newspapers were published in *Gymnasien*. One such paper submitted to Culture Ministry officials contained an article that mocked the actions of the Hessian assembly and included a Latin quotation in its critique. More common, however, were newspapers that underscored their close relationship to the school's student government organizations and outlined their mission to provide a voice to pupils. For example, Hannelore Pistorius, a leader in the student government of the Immanuel-Kant-Schule in Rüsselsheim, used the front page of *Der Rüssel* to explain what she deemed the true mission of SMV to her fellow classmates: "Student government wants—as the name already indicates—to work with the school and not rebel against it. … The goal of SMV is good cooperation and a good relationship between teachers and pupils on one side, and among pupils on the other."[39] As she explained to her readers, it was only with the cooperation of both pupils and teachers that the school's student government had been able to organize sports clubs, several extracurricular committees, a school library, and the paper.

Judging from the submissions of the state's *Gymnasien,* there were two main types of student newspapers in Hessian schools. The first of these was the traditional newspaper, which addressed intraschool issues, as well as national and international news and sports. The other kind of paper more closely resembled a literature journal, which featured essays, stories, and poems from pupils alongside school news and announcements. Regardless of content, the disclaimer of the inaugural issue of Wiesbaden's *disciplus* held true for all student publications: "A student newspaper may in no way be compared with a daily paper. It is only an organ 'from pupils for pupils' and in regard to editorial matters, makes no claim to perfection."[40] Interestingly, *disciplus,* which won second prize in the state's inaugural newspaper contest in 1957, was the combined publication of Wiesbaden's *Gymnasien, Mittel-,* and *Berufsschulen.* Thus even in the more prosperous late 1950s, many papers continued to rely on the combined energies of pupils from various schools.

The Hessian Newspaper Contest indicates the growing importance of student publications in the postwar schools, as well as their educational value. The criteria for the contest reveal that school officials determined papers to be pedagogically valuable on a number of levels. The first of these was "graphic composition and selection of photos." This criterion reflects an increased emphasis on visual learning facilitated by the new generation of textbooks ushered into the schools after the war. More than ever before, textbooks integrated maps, graphs, charts, and photos into lessons to assist the pupil in understanding and retaining challenging concepts. The second point upon which the newspapers were judged was the style and level of writing they exhibited. School officials believed that student papers, whether devoted to journalistic content or literature and poetry, could reinforce writing skills learned in the classroom. The third aspect judges considered in evaluating these papers was the "vibrant reflection of school and youth life." Although a somewhat nebulous concept, it suggests that school authorities hoped that student newspapers would showcase SMV, examine issues of interest to young Germans, communicate school news, and promote better relations between teachers and pupils. The final and most intriguing criterion for the contest was that these publications were to foster political education and instruction in the schools.[41] Organizing the paper, writing articles, editing, and publishing all provided pupils invaluable experience in the everyday responsibilities of democratic citizenship. So, too, did their examinations of contemporary political and social questions. Thus, these papers contributed to the political education of those involved in their publication, as well as those who merely read them.

More often than in Hesse, intraschool issues intersected with larger social and political questions in the student newspapers of the former capital. West Berlin pupils were particularly interested in relations between East and West Germany due to their unique location behind the Iron Curtain. As a consequence, many West Berlin schools operated programs to assist and foster closer relations with their counterparts on the other side of the city. One such initiative was the organization of unofficial visits for West Berlin pupils to East Berlin schools. The Schadowschule, an OWZ in Zehlendorf, organized one such day-long visit in the fall of 1957. After the initial visit to an East Berlin secondary school promoted greater interest, pupils planned a second trip. As the school's newspaper, the *Schüler-Echo*, explained in a front-page story, West Berlin officials rejected their planned excursion. Their explanation: fear of communist influence. The paper responded to this with blatant ridicule:

> We should be allowed to laugh softly: Do the "Gods on Administrative Olympus" really think that critical young people who have lived in a democratically governed city for years could be convinced to become Communists because of a five-hour gathering with pupils in the East? Does one really think that "over there" the schools are exclusively filled with trained functionaries, who have nothing else to do than to convince us of the blessings of Communism?[42]

The paper openly mocked the city's school administration, whose concern about the cultural politics of the East Germans was not wholly unfounded. Readers learned that during the last visit, pupils had talked about music, theater, film, and politics but that "no one had attempted to convince another of the correctness of his claims." In a clear attack on Adenauer's policy regarding East Germany, the article concluded that "the Federal Government refuses to enter into direct negotiations with the German Democratic Republic, because it does not want to give it official recognition. We, however, just want to get to know the people. And no one may forbid us from doing that."[43] This article indicates that pupils in the Schadowschule not only felt obliged to improve relations between the two states, but that they also had the right to speak out against the policies of their government in order to do so.

Student newspapers addressed contemporary political and social questions through traditional articles as well as special editions devoted to a particularly important issue. Occasionally, newspapers would function as a forum in which pupils could examine a specific political question in greater detail. A remarkable example comes from the Arndt-Schule, another OWZ in Zehlendorf. In October 1959, the tenth-grade pupils created a special edition of the paper dedicated to the history of Jews in Germany.[44] Their publication is a valuable source for several reasons. First, it offers insight into how these pupils understood the Nazi regime and the Holocaust. Pupils read five recent scholarly studies of German history, including Eugen Kogon's *SS-State,* and drew from them in their work. These pupils published a startlingly frank discussion of the Final Solution, including photos taken by liberators and detailed accounts of transports, selections, gas chambers, and crematoria. Second, this project, which received funding from the Landeszentrale für politische Bildungsarbeit, indicates the interest of city authorities in furthering political education through the student press. The organization

SCHÜLER-ECHO

SCHÜLERZEITUNG IN DER SCHADOWSCHULE

Nr. 4 / V.Jahrg   Oktober 1957   15 Dpf

Kontakte unerwünscht ?

In der letzten Nummer des "Schüler-Echo" konnten wir davon berichten, daß vier Schüler einer Ostberliner Oberschule für einen Vormittag Gast der 13 1 waren. Wir hatten uns sehr über diesen Besuch gefreut, denn bei den vielen Verbindungen, die unsere Schule zum Ausland unterhält, mußte man befürchten, daß der naheliegendste Kontakt, die Verbindung mit den Menschen im Osten unserer Heimat, vernachlässigt wird. Wir hatten es als natürlich betrachtet, daß wir diesen Besuch erwidern würden und waren deshalb schwer erstaunt, als uns von höherer Stelle mitgeteilt wurde, daß ein offizieller Besuch von Westberliner Schülern im Ostsektor nicht erlaubt werden könnte. Begründung: Gefahr der kommunistischen Beeinflussung. Es sei uns gestattet, leise zu lächeln: Glauben die "Götter im Verwaltungsolymp" wirklich, daß kritische junge Menschen, die jahrelang in einer demokratisch regierten Stadt gelebt haben, durch ein fünfstündiges Zusammensein mit Ostschülern zu überzeugten Kommunisten werden können? Glaubt man wirklich, daß "drüben" auch in den Schulen ausschließlich ausgebildete "Jungfunktionäre" sitzen, die weiter nichts zu tun haben, als uns von den Segnungen des Kommunismus zu überzeugen? Es ist ein alter Aberglaube, daß die Diskussionspartner aus dem Osten gleich mit dialektischem Geschütz anrücken.- Die sind doch selbst noch nicht alle "Hundertprozentige"! Wie war es denn bei unserem Gespräch mit den Schülern? Wir haben uns über Schul- und Jugendprobleme, über Musik, Theater und Film unterhalten - natürlich auch über Politik - aber keiner hat versucht, den anderen von der Richtigkeit seiner Behauptungen zu überzeugen; beide Seiten haben Zugeständnisse machen müssen - genau so wie es bei einer Wiedervereinigung nötig sein wird. Aber das will man bei uns leider

Fortsetzung S.2

Das ist er: Stephen Schultz, 19 Jahre, unser diesjähriger Gastschüler von der Horace-Mann-School. "Unser" Steve ist bestimmt schon allen aufgefallen - seine athletische Figur mit diesem allen Amerikanern eigenen typischen "Etwas".

Einige Wochen weilt er nun schon an unserer Schule und er gibt sich redliche Mühe mit der deutschen Sprache. Natürlich fällt sie ihm, der in New York noch kein Wort Deutsch konnte, sehr schwer, besonders weil die Anleitung durch Lehrer fehlt. So schimpft er, wie viele Amerikaner, auch schon tüchtig: "Deutsche Sprach' - schwere Sprach'!"

Nach seiner Ankunft in Bremen Anfang Juli reiste er einen Monat quer durch ganz Mitteleuropa. Seine Reise führte ihn durch Dänemark, Holland, Frankreich, Italien und Österreich. Er benutzte dabei fast alle Verkehrsmittel: Schiff, Eisenbahn, Bus, Flugzeug, Fahrrad - und per Anhalter. Das letzte machte ihm am meisten Spaß. Von den deutschen Landschaften gefiel ihm der Schwarzwald am besten:" Er ist so typisch deutsch!"   -reichard-

Figure 10. Cover of the *Schüler-Echo*, student newspaper of West Berlin's Schadowschule, 1957. The front-page article "Relations Unwanted?" lampoons city education authorities. Courtesy Heimatmuseum Zehlendorf, Rep. 9, File 452.

undoubtedly viewed the publication as a means to address challenging historical and political questions to interested pupils beyond the confines of the traditional classroom. Third, this newspaper provides evidence regarding what pupils had learned about the problems of German political life before 1945. These sixteen-year-old pupils criticized the "political passivity" of the German people along with their obedience and gullibility. After asserting that the Third Reich was not something that came about overnight but instead was something that had been cultivated by decades of German political indifference, these pupils turned their eyes to the future:

> A second decade like the one that was initiated by Hitler can only be prevented through a change in the attitude of all people in regards to politics. A sense of political responsibility, activity, and constructive criticism—these are the things which alone can contribute to the preservation and strengthening of peace and to the unification of Europe and the world.[45]

These two sentences nicely encapsulate the lessons that the tenth-grade pupils of the Arndt-Schule had taken from their instruction in political education: the importance of political engagement, active participation in the life of the community, and a healthy sense of skepticism.

Student government and student newspapers continued to expand in the West German schools of the late 1950s. As we have seen, SMV became commonplace in the schools of all levels by this point. Student newspapers, admittedly less common in the *Volksschulen* during this period, had emerged in *Gymnasien* and many *Mittelschulen* by the end of the decade. More important than their statistical growth, however, is the fact that these extracurricular reforms contributed directly to political education in the postwar schools. These activities offered pupils the opportunity to gain practical experience with the rights and responsibilities of life in a democratic society. Student government provided pupils with experience in discussing divisive issues and defending their position, respecting the ideas of others, and accepting responsibility for their classroom and school. The essays of Hessian pupils affirm the sentiments of those who participated in the Berlin Student Parliament: it was not *what* SMV did that was significant, rather it was *how* it did it that mattered. The same statement holds true for student newspapers during this period. These publications engaged both intraschool issues, as well as broader social and political events. Pupils involved in these papers learned to work together on the production of the paper, to express their views on a variety of themes, and to challenge authority when the need arose. Whether writing about the undue influence of a teacher in a school election or the foreign policy of Konrad Adenauer, pupils undoubtedly increased their understanding of the topic at hand. Yet it was the process of analyzing the issue, discussing it, and then publishing their conclusions that mattered most. Thus the continued expansion of these reforms in the late 1950s reinforced traditional classroom instruction by providing practical experience in two of the most basic mechanisms of democracy: parliamentary government and an independent press.

Textbooks: From a Study of Theory to Preparation for Citizenship

"You can't judge a book by its cover," goes the old adage. One can, however, gain a good impression of a textbook from its closing remarks. Conclusions often summarize the message of a textbook more succinctly than any introduction or table of contents ever could. Take, for instance, Max Reiniger's *Neue Staatsbürgerkunde* (*New Civics*), used in German classrooms during the 1920s. Following a recapitulation of the defeat of 1918 and Germany's punishment through the Treaty of Versailles, Reiniger concluded his book with a veritable call to arms: "Let me gain strength in heart and hand, to live and to die for the holy Fatherland."[46] Thirty years later, Max Kunow's *Sozialkunde* (*Social Studies*) offered a picture of international cooperation and understanding in its closing pages. After explaining the mission of the United Nations, Kunow's book intoned: "We are indeed all brothers!"[47] The final lines of these two postwar political education texts, one written in the aftermath of the Great War and the other following Hitler's war, represent starkly different conceptions of political education and its place in the world. Both of these texts were supposed to foster knowledge of and respect for Germany's constitution and those who upheld it. Both of these texts were designed to educate new citizens in the aftermath of a defeated regime. Yet, as these closing passages suggest, the content of political education texts after World War II looked quite different from what was taught following Germany's previous defeat.

The transformation of political education textbooks after 1945 is undoubtedly one of the most dramatic reforms in the schools of the Federal Republic. Texts of the interwar era typically consisted of a recapitulation of the Weimar constitution without comment or analysis and a history of Germany's military and political exploits in the nineteenth century. These books often concluded with a biting critique of the Treaty of Versailles and an ambivalent discussion of the democratic mechanisms that now governed the nation. Thirty years later, a new generation of texts sought to prepare the youth of West Germany for their new responsibilities as citizens. Instead of focusing on governmental institutions far beyond the imagination of the young citizen, these books attempted to illustrate the workings of democracy at the local level. Closer in design to the American social studies books of the postwar era, these texts examined not just political issues, but also practical questions related to family, community, economics, and vocation. Pupils were encouraged to discuss and debate controversial questions in the classroom. Their active participation in class was supposed to prepare them more fully for their responsibilities in a democratic state. This newfound emphasis on the rights and obligations of the citizen in a democracy is fundamental to the new generation of texts published in the postwar period.

Six key characteristics differentiate postwar texts from those published during the interwar period. The first and perhaps most obvious of these differences is the focus of the publication. Texts published in the 1920s centered on the state almost without exception. In many ways, the language used to describe the monarchy through the First World War is simply reused in discussions of the republic created after 1918. Postwar texts instead focused on the individual and his place in a democratic society. These books underscored the rights and responsibilities of the individual in the family, community, nation, and indeed, on the planet.

This leads us to a second difference between political education texts before after the war, which is a change in scope. Weimar era texts concentrated almost solely on the national level. Germany stood at the center of these books, which often contained disparaging remarks about neighboring states. Postwar books, on the other hand, offered the pupil broadened horizons; these books emphasized the actions of Germany on a European and global stage. At the same time, they also included examinations of local and regional government, as well as the varied responsibilities of the federal system. A third and related distinction between these two generations of texts is their orientation. The books of the Weimar era were largely historical, as they examined the development of Germany's political institutions, the legacy of its military, and the diplomatic decisions that enlarged its role in the world. The narrative found in postwar texts is quite different, as these publications emphasized the present and looked toward the future. The obligations of citizens in their daily lives became a question of contemporary importance. Likewise, the division of Germany and hopes for reunification prompted texts to consider the role of democracy in Germany's future.

Three additional aspects of postwar political education texts set them apart from their interwar antecedents. These three are arguably more pedagogical in nature, and they further underscored the legitimacy and benefits of democracy in the Federal Republic. The first of these is in the approach of texts to questions of political education. Simply stated, political education in the Weimar Republic was a study of institutions (*Institutionskunde*), such as the Reichstag, the constitution, and the office of the president. The approach of postwar books departed from that of the interwar period by emphasizing the everyday workings of democracy at the community level. Local elections, political parties, and community organizations received increased attention in texts after World War II. So, too, did the rights and responsibilities of life in a democratic society, particularly freedom of speech and an independent press. Another characteristic that must be considered in comparing political education texts is their presentation. Texts from the Weimar era discussed democracy as an abstract principle; pupils learned about democracy as a political form alongside others. This theoretical examination of democracy was further complicated by the overemphasis on acquiring knowledge. The passive memorization of facts, laws, and political structures superseded an understanding of social processes in these publications.[48] Postwar texts, however, underscored the value of practical democracy and offered pupils a variety of opportunities to participate actively in understanding it. Debate, discussion, and group interaction are all hallmarks of postwar texts, which strove to provide pupils first-hand experience with the processes of interaction in a democratic society. Finally, any evaluation of political education texts must consider the tone employed in examining Germany's political development. Texts published after 1918 often displayed a hesitancy to embrace democracy, coupled with an affinity for the lost monarchy. Postwar texts betrayed no doubts that democracy was the best form of government for the Federal Republic. At the same time, though, these books did not conceal the inadequacies of democracy. As Wolfgang Hilligen's classic postwar series termed it, democracy was "the smaller evil" when compared to other systems around the world.[49]

Political education textbooks, or *Staatsbürgerkundebücher*, in the Weimar era suffered from a variety of shortcomings that hindered their effectiveness in preparing young Germans for life in a democracy. One hallmark of Weimar political education texts was their narrow purview; these books examined Germany with little reference to her interactions with neighbors or the global community. Not surprisingly, this fostered a nationalism that steadily intensified throughout the Weimar Republic, particularly as the 1920s came to a close. A 1928 text authored by Ulrich Haacke and Benno Schneider nicely illustrates this underlying current of nationalist sentiment. In a discussion of the League of Nations, the authors explained its advantages to Germany (which joined in 1926) but concluded with an ominous warning: "As long as the ideal of eternal peace among peoples has not become an inviolable reality, then a people (*Volk*) must have strong hearts and be able to keep in sight the other possibility."[50] Hardly a ringing endorsement of international cooperation, this passage suggested that Germany must continue to consider war as an option for solving disputes. The book's closing passage then recounted the country's suffering since World War I and the need for Germans to unify in order to emerge from a lingering state of "misery."[51] This narrative is an unmistakable renunciation of international cooperation and understanding among peoples.

The most passionate writing one finds in Weimar civics texts is usually reserved for denunciations of the Treaty of Versailles. Whereas many volumes literally published the constitution without comment or explanation, the outcome of the Great War merited page after page of outrage and hyperbole. Nowhere was this more striking than in Max Reiniger's *Neue Staatsbürgerkunde*, first published in 1923. In a dry, legalistic tone, Reiniger explained the demise of the *Kaiserreich* and the promulgation of a new constitution in 1919. Following this was an impassioned fourteen-page critique of the Treaty of Versailles. After the war, Reiniger explained, peace was "dictated" to the Germans. The text also devoted attention to the economic reparations due to France, the loss of population, and Germany's lack of sovereignty regarding key military questions.[52] Other Weimar texts displayed similar characteristics, balancing reserved discussion of the institutions of democracy with vigorous criticism of the postwar peace agreements. For example, a 1927 text dedicated five pages to a discussion of the Weimar constitution (and simply reprinted it as an appendix). This same book, however, devoted several more pages to the events that transpired at Versailles, lamenting the removal of culturally German areas from the nation and pondering why the Allies would want to transform Germany from a paying customer into a "moneyless debtor."[53]

Less than thirty years later, a new generation of political education texts entered West German classrooms. These books arrived on the heels of the innovative history texts that appeared in schools at the beginning of the 1950s, from which they drew inspiration. As was true of a number of postwar history texts, many new political education books contained a regional focus and thus achieved a limited circulation. Others were small texts that offered specialized discussions of particular topics or provided only brief summaries of key issues. A few texts, however, targeted a general audience and became staples of the postwar curriculum. Two such series will be featured here: *Der Gemeinde-, Staats- und Weltbürger* (*The Local-, National-, and World Citizen*) by Karl Nebelsiek and *Sehen—Urteilen—Handeln* (*See—Judge—Act*) by Wolfgang Hilligen. These books are useful examples of postwar trends for three major reasons. First, they appealed to educators throughout the Federal Republic. Extending beyond any regional focus, these texts entered classrooms throughout the country during the postwar period. Second, these books enjoyed a long shelf-life. Each book went through multiple editions and stayed in print for a decade or longer. Finally, these two volumes suggest how changes proceeded even within this period. Important, if subtle, differences can be seen in the early editions of Nebelsiek's text and those of Hilligen dating from the mid-1960s.

Nebelsiek's volume can be considered a bridge between the civics texts of the Weimar era and the political education books of the late 1950s. First published in 1951, Nebelsiek's book was one of the trailblazers in the postwar period.[54] Perhaps because of its pioneering role, it retained some of the more problematic characteristics of its predecessors. Like his counterparts before 1933, Nebelsiek emphasized the institutions of the democratic state, devoting great attention to the mechanisms of government. For example, Nebelsiek did an admirable job of explaining the different methods of voting in a democratic society, the different kinds of election systems, and the positions of the different political parties on a variety of fundamental issues. His narrative, however, failed to connect with the experiences and activities of postwar pupils. Theoretical concepts and complicated issues are addressed, but not always in a language or style accessible to pupils in grades seven through twelve. For example, a complicated chart mapping out the political platform of the major West German parties was supposed to help prepare pupils for their future decisions as voters. While Nebelsiek did not repeat the mistakes of Weimar authors and reprint the entire constitution without comment, he did incorporate passages in the text with little analysis of his own.

A second troubling continuity Nebelsiek's text shared with its prewar predecessors was an emphasis on factual knowledge. In the introduction to the first edition, Nebelsiek himself made his attention to facts and information clear, stating that

one of the most important reasons for the lack of openness on the part of youth—and not only just youth!—in regard to political questions is the absence of knowledge of all the things that serve as a precondition for an understanding of political events and with it collaboration on political questions. Phrased crassly, as long as youth do not know the difference between the offices of the federal president, the upper house of parliament, the lower house of parliament, the minister presidents of the individual states, the federal chancellor, etc., one cannot expect them to be interested in the activities of these groups. The goal of this book is to remedy this deficit and with it, to awaken an interest in cooperation on civic tasks.[55]

Few authors would likely have disagreed with Nebelsiek that a fundamental understanding of the institutions of the state and the rights and responsibilities of citizens was indispensable to political education. Yet many postwar educators also recognized the dangers of focusing primarily on facts and figures. They remembered that the pupils of the Weimar Republic had studied democratic institutions and the constitution, but with little practical experience in the classroom, this instruction was to no avail. The goal of these teachers was to strike the proper balance between knowledge and experience.

This emphasis on facts and knowledge notwithstanding, Nebelsiek's volume incorporated a number of important innovations in the field of political education. From its very title, one can see that Nebelsiek's publication signified the start of a new generation of postwar political education texts. Whereas Weimar era texts focused almost solely on Germany and the responsibilities one had to the state, Nebelsiek's book was divided into three roughly equal parts that examined the local, national, and international context of political education. Admittedly, the content of the first two parts could have appeared in civics books of the 1920s, but the third part, the *Weltbürger,* or "world citizen," marked a significant departure from the insularity of Weimar. This section chronicled the history of the international peace movement, examined international organizations, and discussed human rights and their protected place in the Federal Republic. Particularly remarkable is the section entitled "The United States of Europe" (*Die Vereinigten Staaten von Europa*), in which Nebelsiek traced the history of European cooperation and underscored its importance in the postwar world.[56] This section discussed economic developments in which European countries were involved together (the European Recovery Plan, the Schuman Plan, and the Organization of European Economic Cooperation). In addition to these specifically European developments, the text also devoted attention to global issues of transportation, agriculture, religion, and culture.

Further contributing to the active preparation of West German pupils for their responsibilities as citizens were the innovative pedagogical approaches incorporated into Nebelsiek's text. The inclusion of questions for class discussion and debate—similar to those found in the new generation of postwar history books—constituted perhaps the most striking difference between this volume and its Weimar era predecessors. Despite stressing the importance of knowledge acquisition in his introduction, Nebelsiek provided questions that required the critical analysis and discussion of pupils in the classroom. For instance, after an explanation of the federal system of the West German state, the text encouraged pupils to discuss whether the federal government had enough power or if it had too much authority. In another section dedicated to the Bundestag, pupils were prompted to lead an assembly of their own, which included creating an agenda and holding an election.[57] The third part of the book, focused on international developments, also included a variety of challenging questions that could have sparked interesting discussions. After addressing the work of the international peace movement, Nebelsiek asked pupils a succinct but divisive question: "Refusal of military service: yes or no?"[58] The text also encouraged pupils to discuss and analyze a timely topic with direct relevance to the future development of Europe: "Why the United States of Europe? Why have efforts to create the United States of Europe encountered such great difficulties?"[59]

A successor of the Nebelsiek textbook was the *Sehen—Urteilen—Handeln* series, which first entered classrooms at the end of the 1950s. This series emulated many American social studies texts in its approach and content. Hilligen authored several volumes, each offering specialized instruction for a particular grade level. Editions for pupils in the fifth and sixth grades typically consisted of short stories devoted to a certain issue—elections, family, community, school, work, and taxes, among others. Books created for older pupils resembled the more traditional textbook narrative more closely, yet they still relied on everyday situations to convey lessons about rights and responsibilities in a democracy, the institutions of the state, and one's personal and professional relationships. A testament to its effectiveness, Hilligen's series remained in print into the 1990s.

In order to prepare West Germany's youngest pupils for future experiences in elections, Hilligen chose to focus on the activities of student government in his text for the fifth and sixth grades. In this section, Hilligen offered the story of Heinz, president of his sixth-grade class, whose classmates try to unseat him from his position one afternoon after he has gone home sick.[60] Following the tale were several sections of questions designed to underscore certain issues and prompt debate and discussion. First, the story attempted to teach pupils of their responsibilities in helping administer the school. It was easy to blame Heinz for problems or inadequacies in the classroom; it was much harder, however, to take responsibility themselves and assist him in his work. Second, Hilligen encouraged pupils to discuss how to vote and for whom they should vote. Is voting by raising one's hand a fair way to vote? Should people help others get elected in order to curry favor or influence? Hilligen posed each of these questions with a short anecdote that built upon the original experiences of Heinz. Third, the story asked pupils to think about the responsibilities of their student government organization and how they might better serve the school. Finally, the passage related itself to the broader world of life in a democratic society. It informed pupils that adults frequently engage in similar sorts of votes, from parent-teacher associations to national elections. As a concluding task, the text required pupils to draft a ballot and hold a mock election in class.

Hilligen's books for older pupils are just as remarkable for the reforms they incorporated into their pages. His volume for the seventh to tenth grades offers insight into the variety of themes postwar pupils addressed in the classroom. The book itself was divided into four main parts: "Everyone Needs Others," "The Rules by Which We Live," "The World is Full of Differences," and "How Does the World of Tomorrow Look."[61] The first part consisted of eight chapters in which Hilligen demonstrated the value of laws, family, taxes, insurance, and community. This part weighed the rights of the individual against his responsibilities to others in society. The second part, also eight chapters, addressed the legal and institutional framework of the Federal Republic: division of powers, civil rights, federalism, elections, and the economy. Although this section contained the most traditional (but also indispensable) topics, it engaged them in a new way for postwar pupils. The text related complicated economic and political questions to pupils through more familiar occurrences and encouraged them to discuss these issues with classmates and adults. The third section was arguably the most remarkable. It contained twelve chapters that aspired to prepare a new generation of West German, European, and global citizens. One such chapter was devoted to tolerance and the right to one's opinions, while another compared democracy to dictatorship. Other chapters addressed social and economic questions of the postwar period, particularly those related to the newly founded welfare state. Especially noteworthy is a chapter entitled "Us and the World," in which Hilligen examined the place of West Germany in Europe and the international community. This chapter discussed the UN, NATO, WHO, EURATOM, and the EEC. The fourth and final section—also the shortest with four chapters—investigated new technologies, the role of women in society, and the place of developing nations on the global stage. Thus, simply in its layout, Hilligen's book signified a departure from the German-centered study of institutions so common to texts of the Weimar Republic.

Hilligen's text embodies the types of significant changes underway in the design and content of postwar political education books. For example, chapter seventeen of the *Sehen—Urteilen—Handeln* series for secondary schools focused on the practical values of debate and discussion. It opened with a disturbing passage about two young men who fight one another after disagreeing about the construction of a motor. In the fight, one friend stabs the other with a knife. Questions following the passage prompted pupils to discuss what would happen if they carried on fights like the two men in the story. Additionally, the book asked if it would be better to avoid all fights. "Would it not be better if everyone had the same opinion?"[62] Two pages later, in the highlighted passage that underscored key lessons in each chapter, Hilligen reinforced several key themes.

> Differences of opinion and differing interests must be settled according to rules if we all want to continue to live. Three important rules: Absolutely speak with one another! Only decide once one is informed! See with the eyes of the opponent! One should not trust a political opinion—particularly one's own—if it has not been tested by the opinions of others. This is the best means against slogans and propaganda.[63]

Later in this chapter, Hilligen explained how to organize and lead a discussion and provided several topics for treatment in the classroom. The emphasis in this chapter was on the discussion and peaceful resolution of divisive questions. Pupils learned that "controversial issues should not be settled with raw violence, rather with intellectual resources." The closing discussion prompts for this section included the following: "What can one do if others do not cooperate? When others use violence?"[64] Timeless questions, Hilligen's queries provided practical situations for pupils to consider in addressing broader social and political challenges.

The texts of Nebelsiek and Hilligen illustrate dramatic changes between the political education of the Weimar Republic and the postwar era. Perhaps the most important difference between the Weimar and postwar texts is the emphasis on everyday situations in the latter. Postwar textbooks taught pupils about elections and the rule of law through classroom examples. The books then connected these situations to larger social processes, thus making complicated aspects of democracy accessible to younger pupils. A related reform is the attention paid to human interactions and responsibilities in democratic society. Postwar texts also offered pupils the chance to participate actively in their lessons. As we have seen before, questions for debate and discussion reinforced critical points and required that pupils engage with the situations they encountered. Another development visible in postwar texts was the shift away from traditional German-centric narratives. Both Nebelsiek and Hilligen emphasized European and global issues and placed Germany within a broader international framework. Finally, there is no doubt that these books exhibited an unwavering commitment to democracy and looked forward—not backward—in their discussions of life in a democratic society. A careful evaluation of the new postwar political education textbooks suggests that authors had recognized that the mere memorization of the names of democratic statesmen and important dates in the history of the Federal Republic would not keep the flag flying in Bonn.

The Emergence of *Zeitgeschichte*

A final aspect of the new postwar political education curriculum—and arguably the most controversial—was the emphasis on recent German history and contemporary events. In the years after 1945, American occupation officials deemed instruction in Germany's recent development to be indispensable to democratization efforts. In particular, the period from 1914–1945 proved to be a "hot iron," to use the words of many teachers, which they would have rather left untouched. Older teachers, many of whom had taught already before 1945, subtly (and sometimes not so subtly) circumvented these lessons. West German education officials, however, also recognized the importance of addressing these issues and devoted special attention to them into the curriculum. New guidelines published after the war stressed the significance of instruction in contemporary history and required that history instruction address World War I, the Weimar Republic, the Third Reich, and World War II. Lessons in *Zeitgeschichte* were also supposed to address postwar developments, including the division of Germany, the outbreak of the Cold War, and the emergence of peaceful international organizations. Taught in conjunction with geography and social studies in many schools by the 1950s, *Zeitgeschichte* reinforced and expanded political education in the classroom. Utilizing a variety of innovative pedagogical tools including newspapers, radio programs, and classroom debates, *Zeitgeschichte* instruction highlights many reformist trends in West German education. Even though the subject finally established its place in the schools during this period, it continued to face serious challenges as the decade came to a close.

The study of contemporary history had already entered the schools officially during the occupation. Because of the moratorium on history instruction imposed by American officials immediately after 1945, more than two years passed before the subject was welcomed back into postwar classrooms. Contemporary history, however, entered the curriculum in many areas soon thereafter. In Hesse, Erwin Stein explained the importance of contemporary history in his 1948 and 1949 decrees on political education.[65] For him, the two subjects were inseparable. As a consequence of his decrees, *Zeitgeschichte* slowly made its way into the Hessian schools. For example, in a 1949 report on political education instruction in the Realgymnasium Friedberg, the school's principal informed Stein that pupils analyzed several themes of contemporary history in their lessons. Pupils studied the political parties before 1933 and after 1945, the occupation of Germany, the "Berlin Question," and the United Nations. Likewise, they discussed "the most important events of the past week," major foreign and domestic developments, and debated the significance of events they read about in the German press."[66] Admittedly, this report does not indicate that pupils engaged with more troubling aspects of Germany's recent past such as the failure of the Weimar Republic, the Third Reich, or the crimes of the Nazis. Yet it does indicate that, at least in some schools, teachers employed recent history in political education lessons even before the end of the occupation.

Contributing to this new interest in the recent past during the early years of the Federal Republic was the professionalization of *Zeitgeschichte* as an academic subdiscipline. The founding of the Institut für Zeitgeschichte (IfZ) in Munich in 1949 played an important role in this process. The research and publications of the IfZ in the 1950s fostered the creation of *Zeitgeschichte* as an academic subdiscipline in West German universities, a process that further intensified in the 1960s.[67] The institute's work in this period prompted increased attention to two major events in Germany's contemporary history: Germany's history under National Socialism and the refounding of democracy in 1949. Likewise, the recognition of *Zeitgeschichte* by respected German historian Hans Rothfels and the methodological framework he outlined legitimized the new field and ensured that its inherent subjectivity would be moderated by customary professional historical techniques.[68] The definition of *Zeitgeschichte* by Rothfels and his belief in its academic value lent further support to its development as a subdiscipline in the academy. Finally, the creation of the Bundeszentrale für Heimatdienst in 1952 (renamed Bundeszentrale für politische Bildung in 1963) underscored the importance of political education and contemporary history in the eyes of West German policymakers. This federal office offered financial support to research in these fields and, as we have already seen, promoted the study of political themes and contemporary history in the schools of the Federal Republic. These developments assisted in the emergence of contemporary history by lending the young subject area professional legitimacy, political acclaim, and financial support.

Recognizing the potential value of *Zeitgeschichte* instruction in secondary schools, West German education officials quickly formulated new curricula in the sub-discipline. They believed that *Zeitgeschichte* would be a useful tool for exploring both Germany's contentious twentieth-century history and the emergence of its young democracy. An examination of the 1957 Hessian history curriculum offers valuable insight into what teachers were expected to cover in their instruction. In all Hessian schools, contemporary history was to be addressed in the final class. For the eighth class of the *Volksschule*, the curriculum was slightly abbreviated, since there was less class time available to devote to history instruction.[69] Pupils in the eighth grade therefore studied Germany's development since 1815. Natu-rally, with such a large span of time to cover, required topics could be addressed only briefly. Nevertheless, the curriculum included World War I and its conse-quences, a brief survey of the Weimar Republic, a lengthy review of the Third Reich, and a section on the "New Beginning" after 1945. This final portion of the curriculum focused on the creation of the Federal Republic, the United Nations, the division of Germany, the Soviet Union, the Marshall Plan, and contempo-rary colonial struggles. Although plans had been made for the extension of the *Volksschule* to nine years by this time, the extra year had not yet been made com-pulsory. Hessian Culture Ministry officials, however, recognized that an additional year of schooling would allow for a more comprehensive study of contemporary history. As a consequence, they proposed that teachers plan to introduce new themes into their lessons in the future, such as the role of women in history, the place of the East in German development, and a comparison of social and eco-nomic systems in East and West.

The tenth class of the *Mittelschule* addressed many of the same topics included in the *Volksschule* but in greater detail. Because the *Mittelschule* curriculum ex-tended two years beyond that of the *Volksschule* by the late 1950s, German his-tory could be studied at a more relaxed pace. Hessian requirements for history instruction in the tenth class began with the imperialism of the late nineteenth century and World War I and then moved on to the Weimar Republic (empha-sizing its place in the League of Nations). The third unit—on National Social-ism—was more intensive than that of the *Volksschule* and included treatment of the economic and ideological origins of the Nazi Party, comparative study of dictatorships, concentration camps and the annihilation of the Jews, and total war and defeat. Following this section was a unit on the Soviet Union and com-munism (which extended to the 1956 uprising in Hungary) and another on the division of Germany and Europe after World War II. A brief, final unit examined the world in the nuclear age, focusing on the Cold War, divided nations (Ger-many, Korea, Vietnam), and international peace organizations.[70] As was to be expected in the future ninth class of the *Volksschule,* the *Mittelschule* curriculum required that teachers address key issues in detail. Among those suggested as meriting intensive discussion were the history and problems of liberalism, Soviet socialism and communism and its effects in Eastern Europe, political parties, and the history of colonialism.

The *Gymnasium* undoubtedly offered the greatest amount of time for the study of contemporary history. In their earlier classes, pupils in Hessian *Gymnasien* encountered virtually the same *Zeitgeschichte* curriculum as did their counterparts in the *Mittelschule*. The final years of the *Gymnasium,* which comprised grades eleven through thirteen, provided pupils with the additional opportunity to explore particular events and periods in greater detail. The curriculum for grade thirteen targeted *Zeitgeschichte* specifically (with a unit entitled "Epoch of the World Wars"). Pupils in this class were supposed to discuss such subjects as fascism, Hitlerism, Stalinism, and decolonization. "Turning points" such as the passing of the Enabling Act, Hitler's march into Prague in 1939, the Potsdam Conference, and the blockade of Berlin were included in order to prompt pupils to think critically about contemporary historical events.[71] Thus as one can discern from the curricula of the three main types of Hessian secondary schools, *Zeitgeschichte* had established a place for itself in the history curriculum. Culture Ministry officials encouraged teachers to engage Germany's tumultuous twentieth-century history, devoting an entire academic year to the post–World War I period in the *Mittelschule* and *Gymnasium*. With minor differences in chronological divisions, the *Zeitgeschichte* curricula of the other federal states looked very similar to those of Hesse, indicating widespread acceptance of the new subdiscipline throughout the Federal Republic.

Contemporary history had also become an important component of instruction in the schools of West Berlin by the late 1950s. The responses to West Berlin senator for education Joachim Tiburtius's inquiry on the state of *Zeitgeschichte* and political education in the city's schools at the end of the 1950s revealed both acceptance and reluctance among teachers. The surveys received from the OPZs, OTZs, and the ninth grades of the OWZs indicated that teachers largely completed the prescribed curriculum. History instruction in the eighth grade of the OPZs was supposed to conclude with 1945. The ninth grade of the OTZs ended with 1918, while pupils of the same class were supposed to reach 1850 in the OWZs.[72] Most of these schools reported the successful completion of these requirements. In a final report issued in February 1961, school officials reported success rates of 86 percent in the OPZs, 83 percent in the OTZs, and 90 percent in the ninth grade of the OWZs.[73] This meant that, at least in the OPZs, pupils had already studied the Weimar Republic, the Third Reich, and World War II by age thirteen. These results also suggested that, with prerequisites already fulfilled, there was adequate time for an analysis of the troublesome events of Germany's recent past in the city's other schools. A second and more disturbing trend was found in the responses of the most advanced classes of the OWZs. Their reports highlighted staggering failures to meet the expectations of the modern history curriculum. The twelfth grades of these schools were to review Germany's development in the nineteenth century and conclude with the era of Bismarck, although only 56 percent actually did so.[74] Teachers in these schools selectively fulfilled curricular requirements, including material they deemed acceptable and simply putting aside more troubling themes. This passive resistance on the part of some educators in the city's OWZs hindered pupils from completing their studies of contemporary German history the following year in the thirteenth class.

The individual responses of some history teachers in the city's OWZs may not have surprised city officials, but the widespread extent of problems in the twelfth grade certainly did. None of the city's districts could report that their OWZs had completed the history curriculum as prescribed. The shortcomings of the OWZs in Spandau, Wilmersdorf, and Zehlendorf must have been particularly disturbing to city school officials. In Wilmersdorf, four of the OWZ twelfth-grade classes reported that they had approached German unification but had not yet discussed 1871. The situation was similar in Spandau, with most schools falling well short of 1890. None of the four OWZs in Zehlendorf had yet reached 1871.[75] School officials were particularly disturbed by the report of the 4.OWZ in Zehlendorf, in which they learned that history instruction for that year ended at Christmas because of a teacher's illness. Astonishingly, this class had not yet advanced into the nineteenth century. While the disregard for the curriculum and the failure to examine German history to 1890 was a challenge in its own right, it represented a larger problem. City officials were well aware that delays in the twelfth year of the OWZ meant that key events in twentieth-century German history would be cut out of the final year of history instruction. These delays often resulted in the curtailment of history instruction in grade thirteen, with contentious issues of recent German history pushed aside in order to address less troubling developments prior to 1914.

Did teachers uncomfortable with teaching recent history express their outright resistance to the curriculum? They most certainly did not, at least not publicly or in written form. As noted above, teachers cited a variety of explanations for the failure to achieve the expectations of city school officials. Among the most common explanations for failing to achieve the required objectives in the classroom were: prolonged sickness of the teacher; necessary review of material addressed in previous years; extensive coverage of periods or issues that teachers deemed of particular importance (such as the Middle Ages, Renaissance, or Austrian history); extended class trips; and a lack of understanding regarding how far the "courage to leave things out" extended.[76] Interestingly, some teachers blamed shortcomings in the classroom on the extended coverage they said they devoted to specific contemporary political issues, such as the outbreak of anti-Semitic incidents that had recently occurred. Undoubtedly some of these excuses were valid and made in good faith, yet it is hard to believe that they were sincere in all cases. It is much more likely that, taken together, these reports indicate a dragging of the feet on the part of many teachers in the most advanced classes of the OWZs. It is no coincidence that as of 1960, the highest concentration of teachers aged forty-five to fifty-four was in the OWZs, whereas other schools, particularly the OPZs, were much more likely to have younger educators.[77] These reports indicate that hostility to the new subject remained among some of the oldest and most experienced teachers in the city's schools.

To conclude that *Zeitgeschichte* achieved little success in the postwar schools based on these reports, however, would be too hasty. The experiences of teachers in the OPZs and OTZs of West Berlin, as well as many of the city's OWZs, highlight just how far instruction in recent German history had advanced in the first full postwar decade. The schools of Wedding serve as one example. Frau Gauger, a history teacher in the Konrad-Hänisch-Schule (3.OPZ), reported good experiences with the subject in her classes. Her pupils had studied German and international politics since 1945, the division of Berlin, the Korean War, and the United Nations, as well as pursued comparative work on dictatorship and democracy. Her report emphasized the intermingling of political education and *Zeitgeschichte* in her lessons, and further asserted that not all of her pupils "accepted the events of the recent past uncritically." Many of them, she claimed, "showed great interest in political questions."[78] While other teachers noted that there were always challenges to engaging younger pupils in contemporary history, most agreed that there were significant benefits that could be achieved even in the earlier classes.

Instruction in *Zeitgeschichte* and political education largely achieved its objectives in the OTZs of West Berlin. In terms of *Zeitgeschichte* and political themes, the 1959 report of the Zehlendorf OTZs illustrates the active engagement of pupils with contemporary issues. Pupils discussed and debated a variety of such topics, including the extermination of the Jews during the Third Reich, the Geneva Conference, the election of the federal president, the recent visit of Soviet premier Nikita Khrushchev to the US, and the situation in Laos and Tibet.[79] Pupils in the less affluent schools of Kreuzberg covered a similar array of contemporary issues in their classes. In his 1958 report on political education and *Zeitgeschichte* in the Borsig-Schule, the school's principal, Herr Lyske, asserted that his tenth-grade pupils had completed all requirements outlined for them by the city. In order to encourage the interest and involvement of pupils in these lessons, Lyske noted that the school's teachers utilized a variety of innovative methods. Pupils participated in regularly scheduled discussions of contemporary issues with the assistance of different published sources, gave short presentations on current foreign and domestic problems, and most impressively, organized a class trip to West Germany in order to achieve a better understanding of the recent history and geography of the Federal Republic. Further complementing these assignments were visits to the BSP, the Kreuzberg district council, and local judicial hearings. Taken together, these initiatives in the field of political education and *Zeitgeschichte* prompted Lyske to remark that the school's tenth-grade history teacher, "through a continuing exchange of opinions and experiences ... familiarized pupils in the final year of school with contemporary events in order to give them the impulse to act as a responsible and active citizens in the future."[80]

Even with the high degree of failure in the penultimate classes of the OWZs to meet expectations regarding recent history, there were still signs that these schools had achieved some success. As we learned earlier, many of these schools had founded *Arbeitsgemeinschaften* devoted to examining contemporary political issues. For example, pupils in the Schadowschule founded an extracurricular club dedicated to political film. Having observed several meetings, the school's principal was impressed. He informed city school officials that after the film showings, pupils held "lively discussions that revealed not just a solid understanding of politics but an astonishing political maturity as well."[81] The report of the Arndt-Schule in Dahlem further underscores the differences in *Zeitgeschichte* and political education instruction between the OWZs and the rest of the city's schools. While the principal reported strong support for these subjects, his discussion underscores the emphasis placed on ideology and structure in these schools. In order to better understand contemporary political issues, pupils read the works of Karl Jaspers and "intensively addressed Marxist-Leninist-Stalinist ideology." Likewise, the school organized a group dedicated to examining historical-dialectical materialism.[82] While pupils in the OPZs and OTZs appear to have received greater instruction on the years leading up to 1945, their counterparts in the OWZs of West Berlin arguably engaged in a much deeper study of the postwar period before completing their compulsory education.

One of the most significant factors in the growth of *Zeitgeschichte* in postwar schools was the utilization of a variety of new instructional methods and technologies. Perhaps the most notable of these was the use of radio programs during lessons. Nowhere was this effort more concerted than in West Berlin, where the SFB (Sender Freies Berlin) and RIAS (Rundfunk im amerikanischen Sektor) both broadcasted programming designed to assist in the instruction of contemporary history and political education. The use of radio programs in the classroom, however, was a recent innovation. While RIAS had already begun broadcasting educational programming during the occupation, a year-long program of specialized instruction in the field of *Zeitgeschichte* and political education had never been attempted.[83] Thus the two stations were in uncharted territory when, during the 1957–58 school year, they collaborated on a trial program of twenty lessons targeted at ninth-grade pupils in all of the city's secondary schools.[84] To encourage participation in the program and to provide feedback to the radio stations, Senator Tiburtius requested that pupils in every ninth-grade class listen to two broadcasts per month and that teachers complete evaluations on the content of the programs.

The themes addressed during in the course of the twenty-program schedule can be categorized into five major groups. First, "In the Family and School" examined the variety of social relationships that existed within and beyond the home. Second, "Help in Everyday Life," concentrated on the rights and responsibilities of the individual. Included under this theme were such programs as "I Demand Trust," and "Helper of Humanity." The third category of programs was dedicated to "Work and the Economy." Among the lessons pupils encountered in these broadcasts were "Protection and Assistance on the Job" and "Social Occupations." Fourth was "Living Democracy," which included offerings such as "The Tasks of the Citizen in Political Life," "How a Law is Passed," and "Democracy and Dictatorship." Finally, there were an impressive number of transmissions devoted to "Political Lessons from History and Contemporary Events," such as

"The Weimar Republic," "Hitler Comes to Power," "The Idea of Europe," and "The United Nations."[85] Significantly, the final two groupings accounted for the majority of the broadcasting schedule.

The response of educators to these programs was generally positive. Evaluations completed by teachers indicated that 53 percent found the radio programs to be "necessary for instruction," while 44 percent believed that they could "possibly" be of value. The reasons for the hesitancy on the part of some teachers, typically in the OTZs and OWZs, was that the programs addressed topics that were not always directly linked to the curriculum for that specific grade. Nevertheless, teachers throughout the city explained that such programs were desirable and could be incorporated into classroom instruction. One reason teachers were receptive to the integration of radio programming into the classroom was the fact that it reduced the amount of preparation required before class. A second factor that contributed to the warm reception of educational broadcasts was the fact that they were popular with pupils. Radio programs held the attention of pupils as few teachers could; simply stated, many young listeners found these transmissions to be more interesting than their typical lessons.[86] A third strength of educational radio programming was that it facilitated classroom discussion. After the shared experience of listening together, teachers would typically require their pupils to debate the issues addressed in the broadcast. Finally, these radio programs provided teachers with some degree of content standardization in the field of political education at a time when there was still a fair amount of uncertainty among the city's educators regarding the subject.

While West Berlin teachers expressed support for the use of educational radio programming, they were even more enthusiastic about the main themes of these broadcasts. A poll conducted by city school officials determined that 80 percent of educators supported the topics addressed during the year-long schedule, with an additional 11 percent concurring with reservations.[87] Teachers informed the radio stations and city education officials that the most popular segments were "Trek from the East," "I Demand Trust," and "Must Günther Pay Damages?" Perhaps even more revealing were the dislikes of postwar teachers. Their distaste for programs such as "Elections," "Bundestag Representative," and "Federal President," suggests a rejection of the dry, one-dimensional treatment of the civics themes of yesteryear. Arguably just as astonishing as the laudatory responses of teachers was the extent of participation in the radio broadcasts. Over 2,300 classes had listened to the programs and submitted evaluations.[88] This did not include tenth-grade classes or *Berufsschulen* that opted to participate, nor did it account for multiple classes listening to the programs together. Likewise, classes failing to submit an evaluation are not included in this total. Thus, using the conservative figure of 35 pupils per class and not including those outside the target audience that may have tuned in, an average of 4,025 pupils listened to each broadcast.[89]

The participation of so many pupils in the classroom and the congratulatory responses of teachers prompted city school officials and the radio networks to declare the program a success. Yet once again, this success was uneven, as the incorporation of the educational broadcasts varied among the three main types of schools. Officials and radio programmers were most gratified to learn that the programs had been introduced into classroom instruction in about one-third of the schools. Evaluations from the city's teachers revealed that the combining of radio broadcasts and classroom instruction was most common in the OPZs. Teachers in the OTZs and OWZs agreed that the programs were pedagogically valuable, yet they were less likely to incorporate them into their regular instruction. To them, the radio segments were less directly related to classroom lessons and thus stood somewhat "at the edge of scheduled instruction."[90] There are two possible explanations for the greater unwillingness of teachers in these schools to integrate radio broadcasts more fully into their classes. First, as many teachers asserted, the themes covered in the twenty radio programs did not overlap perfectly with the political education curriculum of the West Berlin schools. The second explanation is much more challenging to substantiate. There may have been a higher degree of resistance among educators in the OTZs and OWZs to employ radio as an instructional tool in the classroom. Some may have seen this as an experiment, while others may have warmed up to the idea only as the school year progressed. In either case, such skeptics might have preferred to keep these broadcasts distinct from their traditional lesson plans. These considerations notwithstanding, city officials concluded that "school radio is a valuable aid to political education."[91] They praised its ability to teach pupils about social and political life, to illustrate ideas and forms of the community and the state, and to bring to life contemporary developments.

The incorporation of city, regional, and national newspapers in postwar classrooms stands as another important reform in the field of *Zeitgeschichte* during this period. Reading these publications provided postwar pupils with a better understanding of contemporary issues and facilitated classroom discussions and debates on a whole host of topics. In his 1958 report to city school officials, the principal of the Ernst-Schering-Schule (OPZ) in Wedding was quite frank about the challenges of exploring recent history and contemporary political themes with ninth-grade pupils. Yet he cited the in-class use of newspapers (as well as educational radio programming) as a valuable pedagogical tool for providing pupils instruction on contemporary issues. Pupils in the final class of the Ernst-Schering-Schule received newspapers once a week, read them, and used articles as the basis for classroom discussions.[92] Likewise, teachers in the OPZs of Tempelhof had no illusions about the challenges of addressing these topics with their pupils. They too reported mixed experiences but informed city officials that newspapers provided a valuable resource to their pupils. In the OPZs and many OTZs of the city, practical professional considerations generated interest in contemporary political and historical issues. The motivation of teachers nevertheless remained the same: to prepare pupils for their new responsibilities as intelligent and informed citizens in West German society.

The schools of Hesse faced many of the same difficulties as their West Berlin counterparts in regard to the addition of *Zeitgeschichte* to the postwar curriculum.

Just as many more experienced teachers resisted the introduction of the subject in their classrooms in the former capital, so too did some Hessian educators. An article published in the *Hessische Allgemeine Zeitung* in early 1960 highlights both the necessity of the subject as well as the difficulties teachers faced. The author, historian Walter Görlitz, explained that the Germans were a "strange people" and that they typically remained silent on historical events that were distressing or embarrassing. He claimed that in the eyes of Germans, it is "the others" who are always guilty. This fact, the author opined, made *Zeitgeschichte* all the more important for the schools, since inadequate instruction in recent and contemporary history had hampered the schools since the end of the war. In concluding his analysis, Görlitz asserted that there could be "no doubt that the knowledge of our recent history must be taught and learned, and that it should lead to an analysis of totalitarian regimes—of the NSDAP of yesterday and the SED of today. That much of this is currently left out, there is no doubt."[93] While the article concentrated on the tensions of teaching *Zeitgeschichte* in the Hessian schools, the challenges it discussed were applicable to virtually all of the schools in the Federal Republic.

The sudden outbreak of anti-Semitic incidents in 1958 and 1959 prompted action in Hesse just as it had in West Berlin. Like his counterpart Senator Tiburtius, Hessian culture minister Ernst Schütte reacted promptly to the increasing scrutiny directed toward political education and *Zeitgeschichte* in the schools. In a 1959 directive, Schütte reinforced the importance of *Zeitgeschichte* and expanded instruction in the subject to social studies lessons in the fifth and sixth grades. In particular, Schütte demanded that these younger pupils gain a more complete understanding of the crimes of the Nazis and the anti-Semitic policies of the regime. He explained the need for this expanded instruction and intensified curriculum by noting that many of the perpetrators of the recent anti-Semitic incidents were "misguided youths." Thus, pupils as young as ten would learn about the "role of the swastika in recent German history" and study the inhuman policies of the Nazis, in particular the extermination measures directed at the Jews.[94] This action was in response to a survey of the Hessian schools—similar to the one initiated by Tiburtius in West Berlin—that illustrated shortcomings in the curriculum as well as gaps between expectations and actual classroom instruction. It is important to note that the actions of Tiburtius and Schütte were not unique. A January 1960 report of the Standing Conference of Culture Ministers (KMK) highlighted a slew of new policies enacted or pending introduction throughout the Federal Republic in response to the anti-Semitic incidents of the late 1950s.[95] The expansion and intensification of political education and *Zeitgeschichte* was indeed a common response of culture ministries throughout West Germany as the decade came to a close.

The state of *Zeitgeschichte* instruction in the postwar schools was admittedly more ambivalent than that of other reforms introduced in the postwar era. As we have seen, there were several reasons that the subject experienced only mixed success in this period. Many experienced teachers, unwilling to engage the troubling issues involved with *Zeitgeschichte*, attempted to avoid the subject. Others complained—no doubt with varying degrees of sincerity—that the scheduled curriculum did not allow adequate time to incorporate contemporary issues. Another possible explanation for the mixed results in this area may be the fact that *Zeitgeschichte* was an even more recent innovation than other postwar reforms. While the subject officially dated back to the immediate postwar period, it did not actually begin to penetrate postwar classrooms in many areas until the early to mid-1950s. This makes it a more recent addition to the curriculum than even student government or civics instruction.

Yet there were notable successes in this field as well. As the surveys of West Berlin schools indicate, pupils in many classes did study Germany's recent history and contemporary world events before completing their compulsory education. And by 1960, Culture Ministry officials throughout the Federal Republic had strengthened the curriculum in response to a spike in neo-Nazi activities. Additionally, new methods for instructing pupils in *Zeitgeschichte* entered the schools during this period. Most notably in West Berlin, radio programming complemented more traditional lessons and encouraged pupils to examine questions of citizenship, professional and social issues, and controversial topics in recent German history. In schools throughout the Federal Republic, newspapers entered postwar classrooms and became another tool for pupils to engage contemporary themes and to increase their understanding of the recent past. These experiences and innovations cemented the place of *Zeitgeschichte* in the postwar curriculum and facilitated its continued growth in the 1960s.

* * * * * *

The late 1950s marked the zenith of Adenauer's power in the Federal Republic. This was a time of conservative dominance, a period perhaps best characterized by the CDU's own slogan for the 1957 election: "No Experiments!" Despite this restorative façade and apparent commitment to the status quo, the 1950s marked an important step in the evolution of the postwar schools, especially in the realm of political education. This subject, which had been heralded by American military officials and German administrators in many areas as early as 1946, finally emerged as a discipline in its own right by 1960. This process, however, did not proceed without difficulties. The emergence of political education in the postwar schools was uneven, with many teachers embracing the subject while others avoided it. There was also uncertainty among educators and administrators as to what precisely constituted political education. Nevertheless, the actions of educators in Hesse and the former capital indicate that the new subject did solidify its place in the postwar curriculum during this era. Many educators conceived of the subject broadly and utilized a variety of methods to prepare their pupils for the responsibilities of citizenship in the democratic state. Thus the social conservatism of Adenauer and the CDU did not halt educational reforms underway since the late 1940s. Change continued beneath the surface of the restorative structure of the postwar schools.

The continuing reform of the schools in the late 1950s was only possible because it built upon changes initiated in the immediate aftermath of the war and the late 1940s. In perhaps no other area is this as clear as is it in the field of political education. First, student government expanded to all levels of schools in this era. Teachers and administrators increasingly linked SMV to learning the responsibilities of democratic citizenship.[96] Complementing the work of student government were student newspapers, which secured their place in many *Mittelschulen* and *Gymnasien* in these years. Another important aid to the expansion of political education in the late 1950s was the new generation of textbooks inaugurated at the beginning of the decade. These texts incorporated a variety of new practices and methods such as group work, discussion questions, and practical examples that facilitated the instruction of political education and prepared pupils for their future responsibilities as citizens. Finally, the study of recent history and contemporary events further reinforced the value of political education in the classroom. Despite lingering tensions regarding the subject, postwar pupils increasingly addressed Germany's troubled twentieth-century history, the crimes of the Nazis and the Holocaust, and the postwar world as the 1950s came to a close. These changes boded well for the future, as educational reform gained an even higher profile in the increasingly politicized Federal Republic of the 1960s.

Notes

1. "Preisausschreiben für Schüler, 1955," File B168, No. 282, Bundesarchiv Koblenz (BAK).
2. "Test der staatsbürgerlichen Bildung. 'Postfach 2000 Bonn' antwortet einer Million Schülern," *Das Parlament* (15 February 1956): 9.
3. R. Geil, "Abschliessender Erfahrungsbericht über das Weihnachtspreisausschreiben für Schulen," (undated, likely spring 1954), 3, File B168, No. 275, BAK.
4. Letter from Willi Bratge to Bundeszentrale für Heimatdienst, "Der unterrichtliche und erzieherliche Wert der Weihnachtspreisausschreiben der Bundeszentrale für Heimatdienst im Hinblick auf die Volksschule," (undated, likely 1956), 1, File B168, No. 282, BAK.
5. "Gutachten zur Politischen Bildung und Erziehung," 10.Protokolle, Anlage 2, 22 January 1955, 5–6, File B154, No. 67, BAK.
6. Ibid., 1.
7. Among the various names for political education in the postwar FRG were *Sozialkunde, Weltkunde, Politische Bildung, Gegenwartskunde, Bürgerkunde,* and in Bremen, the subject *Schulkreis* complemented instruction in *Gemeinschaftskunde.*
8. Politische Unterricht, BRD, 1958, B. Rep. 007, No. 36, Landesarchiv Berlin (LAB). One should note that "political education" figures used here refer to the hours dedicated to "History and Social Studies" in the West Berlin curriculum. Only in the ninth grade of the OPZ was there a separation of the two subjects, with social studies receiving two hours of class time per week independent of history instruction.
9. "Anregungen und Hinweise für Gemeinschaftskunde," Westpreussenschule (2.OPZ), Berlin-Charlottenburg, 10 December 1958, B. Rep. 015, No. 441, LAB.
10. "Anregungen und Hinweise zur Gemeinschaftskunde und politische Bildung im Rahmen des

Geschichtsunterrichts der Abschlussklassen," 10.OPZ Berlin-Reinickendorf, undated (likely December 1958), 3, B. Rep. 015, No. 441, LAB

11. Report from the Gustav-Stresemann-Schule (OTZ) Mittelschule, 24 November 1958, B. Rep. 015, No. 441, LAB.

12. "Anregungen und Hinweise für Gemeinschaftskunde und politische Bildung vornehmlich im Geschichtsunterricht der Abschlussklassen der Oberschule," Schadowschule (OWZ), Zehlendorf, 12 December 1958, B. Rep. 007, No. 36, LAB.

13. "Bericht über Politische Bildung, vornehmlich im Geschichtsunterricht der Abschlussklassen der Oberschule, Schulaufsichtsbereich Tempelhof," 30 December 1958, 13, B. Rep. 015, No. 441, LAB.

14. Johann Zilien, *Politische Bildung in Hessen von 1945 bis 1965. Gestaltung und Entwicklung der politischen Bildung als schulpolitisches Instrument der sozialen Demokratisierung* (Frankfurt, 1997), 334–38.

15. Renate Glufke, "Der Sozialkundeunterricht nach den hessischen Bildungsplänen verglichen mit den früheren Richtlinien," Schriftliche Prüfungsarbeit für die 1.Lehrerprüfung an Volks- und Mittelschulen im Lande Hessen, 1958, 13, Abt. 802, Hessisches Hauptstaatsarchiv (HHstA).

16. Zilien, *Politische Bildung in Hessen,* 253.

17. Ibid., 13.

18. "Erster Hochschulkursus für politischen Unterricht an der Johann Wolfgang Goethe Universität," 1954, Abt. 504, No. 1402, Fiche 8616, HHstA.

19. Schnürmann, "Dritter Marburger Hochschullehrgang für politische Bildung und Erziehung vom 23.September bis 8.Oktober 1957," 1–6, Abt. 504, No. 1402, Fiche 8616, HHstA.

20. Hessisches Lehrerfortbildungswerk Zweigstelle Kassel, "Jahresbericht 1956," 10 January 1957, Appendix 1, Abt. 504, No. 1402, Fiche 8614, HHstA.

21. Zilien, *Politische Bildung in Hessen,* 235–36.

22. Harald Krieger, interview by author, tape recording, Berlin-Dahlem, 7 July 2003.

23. Erich Frister, "Man sollte etwas tun für die 'Politische Bildung'," *Berliner Lehrerzeitung* 13/28, no. 13/14: 288.

24. Kurt Sauerborn, "Welche Aufgaben hat nach Ihrer Ansicht der Schüler in der Schülerverwaltung zu lösen?" 24 January 1955, 141, Abt. 429/1, No. 223–224, HHstA.

25. Eckhard Pilz, "Man hat gesagt, die Demokratie die beste und schlechteste Staatsform sein. Nehmen Sie aus Ihrem geschichtliche Wissen, Ihren Beobachtungen und Erfahrungen dazu Stellung!" 1959, 147–148, Abt. 429/1, No. 214, HHstA.

26. "Lebe anständig! 10 Jahre Berliner Schülerparlament," *Schüler-Echo* 6, no. 6, February 1958, 3, Rep. 11 "Schadowschule," Heimatmuseum Zehlendorf (HZ). See also Dietrich Otremba, "10 Jahre Schüler-Parlament," *Wir machen mit* 6, no. 2 (1 May 1958): 9.

27. "Tagesordnung der 100.Sitzung des RIAS-Schulfunk-Parlaments," 9 December 1958, B Rep. 015, No. 431, LAB.

28. Ibid.

29. "Berliner Schülerparlament. Mitteilungen der Arbeitsgemeinschaft Berliner Schülervertretungen," 15 June 1959, B. Rep. 015, No. 431, LAB.

30. Ibid.

31. "Der Hammerschläger," *Berliner Kurier,* 7 November 1957, in B. Rep. 015, No. 430, LAB.

32. See "Schülerparlament oder Ärtzekongress?" *Berliner Zeitung,* 27 October 1957, in B. Rep. 015, No. 431, LAB.

33. Heinz Wild, "Tätigkeitsbericht der Schülermitverantwortung an der Westendschule (seit Ostern Westendschule I & II) von 1954–1960," 29 June 1960, Abt. 504, No. 915, Fiche 5866, HHstA.

34. "Berliner Schülerparlament. Mitteilungen der Arbeitsgemeinschaft Berliner Schülervertretungen," 15 June 1959, B. Rep. 015, No. 431, LAB.

35. Heinrich Moos, "Welche Aufgaben hat nach Ihrer Ansicht der Schüler in der Schülerverwaltung zu lösen?" 24 January 1955, 9–10, Abt. 429/1, No. 223–224, HHstA.

36. Michael Thomas, "Erziehung zum Staatsbürger," Spring 1959, 188, Abt. 429/1, No. 215, HHstA.

37. "Zwischenbericht von der Umfrage der Berliner Schülerparlaments," June 1959, B. Rep. 015, No. 431, LAB.

38. "Unser neues Thema: Wessen Vertrauen?" *Der Funk*, no. 3, 1955, 1, in Abt. 429/5, No. 1248, HHstA. Emphasis in original.

39. Hannelore Pistorius, "Vom Sinn und Zweck der SMV," *Der Rüssel* 21, November 1957, 1, in Abt. 504, No. 628, Fiche 3746, HHstA.

40. Helmut Dill, "Zum Geleit," *disciplus* 1, July 1957, 2, in Abt. 504, No. 628, Fiche 3750, HHstA.

41. "Wettbewerb für Schülerzeitungen," Abt. 504, No. 628, Fiche 3750, HHstA

42. "Kontakte unerwünscht?" *Schüler-Echo* 5, no. 4, October 1957, 1, in Rep. 11 "Schadowschule," HZ.

43. Ibid., 2.

44. "Das Judenproblem," *Schülerzeitung der 10.Klasse der Arndt-Schule*, October 1959, in B Rep. 015, No. 451, LAB.

45. "Das Judenproblem in Deutschland 1848–1945," *Schülerzeitung der 10.Klasse der Arndt-Schule*, October 1959, in B Rep. 015, No. 451, LAB.

46. Max Reiniger, *Neue Staatsbürgerkunde I*, 2nd ed. (Langensalza, 1928), 92. It should be noted that Reiniger's book served primarily as a teacher's guide, although in some cases it also entered the classroom as a text for pupils.

47. Max Kunow, *Sozialkunde. 7.Schuljahr* (Wiesbaden, 1953), 110.

48. Zilien, *Politische Bildung in Hessen*, 27.

49. Wolfgang Hilligen, *Sehen—Beurteilen—Handeln. Lese- und Arbeitsbuch zur Politischen zur Politischen Bildung und Sozialkunde*, Teil 2, Ausgabe A, 6th ed. (Frankfurt, 1964), 148.

50. Ulrich Haacke and Benno Schneider, *Dein Staat und Dein Volk. Eine Staatsbürgerkunde* (Leipzig, 1928), 116.

51. Ibid., 123–24

52. Max Reiniger, *Neue Staatsbürgerkunde II* (Langensalza, 1923), 43–57.

53. H. Kolbe, *Vom Volksthing zur Reichsverfassung. Eine Einführung in die Entwicklung des deutschen Staats-, Wirtschafts- und Gesellschaftsleben als Grundlage staatsbürgerlicher Bildung und Erziehung* (Langensalza, 1927), 33–35.

54. Karl Nebelsiek, *Der Gemeinde-, Staats- und Weltbürger. Ein Handbuch der Bürgerkunde und Sozialkunde (Gemeinschaftskunde)*, (Oldenburg, 1951).

55. Karl Nebelsiek, *Der Gemeinde-, Staats- und Weltbürger. Ein Handbuch der Bürgerkunde und Sozialkunde (Gemeinschaftskunde)*, 2nd ed. (Oldenburg, 1953), 3–4.

56. Ibid., 271–75.

57. Ibid., 156.

58. Ibid., 243.

59. Ibid., 275.

60. Wolfgang Hilligen, *Sehen—Beurteilen—Handeln. Lese- und Arbeitsbuch zur Sozialkunde im 5. und 6.Schuljahr*, 2nd ed. (Frankfurt, 1958), 23–26.

61. Hilligen, *Sehen—Beurteilen—Handeln*, Teil 2, Ausgabe A, 6th ed. (Frankfurt, 1964), 309–10.

62. Ibid., 118.

63. Ibid., 120.

64. Ibid., 125.

65. "Lehrpläne für den politischen Unterricht in den Schulen des Landes Hessen," 21 August 1948, *Amtsblatt des Hessischen Ministeriums für Kultus und Unterricht*, vol. 1, no. 6 (October 1948): 149–70; "Richtlinien für den politischen Unterricht," 30 June 1949, *Amtsblatt des Hessischen Ministeriums für Kultus und Unterricht*, vol. 2, no. 7 (July 1949): 227–58.

66. Letter from Nicolai, Director of the Realgymnasium Aufbauschule Friedberg to Erwin Stein, Hessian culture minister, "Gemeinschaftskunde; politischer Unterricht," 4 April 1949, Abt. 504, No. 1436, Fiche 8855, HHstA.

67. Horst Möller, "Das Institut für Zeitgeschichte und die Entwicklung der Zeitgeschichtsschreibung in Deutschland," in *50 Jahre Institut für Zeitgeschichte,* ed. Horst Möller and Udo Wengst (Munich, 1999), 44.

68. Eric J. Engstrom, *"Zeitgeschichte* as Disciplinary History—On Professional Identity, Self-Reflexive Narratives, and Discipline-Building in Contemporary German History," *Tel Aviver Jahrbuch für deutsche Geschichte* 29 (2000): 399–400. See also Christoph Klessmann, *Zeitgeschichte in Deutschland nach dem Ende des Ost-West-Konflikts,* Stuttgarter Vorträge zur Zeitgeschichte, ed. Gerhard Hirschfeld, vol. 5 (Essen, 1998), 5–6.

69. See "Bildungspläne für die allgemeinbildenden Schulen im Lande Hessen, B. Das Bildungsgut der Volksschule," *Amtsblatt des Hessischen Ministers für Erziehung und Volksbildung,* vol. 10, special no. 2 (February 1957): 172–73.

70. See "Bildungspläne für die allgemeinbildenden Schulen im Lande Hessen, B. Das Bildungsgut der Mittelschule," *Amtsblatt des Hessischen Ministers für Erziehung und Volksbildung,* vol. 10, special no. 3 (March 1957): 349–50.

71. See "Bildungspläne für die allgemeinbildenden Schulen im Lande Hessen, B. Das Bildungsgut des Gymnasiums," *Amtsblatt des Hessischen Ministers für Erziehung und Volksbildung,* vol. 10, special no. 4 (March 1957): 476–81.

72. Ibid.

73. Letter from Senator für Volksbildung, Joachim Tiburtius, an die Schulaufsichtsbeamten in den Bezirken und in der Hauptverwaltung, 3 February 1961, 1, B. Rep. 015, No. 451, LAB.

74. Ibid.

75. "Meldungen der Bezirksschulämter über die Erreichung des Anschlusses an den Stoff der folgenden Klasse im Geschichtsunterricht der 8. Klasse OPZ, 9.Klasse OTZ, 9. und 12.Klasse OWZ in Schuljahr 1959/60," 27 June 1960, 4, B. Rep. 015, No. 451, LAB.

76. Letter from Senator für Volksbildung, Joachim Tiburtius, to Schulaufsichtsbeamten in den Bezirken und in der Hauptverwaltung, 3 February 1961, 1, B. Rep. 015, No. 451, LAB.

77. See appendix 50, *Denkschrift zur inneren Schulreform—langfristige Planungen* (Berlin, 1962).

78. Report of the Konrad-Hänisch-Schule (3.OPZ), Klasse 9–3, Frau Gauger, undated (likely December 1958), B. Rep. 015, No. 441, LAB.

79. Dr. J. Klingebiel, "Gemeinschaftskunde (Politik); hier in den OTZ," Berlin- Zehlendorf, 10 December 1959, 2, B. Rep. 015, No. 451, LAB.

80. "Anregungen und Hinweise für Gemeinschaftskunde und politische Bildung vornehmlich im Geschichtsunterricht der Abschlussklassen der Oberschule," Borsig-Schule, Herr Lyske, 15 December 1958, B. Rep. 007, No. 36, LAB.

81. "Anregungen und Hinweise für Gemeinschaftskunde und politische Bildung vornehmlich im Geschichtsunterricht der Abschlussklassen der Oberschule," Schadowschule (OWZ), Zehlendorf, 12 December 1958; B. Rep. 007, No. 36, LAB.

82. "Anregungen und Hinweise für Gemeinschaftskunde und politische Bildung vornehmlich im Geschichtsunterricht der Abschlussklassen der Oberschule," Arndt-Schule (OWZ), Dahlem, 13 December 1958, B. Rep. 015, No. 441, LAB.

83. For an excellent study of the role of RIAS in postwar Berlin, see Herbert Kundler, *RIAS Berlin, eine Radio-Station in einer geteilten Stadt* (Berlin, 1994).

84. "Schulfunkversuchsprogramm für Gemeinschaftskunde und politische Bildung im 9.Schuljahr 1957/58," 15 August 1958, 1, B. Rep. 210, No. 1658, LAB.

85. Ibid., 8, 11.

86. Oskar Foerster, "Anschauen—Erleben—Stellungsnehmen in der Erziehung zum Staatsbürger. Zum Berliner Schulfunk-Versuchsprogramm für politische Bildung," *Berliner Lehrerzeitung* 11(26), no. 17 (30 September 1957): 353–55.

87. Schulfunkversuchsprogramm für Gemeinschaftskunde und politische Bildung im 9.Schuljahr 1957/58," 15 August 1958, 8, B. Rep. 210, No. 1658, LAB.

88. This statistic, cited in the report, is somewhat misleading, as it refers to the number of evaluations completed in total. This means that 115 classes listened to a program on average.

89. See appendices 13 and 39, *Denkschrift zur inneren Schulreform—langfristige Planungen* (Berlin, 1962).

90. "Schulfunkversuchungsprogramm für Gemeinschaftskunde und politische Bildung im 9.Schuljahr 1957/58," 15 August 1958, 11, B. Rep. 210, No. 1658, LAB.

91. Ibid., 14.

92. "Bericht über die Erfüllung des Bildungsplanes und der im Dbl. III/57 No. 55 gegebenen Hinweise zur Gestaltung des Geschichtsunterricht in den Abschlussklassen der Oberschulen," Ernst-Schering-Schule, 16 December 1958, B. Rep. 015, No. 441, LAB.

93. Walter Görlitz, "Unglückliche Geschichtslehrer," *Hessische Allgemeine Zeitung,* 2 February 1960.

94. "Unterricht in Zeitgeschichte," 8 January 1960. Draft version. Abt. 504, No. 1031b, Fiche 6502, HHstA.

95. "Behandlung der jüngsten Vergangenheit im Geschichts- und sozialkundlichen Unterricht in den Schulen," 20 January 1960, Abt. 504, No. 1226a, Fiche 7516, HHstA. See also "Erklärung aus Anlass der antisemitischen Ausschreitungen," 30 January 1960, Abt. 504, No. 1226a, Fiche 7516, HHstA.

96. "Lebe anständig! 10 Jahre Berliner Schülerparlament," *Schüler-Echo* 6, no. 6, February 1958, 3, Rep. 11 "Schadowschule," HZ.

Chapter 4

REFORM REIGNITED

Ambitious Efforts in the New Decade, 1960–1965

*I*n a March 1961 essay written in response to the theme "Why German-American Friendship?" Margarete Meyer, a pupil in the Mittelschule Dillenburg, recounted the brief history of German postwar democracy. "Today we still find ourselves at the beginning of German democracy," she noted. "The Americans, however, who as experienced democrats have stood up for their freedom, can help us bolster and strengthen our young democracy." Nevertheless, Meyer argued, democracy could not simply be handed to the Germans, nor could the Germans depend solely on the Americans to protect the fledgling republic. She boldly claimed, "That does not mean that we would like to submit ourselves to the dependence of the Americans."[1] Germans, she asserted, must be responsible for their own democracy. They must also work with their allies to defend themselves against those who would seek to destroy it. Yet military strength alone could not protect the Federal Republic from the threat of the "eastern dictatorship." The preservation of democracy would require an appreciation of (West) German citizenship, since, as Meyer shrewdly inquired, what good was it for a citizen to protect something by force that he did not truly understand? It was thus through a recognition and acceptance of the responsibilities of citizenship, Meyer concluded, that young West Germans could best safeguard the new German democracy.

At the same time that pupils from the Hessian *Mittelschule* pondered the influence of the trans-Atlantic relationship in the Federal Republic, the recently promoted Carl-Heinz Evers was working on his own text in the former capital. In conjunction with several local educators, Evers, who became school superintendent for West Berlin in 1959 and would succeed Joachim Tiburtius as senator for education in 1963, drafted an ambitious long-term plan for reform in the schools.[2] His *Denkschrift zur inneren Schulreform* (Memorandum on Internal School Reform), presented to the city's House of Representatives in January 1962, underscored the value of political education, rejected any sort of ideological indoctrination, and encouraged the instruction of "democratic ways of life" through classroom activities.[3] Evers's text was unique in its recognition that democratic school reform could only be realized if material and organizational changes complemented curricular and pedagogical innovations. Thus, the memorandum called for smaller class sizes, new facilities, an increase in the number of teachers, the use of "modern teaching materials," and an intensification of instruction in *Zeitgeschichte*.[4] Evers envisioned his plan as "an educational model that attempts to carry out democracy."[5] Numbering more than two hundred pages (and accompanied by almost 150 pages of additional charts and tables), the memorandum represented a bold plan for the future of education in West Berlin, and by extension, the Federal Republic.[6]

These two episodes highlight the continuing process of reform underway in the West German schools as the 1960s began. They also reflect the two levels on which—more so than at any point since the end of the war—school reform operated. The first of these was that of the individual school, with pupils and teachers continuing their work with innovations such as student government, school newspapers, and political education. The reforms that sprouted in the first postwar decade evolved and intensified throughout the early 1960s. Student government in West Germany continued to expand, while at the same time accepting new responsibilities and engaging a growing variety of issues. The same is true of student newspapers, which sustained their growth in the *Gymnasien* and gradually increased their presence in the country's *Volksschulen* and *Mittelschulen*. History textbooks, too, experienced continued innovation in this period, as many reexamined twentieth-century German history with renewed vigor. Building on reforms inaugurated in the first generation of postwar texts, these books provided greater analysis of the Weimar Republic, the Third Reich, the Holocaust, and divided Germany. Finally, political education retained its position as an important, if contentious, subject area in the postwar schools. With Germany standing at the center of the Cold War battlefield, geopolitical tensions, East-West relations, and the rights and responsibilities of democratic citizenship continued to prompt discussion and debate in postwar classrooms. The study of political education, however, was not confined only to pupils. A concerted effort to prepare teachers for providing instruction in the subject resulted in the creation of several new continuing education programs for teachers throughout the Federal Republic.

The second level of reform underway in this period was at the state level. The first half of the 1960s witnessed a flurry of policymaking by school authorities and Culture Ministry officials. With the notable exception of the immediate postwar period, there had been surprisingly few major policy or curriculum revisions since 1945. This changed dramatically in the early 1960s, as West Berlin and Hesse each enacted significant pieces of educational policy that altered the very foundation of their respective school systems. In West Berlin, school authorities introduced the *Vorläufige Richtlinien für die politische Bildung an der Berliner Schule* (Interim Guidelines for Political Education in the Berlin Schools) in 1960 and the aforementioned Memorandum on Internal School Reform two years later. Arguably less sweeping in scope, important new policies also entered into the Hessian schools in this period. Culture Minister Ernst Schütte authored two directives delineating new rights for student newspapers and student government in 1964 and 1965, respectively. In the case of Hesse, these new policies have prompted at least one historian to claim that 1965 officially marked the end of the postwar period in terms of education.[7]

It is impossible to understand the motivations and goals of West German educators and school officials without considering the context in which they operated. As chapter 3 explained, a rash of anti-Semitic incidents turned the spotlight on education once again by 1960 after several years of relative calm. Calls for reform intensified throughout the first half of the 1960s, with the construction of the Berlin Wall, the Adolf Eichmann trial in Jerusalem, the "Spiegel Affair," and the public discussion of Germany's educational "catastrophe" all contributing to the renewed attention given to the schools. With the wall now dividing Berlin, officials in the western part of the city believed it was more important than ever before to promote democratic reforms in the schools. School authorities hoped to create the most dynamic, flexible, modern, pupil-centered system in West Germany. The Eichmann trial reawakened debates on how *Zeitgeschichte* and political education should be taught in the German schools. The "Spiegel Affair" prompted many to reevaluate the limits placed on the German press.[8] This debacle fostered the climate in which Hesse enacted its landmark 1964 directive granting student newspapers freedom from censorship. Finally, Georg Picht's essay series in *Christ und Welt,* although directed toward the economic implications of a school system unable to prepare qualified and competitive business leaders, placed education once again under public scrutiny.[9] These developments—and more importantly, what they revealed about German society—guaranteed that education would remain a contentious issue throughout the next decade.

Examining the state of education twenty years after the war, there can be little doubt that the Federal Republic had addressed many of the challenges dating from as far back as the empire. In fact, the events of this period suggest that education reform in West Germany had come full circle in at least two notable ways. First, whereas schools had initiated many of the first postwar reforms in response to criticisms from American officials, this new impulse for change originated entirely from German educators. They did not voice their views in order to promote some sort of Americanization; rather, they advocated reforms as a means to make the schools more compatible with their conception of the role of the school in a democratic society. Second, those Germans advocating reform were not marginalized by conservative forces as had been the case during much of the Weimar Republic. Quite the contrary, reformers engaged in debate with their critics—whether on the pages of pedagogical journals or on the floors of legislative assemblies—and rebuffed efforts to curtail the rights of pupils or to limit the content of political education or history instruction. In short, the experiences of the early 1960s underscore the great amount of change implemented since 1945. Just as importantly, they also illuminate the commitment of postwar educators and pupils to the values of the young democratic state.

Reform from Above: Culture Ministries Legislate Sweeping Change

School officials in both West Berlin and Hesse introduced a flurry of new educational policies at the dawn of the new decade. These new regulations served as a backdrop against which reform intensified in the early 1960s. The new plans enacted in West Berlin were undoubtedly the broadest in scope. Senator for Education Joachim Tiburtius's 1960 Interim Guidelines for Political Education in the Berlin Schools contained a detailed political education curriculum to be introduced in all of the city's schools. Even more sweeping was Evers's 1962 Memorandum on Internal School Reform. This document, a Social Democratic blueprint for educational change, demanded both organizational and curricular reforms. Evers deemed his recommendations to be critical to the continued democratization of the West Berlin schools. Hessian culture minister Ernst Schütte initiated several more focused policy changes in the schools during his tenure (1959–1969). Two of his most significant directives related to student government and the student press. In 1964, Schütte granted unhindered freedom of the press to Hessian student newspapers. A year later, he loosened the constraints placed on SMV by Stein's 1948 directive. Taken together, these initiatives signaled a renewed commitment to educational reform at the highest levels, which both fostered changes already underway and encouraged further innovation.

What explains the series of new educational policies introduced in this period? As we have already seen, the reforms of the occupation era were followed by a decade of relative calm in terms of bold new educational policies or directives. Change may have continued in the schools, but it was not sparked by forces from above. This is not to say that state-level school officials did not effect change in the schools, but their actions were less visible and their demands less ambitious. This changed by 1960 with the renewed attention devoted to education on the heels of a rash of anti-Semitic incidents in the Federal Republic. The Eichmann trial, the "Spiegel Affair," and Georg Picht's criticisms in *Christ und Welt* undoubtedly added fuel to educational debates already underway. In addition, the schools had undergone an infusion of new blood since the war. By this point, a young generation of teachers with only a faint memory of the Third Reich had begun entering West German classrooms.[10] Along with being younger and untainted by their actions during the war, these new teachers were also better trained to teach history and political education. Some had even participated in SMV or exchange programs during their school years. All of these factors contributed to the climate of reform that once again made education a front-page issue.

Issued in April 1960, the Interim Guidelines for Political Education in the Berlin Schools offered a detailed curriculum in political education for all West Berlin pupils. This document spelled out the major themes to be addressed in grades four through six of the *Grundschule,* as well as the OPZ, OTZ, and OWZ. Tiburtius, who at this time had been the city's education chief for almost a decade, was anything but subtle in explaining the need for these guidelines. As if to emphasize his goals, he referred to "democracy" three times in the very first sentence of the introduction. He argued that "political education in the school should awaken the will and capacity to make political decisions, to conduct oneself democratically, and to cooperate in democratic society and the democratic state."[11] The senator for education then explained that this could only be achieved through an understanding of Germany's recent history. A thorough knowledge of Nazi Germany, World War II, and the communist regimes on the eastern border of the Federal Republic was indispensable to achieving these goals. Thus in the introduction of his guidelines, Tiburtius emphasized the value of *Zeitgeschichte* in the schooling of the country's youngest citizens.

First and foremost, the Interim Guidelines outlined major themes for each grade and related topics that were also to be incorporated into lessons. In the *Grundschule,* pupils in grades four and five were required to learn about the basic responsibilities of adulthood and of life in the school, the fundamentals of work and the economy, and the institutions of the democratic state. More specifically, the guidelines recommended that pupils elect a class president and organize a school library in order to gain a greater understanding of the operation of the school. They also suggested that a class visit to the mayor and the city's administrative offices would help pupils better appreciate the mechanisms of democratic government. For the sixth grade, Tiburtius proposed that pupils learn about specific occupations, their responsibilities in the school and at home, the Basic Law and their rights and duties as citizens, and the organization of the federal system. While these concepts were rather abstract, the guidelines offered further details for how *Zeitgeschichte* could be incorporated into these lessons. For instance, in grades five and six, they advised teachers to include the Star of David and the swastika in classroom instruction regarding the state and individual rights.[12]

The guidelines concentrated the greatest attention on the political education of pupils in grades seven through nine. For the majority of pupils, this would serve as the culmination of their education before entering into occupational training. In grade seven, pupils would study the district in which they lived, the various forms of political organization (such as monarchy, dictatorship, democracy), and the basic social welfare institutions of the Federal Republic. In grade eight, political education entered more contentious territory. Among the subjects addressed in this grade were the different political parties and their platforms, significant national organizations such as unions and professional groups, the constitution of Berlin, the press and radio, and the legal rights of young citizens. The culminating grade of instruction in the OPZ emphasized both a mastery of the major institutions of political life and the practical application of pupils' knowledge toward contemporary economic, legal, and social issues, as well as national and international political topics.[13] City officials believed that these lessons would provide a sound foundation upon which young Germans could fulfill their responsibilities as knowledgeable citizens.

One of the most important innovations contained in Tiburtius's document was an unequivocal commitment to *Zeitgeschichte* instruction for all students. This meant that the inclusion of contemporary historical and political themes would concentrate on grades seven through nine of the OPZ. In the seventh grade, pupils studied the persecution of the Jews under Hitler, resistance to totalitarianism in Nazi Germany and Eastern Europe, and concentration camps. The contributions of the Weimar Republic and the crimes of the Third Reich received detailed treatment in grade eight. Of particular importance was the call for a frank discussion of Nazi extermination policies during the war. The following year, the curriculum called for pupils to engage such topics as tolerance and the reconciliation of peoples, the contributions of Jews to Germany, Nazi concentration camps, and the struggle of democracy in Germany against National Socialism and Communism.[14] These suggestions indicate two major goals on the part of Senator Tiburtius. First, city officials stressed the value of international cooperation and understanding. The United Nations, NATO, Red Cross, and European Economic Community all held a prominent place in the curriculum. Second, in response to shortcomings in history instruction illustrated by class surveys, the Interim Guidelines demanded a frank and thorough treatment of the Weimar Republic and Third Reich. It is unlikely that discussion of the Weimar Republic and the Third Reich extended to all three grades of the OPZ, as the Interim Guidelines prescribed. City officials likely envisioned the repetition of these themes in the curriculum for grades seven through nine as one way to weaken the influence of isolated educators who might seek to circumvent the new regulations.

Another indication that Tiburtius aspired to move beyond the limitations of previous political education could be found in the section entitled "Further Methodological Recommendations." In this segment devoted to pedagogical methods, he made clear that political education extended far beyond the bounds of instruction provided in *Gemeinschaftskunde* classes. The relationship between pupils and school personnel, the approaches employed in the classroom, and the exercise of discipline were just a few of the instances the report cited as contributing to the preparation of young Germans familiar with and respectful of democracy. Student government and student newspapers also received praise for helping pupils learn "how to behave democratically" (*demokratische Verhaltensweisen*) and collect democratic experiences necessary for their duties as citizens.[15] Further contributing to these goals, the report explained, were group work, *Arbeitsgemeinschaften*, and the use of nontraditional teaching materials. It is interesting to note that a decade after the end of the occupation, West Berlin education authorities found themselves praising many of the same activities and methods that had been recommended by OMGUS officials and advocating still further reform. This example illustrates more clearly than most the nativization of the reform process, as German education authorities had come to endorse the very same types of practices first advocated by their postwar American occupiers.

In addition to the growing national concerns about education at this time, local factors and personal motivations played a key role in the publication of Tiburtius's guidelines in 1960. First, they were a response to the surveys received from the city's schools that chronicled their activities in political education. There were many successes, as we have seen, but there were also a number of classes that slipped through the cracks and fell short of expectations. Second, these guidelines were an attempt to combat the lingering confusion over what should be taught in the context of *Gemeinschaftskunde,* as the course was known in the former capital. Teachers could no longer explain away their avoidance of certain topics by claiming ignorance. A third impetus was Tiburtius's realization that the schools of the Federal Republic were ripe for new initiatives. The *Rahmenplan,* issued by the Deutscher Ausschuss für das Erziehungs- und Bildungswesen (German Committee for Education and Schooling) in 1959, was a call for changes to the organization and curriculum of the West German schools.[16] It undoubtedly contributed to the rejuvenation of the reform movement in culture ministries and state assemblies throughout the Federal Republic. Finally, one cannot discount the idea that Tiburtius hoped to author a plan that could serve as a model for other states to emulate. There was the historical precedent of Berlin leading the way in terms of educational reform initiatives. Even though he belonged to the CDU, Tiburtius may have envisioned the Interim Guidelines as a means of preempting more conservative proposals that might be issued by his colleagues in the south and southwest.

More important than the city's school administration support for the new initiative was its acceptance by the teachers of West Berlin. Letters to city school authorities indicate that teachers were less interested in the theoretical concepts behind the policy than they were in its practical application. For example, the Hermann-Hesse-Schule (an OWZ located in Kreuzberg) submitted a report to city officials informing them of which themes had proven most interesting to pupils. In particular, eleventh-grade pupils expressed the greatest interest in topics that related to the individual and his relationship to the world (the constitution, rights in a democratic state, and totalitarianism). Contemporary political and social questions also attracted their attention, with such issues as parliamentary elections, the United Nations, and the European Free Trade Association atop the list. Pupils "heatedly debated" the construction of the Berlin Wall, although the report noted that they had become somewhat disinterested in the division of Germany.[17] Consistent with the desires of city officials, pupils in the Hermann-Hesse-Schule not only read about and listened to topics of contemporary political significance but also discussed and debated them as part of their class instruction.

Another important aspect of the Interim Guidelines that prompted a response from teachers and school administrators was the concept of political education as a "teaching principle" extending to various subjects. An excellent example how educators sought to integrate this concept into the classroom is provided by the

Borsig-Schule (OTZ). The school's report to city school officials detailed its plans to incorporate specific issues of political relevance into several subjects for the coming year. For the month of January 1963, the school's teachers had chosen "The Jews in the Past and Present" as the theme for political education instruction. In history classes, pupils would study the Zionist movement, the history of anti-Semitism in Europe, the persecution of the Jews in the Third Reich, and the founding of Israel after the war. Teachers of language and literature would include Jewish authors, works, and themes in their lessons, such as Gotthold Lessing's work *Nathan der Weise* (*Nathan the Wise*). In part because it personalized the experiences of Jews during the Third Reich, *The Diary of Anne Frank* became a regular assignment in the Borsig-Schule as it did in schools throughout the city. School administrators and teachers, attempting to integrate their chosen theme as a "teaching principle," also addressed the role of Jews in other subjects. Physics classes would highlight Jewish Nobel Prize winners, particularly Albert Einstein and Gustav Hertz. Music teachers would showcase the work of Jewish musicians, such as Felix Mendelssohn. Finally, geography instruction would feature Palestine and the tensions between Jews and Arabs in the Middle East.[18] Plans for March 1963 outlined a curriculum on "The Individual and the Community," in which pupils would engage with the theme in history, literature, biology, home economics, art, and geography classes.

A second document calling for even broader reform in the West Berlin schools, Carl-Heinz Evers's Memorandum on Internal School Reform, appeared two years later. Evers, West Berlin's school superintendent who would soon become the city's senator for education, built upon the proposals outlined by Tiburtius and called for even broader and more ambitious reforms. This treatise outlined an extensive list of reforms, calling for changes throughout the educational system over the next five years in regards to professional training, class sizes, facilities, curriculum, and pedagogy.[19] Evers sought to promote "inner reform," but he realized that "external" changes (that is, material, professional, and financial) were necessary for the achievement of his goals. There were several of these "external prerequisites" that he stressed in his tome. First, class sizes would have to be reduced. In the *Grundschule,* class averages of 47 were to be reduced to 40, while the goal in the OPZs, OTZs, and OWZs was to move from 41 to a more manageable 35 pupils.[20] Second, Evers called for the addition of nine hundred teachers to the city's schools over the coming five years.[21] Third, the plan proposed additional funds for the schools so that pupils could keep texts that would be of use over multiple years, such as atlases and grammar books. A fourth "external" reform demanded by Evers was the purchase of "modern teaching materials" for the school, such as wall maps, slide machines, models, film projectors, radios, and tape recorders. Finally, the memorandum underscored problems with the educational facilities in the former capital. Evers specifically highlighted the need for new furniture for classroom use, citing pedagogical and health reasons.[22] This list of organizational changes was designed to facilitate the inner reforms that Evers deemed necessary.

When it came to "inner reforms," the memorandum was less precise that it had been on "external" policies in outlining its agenda. In essence, Evers's report reaffirmed changes already underway in the schools and called for their expansion. This was certainly the case in the field of political education, which Evers believed to be a critical part of the school's educational mission. In one draft of the document, he went so far as to describe *Gemeinschaftskunde* as the equivalent of religious education in the confessional schools.[23] Although he used different language in the final version, Evers's conviction that political education stood at the center of the school's mission remained unchanged. To fulfill the tasks of political education in the West Berlin schools, Evers cited the important role of student government. The memorandum proposed that teachers and administrators continue to expand the scope of responsibilities assumed by SMV. The document also emphasized the importance of a more informal relationship between teacher and pupils predicated on respect instead of fear. Teachers also required greater preparation in the field of political education, if they were to be effective and knowledgeable in the classroom. Finally, group work received a great deal of attention as an innovative pedagogical approach that broke down traditional barriers and facilitated pupil-oriented instruction.[24]

There can be little doubt that the construction of the Berlin Wall intensified Evers's concerns about school reform. The East-West conflict and the communist challenge to democracy in the Federal Republic loom large in the memorandum, which was already being drafted when the East German regime erected the wall in August 1961. In an indirect reference to the wall itself, the report reminded readers that Berlin was no longer a place where people from both sides of Germany could meet. Consequently, Evers argued that the West Berlin school system should serve as a model and example. Echoing Adenauer's hopes that the Federal Republic would function as a magnet pulling East Germany toward the West, Evers stated that a "modern democratic school system will work as an attractive force and as an example on free and unfree people."[25] And in a rousing closing sentence, Evers employed the same sort of language used in postwar history and civics texts in positioning Germany in a larger community of democratic states: "It testifies to the will to live and to have faith in tomorrow, when Berlin takes resolute action for the future with the improvement of its school system—for our city, for our *Volk*, and for the community of free peoples to which we belong."[26] The city of West Berlin, Evers intimated, had a responsibility to democratic education that it fulfilled in the name of the Federal Republic—and indeed—the free countries of the Western world.

The aggressive young superintendent argued that the plans outlined in the memorandum were imperative for several reasons. As mentioned above, Evers envisioned Berlin as a model for the educational policies of other federal states. In comments he prepared for the House of Representatives, he stressed the fact that no other states had yet formulated such ambitious long-term policies for their educational systems. Second, Evers emphasized that the reforms embraced in his memorandum coincided with those supported by the Standing Conference of Culture Ministers (KMK). The KMK, he argued, "followed the work of Berlin with great interest and recognized the city's potential as a model."[27] Coordinated by Evers, a member of the SPD, the document also revealed that the party's educational platform resembled the proposals of the KMK and the Deutscher Ausschuss more closely than that of the CDU. Third, he argued that the schools could only succeed in their mission to prepare young democratic citizens if physical and material changes accompanied curricular and pedagogical ones. Evers made this clear, asserting that "it must be recognized that many pedagogical plans are bound up with the enactment of a host of improvements in external educational conditions."[28] Finally, Evers believed that the memorandum underscored West Berlin's commitment to democracy and Western educational values. At the same time, it encapsulated the city's resolve to stand up to the challenges of life behind the Iron Curtain and illustrated its trust in the future. Thus the memorandum was part educational blueprint, part party platform, and part anticommunist propaganda.

As could be expected, the response of the teaching profession to Evers's memorandum was largely positive. In terms of its desire to contribute to the strengthening and further democratization of the West Berlin schools, support from the city's educators was almost unanimous. Certainly, younger teachers, such as those who had collaborated on the memorandum, embraced its emphasis on political education as well as its recommendations for a less formal relationship between pupil and teacher. SPD supporters saw the document as a manifestation of the party's educational platform in its calls for the expansion of the teaching profession and the reduction of class sizes. The city's most active teachers union, the BVL, approved of most of Evers's suggestions. It commended Evers for his efforts to "intensify the work of the Berlin schools and to improve their results." Specifically, the BVL praised the proposed increase in teaching positions (10 percent over five years), the reduction in class sizes, and the addition of optional courses to the curriculum.[29] Finally, those that envisioned Berlin as an educational role model for the rest of the Federal Republic hailed the plan as a success. Frustrated that the city could not serve as the country's political capital, many conceived of Evers's recommendations as a way to help Berlin regain its position as a cultural and educational center. Furthermore, some educators envisioned the memorandum as "an expression of our confidence in the victory of the democratic way of life, as well as [a sign of] the will to live of this city, which is continually threatened by communist totalitarianism."[30] The ambitious tome indeed appealed to a wide audience upon its presentation to the public in January 1962.

In the span of just a few years, Evers's plans had already begun to recast the composition of the teaching profession in the former capital. As of May 1960, 29 percent of teachers in the OPZs were thirty-four years of age or younger. In the OTZs the figure was 17 percent, and in the OWZs it was 20 percent. Significant progress had already occurred since the end of the occupation, when only 18 percent of teachers in all schools were under the age of forty. Yet Evers's memorandum intensified this process through increasing the number of teachers in the city's schools. For example, the number of students training to enter the *Volksschulen* and *Mittelschulen* rose by 64 percent in West Berlin from 1960 to 1962, with most of these newcomers well below the average age of their future colleagues.[31] The expansion of the teaching profession also resulted in a modest increase in female educators in the city's schools. In the *Grundschulen,* the number of female educators rose 6 percent from 1960 to 1964. Likewise, women increased their presence in the West Berlin secondary schools. Their representation in the city's OPZs grew from 35 to 39 percent in the first half of the 1960s.[32] A less remarkable increase of 2 percent was recorded in the city's OTZs. Only in the OWZs did the number of female educators remain unchanged, with women constituting 40 percent of the teaching corps. Thus in less than half a decade, Evers's ambitious plans for educational reform in West Berlin had already begun to bear fruit in the form of a younger, more diverse teaching profession.

Hessian officials also introduced a number of important new educational reform policies during this period that supported postwar innovations already underway. One of the most striking decisions was the 1964 directive granting unlimited freedom of the press to student newspapers. Issued less then two years after the "Spiegel Affair," this landmark decision made Hesse the first state in the Federal Republic to grant such freedom to student publications. Culture Minister Ernst Schütte reached his decision after several pupils challenged the authority of his ministry to censor their publications. The Culture Ministry had increasingly censored student newspapers as the outbreak of anti-Semitic incidents in the late 1950s and early 1960s prompted greater coverage of social and political topics. Even though many educators and pupils believed that discussion of such events reinforced political education, it nevertheless contradicted the policies introduced by Erwin Stein after the war. The situation was finally resolved in 1964, after pupils in an Eschwege *Gymnasium* convinced the Hessian Culture Ministry to distinguish between student newspapers and school newspapers.[33] Schütte's directive did precisely that; it differentiated between a school newspaper (the official organ of the institution) and a student newspaper (an independent publication of pupils) and exempted the latter from the censorship of school authorities.[34] Hesse was the first West German state to differentiate between the two types of publications and guarantee freedom of the press to student newspapers, but its decision can be seen as a spark that ignited the gradual liberalization of policies in other areas beginning in the late 1960s.

Another Hessian education directive captured headlines one year later. Schütte's 1965 decision to loosen the restrictions placed on SMV by Stein during the occupation signaled a willingness to permit pupils greater liberties in their student government organizations. As chapter 2 indicated, Culture Minister Stein limited the scope of SMV in his 1948 directive. Unlike West Berlin, Munich, Hamburg, and Stuttgart, citywide student government parliaments were banned in Hessian cities. Thus throughout the 1950s and the first half of the 1960s, there was a lingering tension between the practical lessons for citizenship in a democracy learned through SMV and the explicitly political aspect it represented. Whereas Hesse may have been a pioneer in some aspects of education during the postwar period, student government was not one of them. In 1963, the KMK issued new guidelines on the need for consensus among administration, faculty, and pupils on the role of student government within the school. This decision, coupled with a close study of the policies of other states in regard to SMV, prompted Schütte to issue his directive, which enhanced the role and responsibilities of student government in the Hessian schools.[35]

The new rules governing student government—although not a complete renunciation of the 1948 decree—encompassed six significant policy changes. First and foremost, the directive improved the position and power of pupils elected to student government offices. They now enjoyed greater rights and responsibilities in their work in the school. Second, the 1965 decision mandated the use of parliamentary rules (such as the secret ballot) in SMV activities. Third, it permitted the creation of student government organizations that extended beyond the confines of the individual school, which constituted a significant change in policy. Fourth, the role of SMV advisor became a regular service position. This policy change was of greatest significance to teachers, since it increased the importance (as well as the prestige and compensation) of the position. Fifth, and also most meaningful to educators, was the removal of legal responsibility for SMV activities from the faculty advisor. This policy, which had made teachers financially responsible for SMV activities, had unarguably discouraged many educators from becoming involved in student government. Finally, the 1965 directive contributed to the better material outfitting of SMV, mandating that schools supply both funds and classroom space to student government organizations.[36] These policy changes constituted a liberation of SMV from the restrictions placed upon it by Stein in the late 1940s. Considered in conjunction with the student newspaper directive of a year earlier, it signaled a new era in the Hessian schools.

School administrators in West Berlin and Hesse each issued meaningful policy changes during this period that promoted continued reform. In the former capital, the plans were more sweeping, with city officials demanding more extensive instruction in political education, *Zeitgeschichte*, and history in addition to fundamental improvements in class sizes, facilities, and materials. Directives in Hesse were more focused, addressing lingering conflicts in student government and the student press. Officials in both areas sought to remedy problems and tensions exposed by political and social events of the early 1960s. Examined apart from other reforms underway in the schools, these initiatives could be dismissed as admirable but quixotic pieces of legislation issued by image-conscious administrators. Yet as we will see, these directives and guidelines reinforced changes underway in the schools and facilitated further reform. Impressive in their own right, these policy decisions take on greater importance when considered as part of a broadening commitment to educational reform in the Federal Republic.

Student Government and Student Newspapers Broaden Their Horizons

"Our school is distancing itself slowly—but in growing fashion—from the pure 'learning school' of the conservative and authoritarian style and increasingly approaching the type of 'working school' in which group work plays an essential part."[37] This required, as the pedagogue noted in his article, a redefinition of the role of pupils in the school that appropriated them greater responsibility for classroom instruction. Published on the front page of *Wir machen mit,* a national magazine devoted to student government, these words and the experiences and suggestions that followed encouraged *Volksschullehrer* to continue their work with SMV in the schools. This 1964 article also highlighted the multitude of activities in which pupils in grades one through four now engaged: operation of the class library, organizing special meals, composing plays and inviting others to attend their performance, and scheduling special athletic contests and field trips. These activities intensified in grades five through eight, with the election of school officers, monthly or biweekly meetings, monitoring responsibilities in the halls and on the playground, and the administration of school contests. Regular readers of *Wir machen mit* would also have remembered that a *Volksschule* in Lehrte (in the state of Lower Saxony) had received the 1962 prize for the best student newspaper in the FRG.[38] At the same time, renewed calls for the intensification of SMV in the *Volksschule* appeared in the *Berliner Lehrerzeitung.* It reminded the city's teachers that pupils in these schools had organized fundraisers, decorated the halls with photos representing political topics, and orchestrated field trips.[39] Developments such as these illustrate the sustained expansion of student government in the 1960s, even in the most challenging of environments.

Student government and student newspapers developed, expanded, and accepted greater responsibilities in schools of all levels in the new decade. Despite having made inroads into the *Volksschulen* during the 1950s, SMV continued to face substantial obstacles in these schools. Some limitations—such as the shorter amount of time pupils spent together in the classroom—could not be overcome. Nevertheless, student government in the West German *Volksschulen* intensified and entered into an increasing number of schools throughout the first half of the 1960s. At the same time, the student government organizations of *Mittelschulen* and *Gymnasien* engaged in a widening array of activities. They also refused to shy away from controversial political and social topics. The same held true for the student newspapers of these schools, which aggressively followed political issues while often challenging the limitations placed upon them by Culture Ministry officials or school administrators. Although new state-level educational policies fostered an environment of reform, they were not the key factor in the growth of SMV and student government during this period. The impulse for change—as had been the case throughout much of the postwar period—originated among teachers, administrators, and pupils interested in revitalizing the West German schools.

A 1960 survey conducted by the Berlin Student Parliament (BSP) and targeted at the *Gymnasien* of West Germany provided evidence that SMV had established deep roots and that pupils had assumed a variety of important responsibilities in these institutions. Arguably the most important role of student government was its involvement in the political education of pupils. Although the twenty-nine teenage representatives who participated in the survey indicated varying experiences with classroom instruction in the subject, three-quarters reported the existence of *Arbeitsgemeinschaften* dedicated to political and social issues in their schools.[40] Themes which had garnered the attention of pupils included: East-West relations, the Weimar Republic, the Third Reich, and perhaps most intriguingly, "coming to terms with the past and present." In conjunction with these groups, pupils had organized a host of activities such as film showings, trips to concentration camps, weekend meetings on political topics, and schoolwide discussions devoted to political problems.[41] Also related to political education was the creation of partnerships between West German pupils and their counterparts abroad. More than two-thirds of the survey's respondents reported some form of international partnership between their school and a foreign institution. Their replies revealed a diverse map of international relations, with West German *Gymnasien* reporting connections with six American schools, five French, four British, three American institutions in Germany, one Japanese, and one class in Israel.[42] The impressive level of participation in foreign partnerships by the survey's respondents—19 of 27 schools—exemplifies a broader interest among West German pupils in communicating with peers abroad. Furthermore, these activities illustrate the extent of other innovations in the postwar schools. The fact that student government organized or led these initiatives in the majority of cases suggests that SMV had assumed a more active role in the lives of pupils in the *Gymnasien* of the Federal Republic.

Another important issue addressed by the 1960 survey was the prevalence of student newspapers in the postwar schools. All but one school reported having a newspaper, with two respondents explaining that their institutions participated in a citywide publication (in Mainz and Bremerhaven). Significantly, the survey revealed that on the whole, pupils and their faculty advisors enjoyed good relationships. In only two cases was the participation of a teacher rejected by the staff of a paper. The relationship between the newspaper and SMV differed in the schools surveyed for the report. In some, the paper was the official organ of student government, while others reported that the two were separate. Regardless of the relationship, there were several areas in which the two organizations typically collaborated: financial partnership, participation of the editor in SMV sittings, attendance of the school president at editorial meetings, and a certain amount of space in each publication dedicated to student government activities.[43] Student newspapers worked in association with student government to publish "interesting topics for discussion [and] the publication of provocative pieces that elicited opposition."[44] These results indicate that student newspapers had established a secure place in the *Gymnasium* and contributed to the engagement of pupils with important, contemporary issues.

Further illustrating the continued expansion of student government and its activities during this period is the Berlin Student Parliament. The 1961–62 school
year had been a tumultuous one for the BSP, due to both internal and external
developments. In July, the parliament refused to confirm the appointment of the
three copresidents, thus forcing them to step down. One month later, the BSP
responded to the construction of the Berlin Wall with a special session in which
it passed a resolution denouncing the separation of the city. These troubling
events notwithstanding, the BSP could still claim several noteworthy achievements in its year-end report. In May 1961, representatives of the BSP traveled to
the national SMV conference and took part in discussions with colleagues from
throughout West Germany about the place of student government in the schools.
To observe the anniversary of the 17 June 1953 uprising, eighty BSP members
visited the Hamburg Student Parliament and spoke about their organization and
everyday life in the former capital. For Christmas, the parliament collected over
DM 1,600 for charity and organized a holiday party for senior citizens. The
highlight of the year's activities, however, occurred on 25 November 1961.[45] At
an evening reception at the Free University, the leadership of the BSP accepted
the Friedrich-von-Schiller Prize, awarded for the pupils' efforts in working for
German reunification. In the closing lines of the annual report, BSP copresident
Norbert Meisner asserted that even more important than these events was "the
steadiness of the work of the BSP and, moreover, the SMV work in the schools.
It is truly this work that confers legitimacy to our student parliament with its
democratic construction."[46]

One of the main tasks of the BSP, as its members often noted, was to assist in
the education of the city's pupils. An April 1962 meeting between members of
the parliament and its committee of teacher advisors underscores the nature of
the BSP's efforts in this area. Committed to the political education of pupils in
the West Berlin schools, a subcommittee of the parliament outlined its plan for
the coming school year. First, the group of twenty parliament members reiterated its support for the creation of political education *Arbeitsgemeinschaften* in all
schools. To assist in this process, the BSP planned to survey those schools with
such organizations, publish a report on their findings, and partner established
groups with others attempting to found such organizations. Second, in conjunction with the city's student press, the BSP resolved to publish a commemorative
newspaper on the first anniversary of the construction of the Berlin Wall. This
paper, to be distributed to schools throughout the Federal Republic, would contribute to instruction in contemporary political education while at the same time
furthering relations between the BSP and the schools of West Germany. Finally,
the committee discussed several additional activities designed to improve political education, including collaborative projects with student government groups
from other cities and exchanges with schools throughout West Germany.[47] This
meeting highlights the various activities of the BSP and its role in the political
education of postwar pupils. It also illustrates the wider participation of the BSP
in the instruction of pupils throughout the Federal Republic. A more subtle sig-

nificance can be found in the organization of the meeting itself. The presence of teachers at the meeting underscores the collaborative nature of these activities. This partnership between teachers and the young parliamentarians made the ambitious plans of the BSP more attainable and may have further legitimized them in the eyes of more skeptical educators.

Remarkable though the activities of the BSP were, the expansion of SMV in the *Volksschulen* is arguably the most notable development in the field of SMV during this period. As noted above, many of the activities and responsibilities of student government in the *Gymnasien* and *Mittelschulen* had gradually begun to appear in the upper grades of the *Volksschulen* as the 1950s came to a close. The expansion of SMV in these schools intensified in the 1960s, however, with West German educators recognizing the educational value of student government in their classroom instruction. One indication of this blossoming support for SMV in the *Volksschule* is found in the proceedings of the 1963 national conference on student government held in Kaiserslautern. In a workshop dedicated to the SMV in the *Volks-, Mittel-,* and *Berufsschulen,* teachers discussed the capabilities of younger pupils to learn the lessons of citizenship and responsibility from student government.[48] Summarizing the group's conclusions, participating educators explained that it was no longer reasonable to assume that these pupils lacked the maturity and sense of responsibility necessary for SMV. Introducing student government to pupils at an early age was important, they added, because "this will make later involvement in SMV easier and more fruitful, because the growing pupil will already be familiar with [this process]."[49] Decorating the classroom, orchestrating school events, assembling care packages for people in East Germany, and assisting even younger pupils with similar activities were all appropriate activities for those in the elementary schools. Many teachers concluded that through such tasks, even the youngest pupils could acquire a sense of responsibility and an understanding of their role in the community.

An impressive example of the integration of student government outside the *Gymnasium* comes from the 12.Grundschule in Borsigwalde (Berlin-Reinickendorf). In a 1964 report sent to the West Berlin senator for education, a teacher from the school explained how SMV complemented political education beginning in the first four grades. Those involved in SMV encountered both external and internal aspects of democracy. Pupils in these grades gained first-hand experience with agendas, bills, and the rules of order. Likewise, they participated in a wide array of activities designed to sharpen their sense of responsibility. Among those cited by the school's teacher in the report sent to city officials were coadministration of the school library and sports equipment, organization of school contests, participation in supervisory roles in the classroom, and volunteer projects related to improving the community. Just as important as the enlarged sense of responsibility gained from involvement in SMV were broader lessons regarding how a citizen acted and behaved in a democratic society. Learning to express and defend their beliefs, working with classmates, listening to dissenting opinions, voicing criticism, and being tolerant of others were all behavioral practices that participation in student government offered to even those pupils in grades one through six.[50] These explicit and implicit lessons reinforced the *Gemeinschaftskunde* curriculum and crystallized many of the abstract goals teachers and administrators assigned to the young discipline.

As impressive as the benefits of SMV were, they were not universal. Not all pupils could—or would—participate in the organization. Yet, as the teachers of the 12.Grundschule in Borsigwalde asserted in their report, the educational rewards offered by student government could be distributed to all pupils in the classroom. Referendums were common during instruction in order to make decisions regarding sports activities, assignments, and field trip destinations. The purpose of this, the report explained, was to provide pupils with an understanding of how elections worked, as well as an appreciation for majorities, minorities, victory, and defeat. For larger decisions, such as student government elections, the class engaged in abbreviated campaigns prior to voting. These activities prepared pupils for future encounters with advertisements and propaganda. The report added that pupils also benefited from these activities through learning to exercise a critical attitude toward political events and defending their personal opinions.[51] Naturally, these activities could not be as advanced as those employed in the upper grades. The topics addressed nevertheless exhibited a commitment to student government and, at the same time, a desire to instill the values of citizenship in pupils through active classroom participation.

The report of the 12.Grundschule in Borsigwalde raises an important point regarding participation in student government activities. Naturally, all pupils did not become involved directly in SMV. In order to gauge the involvement of pupils in student government, it is useful to conceive of a spectrum consisting of several gradations of participation. This is particularly helpful in considering the impact of SMV in the late 1950s and early 1960s, as it expanded deeper into the *Volksschulen*. Those most involved in student government undoubtedly constituted a small minority of postwar pupils. These "leaders" typically held top positions in citywide student parliaments and school councils. Below those most involved in SMV was a larger group of that could be termed "active participants." These pupils authored stories for student newspapers, served as class presidents in school councils, and represented their institutions in citywide organizations. A much larger section of the pupil population could be characterized as "tolerant observers" of student government. These young people might have read the paper, voted in school elections, attended SMV-sponsored activities, and complained to their representatives when they had a problem. A final segment of pupils, smaller in number but not insignificant, could be considered "apathetic bystanders." This group was disinterested in student government and avoided involvement in its activities.

The fact that only a limited number of pupils can be considered to have been the most actively involved in student government does not diminish its important role in postwar school reform. As in the case of the 12.Grundschule in Borsigwalde, the activities of those who might be considered "leaders" and "active participants" created an environment in which others benefited. This democ-ratizing participatory minority organized class and school functions, published newspapers, and expressed the views of their fellow pupils in parliamentary meet-ings. They also worked to improve relations between administrators and pupils. Their participation in the life of the school helped ensure that teachers did not retain their traditional unquestioned place of authority in the classroom. SMV activities might have been planned and executed by a small minority, but their effects disseminated among virtually all young Germans enrolled in the postwar schools. Pupils uninterested in standing for office nevertheless had the chance to read campaign posters, hear debates, vote, and remain informed of SMV proj-ects. Those who would never submit a story to the school newspaper still had the opportunity to read news relevant to their interests, engage the opinions of their classmates, and draw conclusions based on their own analysis.

Student government had made considerable progress at all levels of schools by this period, but it nevertheless continued to face a number of challenges. Argu-ably the most significant difficulty was a sense of indifference toward SMV and its activities on the part of some pupils. For example, a 1964 survey conducted among sixty pupils in a *Gymnasium* in the southern German town of Calw (in the state of Baden-Württemberg) revealed that many were unfamiliar with the responsibilities of SMV. Almost a third of those polled believed that student gov-ernment was for "elites." Less than 40 percent were willing to become involved in the school's SMV. Only 60 percent claimed to be pleased with their student government, yet there were virtually no suggestions for improvement. This pas-sivity on the part of many pupils frustrated those involved in the school's SMV, including the editors of the school's student newspaper, *Der Weisheitszahn:*

> On the one hand, pupils are—perhaps rightly—entitled to have a truly poor opinion of SMV. Many blame school administrators and teachers for an overly authoritarian system. On the other hand, they [pupils] do not feel compelled to improve the SMV they criticize. It is really unimportant to them, and apparently they do not have the desire for a better SMV for the most part.[52]

The author closed his article with feigned satisfaction. "Everyone for himself. To an insignificant student body, an insignificant student government."[53] As had been the case for years, those pupils active in SMV lamented the fact that they re-ceived criticism from counterparts who were unwilling to contribute themselves. The broader impact of this participatory minority's actions on pupils who were less involved was not always immediately visible, particularly to those who were most invested in the process.

Another challenge with which SMV still grappled in the early 1960s was the role of faculty advisors. While most advisors sought to find a balance between ad-vising and directing pupils, not all were successful. Whether due to benevolence or hostility, some advisors overreached their bounds and became the driving force behind the activities of SMV in some schools. As a result, pupils involved in some student government organizations were no longer able to represent faithfully the interests and ideas of their classmates. Predictably, such advisors often elicited the hostility of pupils who saw SMV as a puppet of school officials. One such example comes from the Carl-Zeiss-Schule (OTZ) in West Berlin. In a scathing article in the school newspaper, the publication's editor Bernd Zanke criticized the school's SMV on the occasion of a new advisor taking responsibility for the organization.[54] Because of the close relationship between the advisor and school president, he claimed, the rest of the pupils involved in SMV were marginalized. Thus, Zanke argued, it should have been little surprise that no one volunteered to run for office in the recent elections. Only due to the prodding of the school's teachers had three candidates agreed to run. Since the leadership of student government consisted of three copresidents, this meant that there was simply a referendum on the three pupils instead of an actual election. Whether Zanke was a disgruntled former SMV member with an axe to grind, an investigative journalist looking to make a splash, or just a typical frustrated pupil is unclear. What his article does indicate, however, is that at least in some schools, the overinvolvement of advisors—for whatever reason—alienated some pupils from student government.

With the continued growth of student newspapers throughout this period, new challenges arose as they increasingly turned their attention to larger social and political topics. Perhaps the most pressing issue was the question of censorship. The national SMV publication *Wir machen mit* reveals that pupils were not of one mind in how to respond to pressure exerted on them from above. In an ongoing forum dedicated to precisely this question of the freedom of the press, pupils expressed a variety of opinions. For example, Hartmut Brinkmann, a staff member of *Diagonale*, a school paper in Wolfsburg, advocated a system of self-censorship.[55] If student journalists were cautious about what they printed, there would be no need for teachers and administrators to extend their reach beyond traditional advisory duties. Brinkmann conceived of this "self-control" as an extension of the growing responsibilities pupils accepted in the school. Published alongside Brinkmann's opinion was a report on a forum held in Lower Saxony on the question of student press censorship. An Oldenburg pupil reported that the conference—made up of student newspaper editors, a faculty advisor, members of the Lower Saxony "Friends of SMV," and a publishing house chief from Bremerhaven—had advocated the extension of the freedom of the press to school newspapers.[56] As long as newspapers published the truth, the group concluded, there was no need to belabor the question of censorship. Posing a clear challenge to the position of the chancellor, the pupil who authored the article asserted that "if freedom of the press is not misused, then Adenauer's claim that 'the press is much too critical' is invalid, because criticism becomes a responsibility that gives the press power. All of these laws apply to a student newspaper exactly as they do to the 'big press.'"[57]

While these debates indicate that there was a lack of unanimity on the question of censorship, they do underscore a number of broader trends. First, in the spirit of the political instruction they received, these pupils engaged in debate and discussion about contemporary political and social issues. Second, they questioned authority and challenged the policies and actions of leaders in their school, state, and nation. Finally, the sentiments of pupils (and many adults) that student newspapers should enjoy the same liberties as the conventional press were slowly coalescing into a small protest movement. It is due in part to this rising tide of opinion that Hessian officials would grant freedom of the press to Hessian student publications a few years later. Thus, these debates offer additional evidence of the educational value of the student press for imparting self-reliance, critical thinking, a tolerance for other opinions, and a willingness to challenge limitations created by external authorities.

Questions of censorship aside, student publications became increasingly common throughout all of the West German schools during this period. The reports of the individual schools to Senator Tiburtius's query on the state of political education in West Berlin suggest that many OPZs and OTZs had founded newspapers by 1961. These may not have been as regular or as substantial as those published in the OWZs, but the educational benefits of producing the paper were no less significant. One factor in the emergence of the student press in the OPZs and OTZs during this period was the explicit recognition of the educational value of such publications in major policy initiatives. In the former capital, both Tiburtius and Evers advocated student newspapers as an educational tool for political education. A second factor was the increasing interest of pupils in both broader social and political issues and in expressing their ideas in print. This is arguably a result of the increased political education pupils received in the classroom as the 1950s came to a close. Finally, by the early 1960s, increasing numbers of young teachers entered into postwar classrooms. These educators were much more willing to employ new methods, and some had even had personal experiences with student newspapers from their school days. Thus, there were a variety of factors that influenced the development of the student press during this period, with initiatives at the local level reinforced by policy issued by governmental authorities.

The expansion of the student press beyond the *Gymnasien* in Hesse can be attributed to many of the same reasons. In addition to the factors ascribed to West Berlin, two notable developments assisted the spread of student newspapers along the Rhine. As mentioned above, the establishment of a statewide contest in 1957 helped solidify a place for student newspapers in all schools. The legitimization of such publications through this contest facilitated the development of the student press in *Volksschulen* and *Mittelschulen*. Further reinforcing this trend was the Junge Presse Hessen, an organization consisting of interested pupils, teachers, and other community members that assisted the student press. This group conducted conferences, held seminars, and distributed copies of student publications throughout Hesse. Their work aided the activities of motivated pupils and teachers in schools of all levels. The clear endorsement of the Culture Ministry through contests and legislation, the financial and instructional assistance of the Junge Presse, and the growth of student government in the schools all contributed to the development of student newspapers in the *Volksschulen* and *Mittelschulen* of

Hesse. Although they were not without their problems, student publications in the Hessian schools enjoyed the same level of growth as their counterparts in the former capital during the early 1960s. The sustained development of student publications in West Berlin and Hesse underscored the continuing process of curricular reform underway in the schools as well as the emphasis placed on practical experience.

History Textbooks Reexamine Germany's Traumatic Twentieth Century

The testimony of Auschwitz commandant Rudolf Höss at the Nuremberg Trials must have shocked the pupils in the *Realschulen* and *Mittelschulen* who encountered it in their new history textbook. In a three-page section entitled "Organized Mass Murder," these ninth and tenth graders read the infamous 1941 Hitler order legitimizing murder and pillage in the Soviet Union, learned of Zyklon B and its use in the gas chambers, and saw pictures of the emaciated bodies of prisoners discovered by British troops at Bergen-Belsen.[58] Most striking, however, were the words of Höss, which revealed how Jews were unloaded from transports, robbed, dehumanized, and then led off to their deaths. Pupils reading the text were likely stunned by Höss's cold detachment in describing the systematic murder of prisoners in the gas chambers. "After twenty-eight minutes, there were a few who were still alive. Finally, after thirty-two minutes, everyone was dead."[59] Whereas the crimes of the Third Reich had, in most cases, been neatly packed away or treated only indirectly throughout most of the 1950s, textbooks appearing in the schools around 1960 engaged even the most horrific actions of the Nazi era. Refusing to turn a blind eye to the more disturbing or contentious topics of the past century, the frank treatment of Germany's development before and after 1945 in these textbooks contributed to the broader political education curriculum of the postwar era.

Most teachers and administrators believed that a straightforward treatment of Germany's tumultuous twentieth century was a necessity for the education of West Germany's youngest citizens. The textbooks of the early 1950s constituted a first step in this direction, as postwar authors constructed a new trajectory of German history as a long-standing struggle for liberty and democracy.[60] These books integrated new sources and techniques into their pages in an attempt to dissolve the traditional authoritarian classroom relationship between teacher and pupil. Some broached the most troubling events of the recent past, such as Nazism, war, and the Holocaust.[61] Yet the majority of texts published in the early 1950s marginalized or obscured the most controversial and complicated aspects of Germany's twentieth-century development.[62] If a limited number of new history texts published in the first postwar decade constituted a step in the right direction, the silences of others underscored the fact that an honest engagement with all aspects of Germany's recent experiences required more time.

A number of developments contributed to the new history textbooks published in the early 1960s. Perhaps most important was the renewed emphasis on political education at the dawn of the new decade. In particular, new guidelines published by the KMK in 1959 and 1960 refocused attention on the instruction of *Zeitgeschichte* in the classroom. The committee's report on the treatment of the recent past in history and political education courses once again raised questions about how to address Germany's troubled twentieth century.[63] A second, related development was a reinvigorated public discussion of the recent past and how it was taught in the schools. Articles published in both pedagogical journals and the general press underscore the prevalence of these concerns among the population. A third factor encouraging a new attitude toward the teaching of Germany's recent history was the influx of younger educators into the profession at this time. As we have already seen, a concerted effort to increase the number of teachers in the schools during this period complemented the natural renewal of the profession through retirement. These gradual processes of professional renewal, curricular reevaluation, and social awakening finally began to produce tangible results a decade after the occupation had come to a close.

The history textbooks of the early 1960s nicely illustrate the continuing reform underway in the history curriculum of the West German schools. First, they perpetuated innovations initiated in the books of the early 1950s through their use of discussion questions, incorporation of primary sources, and increasing attention to social history. Second, history texts published in this period made a sincere effort to engage the most troubling issues of the German twentieth century, specifically the Weimar Republic, Third Reich, Holocaust, and division of Germany. Third, these books represented an attempt to prepare a new generation of Germans for their responsibilities as citizens—not just of a young democratic state, but of a world facing enormous political, social, and economic challenges. Through a detailed examination of international cooperation, decolonization and Third World development, and the divisions caused by the Cold War, pupils learned about their duties in relation to their countrymen in East and West as well as to their fellow human beings around the globe. Taken together, these reforms constituted another concerted effort on the part of the West German schools to instill in pupils an understanding of democracy, a willingness to accept their responsibilities as citizens, and an awareness of how the events of the past affected their lives in the present.

In order to examine how they conveyed these critical lessons, this section will concentrate on two major history texts published during this period and used throughout the Federal Republic. The first of these is Hans Heumann's 1961 text *Unser Weg durch die Geschichte* (*Our Path Through History*).[64] The other text is the final volume of Hans Ebeling's *Die Reise in die Vergangenheit* (*A Journey Into the Past*) reprinted in 1964.[65] This book belonged to a new collection published as a successor to Ebeling's celebrated *Deutsche Geschichte* series, which had first entered the schools in the early 1950s. These two examples provide a window into the history instruction of pupils in the eighth through tenth grades in all three levels of schools—the *Volksschule* (or *Hauptschule*), the *Mittelschule* (or *Realschule*) and the *Gymnasium*. Likewise, they permit one to make generalizations on the teaching of history, since these books were used in schools throughout West Germany. Focusing on select examples from these texts that address the Weimar Republic, Third Reich, and postwar world allows one to trace the development of reforms in the postwar history curriculum.

Published in 1961, Heumann's *Unser Weg durch die Geschichte* incorporates several postwar pedagogical reforms in its design and presentation of material. The book included maps, charts, and photos that reinforced content presented in the text as a means to engage the young reader. Like its predecessors, this volume also utilized review questions as a means to stimulate critical analysis on the part of pupils. For example, a section examining the construction of the Nazi state asked them to list the basic rights of citizenship that Hitler had denigrated based upon their knowledge of the Basic Law. The questions that followed required pupils to discuss the responsibilities of the press and political parties in a democratic state.[66] Another indication that this book reflected the proliferation of reforms ushered into textbooks following the war was the inclusion of several challenging primary sources in its pages. Returning to the book's treatment of the crimes of the Third Reich, Heumann provided a passage from Eugen Kogon's *SS-State*.[67] This served as first-hand testimony in regard to the horror and suffering experienced by Jews, political prisoners, and others behind the gates of Nazi concentration camps. Additionally, the book allowed pupils to read passages from *Mein Kampf,* Hitler's speeches and private correspondence, and tellingly, local administrative reports detailing the suffering of civilians in German cities following Allied bombing raids. This final source underscores the interest of this volume in departing from the traditional political narrative of German history texts. Placing the stylized symbol of a family in the margins of the book as a way of denoting social history passages, Heumann examined such topics as the plight of workers and artisans during the inflation of the 1920s, the wartime hardships experienced on the home front, and expellees from the East after 1945.

The emphasis on such sources, methods, and themes in *Unser Weg durch die Geschichte* facilitated the book's direct engagement with Germany's troubling twentieth-century history. Heumann's book integrated passages from the Nuremberg Laws and photos of Jews wearing the Star of David in order to explain the Nazis' persecution of Jews to younger readers. The goal of this volume, however, was more than just instilling factual knowledge in the eighth- and ninth-grade pupils who read the text. Heumann's book endeavored to connect Germany's troubling past to its democratic present. In a passage that nicely highlights the interrelatedness of contemporary history and the lessons of democratic citizenship, the book prompted pupils to consider the enormity of the crimes committed against the Jews and then reconcile them with the laws of the postwar democratic state.[68] The questions that followed required pupils to continue thinking about anti-Semitism and the Third Reich and their contemporary meaning for West Germany, including the basis of the Church's resistance to the Nazis and the legal proceedings against former concentration camp guards and officials. Even more poignant was the concluding question, which prompted pupils to consider how the appearance of swastika graffiti in 1960 had damaged West Germany's image among its neighbors and what they might be able to do about it.[69] Just as important as becoming familiar with the dark years of the Third Reich was investigating the Nazi legacy and its lasting impact on the Federal Republic.

Turning to the postwar period, Heumann's book emphasized the need for young Germans to contemplate their future responsibilities on the international stage. The most prominent of these themes was the movement toward European integration. From the destruction of the war had emerged a new movement toward European unity, one which its architects hoped would prevent such horrible conflagrations in the future. While the fathers of European cooperation were politicians from another era, this 1961 text underscored the vital role that young people would play in the coming decades:

> We hope that the economic unification of Europe will also promote its political unification. According to a good quote from a European youth meeting: "Germany is our motherland, but Europe must become our fatherland."... Europe's young people must discover one another. That is the best foundation upon which statesmen can gradually realize the economic and political unification of Europe.[70]

Only the active participation of Germany's youth—and indeed the young people of all European countries—could ensure a peaceful future for the continent. Reiterating this point were two photos depicting the dramatic change in Franco-German relations in the past century. The first picture showed German troops besieging the French at Sedan in 1870. Directly below this was a contemporary photo of young French and German soldiers smiling, shaking hands, and exchanging gifts as they traveled by train to a joint military exercise. Treaties might forge closer economic unity, but it would require a much deeper change in thinking among European youth in order to accomplish the complicated process of true political and social integration.

Another widely used textbook in this period was Hans Ebeling's *Die Reise in die Vergangenheit*. Ebeling, who had already established himself as a leading textbook author by virtue of his multivolume series for elementary and secondary schools published a decade earlier, envisioned this project as an updated and expanded European survey for West German pupils.[71] Perhaps better than any other text of the period, the final book of his series (volume 4, entitled *Our Era of Revolutions and World Wars*) encapsulates the reforms in method and content that became the benchmark for books during this period.[72] Originally published in the late 1950s, the 1964 revised edition contained extensive coverage of the persecution of the Jews during the Third Reich and a more nuanced examination of the Nazi state that assigned responsibility to more than just one man. Also noteworthy is Ebeling's attention to the successes of the Weimar Republic. Moving beyond the oft-repeated refrain of a flawed democracy that died an unceremonious death, his text highlighted important advances achieved in Germany's first republic, including women's suffrage, the enshrinement of constitutional liberties, brief economic stability, and the creation of a common *Grundschule* for all elementary pupils regardless of wealth or status. Further reinforcing these innovations was Ebeling's incorporation of primary sources, allowing pupils to read historical records and draw their own conclusions. He included not only speeches and writings but also unemployment figures, inflation statistics, and election results in his analysis. Ebeling's textbook illustrates how far history instruction in Germany had evolved since the ban on history instruction imposed by OMGUS had been lifted in the last years of the occupation.

Undaunted by the contentious nature of Germany's recent history, *Die Reise in die Vergangenheit* directly examined the origins of National Socialism and World War II. Perhaps even more controversial was Ebeling's treatment of the Holocaust and the role of the German population in the murder of Europe's Jews. He recognized the need to deal explicitly with the Holocaust, particularly in light of the unwillingness of many older Germans to discuss it. In a cautious evaluation that must have preempted the questions of many pupils, Ebeling explained that

> most German citizens had heard here and there of the existence of concentration camps and other things. Only a few, however, could imagine the things that went on in them, since every watchman and released prisoner was bound to the strictest silence. Few German citizens realized the extent of the mass extermination. The shocking extent of the crimes was only revealed at the end of the lost war. And on the other side, foreign countries could not understand how Germans allegedly could not know anything about them! Even today there are many who do not want to know anything about these crimes. *But it is folly and cowardice to close oneself off from the truth.*[73]

The sentences that followed encouraged pupils to visit memorials, graves, or buildings commemorating these horrible crimes and to "keep these memories alive." Like other history texts of this period, Ebeling addressed not only the troubling events of the past but also their contemporary relevance. Just as important as pupils knowing about recent history was their recognition of how the past influenced their current responsibilities as Germans, Europeans, and human beings.

In an effort to reinforce political education instruction, Ebeling's volume incorporated many themes regarding citizenship and responsibility. This decision was likely sparked by continuing debates among educators regarding how political education should be integrated into the curriculum. In addition to the moral lessons that should be drawn from the Holocaust and Third Reich, pupils encountered a variety of political and social themes in the lengthy postwar section of the book. In regards to the construction of the Federal Republic, Ebeling reminded pupils of the duties given to them by the Basic Law. Even as young citizens, postwar pupils were obliged to "shape the Federal Republic into a true democratic and social constitutional state; to achieve the reunification of the *Volk* in freedom; and to always remain an upright member of the great community of nations of the world."[74] Pupils did not just read the constitution; they instead learned how its words should guide their actions as citizens. This marked a dramatic shift from the books of the Weimar period by attaching practical significance to a document that must have struck many pupils as distant and unrelated to their lives.

The greatest strength of Ebeling's text was undoubtedly his use of primary sources in constructing his narrative. As a tool to display the suffering endured by people interned by the Germans during World War II, Ebeling reprinted passages from the diary of Erich Moen. A young Norwegian, Moen was imprisoned in February 1944 for distributing an underground newspaper in his homeland. His diary conveyed to pupils the daily suffering prisoners endured, as well as the fear, hatred, and anxiety that often consumed them during their imprisonment.[75] Ebeling also utilized primary sources to explore the construction of the Nazi state. His text included passages from the Enabling Act, the Nuremberg Laws of 1935, the Hitler Youth Law, and Hitler's public addresses. In an innovative section that compared "Speeches and Affirmations" with "Orders and Deeds," Ebeling poignantly juxtaposed Hitler's peaceful rhetoric with personal correspondence and military orders that exposed his goals of rearmament, expansion, and conquest.[76] Finally, Ebeling's text used the words of those who fled from East Germany to the Federal Republic to convey the everyday hardships of the postwar division. In a particularly moving section, pupils read the story of a family who exited the GDR via the S-Bahn in Berlin. The mother and children made it through, but the father, a farmer, was pulled out of the train at Friedrichstrasse and arrested. This harrowing experience and the suffering it caused for the family made the political division immediate and tangible even for the youngest readers.[77]

As a final means to document the extent of changes ushered into history texts during this period, one can compare revised editions of the same text from the late 1950s and early 1960s. The transformation of two history readers designed for pupils in the *Volksschule* elucidates the efforts of authors and publishers to engage the most troubling aspects of modern German history. These examples highlight the process of reevaluation underway in the early 1960s regarding how younger pupils in the *Volksschule*, particularly those in the fifth through seventh grades, should learn about the Holocaust. The first of these comes from a series of short history texts entitled *Trögels Lesehefte* (*Trögels Reading Exercises*). Volume 12 of the series, titled *Hitler and the Second World War*, exposed pupils to the excesses of the Third Reich, the course of the war, and its effects on German society.[78] Published in 1958, the second edition of this text offered only cursory comments on the experiences of Jews in Nazi-dominated Europe, noting that there were boycotts of Jewish-owned businesses and concentration camps constructed to imprison them. The book, however, provided no discussion of the extermination of the Jews nor did it examine their daily life in Nazi Germany. Much more disturbing was the fact that the detailed chart of World War II casualties included as an appendix did not include European Jews who lost their lives. This sanitized portrait of the Jews' experiences during the Third Reich changed dramatically in the third edition published in 1960. Pupils reading this new edition encountered an entirely new four-page section entitled "The Jews Are Cruelly Persecuted."[79] In this section, the author described the sufferings of Anne Frank to the young pupils. He emphasized the fact that she was a young German girl, no different from many of them.[80] Following the experiences of Anne Frank, the text moved on to a description of the concentration camps provided by a former SS guard, Kurt Gerstein. The use of his actual letters detailing the use of gas chambers may have shocked some pupils, but at the same time, such sources offered an honest, if brutal, glimpse into the reality of the camps.[81] Finally, the appendix at the end of the book took into account the murder of Europe's Jews, informing readers that over 5.5 million of them had perished during the war.

Another historical reader representing this dramatic change in how textbooks exposed younger readers to the horrors of the Holocaust comes from the widely used history reader *Einst und Jetzt* (*Then and Now*). The third edition of the book, which appeared in 1956, presented a convoluted discussion of the Jews' suffering under the Nazis.[82] A section entitled "People in Fear and Misery" chronicled life during the Third Reich and explained that Hitler "sent the Jews to concentration camps and incinerated their synagogues." In one of the few instances where it cites specific statistics, the book asserted that 335,000 Jews were murdered in 1944. There is no mention of the millions killed before this point. Interestingly, the book combined this passage with a discussion of the "democratic- and social-minded Germans" who spoke out against these crimes. There is no discussion of the treatment of Jews in the concentration camps, their social persecution, or their mass murder through 1945. The tenth edition of the *Einst und Jetzt* text, published in 1963, offered a very different description of the Third Reich and the Holocaust. In this version of the text, the extermination of the Jews is spelled out in no uncertain terms—the concentrations camps and gas chambers are discussed in detail. Pupils also learned that six million Jews died at the hands of the Germans and their accomplices during the war. Another important change in this depiction was the portrayal of the German populace. This volume explicitly connected the support of the German public to Hitler and his ambitions. Perhaps most revealing was a passage addressing the reluctance of many adults to discuss these topics. The authors of *Einst und Jetzt* encouraged their readers to talk about these troubling events with their parents, and to press them for answers even if they avoided the questions or feigned ignorance.[83] One can only speculate as to how many parents and grandparents responded to the penetrating inquiries of their children and grandchildren.

West German history textbooks experienced a minor renaissance in the early 1960s, as they finally accepted their responsibility for conveying the totality of the recent past—both good and bad—to their readers. In order to achieve this goal, these books utilized a diverse assortment of primary sources that allowed pupils to evaluate the words and deeds of their parents' and grandparents' generations. Texts published in this period also explicitly engaged the most contentious issues in Germany's twentieth-century history in great detail. Troubling themes were no longer glossed over or obscured by an overemphasis on less controversial topics. Discussion questions and the incorporation of primary materials placed greater responsibility on the pupil and weakened the traditional dominance of the teacher in the classroom. Analysis of the Third Reich and postwar world reaffirmed the value of *Zeitgeschichte* instruction dedicated to helping pupils understand the contemporary world and the how the legacy of the war influenced their lives. Finally, discussions of the recent German past and the expanded perspective of the postwar world reinforced political education that attempted to convey a new sense of citizenship to West German pupils. The fact that these reforms became the standards for history textbooks by this period indicates the extent of reform in the Federal Republic. By no means perfect, this new generation of texts represents dramatic changes since the end of the war. In fact, books published in the early 1960s display considerable reforms in terms of content and method from their predecessors of just a few years earlier.

Political Education—Not Just For Pupils

Before departing Bonn for his vacation in August 1963, Konrad Adenauer requested a detailed examination of the state of political education in the schools of the Federal Republic. Completed a few weeks later, the document painted a positive but uneven picture of postwar accomplishments in the subject. The report explained how political education had become a new subject in its own right (*Sozialkunde*) as well as a principle of instruction (*Unterrichtsprinzip*) that extended across history, geography, German, and other disciplines. Adenauer must have been pleased to learn that political education had come to address a variety of contentious and significant issues, such as twentieth-century German history, European unity, international cooperation, communism, and human rights. Despite these advances, Adenauer was informed that problems still remained. In particular, the report informed the chancellor of the incongruous preparation of teachers in different schools. Educators in *Gymnasien* and many *Mittelschulen* received better preparation in the field than their colleagues in the *Volksschulen*. Another difficulty was the uncoordinated curricula in political education. Requirements varied for instruction and preparation in political education from state to state. The report nevertheless concluded that new initiatives introduced in the 1950s had greatly strengthened the subject in the West German schools. Radio programs, conferences, national contests, the newspaper *Das Parlament,* and other publications all contributed to classroom instruction in the subject.[84] Likewise, the work of the Federal Office for Political Education and its state-level counterparts complemented the work of postwar educators. Challenges in the field of political education still remained, yet on the eve of his resignation, Adenauer must have been satisfied with the numerous reforms initiated on his watch.

The report prepared for Adenauer offers a succinct evaluation of both the achievements and the lingering shortcomings in the field of political education in the early 1960s. As chapter 3 showed, content and pedagogical method had dominated discussions of political education in previous years. The dossier prepared for Adenauer indeed cites many activities begun in the latter half of the 1950s in its praise for new initiatives in field. While the young subject continued to attract attention in the early 1960s, content and pedagogical method were increasingly overshadowed by a new issue: the preparation of teachers. Educators, administrators, and politicians throughout the Federal Republic agreed that a generation of new texts and the use of innovative methods would be useless if teachers were not adequately prepared to provide instruction in the subject. Thus, the emphasis of those interested in political education in the early 1960s shifted toward the preparation of those providing instruction in the classroom. This period witnessed the creation or expansion of countless teacher training programs in the states designed to provide educators with a stronger foundation in the subject. There was widespread agreement in West Germany that only if the training of teachers matched the zeal for reform could political education contribute to the preparation of young Germans for the responsibilities of democratic citizenship.

Nowhere was the commitment to improving the training of teachers in political education stronger than in West Berlin. The most vivid indication of this comes from Tiburtius's 1960 Interim Guidelines for Political Education in the Berlin Schools. Among the many ambitious goals the senator outlined in this treatise was the requirement that all secondary schools have at least one teacher complete mandatory continuing education courses in political education.[85] The requirement for *Grundschullehrer,* issued later that year, was less onerous than that outlined for secondary school educators in April. Senator Tiburtius informed school officials in all of the city's districts that teachers in the *Grundschulen* would have to complete a minimum of one three-day seminar on political education. The new requirements of secondary schools, however, likely shocked administrators throughout the city. Tiburtius's decision that at least one teacher in every secondary school in the city—OPZ, OTZ, and OWZ, as well as *Berufsschulen*—complete a one-year political education course at the Otto Suhr Institute (located at the city's Free University) symbolized a major commitment of time and resources to the subject. This program constituted a substantial increase in the weekly workload of teachers, with participants required to attend several hours of lecture and discussion every week.[86] In recognition of this new responsibility, the teaching load of those participating in the seminar was to be reduced accordingly. This 1960 decision was an attempt to raise the level of training for teachers of the subject in the city and to standardize it at the same time. It was not only ambitious—it was also successful. Within a few years, virtually every secondary school in the city could claim at least one teacher who had completed the advanced training.

The variety of opportunities available to West Berlin teachers to continue their study of political topics in this period was certainly remarkable. The 1961 listings for continuing education in political education, published on the heels of Tiburtius's directive, offer programs of varying lengths to teachers in all levels of schools. In June 1961, city school officials offered three-day courses (consisting of six lectures) to teachers in the *Grundschulen,* OPZs, and OTZs. Over 135 teachers had registered for the courses, which would be held in Reinickendorf, Charlottenburg, Schöneberg, and Steglitz. For teachers in the *Berufsschulen* and the OWZs, there were five-day courses (consisting of ten lectures) available on political topics. In addition to these programs, the city announced a seminar entitled "Contemporary History in Class," which consisted of twelve lectures and was open to any interested teacher. Finally, there was the aforementioned year-long course at the Otto Suhr Institute, which targeted teachers in the OPZs and OTZs during the 1961–62 academic year.[87] This intensive program received support from both the city school administration and the State Office for Political Education. Notably, the involvement of the Otto Suhr Institute in the continuing education program meant that the city's teachers received instruction from leading political scientists. Either as part of the multiday seminars or the year-long program at the institute, pioneers in the field such as Ernst Fraenkel, Ossip Flechtheim, and Gert von Eynern participated in the new effort. The diverse course options, the multitude of themes addressed, and the quality of the instruction appealed to the needs and interests of the city' s teachers, while at the same time promoting their professional development.

Mandating the participation of the city's teachers in such a program was the easy part. Much more difficult was determining what they would study. The multiday courses could naturally offer only a cursory examination of major issues. Yet even in these abbreviated courses, participants discussed many of the contentious issues of the period. For example, a five-day course offered to trade-school teachers in April 1961 entitled "The State and Social Structure of the Federal Republic" engaged a multitude of contemporary political and educational issues.[88] Among the topics addressed in the week's lectures were: internal and external threats to the multiparty state; the protection of democracy; the Federal Republic and Israel; the role of political education in the *Berufsschule*; and the didactics of social studies instruction through specific examples. Faculty members of the Otto Suhr Institute directed these seminars to encourage the trade school teachers in attendance to move beyond myths and stereotypes and to question assumptions and unchallenged myths in the classroom. Conversations between participants and the seminar's director, Hans-Georg Hartmann, indicate that they did exactly that. During their meetings, the twenty-nine teachers attending the course challenged the black-and-white dichotomy of the National Socialist state. They discussed criticisms that political education weakened the instruction of traditional subjects in the *Berufsschule.* Practical methods to reinforce the lessons of political education in the everyday operation of the classroom also received attention.[89] Although only a five day-course, the themes addressed in the sessions exposed teachers to divisive issues related to contemporary history, pedagogy, and foreign policy.

The reports of those who directed the continuing education seminars reveal that participants displayed a sincere commitment to improving political instruction in the school. Discussing his experiences as leader of a three-day seminar for *Grundschullehrer* in 1960, Dieter Grosser stated that teachers responded enthusiastically to a lecture on the pedagogical difficulties of teaching political education in the elementary school.[90] Both he and the participants lamented the fact that the seminar did not allow more time for these issues. Realizing that short seminars could not alleviate the lack of preparation of many West Berlin teachers in political education, Grosser emphasized the importance of such continuing education offerings as a catalyst for self-improvement. With most participants already aspiring to expand their knowledge and abilities in the discipline, Grosser asserted that these sessions were most valuable for sparking further interest in political education and promoting study on an independent basis.[91] A commitment to the democracy of the Federal Republic, a willingness to engage political issues in class, and a basic knowledge of the discipline represented a kind of educational trifecta to Grosser and his colleagues who worked with the city's teachers. Yet Grosser realized that the continuing education seminars could encourage and foster these sentiments, but they could not mandate them. Only through a partnership between administration and teachers would the improved preparation of the city's teachers in political education become a reality.

Did the ambitious schedule of themes engage the participating teachers or did it simply overwhelm them? A letter of appreciation sent to Senator Tiburtius by one of the participants in an April 1961 course suggests the former to be the case. Karl Thomsik, a trade school teacher in Charlottenburg, wrote that the course was a "valuable enrichment and expansion of topical and methodological knowledge" in the field of political education. His letter devoted special praise to the lecturers for highlighting the problems of the recent German past, including the failures of the Weimar Republic and the racism of the Third Reich. Thomsik explained that in addition to improving factual knowledge, the course introduced participants to innovative practices and materials they could employ in their daily teaching responsibilities. He informed city officials that "these lectures put the tool in our hand, allowing us to see teaching materials more vividly in a larger context, to observe them in actual reality, and to make clear the interplay of forces in the political realm."[92] Additionally, he and his colleagues had been exposed to a variety of techniques and media for introducing challenging political topics in their classrooms. Thomsik's letter reveals that the five-day course provided instruction for the participating trade school teachers in not just *what* to teach but also *how* it could be taught. Mastering the material was only half the battle for educators; they had to learn how to convey their knowledge to pupils in the classroom. Thus, the use of not just critical texts in the field, but also films, tapes, and other materials represented an important part of the course. This emphasis on new instructional materials in the field of political education nicely underscores the emergence of these items as pedagogical tools in preceding years.

The cornerstone of the city's teacher training efforts in the field of political education during this period was undoubtedly the year-long program at the Free University's Otto Suhr Institute. This program, introduced in the 1960–61 academic year for teachers in the OWZs and *Berufsschulen*, represented West Berlin's renewed commitment to political education in the schools.[93] Having recognized that requirements for teachers in the subject had long been inadequate, city officials constructed this program to remedy the shortcomings in the traditional training teachers received during their study before entering the classroom. Thus the one-year course at the Otto Suhr Institute enhanced the knowledge of experienced educators already employed in the city's schools and also exposed them to new pedagogical techniques and approaches. Broader knowledge of recent history and political themes constituted a major priority of the program, but city officials also sought to encourage greater debate and discussion within the schools. Tiburtius was convinced that his new requirements for teachers from throughout the city to enroll in the program would have a major impact in just a few years.

Naturally, the year-long courses at the Otto Suhr Institute promised a much more intensive study of political themes than shorter, less comprehensive programs. The syllabus for the 1961–62 year-long course for teachers in the city's OPZs and OTZs provides insight into the themes examined and methods employed in these seminars. Faculty members of the Otto Suhr Institute who provided the lectures focused on broader, more theoretical issues during the first semester, addressing such topics as "The Ideological Components of the Criticism of Democracy" and "The Idea and Reality of Political Parties in a Pluralistic Society."[94] The lectures scheduled for the second semester addressed more concrete issues that teachers would likely discuss in their own classrooms. Class sessions devoted to "The Creation of the Weimar Republic," "The SS-State," and "The Eichmann Trial and National Socialist Jewish Policies," prepared the city's teachers to engage these contentious topics with their pupils.[95] In response to the requests of participants in the program the previous year, the second half of the course also included a series of four lectures dedicated to contemporary issues. Lectures, although important, only constituted one component of the year-long course. The typical schedule for the 152 educators participating in the 1961–62 program included two ninety-minute lectures during their weekly meeting, a ninety-minute period devoted to discussion and group work, and a concluding forty-five-minute session devoted to further group work and discussion or a faculty-led colloquium. Thus, the activities scheduled for the teachers in the program were similar to those city officials hoped participants might pursue in their own classrooms.

The Hessian commitment to preparing teachers for political education was no different than that of West Berlin, although continuing education offerings changed less dramatically along the banks of the Rhine. The reason that Hessian officials did not initiate such a revolutionary curriculum of continuing education in political education is because of the wide array of courses already available to teachers through the Reinhardswaldschule and other institutions. Nevertheless, the programs offered in the early 1960s reflect an intensifying concern about the preparation of Hessian teachers in the young discipline. Arguably the cornerstone of Hessian efforts to promote continuing political education was the university seminar offered to both professional educators and teachers-in-training in Frankfurt. The eighteenth and nineteenth courses, held during the spring and autumn semesters of 1964, welcomed 64 teachers from *Volksschulen* and *Berufs-*

schulen who studied alongside 121 future colleagues who had yet to complete their training. The lectures they attended constituted a mixture of more traditional political themes emphasizing leading personalities and institutions and less conventional topics including *Zeitgeschichte* and pedagogical approaches. Class meetings dedicated to Bismarck, Lenin's early writings, and a study of economic relations certainly fell into the former group. Arguably more interesting to those participating in the course, especially those already working in Hessian classrooms, were lectures on changes in German political education since 1890 and the sociology of the German educational system since 1914.[96] These seminars provided participants an understanding of the concepts, events, and figures indispensable to a teacher of the subject, as well as a background in the ideas, methods, and techniques used to convey material to pupils.

In addition to the university seminars, there was a multitude of other political education training options available to Hessian educators during this period. The combined efforts of the Hessian Office for Political Education and the Reinhardswaldschule produced a series of courses open to teachers of all levels. Among the courses available in 1964 were: "American Society Today"; "The Role of the Social Partner in Instruction"; and "Conflict with Communism." As one can see from this brief list, Hessian institutions addressed both contemporary topics as well as pedagogical and theoretical issues. Another event held at the Reinhardswaldschule was a conference in which teachers were invited to discuss their experiences in the classroom with experts in the field of political education. Courses and conferences, however, were not confined only to Frankfurt and the Reinhardswaldschule. The *Volkshochschule* in Friedrichsdorf offered several workshops on political education in the trade school, teaching political attitudes and approaches and techniques of political instruction. Enrollment in these meetings was modest, with approximately twenty teachers participating in each session. In Wiesbaden, the Hessian Office for Political Education partnered with the Deutsche Gesellschaft für die Vereinten Nationen (German Society for the United Nations) in sponsoring a political education seminar open to teachers of all grades from throughout the Federal Republic.[97] Although not mandated to complete continuing education courses as in West Berlin, Hessian teachers nevertheless encountered a wide variety of opportunities for further training in political education.

Another important factor explaining the intensifying interest in political education in Hesse during at this time was the addition of the ninth school year to the *Volksschule*. As a consequence, there was an expansion of the political education curriculum, with the ninth grade allowing for greater instruction in the subject. A 1964 Hessian Culture Ministry report cited the "great importance" of political education in the *Gymnasium* and the additional attention to the subject in the newly established ninth-grade *Volksschule* classes as the explanation for a particular emphasis on the subject in continuing education offerings.[98] In accordance with the different needs and themes of political education in the *Gymnasium, Mittelschule,* and *Volksschule,* Hessian authorities worked to expand seminar offerings for educators in all schools. As a result, Hessian authorities organized new week-long courses specifically targeting educators in the *Volksschulen* and *Mittelschulen*. One such course introduced teachers to the content and form of political education in the *Realschule,* while others prepared *Volksschullehrer* for the challenges of political instruction in the ninth grade.[99] This trend of growing opportunities for Hessian teachers in political education continued unabated the following year with twenty-five week-long seminars devoted to political education in the *Volksschule* and *Mittelschule* scheduled. In addition, teachers in the Frankfurt area could participate in two continuing seminars that held weekly meetings: the pedagogy of political education and the history and meaning of Judaism.[100] The breadth and variety of the course offerings indicate that there was an interest among school officials to ensure better prepared teachers in the classroom. On the other side of the equation, the participation of teachers in these noncompulsory programs suggests a widespread commitment to improving their training in the field.

Political education was no less important in the early 1960s than it had been in the last half of the 1950s. Yet the focus shifted from new textbooks and classroom techniques toward improving the professional training of West German educators. This is not to say that other issues were ignored; rather, it indicates that postwar educators recognized that only if earlier innovations were coupled with improved teacher training in the subject would political education fulfill its responsibilities to pupils. Innovative new teacher training courses and seminars offered educators the opportunity to improve their knowledge in the subject. These programs, initiated within the traditional organization of the German school system, nevertheless broadened the horizons of participants, fostered their interest in political topics, and exposed them to new materials and techniques for use in the classroom. As ambitious and rewarding as these programs may have been, their impact would have been greatly weakened had it not been for the interest and commitment of postwar teachers. The involvement of educators in these programs symbolized the widespread awareness that only with additional training would they be able to meet the demands of teaching political education in the classroom. Thus despite the uneven preparation of educators, the disparate curricula throughout the Federal Republic, and continued debate over what merited inclusion in the classroom, reforms in the field of political education continued unabated in this period. Reform from above—in the form of new professional training courses and seminars—coupled with change from below—as seen in the growing commitment of teachers to improving their understanding of the subject—led to improved classroom instruction in political education from a more experienced and knowledgeable corps of educators.

* * * * * *

In the face of increasing public concerns regarding the school system, West German educational authorities issued a number of new policies as the 1960s began. Prompted by political, social, and cultural developments inside and outside of the

Federal Republic, these initiatives constituted an attempt to meet the challenges of the new decade. In West Berlin, two significant policy initiatives directly addressed the role of the schools in fostering democracy in the Federal Republic. The 1960 Interim Guidelines for Political Education in the Berlin Schools mandated expanded political education for the city's pupils, the integration of *Zeitgeschichte* into the curriculum, and the utilization of group work and extracurricular activities in order to encourage the development of democratic attitudes and ideals. Carl-Heinz Evers published his Memorandum on Internal School Reform two years later, which called for significant reforms intended to strengthen democracy in the schools in the face of the new barrier that divided the city. Less expansive but no less meaningful were two pieces of groundbreaking educational policy promulgated in Hesse during these years. Following several challenges to the restrictions placed on the student press by the Culture Ministry and school officials as well as the fallout from the "Spiegel Affair," Hessian authorities officially distinguished between school newspapers and student newspapers and liberated the latter from censorship in 1964. The following year, a new decree on student government improved pupils' responsibilities in the schools, permitted the formation of supraschool organizations and relieved the faculty advisor from the financial and professional onus of working with SMV. Considered together, these policy initiatives illustrate a renewed commitment to the ideals of educational reform among postwar school authorities in the new decade.

Legislation alone, however, cannot dictate change in the classroom. In order to evaluate how change manifested itself in the West German schools, one must consider the involvement of pupils and teachers. In the realm of student government and student newspapers, arguably the most significant development in this period was the growth of both institutions in the *Volksschulen*. Whereas SMV and newspapers had begun to make inroads into these schools in the previous decade, it was only after 1960 that one could claim that they had established a secure place in the *Volksschulen, Mittelschulen,* and even many *Grundschulen,* in addition to the *Gymnasien.* In regard to classroom materials, textbooks published during this period illustrate the continued reform of history instruction. Books entering West German classrooms in the early 1960s enlarged upon pedagogical innovations first introduced in the previous decade. These texts posed challenging questions for classroom debate and discussion, and they—more than ever before—incorporated a broad spectrum of primary sources for pupils to evaluate. Transcending the confines of many of their predecessors, these publications also directly engaged the most contentious and problematic episodes in recent German history, including the demise of the Weimar Republic, the Third Reich, the Holocaust, and the division of Germany. A final innovation came in the form of expanded political education for the teaching profession. Policymakers, administrators, and educators collaborated to create a multitude of new courses and seminars for teachers of all levels. Admittedly, education officials did not significantly alter the organization of professional training, but these additions constituted important reforms initiated within the structure of the existing system.

The early 1960s marked a period of transition in the history of West German education. New public attention to educational questions once again brought the schools into the spotlight. Yet more important than this heightened scrutiny were the continuing reforms at work in postwar classrooms. West German authorities initiated a number of new policies designed to promote pedagogical and professional change in the country's schools. Their proposals, as we have seen, were often warmly received by an ever-younger teaching profession, the majority of whom had entered into the schools after the war. In addition, teachers of all ages were improving their knowledge of political education, a subject whose emergence had helped redefine the goals of the postwar schools. Add to this the fact that a new generation of pupils who had been born and raised in a democratic state filled the classrooms and it becomes clear that the schools were undergoing a metamorphosis during this period. In light of these developments, one can reasonably argue the mid-1960s indeed marked the close of the postwar era in the West German schools.

Notes

1. Margarete Meyer, "Warum deutsch-amerikanische Freundschaft?" 23 March 1961, Abteilung 504, No. 3380, Hessisches Hauptstaatsarchiv, Wiesbaden (HHstW).
2. Among those educators working on the text with Evers was Horst Kollat, who had devoted great energy to the BSP. See Horst Kollat, interview by author, tape recording, Berlin-Reinickendorf, 23 April 2003.
3. *Denkschrift zur inneren Schulreform—langfristige Planungen* (Berlin, 1962).
4. Otto Wenzel, "Die Denkschrift zur inneren Schulreform. Berlin führt als erstes Bundesland langfristige Planungen auf dem Gebiete des Schulwesens ein," *Berliner Lehrerzeitung* 16 (31), no. 3 (15 February 1962): 49–52.
5. Letter from Carl-Heinz Evers, Landesschulrat, to Willy Brandt, SPD Landesvorsitzenden, 21 November 1961, B. Rep. 015, No. 141–142, Landesarchiv Berlin (LAB).
6. The original report can be found in the Landesarchiv Berlin, Signatur P698. This study, however, will refer to the widely distributed published edition, which contained the complete report in significantly fewer pages. This explains apparent discrepancies in page number references.
7. Johann Zilien, *Politische Bildung in Hessen von 1945 bis 1965. Gestaltung und Entwicklung der politischen Bildung als schulpolitisches Instrument der sozialen Demokratisierung* (Frankfurt, 1997), 409.
8. The German news magazine *Der Spiegel* published an article in a 1962 edition that expressed sharp criticism of Chancellor Adenauer's government. Police arrested the editor, on a vacation in Spain, and searched the offices of the magazine. Many Germans viewed this incident as eerily similar to the actions of the Gestapo twenty years earlier. The "Spiegel Affair," as it has come to be known, ultimately contributed to Adenauer's resignation after fourteen years as chancellor.
9. The publication of Georg Picht's essays on the educational crisis in Germany's schools appeared in *Christ und Welt* in 1964. Picht was most concerned with what he perceived to be a lack of professional training at the university level. Even though this argument did not directly engage

with questions of democratization or secondary school reform, it became part of a bigger discussion on the state of education in the Federal Republic. For a complete collection of his essays, see his 1964 volume *Die deutsche Bildungskatastrophe* (Freiburg im Breisgau, 1964).

10. Zilien, *Politische Bildung in Hessen*, 253.

11. "Vorläufige Richtlinien für die politische Bildung an der Berliner Schule," 14 April 1960, 4, B. Rep. 015, No. 451, LAB.

12. Ibid., 8–9.

13. Ibid., 5–6.

14. Ibid.

15. Ibid., 11–12.

16. The *Rahmenplan,* which in reality was nothing more than a set of recommendations, encouraged greater standardization among the school systems of the various states. Believing that West Germany's schools deviated from those of her neighbors, the committee urged organizational reforms to align the educational system more closely to what it considered European societal norms.

17. Letter from Hermann-Hesse-Schule, 21 May 1962 in "Bericht zu den Vorläufige Richtlinien, Kl. 11 s/m, 1961/62," Anlage G, B. Rep. 015, No. 514, LAB.

18. "Auszugsweise Abschrift der Niederschrift über die Konferenz der Borsig-Schule (2.OTZ) vom 16.5.62," B. Rep. 015, No. 514, LAB.

19. *Denkschrift zur inneren Schulreform—langfristige Planungen* (Berlin, 1962).

20. Ibid., 38.

21. Ibid., 49.

22. Ibid., 43–44.

23. Draft of "Denkschrift zur inneren Schulreform; Künftige Planungen auf dem Gebiet der politischen Erziehung und des politikkundlichen Unterrichts," 20 January 1961, B. Rep. 015, No. 142, LAB.

24. Ibid., 12.

25. Ibid., 51.

26. Ibid.

27. "Exposé für einleitende Bermerkungen des Herrn Senators in der Senatssitzung am 21.11.1961," B. Rep. 015, No. 141–142, LAB.

28. Ibid.

29. Response to "Denkschrift" from Berliner Verband der Lehrer und Erzieher, 25 June 1962, B. Rep. 015, No. 141–142, LAB.

30. Otto Wenzel, "Die Denkschrift zur inneren Schulreform," *Berliner Lehrerzeitung* 16(31), no. 3 (15 February 1962): 49–52.

31. In Hesse, the increase was a less dramatic—but by no means unremarkable—31 percent over the same period. The rest of the FRG—with the exception of Saarland and Schleswig-Holstein—experienced similar increases. See *Denkschrift zur inneren Schulreform,* appendix 50; See also Table 1, "Pädagogische Hochschulen und andere Anstalten und Einrichtungen für Ausbildung von Lehrern an Volksschulen, Sonderschulen und Mittelschulen sowie an berufsbildenden Schulen (ohne Handelslehramt) 1954 bis 1962," Lehrernachwuchs (undated, likely late 1962), B. Rep. 015, No. 398, LAB.

32. *Denkschrift zur inneren Schulreform,* appendix 50; also Statistisches Landesamt Berlin, *Statistisches Jahrbuch Berlin 1965* (Berlin, 1965), 108–11.

33. Zilien, *Politische Bildung in Hessen,* 404.

34. "Schülerzeitungen und Schulzeitugen," 13 August 1964, *Amtsblatt des Hessischen Ministeriums für Kultus und Unterricht,* vol. 17, no. 8 (August 1964): 526–28.

35. "Richtlinien über die Schülermitverantwortung (Schülermitverwaltung)—SMV an allen hessischen Schulen mit Ausnahme der Höheren Fachschulen, Ingenieurschulen, Pädagogischen Fachinstitute und Hessen-kollegs," 31 December 1965, *Amtsblatt des Hessischen Kultusministeriums,* vol. 19, no. 1 (1966): 103–8.

36. Zilien, *Politische Bildung in Hessen*, 396–99.

37. J. Winckler, "SMV in der Volksschule," *Wir machen mit* 12, no. 1 (March 1964): 1–2.

38. "SMV—Niedersachsen: Beste Schülerzeitung," *Wir machen mit* 11, no. 4 (December 1963): 7.

39. Erwin Holzem, "Schülermitverwaltung—Schülermitverantwortung," *Berliner Lehrerzeitung* 18 (33), no. 22 (30 November 1964): 529–30.

40. "Erfahrungen und Anregungen aus der Praxis der Schülermitverwaltung gesammelt auf der Bundestagung Deutscher Schüler-Vertretungen in Arnoldshain/Taunus vom 7.-11.Juni 1960," B. Rep. 015, No. 430, LAB. It should be noted that this survey included responses from all of the western states except Bavaria.

41. Ibid., 2–3.

42. Ibid., 5.

43. Ibid., 8–9.

44. Ibid., 9.

45. Norbert Meisner, "Jahresbericht 1961/62," *Mitteilungen der Arbeitsgemeinschaft Berliner Schülervertretungen*, 8 May 1962, in B. Rep. 015, No. 348, LAB.

46. Ibid., 3.

47. Report of the Berliner Schülerparlament, April 1962, B. Rep. 015, No. 348, LAB.

48. "Niederschrift der XII. Bundestagung der Schülermitverwaltung 1963 in Kaiserslautern: Die SMV im Schulalltag," *Wir machen mit* 11, no. 4 (1 December 1963): 17–24.

49. Erika Schwind, "SMV an *Volks-, Mittel-,* und *Berufsschule,*" *Wir machen mit* 11, no. 4 (1 December 1963): 20.

50. "Zur politischen Bildung," 12.Grundschule Borsigwalde, 21 September 1964, B. Rep. 015, No. 448, LAB.

51. Ibid.

52. "Schüler über die SMV. Das Ergebnis einer Umfrage," *Wir machen mit* 12, no. 2 (1 June 1964): 1.

53. Ibid.

54. Bernd Zanke, "SMV—Unter die Lupe genommen," *Der Zeissianer*, October 1964, 7, in uncataloged holdings of Archiv zur Geschichte von Tempelhof and Schöneberg.

55. Hartmut Brinkmann, "Zensor oder Berater," *Wir machen mit* 7, no. 2 (1 June 1959): 19.

56. E. Piotrowski, "Über allem muss die Wahrheit stehen," *Wir machen mit* 7, no. 2 (1 June 1959): 19.

57. Ibid.

58. Eduard Steinbügl, *Geschichte der neuesten Zeit für Mittelschulen und Realschulen* (Munich, 1962), 96–98.

59. Ibid., 98.

60. Investigating the perspective employed by West German textbooks in regard to the tumultuous history of the twentieth century, sociologists have argued that dealing with the crimes of the recent past was "not the only or in some cases even the main dynamic element in portrayals of the nation." See Julian Dierkes, "Teaching Portrayals of the Nation: Postwar History Education in Japan and the Germanys," (PhD diss.: Princeton University, 2003).

61. A 1961 evaluation of West German history texts indicated that at this point—fifteen years after the war—most books addressed Nazi crimes directly in their pages. Texts even incorporated the most controversial subjects, such as the mass murder of the Jews, although they did not always examine these themes in detail. See Karl Mielcke, *1917–1945 in den Geschichtsbüchern der Bundesrepublik* (Hannover, 1961).

62. See Norbert Frei, *Adenauer's Germany and the Nazi Past: The Politics of Amnesty and Reintegration* (New York, 2002), xiii. Frei remarks on the limited support of Germans for "reeducation" both during the occupation and beyond.

63. See "Der neuesten Zeit (zumal der Periode des Nationalsozialismus) im Unterricht, Neufassung des Aktenvermerks vom 20.1.1960," undated (likely late January 1960), Abt. 504, No. 1226a, HHstA; also "Erklärung aus Anlass der antisemitischen Ausschreitungen," 30 January 1960, Abt. 504, No. 1226a, HHstA.

64. Hans Heumann, *Unser Weg durch die Geschichte. Vom Wiener Kongress bis zur Gegenwart* (Frankfurt, 1961).
65. Hans Ebeling, *Die Reise in die Vergangenheit*, vol. 4, 4th ed. (Braunschweig, 1964).
66. Heumann, *Unser Weg durch die Geschichte*, 103.
67. Ibid., 105–6.
68. Ibid., 106.
69. Ibid., 107.
70. Ibid., 152–53.
71. For a discussion of the influence of Ebeling as a textbook author and educator during the early 1960s, see Elizabeth Ebeling, *Erinnerungen an Hans Ebeling: 1906–1967* (Braunschweig, 1997).
72. Ebeling, *Die Reise in die Vergangenheit*, vol. 4, 4th ed.
73. Ibid., 205. Emphasis in original.
74. Ibid., 261–62.
75. Ibid., 208–12.
76. Ibid., 220–25.
77. Erika von Hornstein, *Die deutsche Not. Flüchtlinge berichten* (Cologne, 1960), quoted in Ebeling, *Die Reise in die Vergangenheit*, vol. 4, 4th ed., 271. Ebeling included this citation in the back of his text as a book recommended for pupils interested in learning more about the subject.
78. Willi Adam, *Trögels Lesehefte*, vol. 12, *Hitler und der zweite Weltkrieg*, 2nd ed. (Ansbach, 1958).
79. Willi Adam, *Trögels Lesehefte*, vol. 12, *Hitler und der zweite Weltkrieg*, 3rd ed. (Ansbach, 1960).
80. Ibid., 23.
81. Ibid., 24.
82. Waldemar Hoffman and Georg Müller, *Einst und Jetzt. Geschichtserzählungen für das Fünfte und Sechste Schuljahr*, 3rd ed. (Frankfurt, 1956).
83. Waldemar Hoffman and Georg Müller, *Einst und Jetzt. Geschichtserzählungen für das Fünfte und Sechste Schuljahr*, 10th ed. (Frankfurt, 1963) 113–116.
84. Helmut Grosse, "Bericht über die politische Bildung an den Schulen in der Bundesrepublik," 14 September 1963, File B106, No. 21605, Bundesarchiv Koblenz (BAK).
85. See "Vorläufige Richtlinien für die politische Bildung an der Berliner Schule," 14 April 1960, B. Rep. 015, No. 451, LAB.
86. Letter from Senator für Volksbildung to Bezirksämter of Berlin, "Politische Weiterbildung der Lehrer," 18 October 1960, B. Rep. 015, No. 167–169, LAB.
87. "Lehrgänge für die Lehrerweiterbildung im Rj. 1961," 18 November 1960, B. Rep. 015, No. 165–166, LAB. See "Mitteilung für die Presse—Beendigung des einjährigen Universitäts-Sonderkurses für politische Bildung der Berliner Lehrer," 6 March 1961, B. Rep. 015, No. 167–169, LAB.
88. Hans-Georg Hartmann (Gewerbeoberlehrer) "Abschlussbericht über den 5-Tage-Kursus zur politischen Lehrerweiterbildung v. 24.04 bis 28.04.1961," B. Rep. 015, No. 165, LAB.
89. Ibid., 6.
90. Dieter Grosser, "Bericht über den Lehrgang zur politischer Weiterbildung von Grund- und Sonderschullehrer des Bezirks Charlottenburg (24.-26.10, 1960)," 26 October 1960, B. Rep. 015, No. 165, LAB.
91. Ibid.
92. Karl Thomsik, "Fünf-Tage-Kursus: Staatliche und gesellschaftliche Struktur der Bundesrepublik Deutschland vom 24.4 bis 28.4.61," 18 June 1961, B. Rep. 015, No. 165, LAB.
93. "Mitteilung für die Presse—Beendigung des einjährigen Universitäts-Sonderkurses für politische Bildung der Berliner Lehrer," 6 March 1961, 1, B. Rep. 015, No. 167–169, LAB.
94. Otto-Suhr-Institut an der Freien Universität Berlin, Ein Jahres-Kursus für politische Bildung, Vorlesungsplan für das Sommersemester 1961 (1.Semester), April 1961, B. Rep. 015, No. 167–169, LAB.

95. Letter from Carl-Heinz Evers to Bezirksämter vom Berlin (Abt. Volksbildung/Schulamt), 11 October 1961, B. Rep. 015, No. 167–169, LAB.

96. G. Spath, "Jahresbericht an den Kulturpolitischen Ausschuss über Stand der politischen Bildung an Schulen, Hochschulen, und Universitäten," 19 January 1965, 1, Abt. 504, No. 3159, Fiche 13833, HHstA.

97. Ibid., 2; see also "Politische Bildung an wissenschaftlichen Hochschulen und Schulen Jahresbericht 1965," (undated, likely early 1966), Abt. 504, No. 3159, Fiche 13833, HHstA.

98. "Politische Bildung an wissenschaftlichen Hochschulen und Schulen Jahresbericht 1964," undated (likely early 1965), 3, Abt. 504, No. 3159, Fiche 13833, HHstA.

99. Ibid., 6.

100. "Politische Bildung an wissenschaftlichen Hochschulen und Schulen Jahresbericht 1965," undated (likely early 1966), Abt. 504, No. 3159, Fiche 13833, HHstA.

CONCLUSION

*R*eflecting on the impact of the occupation in his memoir shortly after leaving Germany, General Lucius Clay waxed positive about the future of the German schools. He admitted that changes engineered solely by American officials were not likely to be lasting, but Clay reaffirmed his belief that German educators and administrators would take the initiative in the years ahead. He explained that "the results of an educational program are intangible and almost impossible to evaluate immediately, but they will record the success or failure of our occupation."[1] The need to assess the merits of America's role in postwar Germany based on long-term developments also struck Clay as self-evident. The groundwork laid during the occupation, he believed, would facilitate educational reforms in the decades that followed. Arguably the most important declaration in the general's discussion of the schools was his statement that "lasting reform in Germany must come from within."[2] If the schools were to continue to play a role in the democratization of German society, it would be due to the efforts of German educators, administrators, and pupils.

Authored in 1950, Clay's forecast for Germany's schools proved quite prescient. Exchange programs inaugurated during the occupation expanded in the 1950s and provided Germans practical experience with the workings of a democratic society. Student government and student newspapers offered pupils a wealth of opportunities to acquire personal experience with both the rights and responsibilities of those living in a democracy. A new generation of history and civics textbooks published in the 1950s introduced innovative pedagogical practices to the postwar classroom. Arguably even more important was the new conception of democratic citizenship that appeared in these volumes. The emergence of political education ensured that young Germans would gain a new conception of their role in Germany, as well as their relationship to other countries, regions, and peoples. Postwar training and continuing education courses for teachers improved their knowledge of new subject matter—such as recent history and political education—and also exposed them to innovative teaching methods that became increasingly commonplace in the schools. These postwar reforms indeed made German pupils and teachers alike more "conscious of their rights and freedoms," as Clay phrased it, as well as of their responsibilities and duties as citizens.[3]

The transformation of the educational system continued throughout the next two decades, as Clay had so astutely predicted, because of the efforts of Germans. This was often an uneven process, with varying degrees of reform materializing in the schools of the different federal states. Likewise, pupils experienced reforms differently depending on the type of school they attended. These developments were also contested by different groups in German society. Teachers, administrators, politicians, and pupils all expressed their goals for the postwar schools and—despite consensus on many issues—occasionally clashed over how these might best be achieved. Debates among teachers regarding instruction in contemporary history and articles authored by pupils critiquing the role of SMV illustrate how Germans navigated the choppy waters of educational reform on their own following the occupation. Nevertheless, the driving force behind the reforms that continued throughout the 1950s and 1960s came from within. If it was American officials who had laid the foundation, it was the Germans who had actually constructed and outfitted the schools in which a new generation of young citizens now studied.

The Case for Incremental Change

The evolution of education reform in the fifteen years after the Allied occupation underscores the subtle process of inner democratization underway in the West German schools. The emergence of innovations in the educational system constituted just one component of a much broader process of cultural democratization that began in Federal Republic after the foundation of basic political institutions.[4] Curricular and pedagogical reforms that transpired in the schools during the 1950s and early 1960s were not imposed by OMGUS officials, nor were they a mere replication of American educational practices. West German teachers, administrators, and pupils propelled the process of continued educational reform after 1949, as they continually reevaluated the role of the school in a democratic society. There can be little doubt that some American practices served as inspiration for German reform efforts. For example, West German exchange program participants—teachers and pupils alike—cited American student government as a valuable practice that could be introduced into their schools. Yet the organizations that developed in the German schools reflected indigenous particularities. In the case of student government, for instance, German educators and pupils expanded upon the initial idea and made it uniquely German. Citywide student parliaments serve as but one such example. It was this process of inner democratization, driven by Germans at the local level that ensured educational reform continued—and intensified—in the 1950s and 1960s.

A related development contributing to continued reform in the West German schools was the nativization of reform by the mid-1950s. Whereas American officials had been the initial mouthpiece for school reform after 1945, German educators and administrators gradually accepted this role. One need only read the professional journals published during the 1950s to see how German educators spearheaded efforts for changes in political education, teacher training, and history instruction. The guidelines published by West Berlin senator for education Joachim Tiburtius in 1960 reflect this same phenomenon at the policymaking level. School officials in the former capital promoted a slate of activities—student government, school newspapers, political education, and contemporary history instruction—that had been endorsed by occupation officials just over a decade earlier. Proponents of school reform after the Allied occupation had carved out a new position in the German educational landscape in comparison to the years following World War I. These were not the marginalized, renegade reformers of the 1920s. Advocates of reform in the Federal Republic during the 1950s and 1960s were an active and vocal group that, in most instances, enjoyed the support of powerful politicians, administrators, and cultural elites. This is not to suggest, however, that all reforms were implemented fully or enjoyed complete success. While some reforms entered postwar classrooms rapidly after 1945, others required more time. Nevertheless, the nativization of school reform marked a key development in the democratization of the schools during the early years of the Federal Republic.

Returning once again to the central question of this study, one must ask what specific changes transpired in the West German schools in the two decades following World War II. A new relationship between teachers and pupils emerged in the 1950s that weakened the traditional authoritarian model of classroom instruction. This development was facilitated through the adoption of new pedagogical practices such as classroom discussion, debate, and group work. New textbooks contributed to this process, too, since they deemphasized the position of the teacher and encouraged pupils to become more active in classroom instruction. The rise of student government and student newspapers was important as well, since these activities diminished the role of the teacher and delegated increased responsibilities to pupils. All of these developments signaled a shift in the classroom relationship from the unquestioned authority of the teacher toward the greater independence of pupils.

Another significant reform that transcended disciplinary borders was the preparation of young Germans for their responsibilities as citizens in a democratic society. Political education instruction after the war sought to emphasize democracy as a "way of life," a living, fluid relationship among people in a civilized society. In order to achieve this, educators and administrators encouraged pupils to acquire practical experience with democracy. This process naturally took many forms in the years after 1945. Student government instilled an understanding of parliamentary procedure, majority and minority rights, and voting. At the same time SMV served as a place where pupils worked together, discussed and debated issues, and defended their opinions while still considering the ideas of others. Student newspapers offered many pupils a way to express their sentiments on political, social, and cultural questions. Political education textbooks presented democracy as a local phenomenon, urging pupils to consider their relationships in the family, school, and neighborhood. Social studies teachers throughout the Federal Republic utilized class trips to local government meetings, civic institutions, and political offices as a way to reinforce this perspective. Instruction in *Zeitgeschichte* and history courses examined problems that democracy faced throughout the world and how such challenges might be met. Exchange programs provided West German pupils, students, and teachers the opportunity to observe and participate in the everyday functioning of a democratic society. Overseas travels allowed Germans to learn the value of various civic organizations, as well as the importance of self-initiative, collaboration, and tolerance. These activities made it abundantly clear to postwar pupils that citizenship in a democratic society meant more than possessing a knowledge of the constitution.

Thus almost two decades after OMGUS officials had relinquished authority over the schools and departed for home, one could argue that many of their goals had been achieved. The militarism and fervent nationalism so common in textbooks before 1945 (and before 1933) had largely disappeared. New pedagogical practices, textbooks, and activities redefined the teacher-pupil relationship and weakened the authoritarian nature of the German classroom. New textbooks reconceptualized German history and political development, placing it in a wider European, Western, and global context. Student government and student newspapers offered individuals the opportunity to express their ideas and beliefs and to participate actively in the administration of the school. Finally, political education cemented its place as a key component in the preparation of young Germans for their responsibilities as citizens. The new subject emphasized the practical experience of pupils with the mechanisms and techniques of life in a democratic society. What made the attainment of these goals possible was the fact that a majority of German educators, administrators, and pupils came to believe in the need for these reforms following the end of the occupation. It was the desire of Germans to initiate, continue, and expand reforms in the 1950s and 1960s that explains the educational successes first promoted by OMGUS officials.

One of the central theses of this study has been that postwar educational reform was not a singular, monolithic process. The process of change was often uneven, as pedagogical and curricular innovations often permeated classrooms individually. Reforms also developed in an uncoordinated fashion, as the appearance of new methods and activities varied from region to region. There were unarguably commonalities and broader trends that united the schools, but as we have seen, reforms such as SMV, student newspapers, political education, and teacher training differed throughout the Federal Republic. This was also a gradual process, with reforms maturing throughout the 1950s and early 1960s. For instance, several years passed before new political education texts embodying the ideals of the new democratic state appeared in the schools. Finally, there can be no denying the subtlety of these reforms. They did not constitute a reorganization of the German educational system, as many historians have been quick to point out. And yet, the impact of these pedagogical and curricular changes cannot be overlooked. Their introduction constituted a reconfiguration of the German educational system. Arguably more important than any organizational change, these reforms ushered in a host of new democratic values, relationships, perspectives, and techniques.[5]

Toward 1968

This study has concentrated on a twenty-year period that is often overlooked or characterized as a failure by scholars interested in dramatic organizational change or visible conflict (such as 1968). Even some educators have been dismissive of the subtle reforms afoot during these two decades.[6] Yet the years from the end of World War II to the mid-1960s constituted a significant period of innovation and change in West German education. The student organizations, exchange programs, pedagogical methods, textbooks, and training programs introduced during these years constituted meaningful reform in the schools of the Federal Republic. The impact of these reforms, however, extended far beyond the classroom, and they continued to be felt as the Federal Republic emerged from the postwar era. The curricular and pedagogical reforms introduced during the two postwar decades played an important part in broader social and cultural developments in the years that followed.

Arguably the most immediate influence of postwar curricular and pedagogical reforms was the student movement of the late 1960s. Countless scholars and journalists have focused on the radical political agenda of many of the students, but few have examined the origins of the protests that date back to the 1950s. The preoccupation of historians with the universities has likewise obscured the formative role of secondary education in the lives of the student protesters.[7] Yet it was the education that these young men and women received before 1968 that, at least in part, provided them with the ideas and techniques for their audacious challenges to West Germany's political and social institutions. It may have been university students that sparked much of the conflict in that fateful year, but it was the instruction they encountered in the ten to fifteen years preceding 1968 that laid the foundation for such action.

In order to understand the goals and motivations of the student protesters, one first has to examine the origins of their frustrations. A variety of long-standing tensions came together in the rhetoric of student protesters, which included American involvement in Vietnam, the perceived conformity and materialism of their parents' generation, and an unwillingness to discuss the Third Reich.[8] Not to be overlooked, however, is the widespread animosity toward the West German universities that existed among many students. The universities represented a restoration of pre-Nazi traditions to many students in the 1960s. Students believed that their professors maintained authoritarian powers that were inconsistent with the new democratic values of the Federal Republic. The social conservatism of many professors, coupled with their hostility to calls for reform, did little to endear them to their students. Many youthful protesters felt that professors and administrators did not respect their views, and in some cases, actually curtailed their democratic rights. For these young Germans, the universities represented a bastion of intolerance and authoritarianism that had remained largely untouched by the democratic reforms of the postwar era. Thus, demands for democratic reforms in the universities became central to the rhetoric of those who took to the streets in 1968.

The instruction that student protesters received as secondary school pupils assisted them in their protests in a number of subtle ways. The first of these was the reconceptualization of the role of education and the acquisition of an international mind-set on the part of young Germans. Karl-Heinz Füssl makes precisely this point in his recent study of twentieth-century German-American cultural exchange. Exchange programs, he proposes, offered the young Germans who participated a variety of new ideas relating to the goals of education in a democratic society.[9] Perhaps even more importantly, trips to the US (and other destinations around the globe) instilled a new conception of the world in postwar German pupils and students. This new understanding of Germany and its broader European, trans-Atlantic, and global connections contributed to the international nature of 1968.[10] In this claim, Füssl suggests that exchange programs reconnected German pupils and students to international developments in much the same way that postwar teachers reemerged from the Nazi-imposed isolation of the 1930s and 1940s. The concomitant protests in other major cities around the world helped legitimate the students' demands and their response to West German authorities.

This new international perspective that Füssl illuminates, however, did not arise from exchange programs alone. As we have already seen, a new generation of postwar history and social studies texts situated Germany in an expanded, global context by the 1950s, providing some of the same benefits of exchange programs to a much larger contingent of West German pupils. These young Germans learned about the Federal Republic's connections to Europe, the United States, and the rest of the world in their classrooms on a daily basis. Presumably, postwar German pupils had learned about Vietnam (and other conflicts in Asia) years before they flowed out of university lecture halls and onto the streets. Thus it was a confluence of reforms—not merely the creation of exchange programs—that broadened the horizons of postwar pupils and made the transnational phenomenon of 1968 possible on German soil.

A second manner in which the curricular and pedagogical reforms of the postwar era contributed to the events of 1968 is in the multitude of new techniques and methods introduced in the schools. Specifically, postwar pupils gained practical experience with self-government, a free press, and political affairs in their classrooms. Through such postwar innovations as SMV, student newspapers, and political education, pupils acquired the tools with which they could express their own convictions. These experiences prepared pupils to engage critically with the political questions of the time, discuss and debate competing ideas, criticize and challenge traditional authority figures, propose their own goals, and collaborate with one another on large projects. Student involvement in politics was not a new development in the Germany of the late 1960s, but the origination of that involvement from below was. In 1968, it was the students' views and opinions—and not a political party, government, or interest group—that served as the catalyst. This dynamism and sense of political engagement was cultivated in part through the educational innovations of the postwar era.

Through internalizing the ideas, activities, and language of the instruction they encountered in the classroom, the pupils of the postwar era became the revolutionaries of the late 1960s. Admittedly, some radical groups espoused expressly antidemocratic rhetoric. Yet many others sought to institute change to the existing system, and they employed the practices they had encountered in the schools to achieve their goals. The creation of new student organizations outside the realm of the school could be considered a logical evolution of student government. Student pamphlets, fliers, and journals built on a tradition of a student press that emerged in the 1950s and 1960s. Even attention paid to developments in the US, the Middle East, and the Third World—not to mention elsewhere in Europe—coincided with a new perspective in history and political education texts of the period. This is not to argue that the educational reforms of the postwar era *necessitated* the events of 1968; rather what this project suggests is that university students drew some degree of inspiration from their secondary schooling in organizing and executing their protests. The impetus for the protests of 1968 may have been social conservatism, lingering authoritarian tendencies, and an unwillingness to address the past, yet, fittingly, it was the postwar introduction of various new educational activities and methods challenging these very traditions that helped make such activism possible.

The goals of students taking to the streets in 1968, however, exceeded their ability to implement change. Armed with new ideas and challenging traditional authorities on their own turf, student protesters continually voiced broader, more ambitious demands for reform. In rejecting the authoritarian ideals of their parents' generation, they conceptualized their calls for change in accordance with an entirely new set of ideals acquired, at least in part, in the schools over the previous decade. In a sense, their protests represented a revolution of rising expectations, one which could never hope to be fulfilled. Nevertheless, the actions of students showcased the power of individuals in a democratic society, allowing them to utilize the experiences they had collected as pupils. This process of participatory democracy that played out on the streets in 1968 spread to other areas of society and institutions in the years that followed.[11] Its legacy continued to shape the FRG long after the students returned to their lecture halls.

It was only due to the combination of successes and failures of postwar educational reform that the events of 1968 could have occurred. Had educational reform initiatives succeeded in purging the conservative, often politically tainted academic remnants of the Third Reich from the universities, there would have been little cause for the students' frustration. Had university administrators been more receptive to working with students and listening to their demands, there would have been less fuel for the protesters' fury. In short, if reform had been wholly successful, who or what would have been the focus of the students' anger? At the same time, the potent formula for 1968 required the success of many postwar educational innovations. Only with the curricular and pedagogical reforms of the postwar era could university students have acquired the rhetoric, techniques, and ideas necessary to formulate their challenge. Taking part in democratic organizations as pupils, traveling outside Germany, and debating and discussing contentious issues in the schools all provided invaluable experience to the former secondary school pupils now expressing their discontent. Experiences as pupils in the classrooms of the late 1950s had now translated into action on the streets of the late 1960s. Had the reform of the German educational system been more or less successful twenty years after the war, Germany's 1968 experience would likely have been considerably different.

Citizens Not Subjects

More than a decade after the end of the Second World War, Otto Friedrich Bollnow, a leading German pedagogue, evaluated the state of the German educational system. He asserted that a "general fatigue" had fallen upon educational thought in Germany. "Sluggishly, without any new impulses, pedagogy is dragging itself along."[12] This was hardly an endorsement—or even an acknowledgement—of the subtle reforms already underway in the postwar schools in the mid-1950s. Fifteen years later, in 1970, another influential German educator confirmed this picture of the West German educational system. There had been "sketches and attempts" to alter the schools, Caspar Kuhlmann admitted, but he concluded that no such thing as educational reform had actually taken place.[13] From these diagnoses, one would believe that Germany's defeat, the subsequent American occupation, the creation of a stable democracy on German soil, and the new generation of pupils and teachers who entered the schools had had virtually no impact on the educational system. The schools of a peaceful and prosperous Federal Republic, one could extrapolate from the comments of Bollnow and Kuhlmann, could barely be distinguished from those of Germany three, four, or five decades earlier.

This project has challenged these and subsequent affirmations of the stagnant, restorative nature of the postwar educational system. The continued existence of a three-track school system did not prevent the introduction of curricular and pedagogical reforms. Attempts to alter the schools did not end with the creation of the Federal Republic in 1949. The years of Adenauer's chancellorship were not solely a time of orthodoxy and unquestioned obedience to traditional authority. Nor did they mark a time of complete amnesia in regard to the events of the recent past. Finally, the events of 1968 did not materialize from thin air. The activism of students could be viewed as an effect much more than a cause, when one considers the significant reform of the educational system in preceding years. In light of these claims, this study serves as a plea for further reconsideration of the early years of the Federal Republic. The traditional picture of conservative 1950s West Germany becomes less harmonious and more complicated when viewed through the lens of the schools.

The schools played an indispensable role in the broader process of cultural democratization underway in the early life of the Federal Republic. Few observers recognized this as clearly as West Berlin senator for education Carl-Heinz Evers. In an April 1964 speech before SPD party members in the former capital, Evers reminded his listeners of the key role education played in German society. In an impassioned address, Evers asserted that

> education is the precondition for everything else. There would be no healthy, growing economy; there would be no thriving democratic community with responsible citizens; there would be no cultural variety and no personal self-realization of people, if the basis of all of these things, the educational system, gave way. The realm of freedom that is granted to us would remain empty![14]

These words nicely parallel those written by General Clay almost fifteen years earlier. The democratization of the educational system in the postwar decades had created a new generation of Germans cognizant of their rights and responsibilities as citizens. So, too, had it contributed to broader cultural developments such as a support for the freedom of the press, respect for (as well as participation in) the institutions of democracy, and critical engagement in political affairs. Finally, a renewed emphasis on the individual slowly eroded earlier traditions that stressed the community and the subordination of personal aspirations for the good of the state. As the words of Evers suggest, the most important exercise in which pupils engaged in their postwar classrooms was not math, history, biology, or foreign language instruction. The greatest lesson instilled in postwar West German pupils was indeed one that they may well not have realized they were learning at the time: how to conduct oneself as a responsible citizen in a democratic society.

Notes

1. Lucius D. Clay, *Decision in Germany* (Garden City, NY, 1950), 303.
2. Ibid., 305.
3. Ibid., 303.
4. Konrad H. Jarausch argues that this process of "inner democratization," initiated following the occupation, constituted the most decisive step in the creation of a new civil society in the young Federal Republic. See Jarausch, *Die Umkehr. Deutsche Wandlungen 1945–1995* (Munich, 2004), 135, 182–92.
5. As Beate Rosenzweig has convincingly argued, the introduction of a more flexible school system organization was by no means a guarantee for the success of democratic reforms. Japan, she asserts, indeed followed most American recommendations regarding the structure of the educational system. This did not, however, mean that American goals for the democratization of the school system were realized. German schools, on the other hand, which largely evaded or circumvented these same recommendations, experienced inner reform that led to the achievement of many American goals after 1949. See Rosenzweig, *Erziehung zur Demokratie? Amerikanische Besatzungs- und Schulreformpolitik in Deutschland und Japan* (Stuttgart, 1998), 183.
6. A minority of teachers with whom I conducted interviews concurred with this pessimistic impression, stating that their classrooms were not a place in which the subtle democratic reforms of the postwar era could transpire. Yet even these educators admitted that indeed something had occurred, and that long-lasting curricular and pedagogical changes had penetrated the postwar schools. See Ingrid Handt, interview by author, Berlin-Lichterade, 28 April 2003.
7. There are several studies of the events of 1968 that place German events within a broader international context. See David Caute, *Sixty-Eight: The Year of the Barricades,* (London, 1988); Ronald Fraser, *1968: A Student Generation in Revolt,* (New York, 1988); David Kurlansky, *1968: The Year That Rocked the World* (New York, 2004). For recent examinations of Germany's 1968 experience, see Ingrid Gilcher-Holtey, *Die 68er Bewegung* (Munich, 2001); Wolfgang Kraushaar, *1968. Das Jahr, das alles verändert hat* (Munich, 1998); Uwe Wesel, *Die verspielte Revolution. 1968 und die Folgen* (Munich, 2002). Finally, the work of Elizabeth Peifer examines how the events of 1968 have acquired a mythical like status in the political culture of the Federal Republic. See Peifer, "1968 in German Political Culture, 1967–1993: From Experience to Myth," (PhD diss., University of North Carolina at Chapel Hill, 1997).
8. Jarausch, *Die Umkehr,* 219–21.
9. Karl-Heinz Füssl, *Deutsch-amerikanischer Kulturaustausch im 20.Jahrhundert* (Frankfurt, 2004), 21.
10. Ingrid Gilcher-Holtey emphasizes the international nature of the 1968 protests in her work. See Gilcher-Holtey, *Die 68er Bewegung,* 10, 61–62.
11. Kraushaar, *1968,* 320.
12. Otto Friedrich Bollnow, "Das veränderte Bild vom Menschen und sein Einfluss auf das pädagogische Denken," *Erziehung wozu? Pädagogische Probleme der Gegenwart* (Hamburg, 1956), 35, quoted in Saul B. Robinsohn and J. Caspar Kuhlmann, "West German Education," *Comparative Education Review* XI, no. 3 (October 1967): 311–30.
13. Caspar Kuhlmann, "Schulreform und Gesellschaft in der Bundesrepublik Deutschland 1946–1966," in *Schulreform im gesellschaftlichen Prozeß*, vol. 1, ed. Saul B. Robinsohn (Stuttgart, 1970), 1/155.
14. "Bildungsnotstand in Deutschland?" Rede des Senators für Schulwesen Carl-Heinz Evers anlässlich einer öffentlichen Versammlung der SPD am 17.April 1964 im Bezirk Berlin-Zehlendorf, 5; B. Rep. 015, Nr. 695, Landesarchiv Berlin (LAB). One should note that the official title of Evers, who succeeded Tiburtius as head of the schools in West Berlin, changed in 1963 from Senator für Volksbildung to Senator für Schulwesen.

BIBLIOGRAPHY

Archival Sources

Archiv zur Geschichte von Tempelhof und Schöneberg, Historical Archive of Tempelhof and Schöneberg, Berlin
Uncataloged archival holdings on Tempelhof schools.

Bundesarchiv Koblenz, German National Archives, Koblenz (BAK)
B106 Bundesministerium des Innern
B154 Deutscher Ausschuss für das Erziehungs- und Bildungswesen
B168 Bundeszentrale für politische Bildung

Heimatmuseum Neukölln, Neukölln local museum, Berlin
Exhibit materials.

Heimatmuseum Zehlendorf, Zehlendorf local museum, Berlin (HZ)

Arndt Oberschule	Rep 28	Dokument 20
Alfred Wegener Schule	Rep 26	Dokument 11
Droste-Hülshoff-Oberschule	Rep 20, 22	Dokument 99
Schadowschule	Rep 9, 11	Dokument 452
Schule (allgemein)	Rep 1	Dokument 486
Werner-von-Siemens-Oberschule	Rep 21	Dokument 602

Hessisches Hauptstaatsarchiv, Hessian State Archives, Wiesbaden (HHStA)
Abteilung 429/1. Staatliches Gymnasium Wiesbaden (Dilthey-Schule).
Abteilung 429/5. Realgymnasium Wiesbaden (Gutenburgschule).
Abteilung 429/7. Gymnasium Philippium Weilburg.

Abteilung 429/10. Leibnizschule.

Abteilung 504. Hessisches Ministerium für Kultus und Unterricht (1945–1950); Hessisches Ministerium für Erziehung und Volksbildung (1950–1963); Hessisches Kultusministerium (1963-).

Abteilung 546. Landeszentrale für Heimatdienst (-1958); Landeszentrale für politische Bildung (1958-).

Abteilung 802. Wissenschaftliche Prüfungsarbeiten.

Abteilung 1178. Nachlass Erwin Stein.

Landesarchiv Berlin, Berlin State Archives (Reinickendorf) (LAB)

B Rep. 007. Senatsverwaltung für Volksbildung.

B Rep. 015. Senatsverwaltung für Schule, Beruf, Bildung, und Sport.

B Rep. 202. Bezirksamt Tiergarten von Berlin.

B Rep. 203. Bezirksamt Wedding von Berlin.

B Rep. 207. Bezirksamt Charlottenburg von Berlin.

B Rep. 210. Bezirksamt Zehlendorf von Berlin.

B Rep. 213. Bezirksamt Tempelhof von Berlin.

B Rep. 232. German Youth Activities (GYA).

C. Rep. 120. Magistrat von Berlin, Volksbildung

National Archives II, College Park, Maryland (NACP)

Record Group 12. Records of US Office of Education.

Record Group 59. General Records of the Department of State.

Record Group 226. Records of Office of Strategic Services.

Record Group 260. Records of the US Occupation Headquarters, WWII.

Record Group 466. Records of the US High Commissioner in Germany.

Newspapers and Periodicals

Aachener Volkszeitung
American Mercury
Berliner Kurier
Berliner Lehrerzeitung
Berliner Morgenpost
Bildung und Erziehung
Darmstadt Echo
Deutsche Lehrer, Der
Deutsche Schule, Die
Frankfurter Neue Presse
Gesellschaft, Staat, Erziehung
Hessische Allegmeine Zeitung
Hessische Lehrerzeitung
Hessische Nachrichten
Hessischen Beiträge zur Schulreform
Kasseler Zeitung
Marburger Presse
Neckar Echo

Neue Zeitung, Die
New Republic
New World News
New York Times
Offenbach Post
Pädagogische Provinz, Die
Pädagogische Rundschau
Pandora
Parlament, Das
Sammlung, Die
Schule und Nation
Tagesspiegel, Der
Westermanns Pädagogische Beiträge
Wir machen mit

Interviews

Dr. Richard T. Alexander, Jr., 1 October 2004.
Herr Dr. Martin Müller (pseudonym), 27 May 2003.
Herr Reinhart Crüger, 10 June 2003.
Herr Hans-Dieter Dubrow, 26 June 2003.
Prof. Dr. Hartmut Eggert, 21 July 2003.
Frau Ingrid Handt, 28 April 2003.
Prof. Dr. Ulrich Kledzik, 8 May 2003.
Herr Horst Kollat, 23 April 2003.
Herr Harald Krieger, 7 July 2003.
Herr Dr. Joachim Matysiak, 27 June 2003.
Herr Gustav Merseburg, 5 June 2003.
Herr Heine Moos, 10 August 2003.
Herr Gerd Poeschke, 13 May 2003.
Herr Bernd Roland, 23 May 2003.
Frau Marianne Samarellis, 20 May 2003.
Herr Reinhold Skoecz, 28 May 2003.
Herr Wilhelm-Dietrich von Thadden, 19 May 2003.

Published Primary Sources

Adam, Willi. *Trögels Lesehefte*, vol. 12, *Hitler und der zweite Weltkrieg*. 2nd ed. Ansbach, 1958.
——. *Trögels Lesehefte*, vol. 12, *Hitler und der zweite Weltkrieg*. 3rd ed. Ansbach, 1960.
Amtsblatt des Hessischen Ministeriums für Kultus und Unterricht. Vol. 1 (1948).
——. Vol. 2 (1949).
Amtsblatt des Hessischen Ministers für Erziehung und Volksbildung. Vol. 10 (1957).
——. Vol. 17 (1964).

————. Vol. 19 (1966).

Anrich, Ernst. *Deutsche Geschichte, 1918–1939: Die Geschichte einer Zeitenwende.* Leipzig, 1943.

Bader, G. *Geschichte für württembergische Volks- und Mittelschulen.* Vol. 2. Stuttgart, 1932.

Bodesohn, A. *Handbuch der Staats- und Bürgerkunde.* 3rd ed. Wittenberg, 1923.

Brandi, Karl. *Deutsche Geschichte.* Berlin, 1923.

Büro für Politische Studien. *Der Einzelne und der Staat.* Würzburg, 1950.

Denkschrift zur inneren Schulreform – langfristige Planungen. Berlin, 1962.

Ebeling, Hans. *Deutsche Geschichte.* Vol. 2. Edition B. Braunschweig, 1950.

————. *Deutsche Geschichte.* Vol. 5. Edition A. Braunschweig, 1952.

————. *Die Reise in die Vergangenheit.* Vol. 4. 4th ed. Braunschweig, 1964.

Eichelsbacher, August, ed. *Geschichte des deutschen Volkes - Aufgabe für Nordbayern.* Munich, 1927.

EUCOM, OPOT Division, Training and Education Branch. *German Youth Activities Guide.* Germany, 1947.

Haacke, Ulrich, and Benno Schneider. *Dein Staat und Dein Volk. Eine Staatsbürgerkunde.* Leipzig, 1928.

Haacke, Ulrich and Ernst Ziemann. *Handbook für den Geschichtsunterricht an Volksschulen.* Leipzig, 1941.

Heumann, Hans. *Unser Weg durch die Geschichte. Vom Wiener Kongress bis zur Gegenwart.* Frankfurt, 1961.

High Commission (US) for Germany (Office of), ed. *Educational and Cultural Activities in Germany Today.* Reprints from *Information Bulletin.* Frankfurt, 1950.

Hilligen, Wolfgang. *Sehen – Beurteilen – Handeln. Lese- und Arbeitsbuch zur Sozialkunde im 5. und 6.Schuljahr.* 2nd ed. Frankfurt, 1958.

————. *Sehen – Beurteilen – Handeln. Lese- und Arbeitsbuch zur Politischen zur Politischen Bildung und Sozialkunde.* Part 2, version A. 6th ed. Frankfurt, 1964.

Hoffman, Waldemar, and Georg Müller. *Einst und Jetzt. Geschichtserzählungen für das Fünfte und Sechste Schuljahr.* 3rd ed. Frankfurt, 1956.

————. *Einst und Jetzt. Geschichtserzählungen für das Fünfte und Sechste Schuljahr.* 10th ed. Frankfurt, 1963.

Hornstein, Erika von. *Die deutsche Not. Flüchtlinge berichten.* Cologne, 1960. Quoted in Hans Ebeling, *Die Reise in die Vergangenheit.* Vol. 4. 4th ed. Braunschweig, 1964.

Jaitner, Willy, Hans Mann, and Wilhelm Stodt. *Unsere Geschichte Teil II – Vom westfälischen Frieden bis zur Gegenwart.* Düsseldorf, 1953.

Kolbe, H. *Vom Volksthing zur Reichsverfassung. Eine Einführung in die Entwicklung des deutschen Staats-, Wirtschafts- und Gesellschaftsleben als Grundlage staatsbürgerlicher Bildung und Erziehung.* Langensalza, 1927.

Kumsteller, Bernhard and Ulrich Haacke, eds. *Geschichtsbuch für die deutsche Jugend.* Leipzig, 1930.

Kunow, Max. *Sozialkunde. 7.Schuljahr.* Wiesbaden, 1953.

Müller, O. H. *Deutsche Geschichte in Kurzfassung.* Frankfurt, 1950.

Nebelsiek, Karl. *Der Gemeinde-, Staats- und Weltbürger. Ein Handbuch der Bürgerkunde und Sozialkunde (Gemeinschaftskunde).* Oldenburg, 1951.

————. *Der Gemeinde-, Staats- und Weltbürger. Ein Handbuch der Bürgerkunde und Sozialkunde (Gemeinschaftskunde).* 2nd ed. Oldenburg, 1953.

Office of Military Government for Germany, US (OMGUS). *Education and Religion - Monthly Report of Military Governor.* No. 1, August 1945.

————. *Education and Religion - Monthly Report of Military Governor.* No. 2, September 1945.

Office of Military Government for Germany, US – Education and Cultural Relations Division. *Handbook of Education Statistics (U.S. occupied area of Germany).* 1949.

————. *Second Handbook of Basic Education Statistics, U.S. Occupied Area of Germany.* 1950.

————. *Report on Textbook Evaluation, 1945–1949.* 1950.

Otto, H. *Bürgerkunde. Für Schule und Haus.* 3rd ed. Berlin, 1921.

Reiniger, Max. *Neue Staatsbürgerkunde I.* 2nd ed. Langensalza, 1928.

————. *Neue Staatsbürgerkunde II.* Langensalza, 1923.

Scherrinsky, Harald, Elisabeth Berger, and Georg Müller. *Wege der Völker.* Vol. 3, *Ringen um Freiheit.* Berlin, 1950.

Schulze, Gertrud, Wilhelm Puhlmann, Fritz Seelig, Martha Schwarz, and Waldemar Hoffmann. *Wege der Völker.* Vol. 4, *Demokratie im Werden.* Berlin, 1949.

Seitzer, Otto. *Miteinander – Füreinander. Ein Lese- und Arbeitsbuch zur Gemeinschaftskunde für 12–16 jährige Mädchen und Jungen.* Stuttgart, 1951.

Statistisches Amt der Stadt Berlin. *Statistisches Jahrbuch für der Stadt Berlin.* 9th ed. Berlin, 1933.

Statistisches Landesamt Berlin. *Statistisches Jahrbuch Berlin 1965.* Berlin, 1965.

Steinbügl, Eduard. *Geschichte der neuesten Zeit für Mittelschulen und Realschulen.* Munich, 1962.

Stieve, Friedrich. *Geschichte des Deutschen Volkes.* 19th ed. Munich, 1944.

United States Department of State. *Germany 1947–1949: The Story in Documents.* Washington, DC, 1950.

Warneck, Hans and Willy Matschke. *Geschichte für Volksschulen.* Bielefeld, 1943.

Secondary Sources

Albisetti, James. *Secondary School Reform in Imperial Germany.* Princeton, NJ, 1978.

Bennack, Jürgen. "Volksschulbücher der Nachkriegszeit zwischen Erneuerung und Restauration." *Bildung und Erziehung* 9 (1999): 1–15.

Berg, Falko. "Die Lehrerin." In *Nachkriegs-Kinder. Kindheit in Deutschland 1945–1950,* ed. Jürgen Kleindienst: 161–168. Berlin, 1998.

Berghahn, Volker. *Americanization of West German Industry.* New York, 1986.

————. "Conceptualizing the American Impact on Germany: West German Society and the Problem of Americanization." Paper read at The American Impact on Western Europe Conference, 25–27 March 1999, at the German Historical Institute, Washington, DC.

Bettermann, Karl August and Manfred Gössl. *Schulgliederung, Lehrerbildung, und Lehrerbesoldung und der bundesstaatlichen Ordnung.* Berlin, 1963.

Bittner, Stefan. "German Readers of Dewey–Before 1933 and After 1945." *Studies in Philosophy and Education* 19 (2000): 83–108.

————. *Learning By Dewey? John Dewey und die deutsche Pädagogik 1900–2000.* Bad Heilbrunn, 2001.

Blackburn, Gilmer. *Education in the Third Reich.* New York, 1985.

Blessing, Benita. *The Antifascist Classroom: Denazification in Soviet-occupied Germany, 1945–1949.* New York, 2006.

Boehling, Rebecca. *A Question of Priorities: Democratic Reforms and Economic Recovery in Postwar Germany.* Providence, RI, 1996.

Bölling, Rainer. *Volksschullehrer und Politik. Der Deutsche Lehrerverein 1918–1933.* Kritische Studien zur Geschichtswissenschaft, vol. 32, ed. Helmut Berding, Jürgen Kocka, and Hans-Ulrich Wehler. Göttingen, 1978.

Bollnow, Otto Friedrich. "Das veränderte Bild vom Menschen und sein Einfluss auf das pädagogische Denken." *Erziehung wozu? Pädagogische Probleme der Gegenwart, 35.* Hamburg, 1956. Quoted in Saul B. Robinsohn and J. Caspar Kuhlmann, "West German Education," *Comparative Education Review 9, no. 3 (October 1967):* 311–30.

Borgstedt, Angela. *Entnazifizierung in Kalsruhe 1946 bis 1951.* Karlsruher Beiträge zur Geschichte des Nationalsozialismus. No. 5. Konstanz, 2001.

Buchinger, Hubert. *Volksschule und Lehrerbildung im Spannungsfeld politischer Entscheidung 1945–1970.* Munich, 1975.

Buckhout, Gerald L. "The Concept of the State in Modern Germany: History Textbooks, 1918–1933." *Internationales Jahrbuch für Geschichtsunterricht 9* (1963/1964): 15–30.

Bungenstab, Karl-Ernst. *Umerziehung zur Demokratie? Reeducation-Politik im Bildungswesen der US-Zone 1945–1949.* Gütersloh, 1970.

———. "Entstehung, Bedeutungs- und Funktionswandel der Amerika-Häuser. Ein Beitrag zur Geschichte der amerikanischen Auslandsinformation nach dem 2.Weltkrieg." *Jahrbuch für Amerikastudien 16* (1971): 189–203.

Burstyn, Joan, ed. *Educating Tomorrow's Valuable Citizen.* Albany, NY, 1996.

Caute, David. *Sixty-Eight: The Year of the Barricades.* London, 1988.

Clay, Lucius D. *Decision in Germany.* Garden City, NY, 1950.

Dahrendorf, Ralf. *Bildung ist Bürgerrecht.* Hamburg, 1968.

Dewey, John. *Schools of Tomorrow.* New York, 1915.

———. *Democracy and Education.* New York, 1916.

Dierkes, Julian. "Teaching Portrayals of the Nation: Postwar History Education in Japan and the Germanys." PhD diss., Princeton University, NJ, 2003.

Dietrich, Theodor. *Die Pädagogik Peter Petersens. Der Jenaplan: Beispiel einer humanen Schule.* 5th ed. Bad Heilbronn, 1991.

Doering-Manteuffel, Anselm. *Wie westlich sind die Deutschen? Amerikanisierung und Westernisierung im 20.Jahrhundert.* Göttingen, 1999.

Ebeling, Elizabeth. *Erinnerungen an Hans Ebeling: 1906–1967.* Braunschweig, 1997.

Ellwein, Thomas. "Die deutsche Gesellschaft und ihr Bildungswesen. Interessenartikulation und Bildungsdiskussion." In *Handbuch der deutschen Bildungsgeschichte,* vol. 6/1, ed. Christoph Führ and Carl-Ludwig Furck: 87–109. Munich, 1998.

Engelmann, Susanne Charlotte. *German Education and Re-education.* New York, 1945.

Engstrom, Eric J. "*Zeitgeschichte* as Disciplinary History – On Professional Identity, Self-Reflexive Narratives, and Discipline-Building in Contemporary German History," *Tel Aviver Jahrbuch für deutsche Geschichte 29* (2000): 399–425.

Fedler, Patricia. *Anfange der staatlichen Kulturpolitik in Hessen nach dem Zweiten Weltkrieg, 1945–1955.* Wiesbaden, 1993.

Feiten, Willi. *Der Nationalsozialistische Lehrerbund.* Weinheim, 1981.

Frankel, Richard E. *Bismarck's Shadow.* New York, 2005.

Franz-Willing, Georg. *Umerziehung: Die de-Nationalisierung besiegter Völker im 20.Jahrhundert.* Coberg, 1991.

Fraser, Ronald. *1968: A Student Generation in Revolt.* New York, 1988.

Fredericksen, Oliver J. *The American Military Occupation of Germany.* Darmstadt, 1953.

Frei, Norbert. *Adenauer's Germany and the Nazi Past: The Politics of Amnesty and Integration.* New York, 2002.

Friedeburg, Ludwig von. *Bildungsreform in Deutschland. Geschichte und gesellschaftlicher Widerspruch.* Frankfurt, 1989.

Fullan, Michael. *The New Meaning of Educational Change.* New York, 1991.

Führ, Christoph. *Schulen und Hochschulen in der Bundesrepublik Deutschland.* Bonn, 1988.

———. *Deutsches Bildungswesen seit 1945.* Bonn, 1996.

Füssl, Karl-Heinz. *Die Umerziehung der Deutschen: Jugend und Schule unter den Siegermächten des Zweiten Weltkriegs 1945–1955.* Paderborn, 1994.

———. *Deutsch-amerikanischer Kulturaustausch im 20.Jahrhundert.* Frankfurt, 2004.

Füssl, Karl-Heinz and Christian Kubina. *Zeugen zur Berliner Schulgeschichte (1951–1968).* Berlin, 1981.

———. *Berliner Schule zwischen Restauration und Innovation.* Frankfurt, 1983.

———. *Mitbestimmung und Demokratisierung im Schulwesen. Eine Fallstudie zur Praxis von Beratungsgremien am Beispiel Berlins.* Berlin, 1984.

Füssl, Karl-Heinz and Gregory Wegner. "Education Under Radical Change: Educational Policy and the Youth Program of the United States in Postwar Germany." *History of Education Quarterly* 36, no. 1 (1996): 1–21.

Gaab, Jeffrey S. *Justice Delayed: The Restoration of Justice in Bavaria under American Occupation, 1945–1949.* New York, 1999.

Gagel, Walter. *Geschichte der politischen Bildung in der Bundesrepublik Deutschland 1945–1989.* Opladen, 1994.

Geiger, Wolfgang. "Geschichte und Staatsbürgerkunde vor und in der Weimarer Zeit." In *Geschichte und Geschichtsdidaktik vom Kaiserreich bis zur Gegenwart,* ed. Paul Leidinger: 99–109. Stuttgart, 1988.

Geissler, Gert, ed. *Schulreform und Schulverwaltung in Berlin. Die Protokolle der Gesamtkonferenzen der Schulräte von Gross-Berlin, Juni 1945 bis November 1948.* Frankfurt, 2002.

Giese, Gerhard. *Quellen zur deutschen Schulgeschichte seit 1800.* Quellensammlung zur Kulturgeschichte, vol. 15, ed. Wilhelm Treue. Göttingen, 1961.

Giesecke, Hermann. *Hitlers Pädagogen. Theorie und Praxis nationalsozialistischer Erziehung.* Weinheim, 1993.

Gilcher-Holtey, Ingrid. *Die 68er Bewegung.* Munich, 2001.

Gimbel, John. *A German Community Under American Occupation: Marburg, 1945–1952.* Stanford, CA, 1961.

Giroux, Henry. *Schooling for Democracy: Critical Pedagogy in the Modern Age.* London, 1989.

Gleber, Peter. "Die Mär von 'Fremdbestimmten' und 'Widerstandskämpfern'. Entnazifizierung von NS-Bürgermeistern am Beispiel von Fällen von der Spruchkammer Wiesloch." *Badische Heimat* 77 (1997): 85–95.

Grace, Alonzo G. "Education." In *Governing Postwar Germany,* ed. Edward H. Litchfield. Ithaca, NY, 1953.

Hahn, H. J. *Education and Society in Germany.* New York, 1998.

Harrington, John Edward III. "Weimar Educators' Views of American Educational Practices." PhD diss., University of North Carolina at Chapel Hill, 1979.

Hearnden, Arthur. *The British in Germany: Educational Reconstruction after 1945.* London, 1978.

———. *Education in the Two Germanies.* Boulder, CO, 1974.

Heideking, Jürgen. "Mutual Influences on Education: Germany and the United States from World War I to the Cold War." *Paedagogica Historica* 33, no. 1 (1997): 9–23.

Heinemann, Manfred, ed. *Umerziehung und Wiederaufbau: Die Bildungspolitik der Besatzungsmächte in Deutschland und Österreich.* Stuttgart, 1981.

Henige, David. *Oral Historiography.* New York, 1982.

Henke, Klaus-Dietmar. *Die amerikanische Besatzung Deutschlands.* Munich, 1995.

Herdegen, Peter. *Demokratische Bildung. Eine Einführung in das soziale und politische Lernen in den Klassen 5 bis 10.* Donauwörth, 2001.

Herrlitz, Hans-Georg, Wulf Hopf, and Hartmut Titze. *Deutsche Schulgeschichte von 1800 bis zur Gegenwart.* Regensburg, 1981.

Hertz, H. *Studium nach dem Studium.* Bad Honnef, 1987.

Höhn, Maria. *GIs and Fräuleins: The German-American Encounter in 1950s West Germany.* Chapel Hill, NC, 2002.

Homann, Mathias. "Schulalltag im Dritten Reich – Erfahrungen am Kaiser Wilhelms-Realgymnasium." In *Schulreform – Kontinuitäten und Brücke. Das Versuchungsfeld Berlin-Neukölln,* vol. 1, ed. Gerd Radde and Werner Korthaase et al.: 366–84. Opladen, 1993.

Howarth, Ken. *Oral History.* Stroud, UK, 1998.

Hübener, Theodore. *The Schools of West Germany.* New York, 1962.

Hundsdorfer, Otto. "Demokratie lernen. Erfahrungen eines Junglehrers nach dem Krieg." In *Münchner Nachkriegsjahre. Lesebuch zur Geschichte des Münchner Alltags,* ed. Angelika Baumann: 123–33. Munich, 1997.

Jarausch, Konrad H. *The Unfree Professions: German Lawyers, Teachers, and Engineers, 1900–1950.* New York, 1990.

———. *Die Umkehr. Deutsche Wandlungen 1945–1995.* Munich, 2004.

Keim, Wolfgang. "Reformpädagogik als restaurative Kraft." In *Erziehung und Erziehungswissenschaft in der BDR und der DDR,* vol. 1, eds. Dietrich Hoffmann and Karl Neumann: 221–48. Weinheim, 1994.

———. *Erziehung unter der Nazi-Diktatur.* Darmstadt, 1995.

Kellermann, Henry J. *Cultural Relations as an Instrument of U.S. Foreign Policy: The Educational Exchange Program Between the United States and Germany 1945–1954.* Washington, DC, 1978.

———. "Von Re-education zu Re-orientation: Das amerikanische Re-orientierungsprogramm im Nachkriegsdeutschland." In *Umerziehung und Wiederaufbau: Die Bildungspolitik der Besatzungsmächte in Deutschland und Österreich,* ed. Manfred Heinemann: 86–102. Stuttgart, 1981.

Kellermann, P., ed. *Universität und Hochschulpolitik.* Vienna, 1986.

Kilpatrick, William H. *Group Education for a Democracy.* New York, 1940.

Kitowski, Karin. "Ein warmer Hauch der Liebe zu Volk und Staat… Anspruch und Wirklichkeit der Staatsbürgerkunde in der Weimarer Republik." In *Die Liebe zu Volk und Vaterland. Erziehung zum Staatsbürger in der Weimarer Republik,* ed. Karin Kitowski and Rüdiger Wolf: 9–29. Dortmund, 2000.

Klafki, Wolfgang. "Die fünfziger Jahre — eine Phase schulorganisatorischer Restauration. Zur Schulpolitik und Schulentwicklung im ersten Jahrzent der Bundesrepublik." In *Die fünfziger Jahre. Beiträge zu Politik und Kultur,* ed. Dieter Bänsch: 131–62. Tübingen, 1985.

Klessmann, Christoph. *Die doppelte Staatsgründung.* Bonn, 1991.

————. *Zeitgeschichte in Deutschland.* Stuttgarter Vorträge zur Zeitgeschichte, vol. 5, ed. Gerhard Hirschfeld. Essen, 1998.

Klewitz, Marion. *Berliner Einheitsschule, 1945–1951.* Historische und Pädagogische Studien, vol. 1, ed. Otto Büsch und Gerd Heinrich. Berlin, 1971.

————. *Lehrersein im Dritten Reich.* Weinheim, 1987.

Koch, H. W. *The Hitler Youth: Origins and Development 1922–1945.* New York, 1975.

Kopitzsch, Wolfgang. *Gewerkschaft Erziehung und Wissenschaft (GEW) 1947–1975. Grundzüge ihrer Geschichte.* Heidelberg, 1983.

Kraul, Margret. *Das deutsche Gymnasium 1780–1980.* Frankfurt, 1984.

Kraushaar, Wolfgang. *1968. Das Jahr, das alles verändert hat.* Munich, 1998.

Kropat, Wolf-Arno. "Amerikanische oder deutsche Schulreform?" *Nassauische Annalen* 112 (2001): 541–68.

Kuhlmann, Caspar. "Schulreform und Gesellschaft in der Bundesrepublik Deutschland 1946–1966." In *Schulreform im gesellschaftlichen Prozeß,* vol. 1., ed. Saul B. Robinsohn, 1/155. Stuttgart, 1970.

Kundler, Herbert. *RIAS Berlin, eine Radio-Station in einer geteilten Stadt.* Berlin, 1994.

Kurlansky, David. *1968: The Year That Rocked the World.* New York, 2004.

Lamberti, Marjorie. *State, Society, and the Elementary School in Imperial Germany.* New York, 1989.

————. "Elementary School Teachers and the Struggle against Social Democracy in Wilhelmine Germany." *History of Education Quarterly* 32, no. 1 (Spring 1992): 72–97.

————. *The Politics of Education: Teachers and School Reform in Weimar Germany.* New York, 2002.

Lange-Quassowski, Jutta-B. *Neuordnung oder Restauration? Das Demokratiekonzept der amerikanischen Besatzungsmacht und die politische Sozialisation der Westdeutschen: Wirtschaftsordnung – Schulstruktur – Politische Bildung.* Opladen, 1979.

————. "Amerikanische Westintegrationspolitik, Re-education und deutsche Schulpolitik." In *Umerziehung und Wiederaufbau: Die Bildungspolitik der Besatzungsmächte in Deutschland und Österreich,* ed. Manfred Heinemann: 53–67. Stuttgart, 1981.

Layton, Walter. *How to Deal with Germany.* London, 1945.

Limage, Leslie J., ed. *Democratizing Education and Educating Democratic Citizens.* New York, 2001.

Little, J. and Margaret J. McLaughlin, eds. *Teachers' Work: Individuals, Colleagues, and Contexts.* New York, 1993.

Lüdtke, Alf. *The History of Everyday Life: Reconstructing Historical Experiences and Ways of Life.* Princeton, NJ, 1995.

Maase, Kaspar. *Bravo Amerika. Erkundigungen zur Jugendkultur der Bundesrepublik in den fünfziger Jahren.* Hamburg, 1992.

————. "'Americanization,' 'Americanness' and 'Americanisms': Time For a Change in Perspective?" Paper read at The American Impact on Western Europe Conference, 25–27 March 1999, at the German Historical Institute, Washington, DC.

McGinn, Noel, and Erwin Epstein. *Comparative Perspectives on the Role of Education in Democratization.* Frankfurt, 1999.

McInnis, Edgar, Richard Hiscocks, and Robert Spencer. *The Shaping of Postwar Germany.* Toronto, 1960.

McLaughlin, Milbrey W. "The Rand Change Agent Study Revisited: Macro Perspectives and Micro Realities." *Educational Researcher* 19, no. 9 (December 1990): 11–16.

Meier, Ekkehard. "In einer neuen Zeit – Abiturarbeiten 1946 bis 1948," In *Schulreform – Kontinuitäten und Brücke. Das Versuchungsfeld Berlin-Neukölln*, vol. 2, ed. Gerd Radde and Werner Korthaase et al.: 21–28. Opladen, 1993.

Merritt, Richard and Anna Merritt. *Public Opinion in Occupied Germany.* Chicago, 1970.

Meyer, John W. and Brian Rowan. "The Effects of Education as an Institution." *American Journal of Sociology* 83 (1977): 55–77.

Mielcke, Karl. *1917–1945 in den Geschichtsbüchern der Bundesrepublik.* Hannover, 1961.

Möller, Horst. "Das Institut für Zeitgeschichte und die Entwicklung der Zeitgeschichtsschreibung in Deutschland." In *50 Jahre Institut für Zeitgeschichte. Eine Bilanz*, ed. Horst Möller and Udo Wengst: 1–68. Munich, 1999.

Moos, Gerd. "Aus der Mittelstufe unserer Klasse." In *O' KPATHP, Der Mischkrug, Abitur-Zeitung Dilthey-Schule 1953*, ed. Hans-Rudolf Horn et al.: 72–74. Wiesbaden, 2003.

Morgenthau, Henry Jr. *Germany Is Our Problem.* New York, 1945.

Müller, Winfried. *Schulpolitik in Bayern im Spannungsfeld von Kultusbürokratie und Besatzungsmacht 1945–1949.* Munich, 1995.

Neuhäuser, Heike and Tobias Rücker, eds. *Demokratische Reformpädagogik.* Frankfurt, 2000.

Niethammer, Lutz. *Entnazifizierung in Bayern.* Frankfurt, 1972.

———. *Die volkseigene Erfahrung: eine Archäologie des Lebens in der Industrieprovinz der DDR: 30 biographische Eröffungen.* Berlin, 1991.

Nishi, Toshio. *Unconditional Democracy. Education and Politics in Occupied Japan, 1945–1952.* Education and Society, vol. 1, ed. Paul R. Hanna. Stanford, CA, 1982.

Nizer, Louis. *What To Do with Germany.* New York, 1944.

Oelkers, Jürgen. "Pädagogische Reform und Wandel der Erziehungswissenschaft." In *Handbuch der deutschen Bildungsgeschichte*, vol. 6/1, ed. Christoph Führ and Carl-Ludwig Furck: 212–41. Munich, 1998.

Oppenheim, A. N. *Civic Education and Participation in Democracy: The German Case.* Contemporary Political Sociology Series, vol. 2, ed. Richard Rose. London, 1977.

Ottweiler, Ottwilm. *Die Volksschule in Nationalsozialismus.* Weinheim, 1979.

Pakschies, Günther. *Umerziehung in der Britischen Zone, 1945–1949.* Weinheim, 1979.

Parker, Walter. *Teaching Democracy: Unity and Diversity in Public Life.* New York, 2003.

Peifer, Elizabeth. "1968 in German Political Culture, 1967–1993: From Experience to Myth." PhD diss., University of North Carolina at Chapel Hill, 1997.

Phillips, David, ed. *Education in Germany: Tradition and Reform in Historical Context.* New York, 1995.

Picht, Georg. *Die deutsche Bildungskatastrophe.* Freiburg im Breisgau, 1964.

Pilgert, Henry P. *The Exchange of Persons Program in Western Germany.* Bonn, 1951.

———. *The West German Educational System with Special Reference to the Policies and Programs of the Office of the U.S. High Commissioner for Germany.* Germany, 1953.

Poiger, Uta. *Jazz, Rock, and Rebels: Cold War Politics and American Culture in a Divided Germany.* Berkeley, CA, 2000.

Puaca, Brian. "Drafting Democracy: Education Reform in American-Occupied Germany, 1945–1949." MA thesis, University of North Carolina at Chapel Hill, 2001.

———. "'We learned what democracy really meant': The Berlin Student Parliament and School Reform in the 1950s." *History of Education Quarterly* 45, no. 4 (Winter 2005): 615-624.

————. "'Missionaries of Goodwill.' Deutsche Austauschlehrer und –schüler und die Lehren der amerikanische Demokratie in den frühen 1950er Jahren." In *Demokratiewunder. Transatlantische Mittler und die kulturelle Öffnung Westdeutschlands 1945–1970*, ed. Arnd Bauerkämper, Konrad H. Jarausch, and Markus Payk: 305–31. Berlin, 2005.

————. "Navigating the Waves of Change: Political Education and Democratic School Reform in Postwar West Berlin." *History of Education Quarterly* 48, no. 2 (Summer 2008): 244-264.

Reble, Albert. *Lehrerbildung in Deutschland*. Henn, 1958.

Redding, Kimberly. "'We Wanted to Be Young': Hitler's Youth in Post-War Berlin." PhD diss., University of North Carolina at Chapel Hill, 2000.

Rempel, Gerhard. *Hitler's Children: The Hitler Youth and the SS*. Chapel Hill, NC, 1989.

Richie, Donald A. *Doing Oral History*. 2nd ed. Oxford, 2003.

Robinsohn, Saul B. and J. Caspar Kuhlmann. "Two Decades of Non-reform in West German Education." *Comparative Education Review* 11, no. 3 (October 1967): 311–30.

Roehrig, Paul. *Politische Bildung. Herkunft und Aufgabe*. Stuttgart, 1964.

Röhrs, Hermann. "Progressive Education in the United States and Its Influence on Related Educational Developments in Germany." *Paedagogica Historica* 33, no. 1 (1997): 45–68.

Röhrs, Hermann and Volker Lenhart, eds. *Progressive Education Across the Continents*. Frankfurt, 1995.

Rosenzweig, Beate. *Erziehung zur Demokratie? Amerikanische Besatzungs- und Schulreformpolitik in Deutschland und Japan*. Stuttgart, 1998.

Ruge-Schatz, Angela. *Umerziehung und Schulpolitik in der französischen Besatzungszone, 1945–1949*. Frankfurt, 1977.

Rupieper, Hermann-Josef. *Die Wurzeln der westdeutschen Nachkriegsdemokratie. Der amerikanische Beitrag 1945–1952*. Opladen, 1993.

Rust, Val. "The German Image of American Education through the Weimar Period." *Paedagogica Historica* 33, no. 1 (1997): 25–44.

Sarason, Seymour Bernard. *The Predictable Failure of Educational Reform: Can We Change Course Before It's Too Late?* San Francisco, 1990.

Scheibe, Wolfgang. *Schülermitverantwortung*. Berlin, 1962.

Schiller, Dietmar. "Schulalltag in der Nachkriegszeit." In *Schulreform – Kontinuitäten und Brücke. Das Versuchungsfeld Berlin-Neukölln*, vol. 2, ed. Gerd Radde and Werner Korthaase et al.: 29–40. Opladen, 1993.

Schlander, Otto. "Der Einfluß von John Dewey und Hans Morgenthau auf die Formulierung der Re-educationpolitik." In *Umerziehung und Wiederaufbau. Die Bildungspolitik der Besatzungsmächte in Deutschland und Österreich*, ed. Manfred Heinemann: 40-52. Stuttgart, 1981.

Schmidt, Angelika. "Lehrer gesucht – Zur Ausbildung der Schulhelfer und Hilfslehrer." In *Schulreform – Kontinuitäten und Brücke. Das Versuchungsfeld Berlin-Neukölln*, vol. 2, ed. Gerd Radde and Werner Korthaase et al.: 48–53. Opladen, 1993.

Schmoldt, Benno, ed. *Das Schulwesen in Berlin seit 1945*. Berlin, 1996.

Schnorbach, Hermann, ed. *Lehrer und Schule unterm Hakenkreuz. Dokumente des Widerstands von 1930 bis 1945*. Königstein, 1983.

Scholtz, Harald. *Erziehung und Unterricht unterm Hakenkreuz*. Göttingen, 1985.

Schreiber, Wernfried. "Auf den Wege zur universitären Lehrerbildung in Hessen von 1945–1950." PhD diss., Goethe Universität (Frankfurt), 1978.

Schulte, Birgitta M., ed. *Die Schule ist wieder offen: Hessische Schulpolitik in der Nachkriegszeit.* Frankfurt, 1997.

Schulze, W. and Christoph Führ. *Das Schulwesen in der Bundesrepublik Deutschland.* Weinheim, 1966.

Schumann, Dirk. "Authority in the 'Blackboard Jungle': Parents, Teachers, Experts and the State, and the Modernization of West Germany in the 1950s." *Bulletin of the German Historical Institute* 33 (Fall 2003): 65–78.

Schuppan, Michael-Sören. *Berliner Lehrerbildung nach dem Zweiten Weltkrieg. Die pädagogische Hochschule im bildungspolitischen Kräftspiel unter den Bedingungen der Vier-Mächte-Stadt (1945–1958).* Frankfurt, 1990.

Schuster, Armin. *Die Entnazifizierung in Hessen 1945–1954.* Veröffentlichungen der Historische Kommission für Nassau. No. 66. Vorgeschichte und Geschichte des Parlamentarismus in Hessen. Vol. 29. Wiesbaden, 1999.

Shirley, Dennis. *The Politics of Progressive Education: The Odenwaldschule in Nazi Germany.* Cambridge, MA, 1992.

Stachura, Peter. "Das dritte Reich und Jugenderziehung: Die Rolle der Hitlerjugend 1933–1939." In *Erziehung und Schulung im Dritten Reich,* ed. Manfred Heinemann: 90–112. Stuttgart, 1980.

———. *The German Youth Movement 1900–1945.* New York, 1981.

Steffens, U. and T. Bargel. *Erkundungen zur Qualität von Schule.* Neuwied, 1993.

Teicher, Ulrich. "Problems of West German Universities on the Way to Mass Higher Education." *Western European Education* 8, no. 1–2 (1976): 81–120.

———. *"Öffnung der Hochschulen" - auch eine Politik für die achtziger Jahre?* Bremen, 1983.

———. *Changing Patterns of the Higher Education System: The Experience of Three Decades.* London, 1991.

Tenorth, Heinz-Elmar. *Zur deutschen Bildungsgeschichte 1918–1945.* Studien und Dokumentation zur deutschen Bildungsgeschichte, vol. 28, ed. Christoph Führ and Wolfgang Mitter. Cologne, 1985.

———. *Geschichte der Erziehung. Einführung in die Grundzüge ihrer neuzeitlichen Entwicklung.* Weinheim, 1988.

———. "Pädagogisches Denken." In *Handbuch der deutschen Bildungsgeschichte,* vol. 5, ed. Dieter Langewische and Heinz-Elmar Tenorth: 111–54. Munich, 1989.

Tent, James. *Mission on the Rhine: Reeducation and Denazification in American-Occupied Germany.* Chicago, 1982.

———. "Mission on the Rhine: American Educational Policy in Germany, 1945–1949." *History of Education Quarterly* 22, no. 3 (Autumn 1982): 255–276.

Thompson, Paul. *The Voice of the Past: Oral History.* 3rd ed. Oxford, 2000.

Trainor, Joseph C. *Educational Reform in Occupied Japan: Trainor's Memoir.* Tokyo, 1982.

Tsuchimochi, Gary T. *Education Reform in Postwar Japan: The 1946 U.S. Education Mission.* Tokyo, 1993.

Verba, Sydney. "Germany: The Remaking of Political Culture." In *Political Culture and Political Development,* ed. Lucian W. Pye and Sydney Verba: 130–70. Princeton, NJ, 1965.

Vereinigung der Freunde der Dreilinden-Obersschule. *Schulzeit 1939 bis 1999. Festschrift anlässlich des 60-jährigen Bestehens der Dreilinden-Oberschule Berlin-Zehlendorf.* Berlin, 1999.

Wegner, Gregory P. "The Power of Tradition in Education: The Formation of the History Curriculum in the Gymnasium of the American Sector in Berlin, 1945–1955." PhD diss., University of Wisconsin–Madison, 1988.

———. "Germany's Past Contested: The Soviet-American Conflict in Berlin over History Curriculum Reform, 1945–48." *History of Education Quarterly* 30, no. 1 (Spring 1990): 1–16.

Weick, Karl. "Educational Organizations as Loosely Coupled Systems." *Administrative Science Quarterly* 21 (March 1976): 1–19.

Weiler, Hans N., Heinrich Mintrop, and Elisabeth Fuhrmann. *Educational Change and Social Transformation: Teachers, Schools and Universities in Eastern Germany.* The Stanford Series on Education and Public Policy, vol. 18, ed. Henry M. Levin. Bristol, PA, 1996.

Weisz, Christoph, ed. *OMGUS-Handbuch: Die amerikanische Militärregierung in Deutschland 1945–1949.* Munich, 1994.

Werner, Jobst. *Schülermitwirkung in den öffentlichen Schulen Deutschlands nach 1945 unter besonderer Berücksichtigung der Entwicklung in Berlin. Eine Darstellung der Entwicklung in der Zeit von 1945 bis 1994.* Berlin, 1995.

Wesel, Uwe. *Die verspielte Revolution. 1968 und die Folgen.* Munich, 2002.

Wierling, Dorothee. "Three Generations of East German Women: Four Decades of the GDR and After." *Oral History Review* 21/2 (1993): 19–30.

Wilhelm, Theodor. [Oetinger, Friedrich]. *Wendpunkt der politischen Erziehung. Partnerschaft als pädagogische Aufgabe.* Stuttgart, 1951.

———. *Pädagogik der Gegenwart.* 4th ed. Stuttgart, 1967.

Ziemer, Gregor. "Our Educational Failure in Germany." *American Mercury* 62, no. 270 (June 1946): 726–33.

Zilien, Johann. *Politische Bildung in Hessen von 1945 bis 1965. Gestaltung und Entwicklung der politischen Bildung als schulpolitisches Instrument der sozialen Demokratisierung.* Frankfurt, 1997.

Zink, Harold. *American Military Government in Germany.* New York, 1947.

———. *The United States in Germany, 1944–1955.* Princeton, NJ, 1957.

Zymek, Bernd. "Schulen, Hochschulen, Lehrer." In *Handbuch der deutschen Bildungsgeschichte,* vol. 5, ed. Dieter Langewische and Heinz-Elmar Tenorth: 155–208. Munich, 1989.

INDEX

Adenauer, Konrad, 127, 147, 161, 171, 180–81, 201

Adorno, Theodor, 118

Alexander, R. T., 40n124, 41

Alsace-Lorraine, 30

American Field Service, 76

Americanization, 5, 29, 39–40, 46, 155

Amerikahaus, 27, 69

Ann Arbor Council of Churches, 76–77

Anti-Semitism, 119, 141, 146, 155–56, 163, 175–76

Auschwitz, 173

Baden-Württemberg, 38–39, 41, 113–14, 170

Basic Law, 157, 175, 177

Bavaria, 17, 20, 25–26, 30, 38–39, 41, 75, 90, 93
    denazification in, 34
    resistance to American reform proposals, 6, 41n131

Bergen-Belsen, 173

Berghahn, Volker, 5

Berlin Association of Teachers and Educators (BVL), 92, 162

Berlin School Law, 64

Berlin Student Parliament, 8, 56–58, 61n2, 66–70, 120–24, 142, 166–68
    and Berufsschul-Parlament, 69
    See also Rundfunk im amerikanischen Sektor

Berlin Wall, 10, 155, 159, 167

Berliner Lehrerzeitung, 119, 165

Berliner Schülerparlament. See Berlin Student Parliament

Berufsschul-Parlament. See Berlin Student Parliament

Bildung und Erziehung, 8n22, 18

Bismarck, Otto von, 84, 86, 140, 185

Bollnow, Otto Friedrich, 200–201

Bonn, 108

Brandt, Willy, 121–22

Braunschweig, 87

Bremen, 25, 38, 41, 62n13, 113n7

Bremerhaven, 166, 171

Brethren Service Committee, 76

Bundestag, 108, 115, 134

Bundeszentrale für Heimatdienst. See Bundeszentrale für politische Bildung

Bundeszentrale für politische Bildung, 108, 115, 138, 180

Catholicism, 25, 90

Charlottenburg, 114, 182–83

Christ und Welt, 9n27, 155–56

Christian Democratic Union (CDU), 121, 147, 159, 162

Christmas Prize Competition, 108–10, 115

Citizenship, 3, 75, 110, 130, 147, 153–54, 181, 193, 196
    American proposals for, 44–46
    Nazi instruction in, 22–23
    political education for, 94, 157–58
    and student government, 120, 123, 164, 168–69
    and student newspapers, 125–26
    and textbooks, 87, 129–37, 174–75, 177, 193

Civics, 16, 44
    Weimar Republic instruction in, 3, 20–21, 44, 112, 134
    Weimar Republic textbooks, 130–34

Classrooms, 25
    damaged and destroyed, 25–26
    occupied for other purposes, 26
    See also shift instruction

Clay, Lucius, 2–3, 193–94, 201
Cold War 4, 6, 44–45, 47, 110, 137, 154
  and history instruction, 139, 174
Columbia University Teachers College, 29,
  40n124
Confessional education, 6, 90, 161
Curriculum and Textbooks Centers. *See*
  Education Service Centers

Das Parlament, 180
Democratization, 2–4, 8, 10, 39–40, 46,
  155n9, 193–95, 201
  and inner democratization, 9, 194n4
  and teacher training, 89–90
Denazification, 4n7, 15, 32–39, 47
  in Berlin, 35–36
  in Hesse, 34–35
Denkschrift zur inneren Schulreform. *See*
  Memorandum on Internal School Reform
Der Gemeinde-, Staats- und Weltbürger,
  133–35
Deutsche Geschichte, 87–88
Deutsche Geschichte in Kurzfassung, 86–88
Deutsche Gesellschaft für die Vereinten
  Nationen, 185
Deutscher Ausschuss für das Erziehungs- und
  Bildungswesen, 112, 115–16, 159, 162
Dewey, John, 3, 5, 21, 23, 40, 46, 63
Diary of Anne Frank, The, 160
Die deutsche Schule, 8n22
Die pädagogische Provinz, 8n22, 24, 94
Die Reise in die Vergangenheit, 174, 176–78
Diesterweg Press, 32, 85
Doering-Manteuffel, Anselm, 4
Dresden, 90

East Germany. *See* German Democratic
  Republic
Ebeling, Hans, 87
  and *Deutsche Geschichte,* 87–88, 174
  and *Die Reise in die Vergangenheit,*
    174, 176–78
Education and Cultural Relations Division,
  29, 34, 39–41
Education & Religious Affairs (E&RA).
  See Education and Cultural Relations
  Division
Education Service Centers, 31, 82
Ehlers, Hermann, 67n35
Eichmann, Adolf, 155–56, 184
Einst und Jetzt, 179
Einstein, Albert, 160

Enabling Act, 140, 178
Essen, 78
Europe, 40, 46, 59, 81, 115
  integration of, 118, 129, 134–36,
    158, 176, 180, 198
European Atomic Energy Community
  (EURATOM), 136
European Economic Community (EEC),
  136, 158
European Free Trade Association, 159
European Recovery Program. *See* Marshall
  Plan
Evers, Carl-Heinz, 116–17
  as city school superintendent, 153–
    54, 156, 160–63, 172, 187
  as Senator for Education, 201
Exchange programs, 3, 70–80, 166, 193, 198
  multipliers for, 78
  participant surveys from, 75–76,
    78–79
  teenagers involved, 76–79
  See also German Teacher Trainee
  Program
Eynern, Gert von, 182

Federal Republic of Germany (FRG), 9–10,
  59, 71, 78–79, 93, 99, 139, 161, 167,
  201
Flechtheim, Ossip, 182
Ford Motor Company, 77
Fraenkel, Ernst, 182
France, 5, 166
  depiction in German texts, 30, 83,
    132, 176
  occupation zone of, 25n51
Frank, Anne, 160, 179
Frankfurt, 25, 118, 122–23, 184–86
Franz-Willing, Georg, 32
Free University Berlin, 92–93, 167
  teacher training at, 91–93, 181, 183
  See also Otto Suhr Institute
Freie Universität Berlin. *See* Free University
  Berlin
Friedrichsdorf, 185
Fröbel, Friedrich, 21
Fulbright Program, 71, 79
Füssl, Karl-Heinz, 198

Gaudig, Hugo, 23
Geheeb, Paul, 18–19
Gemeinschaftskunde. *See* social studies;
  political education

Geneva Conference, 142
German Democratic Republic, 88, 122–23, 127, 161, 168, 178
German Teacher Trainee Program, 72–76
German Youth Activities (GYA), 28, 43
Gewerkschaft Erziehung und Wissenschaft (GEW), 91
Grace, Alonzo, 29, 39, 41
Great Britain, 5, 115, 166
    occupation zone of, 25, 81n80
Grundschule, 7n19, 40–42, 60, 64, 177
    reform in, 157, 160, 163, 168–69, 181–83
Gymnasium, 6, 40–42, 60, 95, 165–66
    in Hesse, 35, 62–64, 119–20, 123, 139, 163
    in Weimar Republic, 19
    See also Oberschule Wissenschaftlicher Zweig

Haacke, Ulrich, 132
Hamburg, 62n13, 85, 90, 93, 113, 163, 167
Hennig, Arno, 91
Herbart, Johann, 21
Hertz, Gustav, 160
Hesse, 6, 41
    history instruction in, 138–40, 145–46
    Landeszentrale für Heimatdienst, 118, 185
    political education in, 61, 95–97, 117, 184–86
    School Advisory Council, 86
    student government in, 61–64, 119–20, 123–24, 163–64
    student newspapers in, 63, 125–26, 163, 172
    teacher training in, 91–92, 118, 184–86
    See also Gymnasium; Mittelschule; Volksschule
Hessische Allgemeine Zeitung, 146
Hessische Lehrerzeitung, 91
Heumann, Hans, 174–76
Heuss, Theodor, 108–9
High Commission (US) for Germany (HICOG), 71, 79, 95
Hilfslehrer, 35, 89n109
Hilligen, Wolfgang, 132–33
    and *Der Gemeinde-, Staats- und Weltbürger,* 133–35
History instruction. *See* Hesse; West Berlin

History textbooks, 3, 193
    classroom assignments in, 84–85, 87
    and democracy, 80, 83
    postwar discussions of 1848, 83, 86–88
    postwar discussions of German Empire, 84, 86, 176
    postwar discussions of National Socialism and war, 84–85, 88, 175, 177–79
    postwar discussions of the Weimar Republic, 84–88, 176–77
    use of primary sources in, 88, 174–75, 177–79
    vetted by American officials, 30, 81–82
Hitler, Adolf, 15, 22–23, 129, 175
    treatment in textbooks, 31, 42, 84–85, 87–88, 140, 144, 173, 175, 178–79
Hitler Youth, 22, 34n99, 69, 178
Holocaust, 80, 127, 148, 154, 173–74, 177–79, 187
Horkheimer, Max, 118
Höss, Rudolf, 173

Institut für Zeitgeschichte (IfZ), 138
Interim Guidelines for Political Education, 155–59, 181, 187

Jaspers, Karl, 143
Jena, 90
Jena Plan, 21
Jugenheim, 92
Junge Presse Hessen, 172

Kaiserslautern, 168
Karsen, Fritz, 41, 46, 81n80
Kassel, 35, 118
Kerschensteiner, Georg, 21, 23, 46
Khrushchev, Nikita, 142
Kilpatrick, William, 3, 40
Klett Press, 85
Kogon, Eugen, 127, 175
Kreuzberg, 25, 29, 115, 142, 159
Kuhlmann, Caspar, 200–201
Kultusministerkonferenz (KMK). *See* Standing Conference of Culture Ministers

Lange-Quassowski, Jutta-B., 4n7, 33–34
Latin instruction, 31, 41
League of Nations, 132, 139

Leipzig, 90
Lemmer, Ernst, 121
Lessing, Gotthold, 160
Lietz, Hermann, 19
Liliencron, Detlev von, 63
Lower Saxony, 85, 165, 171
Ludwigsburg, 76, 95

Mainz, 166
Marshall Plan, 84–85, 134, 139
Mein Kampf, 175
Memorandum on Internal School Reform,
    154–56, 160–63, 187
Mendelssohn, Felix, 160
Michigan Council of Churches, 76–77
Mittelschule, 40–42, 165
    in Hesse, 139, 153
    See also Oberschule Technischer Zweig
Montessori, Maria, 23
Morgenthau, Henry, 1–2
Müller, Otto, 86–87
Munich, 62n13, 138, 164

National Catholic Welfare Conference, 76
National 4–H Club Foundation, 76
National Grange, 76
National Socialism, 14, 22, 146
    educational policies of, 22
    and teachers, 17, 32–33, 90
    and textbooks, 29, 31, 81
National Socialist Teachers League (NSLB),
    33
Nebelsiek, Karl, 133–35, 137
Neukölln, 25, 27, 36–37, 46
New Republic, 34
New York City, 77
New York Times, 34
Normal schools, 90
North Atlantic Treaty Organization (NATO),
    136, 158
North Rhine-Westphalia, 85
Nuremberg Laws, 175, 178

Oberschule Praktischer Zweig (OPZ),
    41n129, 42, 162–63
    history instruction in, 140–43, 145
    political education in, 113–15,
        157–60
    student government in, 64–66, 69,
        122–23, 172
    student newspapers in, 125, 171
    teachers in, 162–63, 181–82, 184

Oberschule Technischer Zweig (OTZ),
    41n129, 42, 162–63
    history instruction in, 140–45
    political education in, 114–15, 157
    student government in, 64–66, 69,
        171
    student newspapers in, 124–25, 171
    teachers in, 162–63, 181–82, 184
Oberschule Wissenschaftlicher Zweig
    (OWZ), 41n129, 42, 162–63
    history instruction in, 140–45
    political education in, 114–15, 157,
        159
    student government in, 64–66, 69
    student newspapers in, 124, 127–29,
        171
    teachers in, 162–63, 181–84
Occupation, 4–6, 24–32, 40, 46, 79, 81, 92,
    98–99, 193–96
    See also France; Great Britain; Soviet
        Union; United States
Oetinger, Friedrich, 94
Office of Military Government (US) for
    Germany (OMGUS), 7, 15, 194, 196
    and immediate postwar challenges,
        25–26, 29
    teacher training policies of, 89–90,
        93–95
    textbook policies of, 15, 25, 30–31,
        81–82, 86
    views on German education, 40–46
    See also denazification
Oral history, 8
Organization of European Economic
    Cooperation (OEEC), 134
Otto Suhr Institute, 181–84

Pädagogische Hochschule (PH), 91–93
Pädagogische Rundschau, 8n22
Parent-teacher associations (PTAs) 73, 75,
    135
Paulskirche, 86–87
Petersen, Peter, 21, 46
Phillips, Burr W., 44–45, 96–97
Picht, Georg, 9n27, 155–56
Pilgert, Henry, 95
Political education, 3, 69, 89, 110–11, 113–
    14, 167–68, 193–96
    definition of, 116–17
    as educational principle, 113, 117,
        159–60, 180
    postwar textbooks for, 132–37

training for teachers, 180–86
  See also Hesse; social studies; West
    Berlin
Political socialization, 2, 21
Potsdam Conference, 140

Radio programming, 111, 115, 138, 147, 180
  in West Berlin, 143–45
Rahmenplan, 159
Realschule. *See* Mittelschule
Red Cross, 65, 158
Reformpädagogik, 13, 18, 23
Reinhardswaldschule, 97, 184–85
Reinickendorf, 115, 168–70, 182
Reiniger, Max, 130, 132
Reuter, Ernst, 57, 67n35
Rhineland-Palatinate, 85
RIAS-Schulfunk-Parlament. *See* Berlin
  Student Parliament; Rundfunk im
  amerikanischen Sektor
Rosenzweig, Beate, 4, 197n5
Rostock, 90
Rotary International, 76
Rothfels, Hans, 138
Rundfunk im amerikanischen Sektor (RIAS),
  66–67, 143
  See also Berlin Student Parliament
Rupieper, Hermann-Josef, 4

Schichtunterricht. *See* shift instruction
Schleswig-Holstein, 85
Schneider, Benno, 132
Schneider, Hermann, 66–67, 122
Schöneberg, 25, 182
Schülermitverwaltung (SMV). *See* student
  government
Schülerzeitungen. *See* student newspapers
Schulhelfer, 35n106, 37–38,
Schuman Plan, 134
Schütte, Ernst, 146, 155–56, 163–64
Secondary education, 6, 7n19, 41n129
Sedan, 176
Sehen – Beurteilen – Handeln, 133, 135–37
Sender Freies Berlin (SFB), 143
Shift instruction, 27
Smith-Mundt Act, 71
Social Democratic Party of Germany (SPD),
  19n21, 156, 162, 201
Social studies, 3, 82, 89, 94–99, 117, 123,
  130, 135, 137, 146, 196
  American proposals for, 44–45, 77,
    94–95

teacher training for, 59–60, 118, 182
  See also political education
Socialist Unity Party (SED), 115, 146
Soviet Union, 25
  depiction in textbooks, 139–40, 142
  occupation zone of, 25, 91
Sozialkunde. *See* social studies
Spandau, 141
Spiegel Affair, 155–56, 163, 187
SS-State, 127, 175
Staatsbürgerkunde. *See* civics
Standing Conference of Culture Ministers,
  146, 161–62, 164, 174
State Department (US), 70–71, 76–79
Steglitz, 25, 182
Stein, Erwin, 6, 13, 23–24, 61–62, 86, 117,
  138, 163
Strategic Bombing Survey, Field Information
  Agency, Technical (FIAT), 40
Student government, 45, 111, 135, 154, 166,
  193, 195–96, 199
  and faculty advisors, 64, 164, 170–71
  See also Hesse; West Berlin
Student movement, 10, 197–200
Student newspapers, 124, 154, 166, 193,
  196, 199
  censorship of, 171
  See also Hesse; West Berlin
Stuttgart, 62n13, 163
Suhr, Otto, 67n35. *See also* Otto Suhr
  Institute

Taylor, John W., 40n124, 41
Teacher training, 3, 38, 194
  American objectives for, 89–90,
    93–95
  class differences within, 89–91
  and continuing education, 97–98,
    180–86
  in Weimar Republic, 90
  See also Hesse; Hilfslehrer;
    Schulhelfer; West Berlin
Teachers
  age of, 17, 35–39, 91, 162–63
  and women, 35–39, 163
Tempelhof, 116–17, 145
Tent, James, 40
Tewes, Johannes, 18–19
Textbooks. *See* history textbooks; political
  education
Three-track system, 4, 8, 40–41, 47, 59–60,
  111, 144–45, 174–75, 201

Tiburtius, Joachim, 67n35, 93, 121
  and history instruction, 140, 143, 146
  and Interim Guidelines for Political
    Education, 153–54, 156–60, 181,
    195
  and political education, 114–16, 172
  and teacher education, 181, 183–84
Titania-Palast, 67
Treaty of Versailles, 130, 132
Trögels Lesehefte, 178–79

United Nations, 122, 130, 136, 138–39,
    140, 142, 144, 158–59
United Nations Relief and Rehabilitation
    Agency (UNRRA), 40
United States, 5–6, 17, 29, 66, 115, 193–94,
    198
  as model for reform, 23–24, 97, 130,
    135, 194
  exchange programs to, 70–80, 198
  occupation zone of, 25–26
  See also Americanization; German
    Youth Activities; Office of Military
    Government (US) for Germany
United States Education Mission to
    Germany, 43
University of Cincinnati, 73
University of Kentucky, 75
University of Wisconsin, 96
Unser Weg durch die Geschichte, 174–76
Unsere Schule, 82

Volksschule, 7n19, 38, 40–42, 60, 75,
    90–91, 97
  in Berlin, 35–36
  in German Empire, 18
  in Hesse, 34–35, 38, 62, 139, 185–86
  history readers in, 178–79
  and student government, 122–23,
    165, 168–70, 187
  in Weimar Republic, 19
  See also Oberschule Praktischer Zweig
Vorläufige Richtlinien für den politischen
  Unterricht. *See* Interim Guidelines for
  Political Education

Wedding, 142, 145
Wege der Völker, 82–88
Weilburg, 35, 63, 92
Weimar Republic, 13
  constitution of, 20, 86–87, 90, 130,
    132

reform in, 13–14, 19–21, 155, 195
  textbooks in, 29–31, 81, 130
Werdau, 67
West Berlin, 6, 38, 76, 161–62
  Einheitsschule, 92
  history instruction in, 140–45,
    157–58
  Landeszentrale für politische
    Bildungsarbeit, 116, 127, 182
  political education in, 69, 96,
    114–17, 119, 121–22, 156–61,
    181–84
  student government in, 56–58,
    64–69, 120–24, 168–71
  student newspapers in, 116, 124–29,
    171
  teacher training in, 91–93, 181–84
  See also Berlin School Law; Interim
    Guidelines for Political Education;
    Memorandum on Internal
    School Reform; Oberschule
    Praktischer Zweig; Oberschule
    Technischer Zweig; Oberschule
    Wissenschaftlicher Zweig;
    Pädagogische Hochschule
West Germany. *See* Federal Republic of
  Germany
Westermanns Pädagogische Beiträge, 8n22
Westernization, 5
Wiesbaden, 26–28, 62–64, 119–20, 125–26,
    185
Wilmersdorf, 141
Wir machen mit, 165, 171
Wolfsburg, 171
World Health Organization, 136
World War I, 15, 30, 80, 86–87, 130, 132,
    137, 139–40
World War II, 1, 4, 9, 23, 36, 157
  in *Zeitgeschichte* instruction, 137,
    139–40
  See also history textbooks
Wyneken, Gustav, 18–19

Yalta Conference, 25
YMCA, 73, 78
YWCA, 73

Zehlendorf, 27, 66, 115, 127, 128, 141–42
Zeitgeschichte, 111, 137–47, 154, 157–58,
    164, 174, 185, 196
  professionalization of, 138
Zyklon B, 183

1st mtg Intro to PTK
2nd mtg Election

PTK Welcome
  Link to Canvas
  Note re: meetings
  Survey link?

3rd/4th Have them create a PTK
mtg   Constitution
        - What is a member in
          good standing?
        - How to deal w/ those
          under 3.5

on Civil Society (PTK)
  on college campus
Send students to other
  CC PTK mtgs for ideas

Canvas site
  should have local
  transfer scholarship
  info

○ Purpose
● Rel. to non-Honors
○ How to recognize
●
○ Diplomas etc
○ Conference(?)

4th Thanksgiving - How to
    get stuff down

○ 5 Star Status
  - Procedure
  - Requirements
    for scholarships

(intro of 4
 Pillars

Put Buchman
passage next to
other textbooks.
Have students
pick out
"facts"/biased

Mod hist
4 have them compare
Dem/Rep vs. hist
Radicals of 1910c

Fact checking(?)
exercise

Fact checking(?)
more inclusion of
mushono/other
national history